D1484185

Robust Political Economy

NEW THINKING IN POLITICAL ECONOMY

Series Editor: Peter J. Boettke, *George Mason University, USA*

New Thinking in Political Economy aims to encourage scholarship in the intersection of the disciplines of politics, philosophy and economics. It has the ambitious purpose of reinvigorating political economy as a progressive force for understanding social and economic change.

The series is an important forum for the publication of new work analysing the social world from a multidisciplinary perspective. With increased specialization (and professionalization) within universities, interdisciplinary work has become increasingly uncommon. Indeed, during the 20th century, the process of disciplinary specialization reduced the intersection between economics, philosophy and politics and impoverished our understanding of society. Modern economics in particular has become increasingly mathematical and largely ignores the role of institutions and the contribution of moral philosophy and politics.

New Thinking in Political Economy will stimulate new work that combines technical knowledge provided by the 'dismal science' and the wisdom gleaned from the serious study of the 'worldly philosophy'. The series will reinvigorate our understanding of the social world by encouraging a multidisciplinary approach to the challenges confronting society in the new century.

Recent titles in the series include:

The Neoliberal Revolution in Eastern Europe
Economic Ideas in the Transition from Communism
Paul Dragos Aligica and Anthony J. Evans

Employees and Entrepreneurship
Co-ordination and Spontaneity in Non-hierarchical Business Organizations
Ivan Pongracic, Jr.

Media, Development, and Institutional Change
Christopher J. Coyne and Peter T. Leeson

The Economics of Ignorance and Coordination
Subjectivism and the Austrian School of Economics
Thierry Aimar

Socialism, Economic Calculation and Entrepreneurship
Jesús Huerta de Soto

The Political Economy of Hurricane Katrina and Community Rebound
Edited by Emily Chamlee-Wright and Virgil Henry Storr

Robust Political Economy
Classical Liberalism and the Future of Public Policy
Mark Pennington

Robust Political Economy

Classical Liberalism and the Future of Public Policy

Mark Pennington

Reader in Public Policy and Political Economy, Department of Politics, Queen Mary, University of London, UK

NEW THINKING IN POLITICAL ECONOMY

Edward Elgar
Cheltenham, UK • Northampton, MA, USA

Published by
Edward Elgar Publishing Limited
The Lypiatts
15 Lansdown Road
Cheltenham
Glos GL50 2JA
UK

Edward Elgar Publishing, Inc.
William Pratt House
9 Dewey Court
Northampton
Massachusetts 01060
USA

A catalogue record for this book is available from the British Library

Library of Congress Control Number: 2010927652

Mixed Sources
Product group from well-managed
forests and other controlled sources
www.fsc.org Cert no. SA-COC-1565
© 1996 Forest Stewardship Council
FSC

ISBN 978 1 84542 621 7 (cased)
ISBN 978 1 84980 765 4 (paperback)

Typeset by Cambrian Typesetters, Camberley, Surrey
Printed and bound by MPG Books Group, UK

This book is dedicated to the memory of Elizabeth Ellen Etheridge

Contents

Acknowledgements

There are a number of people and institutions whose support I would like to acknowledge. John and Christine Blundell for their encouragement and friendship and for providing an office at the Institute of Economic Affairs, during my sabbatical year in 2007. John and Christine are embarking on journeys new and I wish them all the best for the years to come. I will never forget the warmth they have shown me since our first meeting in 1993 when I began my own journey into classical liberalism as a 23-year-old PhD student. The Earhart Foundation is owed my gratitude for the provision of a grant that enabled the completion of this book. Thanks are also due to Queen Mary, University of London, for the provision of sabbatical leave during which a large part of the book was completed. The arguments presented in various parts have benefited from conversations with, among others, Philip Booth, Paul Gunn, Paul Lewis, Jeffrey Friedman, John Meadowcroft and Adam Tebble. Peter Boettke, the editor of this series, and Edward Elgar the publisher, are due particular thanks for their support and patience. I owe a special thank you to Nigel Ashford, Elaine Hawley and all the staff at the Institute for Humane Studies, George Mason University. It can be a little lonely espousing classical liberalism in a British university and for someone who tends towards the solitary life the ideas and personalities at the Institute offer me that much needed sense of 'belonging'. I thank Guillaume Loyau for the concept behind the cover design. Finally, I would like to thank my mother and Gerard Roscoe for their love and support in UpHolland, Lancashire. It will always be my home.

1. Introduction: classical liberalism and robust political economy

INTRODUCTION

Contemporary debates in political economy have been shaped by reactions towards 'neo-liberalism'. From reform of the welfare state to discussions over international trade and the environment, many commentators have discussed the apparent ascendancy of a belief in 'free markets' and the minimal state. The impression generated by such commentary is that following the collapse of the socialist project in Eastern Europe and elsewhere, opposition to neo-liberalism, or classical liberalism as it should really be known, has been marginalised in the political landscape.

A cursory glance at the trajectory of public policy, however, reveals a different picture. While the 'privatisation' movement of recent years may have slowed the advance of post-war social democracy, many policy areas have exhibited a marked resistance to liberalisation or have seen a further expansion in the role of government. The financing and delivery of health and education remain, for example, the overwhelming preserve of governments in most liberal democracies with even minor attempts to introduce market forces making little headway. In the realm of international trade, continued adherence to agricultural protectionism and widespread support for financial aid as the key to securing prosperity in developing economies confirms a lingering attachment to interventionist principles. Environmental policy has proven even more resistant to classical liberal ideas with a massive growth of regulatory initiatives. And, as if this were not enough, the unprecedented scale of government activism that followed the 'financial crisis' of 2008 hardly suggests that the grip of 'market fundamentalism' has been particularly secure.

The speed with which governments have sought to expand their powers in response to the recent financial crisis reflects a longer-term drift of ideas and opinion that far from supporting classical liberal ideas has actively sought to undermine them. In economics, for example, the dominant neo-classical tradition provides increasingly sophisticated rationales for government interventions ranging from product regulation to environmental taxes. Political theorists meanwhile question the philosophical and moral assumptions of classical liberalism, arguing that many of these are based on a crude form of individualism which undermines norms of solidarity and distributive justice. If there is a dominant position in contemporary social science, therefore, it is characterised explicitly or implicitly by hostility to classical liberalism and support for 'social democracy' at the national and the international scale.

In view of these developments, this book aims to challenge many of the arguments levied against classical liberalism in contemporary political economy and to restate the case for a movement 'towards the minimal state'. The aim of the book is not to present a 'new' contribution to political economy per se, but to synthesise existing arguments within an analytical framework – 'robust political economy' – that demonstrates the ongoing relevance of classical liberal principles to some of the most pressing questions of the day. In completing this task, the book draws on a range of literature from economics and political theory with a particular focus on 'comparative institutions' reasoning. This introductory chapter commences by setting out the principle of institutional 'robustness' on which comparative institutions analysis is based. It then outlines the case for classical liberalism as meeting the requirements of 'robust political economy'. The final section sketches the major challenges to the robustness of classical liberalism addressed in the chapters that follow.

COMPARATIVE INSTITUTIONS ANALYSIS AND ROBUST POLITICAL ECONOMY

Political economy is concerned primarily with the comparative performance of social and economic institutions. Human action always takes place in a specific institutional milieu and the conditions that people face under different institutions affect the character of their behaviour and the resultant social outcomes. Within this context, a 'robust' set of institutions may be defined as one that generates beneficial results even under the least favourable conditions (Leeson and Subrick, 2006). Such conditions may arise as a consequence of human imperfections. If people are 'perfect' or at least 'perfectible' then questions of comparative institutional analysis may cease to arise – one would expect beneficial outcomes irrespective of the institutional framework. If, however, people are 'imperfect' in a variety of ways, then questions of institutional robustness assume centre stage. Certain institutions may be better placed than others to withstand the stresses and strains wrought by the relevant human weaknesses.

In the context of institutional analysis there are two human imperfections that must be accounted for when considering the robustness of alternative regimes. The first of these is the 'knowledge problem'. Human beings are limited in their cognitive capacities and as a consequence even the most intelligent and far-sighted people are relatively ignorant of the society in which they are situated (Hayek, 1948a; Simon, 1957). Given the imperfections of human knowledge, the consequences of any particular action, either for the actors concerned or for the wider society, will at any given time remain uncertain. Robust institutions should therefore allow people to adapt to circumstances and conditions of which they are not directly aware, and under conditions of 'bounded rationality' must enable them to learn from mistakes and to improve the quality of their decisions over time.

The second human imperfection that must be accounted for is the possibility that people may act out of self-interested motivations (Ostrom, 2006). Actors may follow their own specific goals – material or non-material – rather than some notion of the 'common good' or the 'public interest'. People may not be willing to contribute towards the advancement of their fellows' interests unless they are able to gain some personal benefit from doing so. Incentives may matter, and as a consequence institutions must be judged on their capacity to channel potentially self-interested motivations in a way that generates beneficial outcomes at the societal level. The pursuit of self-interested behaviour under certain institutional conditions may lead to social and economic breakdown, but if institutions are structured in an appropriate manner then even those driven by the most egotistical of motives may act in a way that benefits the society of which they are part.

Given the human imperfections noted above, a robust political economy of institutions and decisions seeks answers to the following three questions:

- Which institutions perform best when people are not omniscient?
- Which institutions perform best when people are motivated by self interest?
- Which institutions perform best when people have limited knowledge *and* are prone to self-interested behaviour?

CLASSICAL LIBERALISM AND ROBUST POLITICAL ECONOMY

The classical liberal answer to the above questions is that the institutions of private or severally owned property, a market economy, and a limited government confined to the resolution of disputes between private parties, are best placed to meet the requirements of a robust regime.

Classical liberalism as it is understood in this book originates in the Scottish enlightenment of Adam Smith and David Hume and more recently is reflected in the work of Friedrich Hayek, Michael Oakeshott and James Buchanan. The fundamental organising principle of classical liberalism is freedom of association and disassociation. People must, according to this view, have the freedom to enter and exit from a variability of human arrangements. These need not exclude authoritarian or communitarian organisations which subscribe internally to 'illiberal' norms, but social actors must be able to leave any group which they have joined voluntarily or have been 'born into' on an involuntary basis. A classical liberal society, therefore, is one where there are multiple authorities and jurisdictions, none of which exercises a total, hierarchical form of power over the others (Kukathas, 2003). An important precondition for such an order is that ownership of property, though not necessarily equal, is widely dispersed between an array of individuals and voluntary associations.

The private or several ownership of property is recognised by classical liberals as a modus vivendi, necessary to cope with the reality of diverse human values. In conditions of limited rationality, the capacity to enter and leave a variety of human arrangements facilitates trial and error learning as people may observe the results that flow from different modes of life. Moreover, the space that private property affords people to experiment with their own favoured ends minimises conflict in conditions where people exhibit different views of the good life. When ownership of property is dispersed there is greater scope to enter voluntary agreements and contracts to secure one's own ends, without preventing other actors from seeking alternative partners with which to pursue theirs. When ownership of property is concentrated in a single centre, by contrast, those who control the relevant agency have the capacity to impose their particular ends on others. From a classical liberal perspective, given the limited nature of human rationality and the possibility of self-interested behaviour such systems are likely to promote conflict as individuals and groups may seek to control the ruling apparatus to implement their own particular vision.

Freedom of association and the observance of private or several property rights are also emphasised by classical liberalism because they permit the formation of what Hayek refers to as 'spontaneous orders' (Hayek, 1982, Part 1). 'Orders' of this nature exhibit patterns of coordination, but the regularities at issue are not the product of deliberate design by agents pursuing a unitary goal. Rather, they are 'emergent' phenomena that arise from the actions of a variety of dispersed agents each pursuing their own separate ends. For classical liberalism the advantages of such orders are threefold and exemplified in a market economy based on dispersed, though unequal ownership of property.

First, spontaneous orders are better placed to cope with conditions of imperfect knowledge and bounded rationality because they draw on and adapt to knowledge embedded in the multiple nodes that constitute them. In markets, for example, dispersed individuals and organisations make bids for property rights and contribute incrementally to the formation of prices that transmit their particular 'bit' of information to the resource owners with whom they trade. The latter may then adapt their behaviour in light of their own preferences and knowledge, and these adaptations may affect subsequent transactions with still other agents in a network of increasing complexity. The price signals that emerge from such a process prompt 'economising behaviour' and enable a degree of coordination that may not be achieved by a central coordinating authority. Under conditions of limited rationality and knowledge, such an authority could not be aware of all the relevant margins for adjustment that are scattered across a diversity of social actors (Hayek, 1948a, 1982).

A second advantage of spontaneous orders is that they allow for experimental evolution. The decentralised exchange of property rights in a market, for example, allows competing production and consumption ideas to be tested simultaneously. Should there be only one decision-making or 'planning' body then any errors are more likely to be systemic. Adaptation in a spontaneous order is also speedier than in a centralised or 'planned' equivalent – actors may learn from and imitate the most profitable models without approval from an overarching authority or majority. Market participants need not be aware of how or why their actions benefit themselves or their fellows in order for systemic improvements to arise. Entrepreneurial discoveries may result from pure chance rather than conscious deliberation. What matters is that production models that meet consumer demands make profits which signal the need for imitation, while loss-makers divert people away from the least promising lines (Alchian, 1959). Consumers meanwhile need not know why they find some products more satisfying than others. All they need do is 'exit' from suppliers they find least satisfactory in favour of those they find more so. In order to function effectively, therefore, the market 'system' requires little cognitive competence from any of its participants (Friedman, 2005).

The previous points refer to the robustness of spontaneous orders in overcoming the 'knowledge problem' and make no assumptions about human motivations – they do not, for example, assume that actors are, or should be, egoistic. A third advantage of such orders, however, is that they provide safeguards against the abuse of power where people do act out of self-interest. As David Hume and, more recently, James Buchanan have argued, people should be modelled 'as if they are knaves' – not because most are egoistic, but because institutional safeguards are needed to constrain a selfish minority (Buchanan, 1986). In the specific case of markets, the 'exit' option may allow people to escape from actors who offer inferior terms of cooperation. Although the distribution of wealth in a market economy is uneven, this inequality is dynamic as resources are continually shifted away from those who fail to put their property to the most valued uses. A system of private property rights provides incentives that may encourage even the most uncooperative or egotistical agents to act in a socially tolerable vein. Where property rights are well defined, the costs of decisions are effectively internalised – actors profit from decisions which benefit their fellows but must bear the costs of those that do not (Alchian and Demsetz, 1973).

These principles of institutional robustness are relevant not only in the context of 'economic' decision-making but also with respect to matters of distributive justice. From a classical liberal perspective, institutions that enable actors to impose a unitary conception of distribution on society are incompatible with a process of evolutionary learning and the principle of free-dom of association. Under conditions of limited rationality there may be substantial disagreement over what constitutes a 'fair' distribution of income and wealth. The results of a classical liberal order cannot be considered 'just' or 'unjust' because they are not based on obedience to a unitary system of commands, but follow from the actions of people associating on the basis of many different distributive norms (Hayek, 1982). The defining character of a 'liberal' system of justice should, therefore, be one of 'ends-independence' – it should not attempt to determine the justice of the results that follow from freedom of association, but should seek to resolve disputes when it is not clear where rights of ownership lie, or whether such rights have been breached. Seen in this light, all actors – even if they disagree about distributive justice – have an interest in maintaining a framework that ensures stability of posses-sions, because it is the latter that enables people to live their lives without coming into permanent conflict with their fellows (Otteson, 2006). From a classical liberal perspective, no central authority may access the knowledge necessary to judge all of the factors that contribute to a particular distribution, and given the possibility of self-interested behaviour no such authority should be trusted to determine the 'just deserts' of others.

If robust institutions are those that cope best with human imperfections then so too must the process of institutional design. In a world of imperfect knowl-edge and limited benevolence people may err when devising institutional structures. A robust political economy should, therefore, allow for evolution-ary learning and provide checks and balances at the meta-institutional level. Thus, while classical liberalism is a theory that claims universal validity in explaining the institutional types best placed to facilitate social coordination, it does not offer a blueprint towards achieving any one institutional form. The processes of evolutionary learning that occur within markets should be opera-tive on multiple levels so that people can exit and enter competing and often overlapping institutional designs (Buchanan and Vanberg, 2002). The state, therefore, although a particularly powerful organisation should be just one of many other similar organisations, constrained in its powers by the existence of competitors.

It is important to specify in this context what a commitment to the 'mini-mal state' actually implies. The most significant point to emphasise is that classical liberalism recognises that states may have an important role to play within a liberal society. Just as hierarchical organisations such as firms may have efficiency advantages over smaller, more individualised production and consumption units in markets, so states or 'state-like' institutions may have comparative advantages when it comes to the maintenance of the rules needed to sustain a liberal order, such as protection of persons and property. The boundaries between those cases where action by state-like entities is required should not, however, be set in stone, but as with the boundaries of firms should be able to shift in response to technological and institutional innovations that enhance the relative effectiveness of alternatives. The ideal of the minimal state, therefore, is a relatively fluid one and does not represent an equilibrium point to which all efforts at institutional reform should be directed.

For classical liberals it is not the existence of state-like entities that should be questioned, but the processes through which these institutions may have arisen. The rules that govern the operation of markets may themselves emerge via a 'bottom-up' process of spontaneous order. In competitive sports, for example, individual teams voluntarily submit to the rules and regulations of particular 'leagues'. While teams compete for spectators and acclaim within such leagues, they also cooperate on dimensions that enhance the attractiveness of their particular league with respect to rivals within the same sport or indeed of competitor sports. Competition operates within a 'nested' structure – individuals and organisations compete against one another, but at a higher institutional level so do the standards and rules subscribed to by different groups of actors. Similarly, individuals and organisations may subscribe to institutional rules provided by states or state-like entities in order to secure advantages, such as greater security of property than might otherwise be available. States themselves meanwhile may subscribe to common norms and standards that may be enforced by supra-national entities. Given the limits of human rationality and the possibility of self-interested action, what matters is whether the institutions concerned are arrived at via a process of consent rather than enforced coordination, and whether there is scope for dissenters to 'exit' at some level in order to subscribe to alternate practices.

In view of the 'knowledge problem' and recognition that 'incentives matter', the requirements of robust political economy represent a regulative standard against which to judge existing institutional practices and proposals for reform. The central tests of proposals for institutional reform should be whether they enhance the scope for evolutionary discovery and the extent to which they offer incentives that constrain the potentially oppressive powers of coercive authority. Many historical institutions, including states and suprana-tional organisations, have resulted from monopolistic imposition rather than consensual evolution and may thus be the subject of critical scrutiny.

CHALLENGES TO CLASSICAL LIBERALISM AND THE STRUCTURE OF THE BOOK

The principles outlined above aim to fulfil the criteria for a robust political economy of institutions and decisions. The claims advanced concerning the robustness of classical liberalism as a political project have not, however, gone without significant challenge and it is the purpose of this book to address some of the most significant objections in this regard. The book is structured in two parts. Part I examines the veracity of recent theoretical challenges to minimal state thinking that have emerged from the fields of economics and political theory. Part II then examines these questions in three areas of public policy that have proven most resistant to liberalisation.

Part I: Challenges to Classical Liberalism

The efficacy of markets in communicating information and generating productive incentives lies at the heart of the case for a framework of open markets and minimal government. The robustness of these arguments is, however, challenged by the 'new market failure' perspective of Joseph Stiglitz and his followers (Stiglitz, 1994). According to Stiglitz, while markets are a necessary component of a well-functioning economy, comparative institutional analysis does not imply support for classical liberalism but for a 'mixed economy' model. From a 'new market failure' perspective, markets are riddled with collective goods and asymmetric information problems which stifle the discovery and communication of information and which prevent the attainment of an efficient equilibrium. Consequently, widespread government action is deemed necessary to improve resource allocation via 'optimality taxes' and product regulation. More recently, this analysis has been reinforced by the path-dependency or network externalities approach of Paul David which argues for further intervention to correct 'market failures' in a wide range of areas afflicted with 'technological monopolies'.

Chapter 2 develops central themes from Hayek's economics and the Virginia school of public choice to argue that new market failure theory does not meet the requirements of robust political economy. On the one hand, this approach reduces comparative institutions analysis to issues of incentives. The 'knowledge problem' enunciated by Hayek is neglected by models that focus on incentives to search for information which is known in principle to be available. From a Hayekian perspective the function of markets is to alert people to unforeseen circumstances and opportunities, a function which cannot be analysed in terms of the equilibrium models central to neo-classical economics. Moreover, insofar as market failure theorists are right to focus on 'incentive compatibility', they fail to apply this analysis to their favoured institutional alternatives. A consistent analysis of collective action and asymmetric information problems reveals that these are often more pronounced in a public sector environment than they are in a regime of 'imperfect markets'.

Chapter 3 turns to critiques of classical liberalism from outside of economic theory. For communitarian political theorists such as Charles Taylor and the followers of Jurgen Habermas, the case for the market economy is based on assumptions of individual self-interest and the notion that 'incentives matter' (for example, Taylor, 1985; Habermas, 1992). These authors contend that classical liberalism neglects the social and moral context in which individual preferences are formed and is preoccupied with the pursuit of efficient 'means' rather than the discovery of new and more elevated 'ends'. A related set of arguments, considered in Chapter 4, claims that market processes and the principle of 'exit' undermine the moral and social capital on which they rely. Liberal economic policies are said to destroy cultural resources that emphasise solidarity and cooperation. According to each of these perspectives, therefore, markets need to be 'kept in their place' by an alternative set of institutions organised on 'voice-based' processes of deliberative democracy.

Communitarian political theory makes some telling points against 'hyper-individualist' and rationalistic forms of social science such as those found in the models of neo-classical economics. As Chapters 3 and 4 aim to show, however, even if one accepts all communitarian criticisms of neo-classical economics, none of these arguments proves effective against the case for a classical liberal regime. On the contrary, the arguments emphasised by Hayek suggest that markets and other 'exit'-based institutions may be better placed to facilitate the discovery of new tastes and values than democratic alternatives, because they allow greater scope for decentralised evolution. Similarly, attempts to sustain norms based on 'solidarity' through the use of government power, far from facilitating social unity may actually increase conflict. On each of these counts, therefore, communitarian arguments fail on their own terms. In addition, however, such theories lack any account of how democratic structures can deal with problems of inadequate incentives. While it is erroneous to assume that people always act out of self-interest, it is equally misguided to assume that democratic institutions are capable of transcending the importance of incentives. Judged by the standards of robust political economy, deliberative democracy may actually reduce the capacity for people to challenge and to question one another's ends, and far from building social capital may undermine adherence to cooperative social norms.

The final challenge to classical liberalism considered in Part I arises from egalitarian political theory. Shifts towards a more unequal distribution of wealth in societies that have undergone a process of economic liberalisation have prompted restatements of the claim that unfettered markets fail to satisfy the criteria of inclusion and social justice. Following Rawls (1971) and

Dworkin (1981), philosophers in the liberal egalitarian tradition argue that income inequalities fail to deliver sufficient compensatory benefits to the worst-off and are incompatible with the principle of 'equality of respect'. For philosophers associated with recent theories of multiculturalism, meanwhile, these economic inequalities are only one component of a much wider range of exclusive social practices (in terms of gender, race and sexual identity) that are reinforced by private market processes (Young, 2000).

Chapter 5 examines the robustness of the egalitarian challenge in terms of the 'knowledge problem' and the 'incentive problem'. Given conditions of limited knowledge and the complex trade-offs pertinent to distributive justice, it argues that the principle of equal respect should not attempt to establish any one set of norms with regard to the distribution of income and social status. Rather, it should support a framework that enables individuals and voluntary associations to learn from a variety of distributive principles. Equality of respect, therefore, must be confined to the enforcement of the norms of 'non-interference' compatible with freedom of association and disassociation. In addition to these knowledge-based constraints, the chapter contends that theories of justice should not impose excessive 'strains of commitment' that fail to recognise the link between ownership and incentives. Within this context, egalitarian theories, which treat both personal talents and natural assets as 'common pool resources', are found to be incompatible with the principle that 'incentives matter'.

Part II: Classical Liberalism and the Future of Public Policy

Having offered a theoretical defence of classical liberalism in Part I, Part II examines some of these issues in more depth, focusing on three areas that have proven most resistant to liberalisation. Each of the chapters sets out a classical liberal agenda to the respective policy issues and then addresses objections derived from 'market failure' economics and both communitarian and egalitarian variants of political theory.

The first of the chapters in Part II deals with the question of poverty relief and the welfare state. Redistributive taxation and the provision of education and health care by the state have been sustained by arguments that suggest market processes are both inefficient and inequitable. Economists focus on informational problems that face service users, while for political theorists the concern is that markets undermine the 'public service' ethos and fail to provide adequate access or decision-making power to those on lower incomes. Chapter 6 shows, however, that while welfare state services do indeed provide informational problems for consumers, these tend to be exacerbated by government provision and regulation. With respect to ethical and political issues meanwhile, communitarian and egalitarian theories are shown to lack a robust account of why – even on their own terms – welfare state institutions should be judged superior to the mosaic of competing associations favoured by the classical liberal approach.

Chapter 7 focuses on the international dimension where much of the debate on 'neo-liberalism' is dominated by discussions over globalisation and trade. For critics, open market policies bring about increasing global inequalities owing to the intensification of competition between developed and developing nations. Drawing on 'path-dependency' theories, such critics support interventionist policies in developing nations combined with large-scale increases in economic assistance from wealthier countries in order to shift the trajectory of development in the poorest parts of the world. This analysis is reinforced by 'cosmopolitan' theories of justice, which argue that in a world of economic interdependence, questions of social or distributive justice should be extended beyond the nation state to encompass global democratic institutions. Chapter 7 questions the robustness of these contemporary development models, highlighting knowledge problems and incentive-based deficiencies in the case for global governance structures. It suggests that global aid agencies lack both the knowledge and incentives to choose an appropriate development path for low-income countries, and contends that the pursuit of distributive justice is likely to empower global elites at the expense of citizens in both the developed and the developing world.

Chapter 8 turns to environmental policy, where most governments remain wedded to an approach that combines command and control regulation with centrally determined pricing schemes. This approach is premised on market failure theories that question the practicality of property rights solutions, and by those who argue that the moral status of environmental goods precludes their allocation on the basis of trade. Chapter 8 challenges these objections. It shows that while transaction costs surrounding the definition and enforcement of property rights provide obstacles to environmental markets, these costs obstruct social democratic processes to a far greater extent. In terms of ethics, the chapter shows that the case for establishing environmental property rights is not confined to arguments from efficiency, but is based on the view that market institutions allow the greatest scope for individuals and civil associations to express their commitments to environmental objectives over other values, including those of material prosperity. Finally, the chapter notes that although there is a class of 'global' environmental problems not readily amenable to robust classical liberal 'solutions', there is little reason to suppose on the grounds of either economics or ethics that centrally directed alternatives are any better suited to the issues in hand.

The book concludes in Chapter 9 with some alternative strategies for institutional reform. There is no one model of how to move towards a classical liberal regime of open markets and limited government. This will vary between countries, with the character of the evolutionary path affected by differences in the cultures and traditions concerned. What is crucial, however, is that policy-makers are equipped with a clear set of principles that should frame the direction of reform. It is the purpose of this book to articulate those principles.

PART I

Challenges to classical liberalism

2. Market failures 'old' and 'new': the challenge of neo-classical economics

INTRODUCTION

Economic theory enjoys a vexed relationship with the classical liberal tradition. On the one hand the writings of Adam Smith are often invoked to illustrate how a complex process of social coordination may occur without guidance from a centralised system of command and control. On the other hand, however, the tools of modern neo-classical economics highlight a wide array of 'market failures' thought to justify corrective government interventions. Even critics of the market economy appear confused about the relationship between economic theory and classical liberal conclusions. For many, the fully rational agents that populate the models of contemporary economics present a distorted view of human nature in order to deduce market liberal policies (for example, Barber, 1984; Ramsey, 2004). What such critics often fail to recognise, however, is that these very models of rationality are also used by contemporary economists to highlight the supposed weaknesses of an unregulated market system and to make the case for widespread government action. As Frank Knight (1982: 57) once remarked: 'Critics of the enterprise economy who do not have a fair understanding of how the machinery works cannot tell whether to criticise it because it doesn't work according to the theory or because it does.'

Much of this confusion about the status of classical liberalism arises from differing interpretations of 'equilibrium' in economic theory. To those working within the mainstream of neo-classical economics the equilibrium standard is a benchmark against which to judge the performance of 'real-world' market institutions. From a classical liberal perspective, however, a robust political economy uses the equilibrium concept as a form of 'ideal typical' analysis to explore how institutions cope with 'real-world' conditions that depart from the equilibrium ideal (Boettke, 1997).

Focusing on the 'knowledge problem' and the 'incentive problem', this chapter argues that contemporary neo-classical policy analysis fails to meet the requirements of a robust political economy. The chapter commences with an outline of the meaning and interpretation of equilibrium in contemporary economic theory and then explores the weaknesses of such theorising in the context of 'market failure' arguments 'old' and 'new'. This includes an examination of the misuses of equilibrium in the 'socialist calculation debates' and in the rise of theories of externalities and collective goods. It also presents an explanation and critique of more recent market failure theories associated with Joseph Stiglitz. Finally, the chapter presents some further reflections on the status of equilibrium theorising and sets out an alternative, evolutionary standard for the robust application of comparative institutions reasoning.

EQUILIBRIUM, EFFICIENCY AND ROBUST POLITICAL ECONOMY

Equilibrium analysis plays a central role in economic theory primarily because the latter has sought to distinguish the conditions in which 'efficiency' prevails. Efficiency is, of course, a contested concept – when people differ in their goals and values then actions which are efficient from the viewpoint of one actor may be inefficient through the eyes of another. Economic theory has sought to avoid this problem of incommensurable values by judging efficiency in terms of the capacity of different institutions to enable the satisfaction of individual preferences. People hold different subjective values, but it is precisely these differences in values that provide opportunities for mutually beneficial exchanges to occur. Within this context, certain institutions may prevent people from realising their preferences efficiently whereas others may make it easier for them to be fulfilled in an efficient manner.

'Pareto optimality' is the usual standard against which the efficiency properties of institutions are judged by mainstream economists. The Pareto criterion is fulfilled when there can be no other arrangement which will leave someone better off without worsening the position of others. This standard implies that all opportunities to expand the social product and to engage in mutual gain have been exhausted and that the only way people may improve their position beyond such a point is through a process of wealth redistribution. The conditions that would have to be met in order for a Pareto optimal equilibrium to be attained by a decentralised market economy were originally enunciated by Leon Walras but were formally articulated in the 1950s by Arrow and Debreu (1954) in the fundamental theorems of welfare economics. These conditions include perfect information on behalf of producers and consumers; perfect competition – where there are large numbers of buyers and sellers none of whom can exercise a significant impact on prices; the costless mobility of resources; and the absence of externalities or external costs.

Although the theorems of welfare economics constitute the core of neo-classical theory, economists within the mainstream paradigm vary in their judgement of whether such analysis supports the case for an unregulated market economy or whether the conditions required are so stringent that no market system could ever hope to achieve them. For those in the Chicago school following George Stigler and Gary Becker, general equilibrium constitutes an accurate description of how a market economy actually works. Producers and consumers act as if they are perfectly informed of exchange opportunities and even the largest firms are thought equivalent to perfectly competitive price-takers given the scale of the markets in which they operate. For critics of 'free markets', however, such as Kenneth Arrow and Joseph Stiglitz, the equilibrium standard provides strong grounds to doubt the efficiency properties of an unregulated capitalist system. 'Real-world' markets depart in so many ways from the perfectly competitive standard that in the absence of government action they result in massive inefficiencies.

Though it remains dominant in contemporary economics, the standard use of equilibrium theory does not meet the requirements for a robust political economy as set out in the introduction to this book. At issue is the failure of neo-classical economics to pay sufficient attention to the manner in which the institutional context of decision-making conditions the outcomes that result. Although equilibrium analysis appears to be concerned with the evaluation of different institutional regimes, the explanatory power of these models rests not on the qualities of specific institutional environments, but on the assumptions that underpin the models at hand. Hayek recognised this tendency as early as the 1940s when he noted that:

> In the usual presentations of equilibrium analysis it is generally made to appear as if these questions of how the equilibrium comes about were solved. But if we look closer, it soon becomes evident that these apparent demonstrations amount to no more than the apparent proof of what is already assumed. (Hayek, 1948a: 45)

Both the Chicago school and its interventionist critics appear guilty of this tendency. In the former case the assumption of perfect information and perfectly aligned incentives leads to the view that markets produce optimal results. In the latter case the assumption of perfectly informed and motivated governmental actors leads to the view that state intervention delivers optimal results. No attempt is made by Chicago school economists to explain how market actors are able to acquire the capacity to coordinate their actions in the appropriate manner – the assumptions of the general equilibrium model are simply conflated with the situation facing real-world market participants. Critics of classical liberal policy conclusions are, however, guilty of the very same tendency. While recognising that real-world markets fail to meet equilibrium standards, no explanation is given of how governmental actors can bring about the necessary equilibrium in place of markets – it is simply assumed that they can.

To question the relevance of general equilibrium in the above vein is not, however, to imply that the concept has no use. What is required is not abandonment of equilibrium as an idea, but of those approaches which treat equilibrium states either as a description of the real world, or as a description of how the world can and should be made to function. A more fruitful way of using the equilibrium concept is as a form of ideal type. As Boettke (1997) has noted, the purpose of ideal types is to gain understanding of the implications that arise owing to departures from the ideal. Departures from ideal typical conditions focus attention on how different institutions cope with the actual conditions that characterise the 'real world' of human interaction. Seen in this light, the task of a robust political economy is not to highlight the failure of social and economic institutions to attain a state of 'perfect' coordination but to provide institutionally grounded explanations for the degree of coordination that we do actually see.

The use of equilibrium as an ideal type forms the basis for the robust application of comparative institutions analysis in public policy. Analysts must, before determining that a particular set of institutions 'fails', offer an account of how and why an alternative set of institutions can do better in addressing the 'knowledge problem' and the 'incentive problem'. It is in this context that classical liberalism draws on insights from the Hayekian and property rights and public choice schools to highlight the relative robustness of unfettered markets. These arguments develop an institutional account of why market processes may be better placed than systems of government planning and intervention to cope with problems of imperfect knowledge and imperfect motivation.

If comparative institutions reasoning forms the core of classical liberalism then it is an approach to public policy that is not widely understood. Nowhere is this more evident than in the continuing application of 'market failure' theory. While it is doubtful that the growth of state intervention has been directly informed by market failure economics, there are few interventions that have not been defended at some point or other on 'market failure' grounds. Two distinct waves of theorising have informed the views of economists in this regard. The first followed the socialist calculation debates of the 1930s and 1940s and included theories of imperfect competition and developments in the theory of externalities and collective goods. The second wave developed in the 1970s and 1980s with the rise of 'information economics' and theories of network externality. From the perspective of classical liberalism neither of these approaches meets the requirements of a robust political economy. The subsequent sections defend the case for classical liberalism against market failure arguments 'old' and 'new', and in doing so highlight the continuing deficiencies of equilibrium theorising in economic analysis.

CLASSICAL LIBERALISM VERSUS 'OLD' MARKET FAILURE THEORY: THE LEGACY OF THE SOCIALIST CALCULATION DEBATES

'Old' Market Failure Theory and the Socialist Calculation Debates

The modern comparative institutions case for the market economy arose out of the socialist calculation debates of the 1930s and 1940s. In the course of these debates Oscar Lange and advocates of 'market socialism' contended that the analytical techniques of neo-classical economics provided a sound basis on which to construct a 'planned' economy. Lange and his followers maintained that there was no theoretical difference between the manner in which capitalist and socialist systems must solve the economic problem. They accepted the argument of Von Mises (1920) that an efficient economic system cannot, *contra* Marx, dispense with the process of monetary calculation in evaluating production plans. Without price signals indicating the relative scarcity of different production goods, decision-makers lack the capacity to determine which input combinations generate the highest-valued outputs. The market socialists maintained, however, that a socialist system was capable of generating the relevant price signals at least as effectively as an economy based on private ownership of productive assets.

According to Lange, if the conditions underlying the neo-classical equilibrium model pertain, then socialist planners could allocate resources efficiently by arriving at an appropriate set of 'accounting prices' (Lange, 1936a, 1936b). Under perfect information the same data that neo-classical models assume are available to market participants would also be available to government planners. Planners, therefore, could perform the function of the 'Walrasian auctioneer', adjusting prices up or down until equilibrium between supply and demand in all markets was achieved. For Lange such procedures would be more efficient than a system based on private property, because 'real-world' markets do not meet the criterion of perfect information and competition, and require the complex paraphernalia of contract which he assumed would not be necessary under a government-administered system.

Lange and his followers contributed to a growing stream of 'market failure' theorising in both the pre- and post-war periods that questioned the capacity of a private enterprise system to meet the optimality criteria specified in the neo-classical model. The continuing growth of large joint stock companies and the elimination of many family-owned enterprises offered superficial support, if not to Marxian notions concerning the 'self-eliminating' tendencies of competition and the 'increasing concentration of industry', then to those who questioned the 'real-world' relevance of perfectly competitive markets

(Chamberlin, 1933; Robinson, 1933). Similarly, the onset and persistence of economic depression in the 1930s appeared to contradict the informational assumptions of a model which suggested that markets are self-correcting mechanisms. Within this context a socialist order, it was assumed, could perform the calculations necessary to achieve Walrasian equilibrium but without the inefficiencies, slumps and concentrations of power that pertain under capitalism.

In the years following the Second World War developments in the theory of externalities and collective goods dealt an additional blow to the classical liberal position. Originally set out by A.C. Pigou in 1920 and developed by James Meade, Francis Bator and Paul Samuelson in the 1950s, these theories suggested that unregulated markets would fail to provide certain mutually beneficial goods and services in the appropriate quantities owing to the widespread existence of 'free-riding' behaviour. If actors can impose costs on others or receive benefits without payment then the price signals generated by a decentralised market fail to reflect the full value placed on the relevant services by society at large. From the perspective of market failure theory a range of services from the supply of public parks and lighthouses to the control of industrial pollution provided solid grounds to believe that the pattern of resource allocation could be improved through targeted government action.

The 'Knowledge Problem': Hayek and the Case for Private Markets

The economic writings of F.A. Hayek may be understood as a response to this first wave of market-failure theory (Caldwell, 2004). In the 1940s Hayek authored a string of papers arguing that the claims made by socialists in the 'calculation debates' revealed more about the weaknesses of the neo-classical paradigm than about the relative robustness of 'real-world' market and socialist economic systems. According to Hayek, Lange's recognition of the formal rules that must be adhered to for Walrasian equilibrium to be achieved said nothing about the relative capacity of different systems to approach anything like this standard.

From Hayek's perspective it could not be assumed that the information necessary for economic coordination could be attained independent of the institutional context (Boettke, 1997). Assuming the existence of objectively 'given' knowledge is to neglect how the relevant knowledge of relative resource scarcities is acquired. It was Hayek's contention that the knowledge needed to determine the content of the price signals necessary for economic calculation could not be generated as effectively, if at all, by a socialist system of central accounting as it could by a system of private property exchange. At the core of this argument was a comparative institutions claim that market processes are better placed to cope with a world in which the conditions articulated in the neo-classical model are absent (Boettke, 1997). There are several dimensions to Hayek's critique of neo-classical theory, each of which points towards the institutional superiority of a liberal market order.

First, according to Hayek the 'data' that contribute to the formation of prices in a market economy are not 'given' to any agency in their totality, but are divided between the many actors that make up the market concerned. A private enterprise system communicates indirectly the elements of this 'division of knowledge' through the medium of price. Individuals and organisations bid for resources on the basis of knowledge concerning personal preferences, the availability of substitutes and entrepreneurial innovations known only to themselves, but in doing so they contribute incrementally to the formation of prices, transmitting their 'bit' of information to those with whom they exchange. The latter may then adapt their own buying and selling decisions in light of this data, which then inform subsequent agents like ripples spreading out in a pool. Thus, the distant actions of an entrepreneur bidding up the price of tin in response to a new source of demand are transmitted through the entire market as those who use tin and its substitutes economise in response to the higher price. Crucially, in order to adjust their production or consumption patterns (substituting more for less expensive alternatives, for example) accordingly, market actors need not be fully aware of the complex network of events that contributes to a rise or fall in price – what they do need to know is that the prices they face have changed. Thus: 'The whole acts as one market, not because any of its members survey the whole field, but because their limited individual fields of vision sufficiently overlap so that through many intermediaries the relevant information is communicated to all' (Hayek, 1948c: 86).

A socialist system would, according to Hayek, be unable to achieve equivalent coordination owing to the inability of any one agency to grasp all the changing conditions of supply and demand facing a multitude of dispersed social actors. Relative to a private market, therefore, a system of government-determined prices will result in a misallocation of resources.

The second aspect of Hayek's challenge to neo-classical theory turns on the assumption that the 'bits' of information possessed by market agents concerning the plans of their exchange partners are necessarily accurate. This assumption is apparent in the notions of perfect information which pervade neo-classical models and that frequently lead to demands to correct 'market failures' when information is 'imperfect'. From a Hayekian perspective, such models assume away the processes by which individuals and organisations improve the accuracy of their expectations over time. The task of attaining coordination occurs under conditions of uncertainty, where information is often contradictory (Hayek, 1948b, 1948c, 1946d). In a market economy individuals and firms make bids for resources reflecting their own subjective interpretations and it is via the generation of profits and losses that these expectations are tested against the objective facts of other peoples' behaviour manifested in decisions to buy or sell at particular prices. It is the signals of profit and loss generated by the clash of competing ideas that enables trial and error learning as participants imitate successful entrepreneurs and learn not to make the same errors as the unsuccessful. Markets are never in equilibrium, but the profit and loss signals generated in disequilibrium encourage the movement of resources towards a higher level of coordination than would otherwise be the case (Kirzner, 1992, 1997). According to Hayek, government planners (democratically elected or otherwise), could never set prices reflecting the perceptions of economic opportunities that are dispersed amongst a myriad of actors who have the freedom to exchange property titles in the market.

Knowledge of market opportunities and discrepancies is dispersed in a lumpy and uneven manner and it is through the inequalities that emerge from the competitive process that entrepreneurs discover which production models to follow and which to avoid. On Hayek's account, therefore, competition can never be 'perfect'. It is because some firms exercise a greater influence on the market than others that a process of imitative learning is set in motion. Entrepreneurial profits which would not exist under perfectly competitive conditions are the symbols that signal the best way of serving the market. Competition is a dynamic process which cannot be captured in a model where all actors are assumed to possess the same data and react passively to the objective stimuli before them. The absence of perfect competition where there are multiple buyers and multiple sellers of homogenous products does not, therefore, constitute 'market failure', but is an essential characteristic of a process where people exercise creative agency in discovering new input–output combinations and where these experiments are 'tested' by the decisions of consumers. By contrast, under 'perfect' conditions: 'Advertising, undercutting and improving ("differentiating") the goods or services produced are all excluded by definition – "perfect" competition means indeed the absence of all competitive activities' (Hayek, 1948e: 96).

Markets are only likely to approach 'perfection' in the neo-classical sense when there is little disagreement and no new knowledge to be spread. In a market for a product such as grain, for example, where it is hard to differentiate between supplies and where techniques are well known, then prices are unlikely to be affected significantly by any one actor (Hayek, 1948e: 103).[1] When products can be produced in a variety of ways, however, when there are a range of potential substitutes and where it takes much longer to discover the appropriate resource combinations, management techniques and organisational forms, then those who create the most suitable methods may generate substantial profits before others are able to emulate their practices. These profits reflect better entrepreneurial foresight in conditions of uncertainty.

Entrepreneurial action is often of the 'price-making' variety where firms duel with one another, launch price-cutting campaigns, fashion new products to open up markets and develop new organisational forms. In order for competition to be effective what is required is that existing market participants are open to challenge from new entrants offering better opportunities than currently available. The alternative to such 'imperfection' is not 'perfect competition' but attempts to set prices and to regulate entry by government licensing boards or equivalents. From a Hayekian perspective the latter stifle the evolutionary processes which enable people to discover the lowest-cost methods of production and those actors in the best position to deliver them (Hayek, 1948e: 100; 1978b). A system of central regulation cannot simulate or replicate such a discovery process because the results cannot be known in the absence of actual competition, however 'imperfect'.

The third and final element of the Hayekian critique centres on the preferences of market participants. For Hayek, the notion of 'given' knowledge is inappropriate not only because of errors in interpreting the demand for different goods and judging production methods, but because the content of people's preferences is also subject to dynamic change. Market agents are alerted to and acquire previously unforeseen tastes and organisational practices by the process of market competition itself. The market process facilitates learning under conditions of 'radical ignorance' where actors on both demand and supply sides become aware of information which they previously did not know was in existence. The latter is captured in the claim that participation in markets is akin to a 'voyage of exploration into the unknown' (Hayek, 1948e: 101). In this sense, Hayek anticipated Schumpeter's notion that capitalism is a process of 'creative destruction' where competition in the form of new technologies and production methods 'strikes at the foundations and very lives' of incumbent firms. Static notions of equilibrium are inappropriate to understanding this process of innovation and evolutionary change (Lavoie, 1985).

These critiques of the 'given' knowledge assumption also challenge the Pigovian-inspired view that government action can easily 'correct' for market imperfections that flow from externalities and collective goods problems. Put simply, the costs and benefits associated with externalities are subjective and are best revealed through the actions of people when confronted with a range of competing alternatives and where there are profit and loss signals to communicate the content of the relevant choices. Just as government planners in general may be incapable of accessing sufficient information to set prices at a socially optimal level, so they may lack the capacity to set environmental taxes, subsidies and regulatory controls at the appropriate rate. This is not to exclude the possibility of genuine 'market failures' that limit the possibility of even 'imperfect' market solutions. There may be some goods the supply of which simply cannot be subject to a process of competitive discovery. At the very least, however, Hayek's views suggest that the burden of proof should be shifted in the direction of those favouring greater government intervention.

The 'Incentive Problem': Public Choice Theory and Government Failure

If Hayek's contributions cast doubt on market failure theory then a further set of questions was highlighted by the rise of the public choice school. Hayek's arguments against socialism make no assumptions about the motivations of public decision-makers – they do not, for example, challenge the idea that politicians and civil servants are 'public spirited', but focus instead on the 'knowledge problems' of planning under conditions of complexity. Public choice analysis, by contrast, relaxes the assumption of public-spirited motivation. Buchanan and Tullock (1962) objected to the 'bifurcated' view of human action implicit in market failure models, which depict people acting out of self-interest in the context of commercial exchange, but assume 'other-regarding' motivations when people enter the political arena. Demsetz (1969) meanwhile argued that market failure theories were guilty of the 'nirvana fallacy'. They compare the 'inefficiencies' resulting from externalities and informational problems in markets with an unspecified alternative where such problems are assumed to disappear. According to Demsetz, a comparative institutions approach requires analysis of the strengths and weakness of 'real-world' though 'imperfect' institutional alternatives. The work of Coase, for example, shows that markets 'fail' when the transaction costs of internalising externalities via the specification of property rights are too high (Coase, 1960). Coase's work also demonstrates, however, that such costs exist in any institutional setting (Dahlman, 1979; Medema, 1994). The question, therefore, becomes one of comparing the relative extent of transactions costs within 'imperfect' markets to those arising under 'imperfect' government intervention. It is in this context that the Virginia school of public choice argues that problems of externalities and high transaction costs that cause market failure may be more pronounced within the context of democratic politics.

Public choice theory recognises that moving responsibility for collective goods from the private to the public sector does not eliminate free-riding behaviour and indeed may create greater problems than those that inhibit the operation of private markets (Buchanan and Tullock, 1962; Mitchell and Simmons, 1994). Specifically, because the results of the democratic process are often non-excludable, people may 'free-ride' on the political efforts of others. To achieve benefits from politics requires collective action, but the larger the numbers who might benefit or bear the costs from such action, the greater the incentives to free-ride. Policies that concentrate benefits on a relatively small number of actors may attract well-organised lobbies that face lower costs of monitoring and disciplining free-riders. By contrast, measures that diffuse benefits across large groups may not bring forth organised support proportionate to the numbers affected, owing to the higher costs of controlling free-riding behaviour in large-number situations (Olson, 1967; 1982; Tullock, 1994). Consequently, the political process may be captured by special interest organisations and in particular producer groups who may concentrate monopolistic benefits and privileges on their members while externalising costs across unorganised sections of the population.

From a public choice perspective, the political process externalises costs because people vote for things that will be paid for by others (Mitchell and Simmons, 1994; Olson, 2000). Access to benefits provided by the state constitutes an 'open access' resource. It is in each individual's interest to support organisations lobbying for policies that concentrate benefits on themselves while financing them with resources taken from the electorate at large. While collectively it may be beneficial to call a halt to such 'rent-seeking' behaviour, no individual or group is likely to do so because the exercise of voluntary restraint would open the way for exploitation by less-scrupulous actors. When the majority of actors recognise this logic, societal interaction may transform from a positive sum game of voluntary exchange into a zero-sum or even a negative-sum game, where people seek to gain predatory transfers from one another (Buchanan and Tullock, 1982; Tullock, 1994).

Collective-goods problems on the 'demand side' of politics are, from a public choice perspective, mirrored by the poor incentives for politicians and civil servants who 'supply' public policies. Because political actors are not 'residual claimants' who can profit personally from the exercise of sound management, they have relatively few incentives to take long-term decisions the benefits of which may accrue when a different party is in power. Politicians cannot choose to retain and then to sell shares in the management of public services and may as a consequence have incentives to act opportunistically either in their own private interests or in those of client groups, rather than in the interests of the polity at large. Incentives towards productive efficiency are hampered further by the monopolistic character of the political process. In the period between elections voters are faced with a 'take it or leave it' scenario where they have limited capacity to escape from the consequences of poor service delivery (Wholgemuth, 1999). The capacity to raise revenue via compulsory taxation creates a 'soft budget constraint' that reduces the incentive to respond to public demands. The softness of this constraint may be pronounced even in the longer term because citizens typically have a very limited number of political competitors from which to choose. Relative to the power of firms in a private market, the capacity of politicians to enforce exclusionary cartels is much greater because the monopoly of force exercised by the state enables those in power to fix the terms of political competition.

'NEW' MARKET FAILURE THEORY: THE CHALLENGE OF INFORMATIONAL ECONOMICS

The classical liberal critique of market failure theory set out above has led to a re-evaluation of the interventionist conclusions that dominated the post-war period. With the failure of East European central planning and more moderate industry specific nationalisations in the capitalist democracies, economic theorists have concluded that neo-classical conceptions of 'market socialism' have little if any relevance to judgements concerning the comparative merits of alternative economic systems. This recognition has not, however, led to the acceptance of classical liberal conclusions. On the contrary, while it is accepted that comprehensive models of state ownership and planning have little to commend them, theoretical developments in the neo-classical paradigm now highlight an entirely new class of 'market failures' which suggest that a 'mixed' system combining private ownership with widespread government intervention can be justified on comparative institutions grounds.

Stiglitzian Economics and 'New' Market Failure Theory

The Nobel laureate Joseph Stiglitz has been at the forefront of innovations which, though highlighting the weaknesses of socialist systems, also point towards the inefficiency of laissez-faire markets. Building on work in the 'economics of information', Stiglitz (1994) challenges the implications previously drawn from the Walrasian and Arrow–Debreu models. On the one hand, Stiglitz rejects the market socialist claim that a central planning board could use the model of general equilibrium as the rule on which to base its decisions. According to Stiglitz, 'real-world' socialist institutions lack the information and incentives to implement this result. Equally, however, Stiglitz questions the relevance of the general equilibrium model with respect to the performance of private markets. Real-world markets rarely, if ever, meet the optimality conditions specified in the Arrow–Debreu theorem so this model cannot justify classical liberal prescriptions. What is needed, instead, is a comparative approach which recognises that while the information and incentives generated by 'real-world' markets do have strengths, such markets are also prone to numerous imperfections requiring corrective government action. Stiglitz, therefore, aims to articulate the principles which can be used to discern an appropriate 'mix' between private markets and government regulation (Stiglitz, 1994: 25).

Throughout his work Stiglitz emphasises that competition has an important role in providing incentives for economic actors to improve their performance, and he attributes the failure of the socialist experiments in Eastern Europe to the weak incentives wrought by the absence of competitive forces. Stiglitz rejects the view that for competition to be effective it must occur in the form of 'price-taking' behaviour in markets where there are large numbers of buyers and sellers. Echoing Baumol and the 'contestable markets' thesis, he recognises that competition on dimensions such as quality and organisational structure as well as price can provide a disciplinary check on producers even when there are far fewer players in the market than under perfectly competitive conditions (Stiglitz, 1994: 112, 132).

This apparent concession to classical liberal understandings is, however, heavily qualified by two specific claims. First, Stiglitz argues that the benefits from competition do not necessarily depend on the private ownership of productive assets (1994: 239). Governments can, for example, set up rival bureaucratic agencies that compete for funds and custom, simulating private markets. Second, Stiglitz claims that while competition is beneficial in some circumstances there are other situations where it is ineffective. There are in particular a large number of areas where competition is limited by natural monopoly effects. While in the past such monopolies were thought to be confined to utilities, where the infrastructural costs involved in the supply of electricity or telecommunications meant that only one or a limited number of producers could supply a given locale, Stiglitz contends that these effects are much more pervasive. They are, he argues, especially pronounced in sectors requiring large amounts of research and development expenditure and where there are increasing returns to scale (Stiglitz, 1994: 140–45).

The above arguments have been buttressed by Brian Arthur and Paul David who focus on the alleged tendency of markets to create monopolies in 'knowledge-based' industries afflicted with the problem of network externalities and 'lock-in' effects (for example, David, 1985). According to this view, when the benefits of consuming a particular good or service depend positively on the number of other individuals who do so (as is the case with computer software or telephone networks, for example) then concentrations of economic power may arise that have little relation to the qualities of the goods provided. What matters is that beyond a critical threshold people will opt for a product on the basis of the number of other consumers already in the relevant 'network', rather than on the superiority of the product itself. In these circumstances competition will not select for the best products but may be affected by random events such as which product is first to establish a foothold in the market concerned.

'Lock-in' and path-dependency arguments have also been reinterpreted to offer theoretical support to Keynesian-style macroeconomic conjectures concerning the propensity of markets to get 'stuck' in alternating spirals of excessive optimism or pessimism (for example, Hill, 2006; Akerlof and Shiller, 2009). According to this view, under conditions of uncertainty, markets exhibit a strong tendency to be dominated by 'irrational' forms of

behaviour in response to sudden events or 'shocks' which exhibit little relationship to underlying economic 'fundamentals'. Instead of making rational
calculations about the likely success of investments the 'herd instinct' domi-
nates, where on the upside people invest in stocks or real estate simply because
everybody else appears to being doing so, and on the downside people withdraw investments in a context of collective pessimism about the prospect for
future returns. Unless government intervenes to regulate these expectations
through various macroeconomic stimuli (for example, regulating financial
markets, raising taxes in a boom, and introducing fiscal stimuli such as tax cuts
or increases in public spending in a slump) then only by chance will an unregulated market show any tendency to coordinate resources effectively.

If classical liberals over-rate competition then from a new market failure
perspective they also over-rate the role of the price system. This conclusion
arises from a focus on misaligned incentives in conditions of costly information. According to Grossman and Stiglitz (1976) information is never perfect
because it is costly to acquire – but there may be insufficient incentives to
acquire an 'optimal' amount of information when the decision to acquire additional data has collective-good attributes. Under socialism, central planners
lack incentives to acquire necessary information because they cannot capture
enough of the gains from doing so – these are taken by society at large.
Equally, however, the informational claims advanced in favour of decentralised pricing systems by Hayek are called into question. Grossman and
Stiglitz understand Hayek to be arguing that the prices generated by markets
provide 'sufficient statistics' for them to coordinate successfully (Grossman
and Stiglitz, 1976: 246; Stiglitz, 1994: Chapter 3). On this reading of Hayek,
people do not need to have any information about the economy at large
because the price system when in equilibrium transmits perfect information to
all market participants in an indirect form. For Grossman and Stiglitz,
however, if markets convey this much information then no one would have an
incentive to acquire any information themselves. Hayekian market prices have
collective-good attributes which allow people to 'free-ride' on the efforts of
others by observing prices and obtaining for nothing what they would otherwise have to search for (Grossman and Stiglitz, 1976: 246–7; Stiglitz, 1994:
Chapter 3). The price system can only operate when traders are able to hide
information from other participants and prices are, as a consequence, 'noisy'.
From this, Grossman and Stiglitz conclude that decentralised pricing systems
cannot achieve full equilibrium without corrective government action.

In addition to problems caused by the externality characteristics of prices,
Stiglitz (1994: 35) emphasises further market failures reflecting asymmetric
information. While Hayek's account of prices emphasises their role in communicating shifting patterns of resource scarcity, Stiglitz also considers prices to
represent a highly imperfect quality control device. If markets are to signal

quality to consumers effectively, then higher-priced products should be of better quality than lower-priced equivalents. Building on Akerlof's work (Akerlof, 1970), however, Stiglitz suggests that when one side of the market lacks information this relationship does not hold. When buyers are unable to judge the quality of the products being sold, they will offer lower prices to reflect the risk of receiving goods of poor quality. As prices offered by prospective consumers are lowered, however, this reduces the propensity of sellers with higher-quality goods to put them up for sale. Thus, in a market with asymmetric information poor products drive out the good. The related problem of 'adverse selection' on the supply side is also invoked in the context of insurance markets. Here, sellers cannot tell the difference between low- and high-risk purchasers and in order to compensate for a potential excess of high-risk consumers, they charge higher prices. As a consequence, low-risk consumers find it hard to find insurance products priced in a way reflecting the actual level of risk that they represent.

Though it recognises the weaknesses of socialism, Stiglitz's approach may be taken to imply a much larger role for the state than was recognised by the 'first wave' of market failure theorising (Stiglitz, 1994: 42–3). While claiming that a socialist system that applied the rules of marginal cost pricing could match the performance of a market system, post-war neo-classical theory maintained that only in a limited number of markets, where competition was highly imperfect or with large external effects, could state intervention actually outperform the market outcome. Stiglitz's arguments, on the other hand, imply that widespread 'market failures' occur whenever the price system is used and that state intervention could, in principle at least, improve efficiency across large parts of the economy. Thus, governments should pursue an active antitrust policy in markets with returns to scale and network effects; they should introduce tax and subsidy schemes to improve the informational properties of prices; and there should be widespread regulation of sectors plagued with asymmetric information including health care, insurance and banking. As such, Stiglitzian arguments represent perhaps the most sophisticated economic rationale for the modern regulatory state.

CLASSICAL LIBERALISM VERSUS 'NEW' MARKET-FAILURE ECONOMICS

Stiglitz and his colleagues claim to have developed important innovations that challenge the policy relevance of the Arrow–Debreu model in favour of a comparative institutions approach, but a close reading of these arguments reveals that the assumptions of the general equilibrium model still constitute the normative benchmark used when recommending specific policies. This is especially evident in the discussion of 'market failures'. If the Arrow–Debreu model is an unrealistic standard to judge between institutional regimes then concepts such as 'imperfect competition', 'natural monopoly' and 'external-ities' need to be redefined. Stiglitz, however, tends to define monopolies and problems arising from imperfect and asymmetric information as 'market fail-ures' precisely because they depart from the conditions laid down in the Arrow–Debreu equilibrium. It is inconsistent to maintain that general equilib-rium conditions cannot exist in the 'real world' but to persist in the judgement that markets 'fail' when they do not match these very criteria. It may, of course, be possible to say that markets 'fail' when judged against some alter-native criteria, but Stiglitz does not elaborate in this regard and neglects to explain how his proposals for intervention overcome problems arising from lack of knowledge and imperfect incentives. As such, from the perspective of classical liberalism, Stiglitz's claims to offer a comparative institutions approach do not meet the standards required by a robust political economy.

Misunderstanding Competition

Consider first 'imperfect' competition and the problem of 'natural monopo-lies'. According to Stiglitz:

> The new view has shown that markets may not be efficient and profits may not be zero. There is potential scope for competition policy both to limit profits and to improve efficiency. The new view stresses the importance of imperfect competition rather than monopoly … It argues that in most markets in modern industrialised countries competition is limited but that the welfare losses from limited competition may be much greater than had previously been thought to be the case. (Stiglitz, 1994: 128)

Given that Stiglitz rejects the 'real-world' relevance of the Arrow–Debreu model, it is far from clear why the fact that 'profits may not be zero' is consid-ered a problem at all. From a Hayekian perspective, owing to the dispersed and lumpy nature of knowledge and the need for learning, profits (and losses) are hardly ever zero. If the general equilibrium perspective does not provide an understanding of how 'real competition' operates as a discovery procedure then it is not obvious why industries with returns to scale or natural monopoly effects should be particular targets for government ownership and/or regula-tion. How are policy-makers to distinguish profits that reflect natural mono-poly effects and other 'imperfections' from those that reflect better entrepreneurial foresight? The characteristics of these sectors prevent the exis-tence of anything approaching a perfectly competitive structure. From a Hayekian perspective, however, and as Stiglitz also recognises, this need not imply that competition is ineffective. As Hayek notes:

> The confusion between the objective facts of the situation and the character of the human responses to it tends to conceal from us the important fact that competition is the more important the more complex or 'imperfect' are the objective conditions in which it has to operate. Indeed far from competition being beneficial only when 'perfect', I am inclined to argue that the need for competition is nowhere greater than in fields where the nature of commodities or services makes it impossible that it ever should create a perfect market in the theoretical sense. (Hayek, 1948e: 104)

In the case of local or regional natural monopolies such as water or electricity supply, for example, it may be that the necessary unit of competition is different. Instead of buyers facing an array of competing sellers within a given locality or region, competition may occur between localities and regions that have different 'monopoly' suppliers. Competition may occur as people vote with their feet for the particular locality or region where they wish to live. Inevitably, this would mean that purchases of such goods are 'bundled-up' with other purchases to a greater extent than in other markets and that competition may be relatively less intense. The alternative to such 'imperfection', however, is not more competition but outright government ownership or the central determination of prices which may reduce the scope of competition still further.

Stiglitz contends that competition can be preserved under public ownership because local or regional utilities may be placed in the hands of equivalent governmental units rather than being 'nationalised' concerns. This assumes, however, that it is possible to know prior to the existence of a private market the territorial extent of natural monopolies. Without a market in which there is the potential for entry and where more efficient firms can drive competitors out of business, then the actual extent of 'natural monopoly' effects may not be revealed. In order to match the results emerging from a private market, public utility suppliers would have to be subject to competitive entry from private suppliers and run the risk of bankruptcy. As Stiglitz himself recognises, however, under public ownership (even if this is at the local government level) new entry from those seeking to challenge natural monopolists is often prohibited (Stiglitz, 1994: 81). More importantly, if the possibility of bankrupting public utilities is to be allowed then it is difficult to see why taxpayers rather than private investors should have to bear these risks. What then is left of the claim that there is scope for government action to 'improve efficiency'?

Public ownership, it should be emphasised, may also stifle technological innovations that undermine natural monopolies. Under private ownership the generation of large profits may signal the need for investment in new technologies that could undermine the existence of monopoly phenomena. Telecommunications monopolies appear to have been undermined in precisely this way, with the advent of new digital and satellite technologies. Seen in this light, the large research and development expenditures that Stiglitz sees as monopoly-generating barriers to entry are often the competitive means necessary to fend off attacks from innovative challengers. There is, for example, evidence that a disproportionate share of innovations occur in smaller firms that subsequently grow into much larger concerns able to challenge incumbents (Mathews, 2006: Chapter 2). Where they reflect genuine start-up or information-related costs, as opposed to state-enforced restraints on trade, 'barriers to entry' do not themselves constitute a source of 'market failure'. The capital costs and the time taken to establish management expertise and public knowledge of one's technology or enterprise are real costs which reflect either a genuine scarcity or a cost already incurred by incumbent producers. These costs cannot be avoided but may only be redistributed from more to less successful firms by government action. If would-be market entrants cannot afford to incur the costs of competing with incumbents then this indicates that entry is not profitable and should not occur. Most new firms operate at a loss for an initial period but those that have identified a genuine market niche will be compensated by higher returns at a later point in time. There is as a consequence no case for start-ups to be subsidised by the state or to be given other privileges at the expense of incumbent market participants (O'Driscoll and Rizzo, 1996: 152).

These Hayekian insights also challenge the Stiglitzian claim that governments can match the results of private competition by granting decision-making autonomy to rival bureaucratic agencies within the public sector. These proposals simply shift the 'knowledge problems' of central planning to another level. Central planners (civil servants and politicians) may not know what the optimal number of competing agencies is and who the relevant competitors should be – these are some of the very facts which must be allowed to emerge from a 'bottom-up' environment where a diversity of investors, personal and institutional, sponsor an array of competing capital projects and organisational forms subject to the entry and exit decisions of consumers. In order to generate an equivalent 'discovery process', public enterprises would need the freedom to set their own prices and terms of employment, the capacity to reinvest their profits where they judge appropriate, and the freedom to take over or purchase rivals without permission from a central hierarchy. They would also need to face entry from rival firms sponsored by any one of a diversity of potential investors, and be subject to the threat of bankruptcy. Stiglitz's arguments are, therefore, subject to pressure from two sides. The more autonomy granted to public enterprises – to buy and sell and to invest at will – the more they acquire the powers of private enterprises and the stronger the argument for their outright privatisation. The less autonomy granted to public enterprises, however, the more they are subject to political controls from different levels of government and the more likely it is that they will be subject to the problems of a centrally planned regime.

'Lock-in', Path-dependency and Macroeconomic Failure

The case of network industries such as computer software illustrates a still further set of problems for the Stiglitzian perspective on competition. The empirical and theoretical basis of the 'lock-in' thesis has been challenged by Leibowitz and Margolis (1990, 1994). Drawing on evidence of industry structure and surveys of consumer guides, they found no evidence of cases where 'lock-in' has eliminated effective competition, and ample evidence that consumers did not prefer the 'locked-out' products. In the 'worst-case' scenarios consumers may have no clear preference between products and professional opinion may be deeply divided over their merits, as in famous cases such as the choice between QWERTY and DVORAK keyboard formats. Although network effects do exist in these markets it remains possible for entrepreneurs to start new networks or niche networks for specialist subsets of consumers which can then whittle down the advantage of incumbents.

Even if evidence of 'market failure' could be sustained in the above cases, however, it is far from clear that interventionist policy conclusions follow. The normative implication of the network externalities thesis is that governments should 'delay the market' in order to preserve product diversity and prevent people from becoming 'locked in' to inferior products. Yet, these arguments beg the question of how policy-makers can know at what point to 'delay the market' or 'how much diversity' is required? The network externality thesis ducks the question of how to assess the likelihood that policy action itself may be the 'random event' or 'accident' that locks society into an inferior path (Lewin, 2001). If the knowledge necessary to avoid 'lock-in' is readily available then market participants may also have access to it and the problem may not arise. If the relevant information is not available to any particular group, however, then competing ideas should be tested against one another. The case for the market economy is based on the notion that entrepreneurs do not have perfect information and that divergent interpretations of the economic environment need to be tested in order for learning to occur. There are no guarantees that this process will produce the most 'efficient' results, but market failure theorists who advocate state intervention to counteract 'lock-ins' do not provide any reasons to suppose that interventions, which are themselves monopolistic, will 'correct' the mistakes concerned.

A similar argument applies in the context of Keynesian macroeconomic applications of the path-dependency thesis. While market actors are often irrational and their behaviour may generate speculative bubbles and slumps, it does not follow that government action can improve on such 'imperfection'. On the contrary, there are strong reasons to believe that policy-makers may also suffer from a lack of information and may be subject to irrational exuberance or pessimism.[2] Indeed, they may be more likely to exhibit such behaviour owing to the majoritarian nature of public policy-making. Though the 'herd instinct' can be very strong, markets may be less subject to path-dependent processes precisely because they do not rely on collective action and majority rule. The most successful market traders are those who 'beat the market' by selling when everyone else is buying and vice versa, and it is the contrarian decisions of such marginal entrepreneurs which may lead, over time, to a corrective process which moves expectations closer to underlying fundamentals. In a public policy context, by contrast, those who wish to pursue a minority path are unable to do so because majority support is required before a change of direction may be implemented. In these circumstances, if the majority (whether a majority of the electorate or of policy 'experts') is pursuing an 'irrational' course, there is relatively less scope for dissenters to act in a way that may prompt a subsequent correction. The possibility of 'systemic' market failure where all major players – such as banks and institutional investors – make the same mistakes cannot be ruled out, but the possibility of such failure may be increased when the prevailing majority opinion is backed by the force of law (Friedman, 2009).

Owing to uncertainty and imperfect information, macroeconomic fluctuations may be an inevitable feature of a market economy, but from a Hayekian perspective these fluctuations are exacerbated by centralised government actions. Although market participants may follow 'herding' conventions to cope with uncertainty, in a 'free market' these conventions emerge through a decentralised process of trial and error in which profits can be made by those actors who break from the convention and modify business practices in the appropriate direction. By contrast, policy-makers such as finance ministers and central bankers have the capacity to affect the operation of markets – by controlling the supply of money, setting interest rates, regulating financial products and boosting government spending – but these centralised actions are not subject to simultaneous competition from rival agents and their success or failure in matching subjective interpretations to underlying conditions cannot be judged through the account of profit and loss (Butos and Koppl, 1997; Butos, 2003; O'Driscoll and Hoskins, 2006). Seen in this light, it is significant that the most severe instances of financial instability have corresponded not with periods of 'laissez-faire' but with increasing moves to centralise the regulation of finance and money. The United States Federal Reserve system was, for example, created to overcome the supposed 'failings' of the decentralised system of private 'clearing house' associations in the nineteenth century. Yet, through a failure to fulfil its basic mission of supplying liquidity during banking 'crises', it presided over the worst depression in US history (Butos and Koppl, 1997; Butos, 2003; O'Driscoll and Hoskins, 2006.).

Recent events may also confirm the foregoing analysis. The worldwide financial crisis of 2008 arguably followed from a series of historical government interventions which exacerbated the potential for systemic failure in financial markets (Friedman, 2009). These included the decision of monopoly central banks to hold down the rate of interest well below what may have been justified by the actual level of private savings – and to do so for a prolonged period of time (Gjerstad and Smith, 2009); the regulatory and fiscal induce-ment of government-backed mortgage companies to relax the lending require-ments for home purchase to low-income families (Wallison, 2009); internationally enforced capital regulations which induced banks to securitise risky mortgages (Jablecki and Machaj, 2009); and the creation of legally protected monopolies in the credit rating business such that the financial success and reputation of these agencies was not dependent on the quality of their risk assessments but on effective immunity from competition (White, 2009). In each of these cases, the homogenising effect of centrally determined policies may have increased the level of systemic risk. The very purpose of such policies is to reduce the behavioural heterogeneity that would otherwise be exhibited by the dispersed centres of decision-making power that constitute a market economy.[3] This argument does not imply that systemic 'market fail-ure' played no role in the crisis, but that such failure may have been magnified significantly by systemic failures in the structure of centrally determined monetary and regulatory policies.[4]

Misunderstanding Prices

The failure to understand the significance of the 'knowledge problem' evidenced in Stiglitz's views on competition and networks is also reflected in his analysis of the price system. The suggestion that markets lead to an under-production of information, because prices enable actors to 'free-ride' on costly data, misinterprets the nature of the 'knowledge problem'. Grossman and Stiglitz (1980) conceive profit as a reward for searching out costly information with problems of 'imperfect' information attributed to a lack of incentives to acquire additional knowledge which is nonetheless 'known' to be available in principle. In this 'rational expectations' model the possibility of pure error is ruled out. It is assumed that any mistakes have already been anticipated but have not been thought worth the cost of avoiding. This approach reflects a more general tendency for neo-classical theories to model problems of uncer-tainty and imperfect information in probabilistic terms. On this account, actors are able to assign probabilities to a range of possible market outcomes when making their own particular decisions. For Hayek, however, the primary func-tion of profit and loss signals is to alert market participants to unforeseen opportunities and circumstances – a problem of 'radical ignorance', which cannot be accounted for by a model of rational 'search' (Lavoie, 1985; Kirzner, 1992; Thomsen, 1992; Boettke, 1997). The range of options that may

be thrown up by the market process and the adaptations they may require
cannot be analysed probabilistically. It is not merely that actors do not know
which possibility out of a 'given' set will occur, but that the set itself is
unbounded and thus unknowable (O'Driscoll and Rizzo, 1996: 4).

Within this context, the type of knowledge that Hayek is concerned with
consists of the tacit 'judgements' and subjective 'hunches' that actors possess
about potential opportunities as they arise from the 'experience' of working in
a particular business or line of trade. Hayek's 'knowledge problem' also refers
to entrepreneurial imagination, where faced with the same set of data some
actors perceive opportunities whereas others see nothing. It is the inability to
'gather' and centralise information of this nature, no matter what incentives
are given to encourage 'search', that may account for the relative failure of
socialist economic systems. Knowledge of this order resides within individual
minds and is embedded in the cultural routines and procedures of different
organisations and their working practices. This knowledge is not subject to
'free-riding' because it is, to all intents and purposes, 'free' to those in its
possession.

On a Hayekian reading, the price system operates under conditions
inevitably characterised by disequilibrium because knowledge is dispersed
between competitors in a lumpy or uneven manner and is not instantly accessible to all. It is by responding to private perceptions of market opportunities that
entrepreneurial action prompts a learning process as profit signals and changes
in price data ripple across the overlapping perspectives of neighbouring market
actors. These processes occur incrementally, as reaction takes time and as each
entrepreneur or firm in the relevant chain of events differs in assessing and
reacting to the new situation and changing data. Although actors may learn
from their competitors by copying and imitating their successes, the capacity to
apply the relevant knowledge correctly is gained through experience and
initially, at least, is specific to those embedded in particular personal or organisational routines. Under conditions of dispersed knowledge and where imitative learning occurs over time there are always 'first-mover' advantages from
acting on private information and hence obtaining larger gains (profits) before
competitors can adapt to the relevant data. In practice, of course, entrepreneurial action in markets combines information gleaned from deliberate search and
the private context-dependent knowledge derived from experience and the
exercise of creative imagination. Knowledge, therefore, is rarely if ever a
collective good in the neo-classical sense of the term (Mathews, 2006: 57).[5]

To recognise that market prices are always in some degree of disequilibrium
is not to undermine the informational role of prices alluded to by Hayek.
Market-failure theorists interpret Hayek to be claiming that price signals are the
only type of information that actors need in making decisions. If prices are in
disequilibrium then according to Grossman and Stiglitz they are incapable of

performing this function because actors cannot tell whether a rise in price is due to an entrepreneurial mistake in bidding up the price of a particular asset or commodity, or whether it genuinely reflects underlying conditions of supply and demand. In the absence of perfect futures markets neither can actors know whether price changes are likely to reflect short-lived or longer-lasting changes in underlying conditions. On this interpretation, prices are far 'too coarse' a signal to be of significant use to decision-makers (Stiglitz, 1994: 93–5).

The problem with this market failure reasoning, however, is that Hayek's argument is not that prices provide all the necessary information but that without price signals generated by decentralised markets, decision-making would be that much harder (Lavoie, 1985; Thomsen, 1992). Prices do not act as 'marching orders' telling people how to act, but they do provide a valuable prompt to decision-makers and reduce the amount of detail required in formulating their plans (Thomsen, 1992: 50–51). Since future-oriented decisions grow incrementally out of past decisions, current market prices (profits and losses) act as 'aids to the mind' that help people to formulate conjectures about the likely course of events and how to adapt accordingly. The 'division of knowledge' embodied in the price system, meanwhile, reflects the actions of dispersed entrepreneurs who specialise in particular markets combining information they glean from prices with other more detailed non-price information acquired from experience in a specific trade. Entrepreneurs may, for example, use their knowledge of technological developments or of trends in local culture to make a judgement about the cause of a price rise and how long it is likely to last. Their subsequent conjectures and forecasts are then tested through the account of profit and loss as those who interpret market conditions more accurately make the most money and exert relatively more control over the subsequent direction of the market. The price signals brought about by this trial and error competition between specialist entrepreneurs, while far from 'perfect', are adequate to enable most other actors who lack specialised knowledge of particular markets to adapt to changing conditions of supply and demand of which they may be relatively ignorant. To suggest that markets 'fail' because the knowledge they convey is 'too coarse' is simply to imply that it would be better if people were omniscient (Friedman, 2006: 483–6). Market-failure theorists, however, have yet to explain how a process of central intervention can deal with the absence of omniscience that characterises the 'real world' of human interaction better than 'imperfect' markets. As Stiglitz himself concedes:

> a full corrective policy would entail taxes and subsidies on virtually all commodities, based on estimated demand and supply elasticities for all commodities (and all cross elasticities). The practical information required to implement the corrective taxation is well beyond that available at the present time (Stiglitz, 1994: 43)

One might add that such knowledge can never be made available to a central authority. It is, therefore, difficult to see what the 'new' market failure perspective adds to practical policy debates, and why insofar as it offers an argument for state intervention it is not guilty of the 'given' knowledge fallacy levelled by Hayek against more orthodox versions of neo-classical theory.

Markets, Entrepreneurial Regulation and Asymmetric Information

Viewed through a Hayekian lens, the information asymmetries that Stiglitz claims undermine the effectiveness of the price system should also be dealt with through processes of trial and error competition. While markets with asymmetric information present problems for buyers and sellers they also bring forth dynamic responses from those seeking to profit by facilitating exchange. As Steckbeck and Boettke (2004) show in their examination of Internet markets – where one might expect information asymmetries to be pronounced (many trades occurring between largely anonymous actors with minimal government regulation) – the profits to be gained from providing a safe and secure environment in which people can trade have encouraged entrepreneurs to vie with one another in supplying low-cost, private systems of verification. These include the provision of online histories, reputational ratings for sellers and the enforcement of sanctions against those who break the rules of particular selling networks. Market failure theory would predict that trade in such markets will be thin, or even non-existent, but the massive growth of online sales provides empirical support for the view that market competition is more robust than neo-classical models imply.

Elsewhere, gains from trade are spotted by entrepreneurs who specialise in checking the trustworthiness of others and who create markets by developing a reputation for supplying appropriate levels of assurance. Institutional innovations such as brand names, franchise outlets and simple reputation-building devices such as money-back guarantees exemplify the manner in which entrepreneurs compete to satisfy consumers on multiple different dimensions, including those of reputation and probity. Similarly, with respect to 'adverse selection', agencies have emerged that specialise in checking the risk status of those purchasing insurance and similar services.[6] Thus, empirical analyses of markets hypothesised to exhibit asymmetric information, such as those for used automobiles, offer little support for the theoretical claim that competition leads to declining product standards (Bond, 1984; Bereger and Udell, 1992). Similarly analysis of markets for health care and other insurance products has failed to find any evidence to suggest that adverse selection impedes the effective operation of such markets (Browne and Dorphinghaus, 1993; Cawley and Philipson, 1999; Chiappore and Salanie, 2000). Where neo-classical theory describes reputation building and other entrepreneurial responses to 'market failure' as 'wasteful' – because they divert resources away from direct production – from a Hayekian perspective, competition on these dimensions is a value-enhancing activity that helps overcome, albeit 'imperfectly', 'real-world' conditions that depart from the general equilibrium model. Market-failure theory offers little or no reason to believe that the costs of overcoming information asymmetries would be lower with government ownership or regulation.

Misrepresenting Coase and Ignoring Public Choice

A final weakness of the new market failure perspective is its neglect of the insights provided by the property rights and public choice schools. Stiglitz, in particular, questions the Coasian argument for the efficiency of private ownership on grounds that it ignores the transaction costs, principal versus agent problems, and information asymmetries that characterise 'real-world' market processes. Thus:

> Coase went wrong in assuming that there are no transaction costs and information costs. But the central contention of this book is that information costs … are pervasive. Assuming away information costs in an analysis of economic behaviour and organisation is like leaving Hamlet out of the play. (Stiglitz, 1994: 174)

Stiglitz does not, however, appear to have read Coase's work very closely and indeed completely misrepresents its main conclusions. What Coase (1989: 179) actually says on this matter is as follows:

> The reason why economists went wrong was that their theoretical system did not take into account a factor that is essential if one wishes to analyse the effect of a change in the law on the allocation of resources. This missing factor is the existence of transaction costs.

Coase could not be more explicit in recognising that transaction costs are positive in any institutional setting (see also Coase, 1960: Medema, 1994). The Coasean argument for privatisation rests on the comparative institutions claim, reinforced by public choice theory, that collective action problems and information asymmetries tend to be more pronounced in the public than in the private sector. Principal versus agent relationships do lead to inefficiencies within private markets. In joint stock companies, for example, shareholders face free-rider problems in disciplining poor management owing to the fact that the rewards from seeking better company performance may be shared with a large number of dispersed owners. In markets, however, these problems are reduced in significance because individual owners retain the option of selling shares in poor performers and buying shares in better performers, and/or investing their wealth in alternative organisational structures – such as owner-managed firms or those where shares are concentrated in a smaller number of institutional investors. People also have strong incentives to acquire more information about their decisions in markets – and thus to reduce information asymmetries – because their capacity to make individual buying and selling decisions is decisive in determining the nature of the product that they receive, with the costs of purchasing errors reflected directly in their net wealth.

In the political process, by contrast, 'exit' is prevented, so the decision to acquire information has collective-good characteristics. An individual's decision to obtain information about the quality of the policies on offer is not decisive in determining what they receive – the latter is entirely a function of how the prevailing majority votes. It is, therefore, rational for voters to be ignorant of political information, an incentive compounded by the high information costs associated with the 'bundle purchase' nature of politics itself. Voters cannot choose between a series of discrete policy options each with its own price tag in the way that private agents may customise their purchasing bundles, but must elect politicians to represent them across the full range of policy interventions. Though the bundling of services also occurs in some private markets where the conditions for 'perfect competition' are absent, this phenomenon tends to be far less pronounced than in representative politics. The sheer scale of the policy bundles concerned makes it harder for voters to judge which particular policies work or fail, than for private consumers to judge the merits of marketed products or to compare the returns on investments (Tullock, 1994; Somin, 1998). Such problems tend to be magnified by the absence of enforceable contract and tort remedies against deception by politicians of the sort available against product manufacturers. In view of these points, it is difficult to see how Stiglitz can sustain the contention that there is no difference between the scale of principal versus agent problems in the public and the private sectors.

EVOLUTION, COMPARATIVE INSTITUTIONS AND THE ECONOMIC CASE FOR CLASSICAL LIBERALISM

This chapter commenced by noting that the economic case for classical liberalism draws on the principles of robust political economy and ideal typical analysis. These principles examine how and why different institutions cope with 'real-world' circumstances that depart from theoretical ideals such as the model of perfectly competitive equilibrium. Implicit in the arguments raised against 'old' and 'new' versions of market-failure theory has been an evolutionary account of the market process. From a classical liberal perspective, market institutions contain valuable selection mechanisms that enable people to cope with knowledge problems and the possibility of self-interested behaviour. In concluding this account, however, it is important to make more explicit the basis of these claims because the application of evolutionary standards in political economy has not gone without challenge.

Classical Liberalism versus the Panglossian Fallacy

By far the most important charge levied against evolutionary arguments, and defences of markets in particular, is that they tend towards the Panglossian fallacy. The latter suggests that whatever is has evolved, and that whatever has evolved necessarily represents the most desirable or efficient state of affairs.

Critics contend that evolutionary arguments collapse into a purely descriptive account which relegates public policy analysis to passive observation. According to this view, if evolutionary forces guarantee the most desirable or efficient results then there is little if any role for those who challenge the status quo. It is further noted, however, that processes based on competitive selection do not necessarily lead to optimal or efficient results. On the contrary, evolutionary processes are subject to random factors and may through path-dependent processes become 'locked' into a suboptimal path. Moreover, whether evolution is considered to produce desirable results depends on the criterion of selection at hand. Terms such as 'survival of the fittest' are of little value unless there is a normative basis to favour a particular criterion of what it means to be the 'fittest'. One might not, for example, want to favour institutions in which the 'fittest' are those who have a comparative advantage in the application of violence. A related argument contends that those such as Hayek who understand social and economic institutions in evolutionary terms are guilty of the 'naturalistic fallacy' – the claim that processes which mimic natural evolution are 'good' precisely because they are 'natural'.

Arguments of this character have often been invoked against evolutionary applications in social theory. In the specific case of economic analysis Stiglitz is aware that evolutionary defences of unregulated markets represent an alternative approach to that of the neo-classical mainstream, but he argues that these accounts claim too much. Thus:

> As important as these arguments are, they are not based on a well-formulated dynamic theory, nor is there a well-articulated normative basis for the widespread belief in the desirability of evolutionary forces – or the often drawn policy conclusion that government intervention in the evolutionary process would either be futile or worse, be a retrograde step. It seems nonsensical to suggest that we should simply accept the natural outcome of the evolutionary process. What does 'natural' mean? How do we know whether or not any particular perturbation that we might propose such as more or less government is, or is not part of the 'natural' evolutionary process? (Stiglitz, 1994: 275)

Although these criticisms are commonly voiced, they misinterpret the classical liberal use of evolutionary principles and their normative significance in a public policy setting. The first point to emphasise here is that classical liberal claims are in fact very modest. In a complex environment, where the limits of human cognition are tightly drawn, processes that facilitate variation and competitive selection are held to increase the chance of discovering better solutions to human problems relative to institutions that reduce the scope for producer and consumer 'exit'. There is no implication in this argument that competitive processes always produce the most efficient or desirable results. It is possible to accept that markets are riddled with the 'inefficiencies' that concern neo-classical economists, but to maintain that such processes may be better placed to discover solutions to their own deficiencies than alternatives which reduce the scope for competitive experimentation. The latter include not only competition in the supply of different goods and services, but also competition between approaches to solving principal versus agent problems, information asymmetries, adverse selection and other 'market failures'. Markets 'fail' because their participants are not omniscient, but it is to attribute a 'god's-eye' view to planners and policy-makers to assume that they are able to overcome these same limitations without an equivalent process of trial and error discovery.

Far from implying uncritical support for the status quo, classical liberalism invokes evolutionary principles as a critical vantage point from which to challenge the robustness of existing institutions and practices. As Hayek (1988: 25) points out, evolutionary processes in the human world are not 'natural' or Darwinian in form, but simulate Lamarckism. Whereas a Darwinian process excludes the transmission of acquired characteristics, socio-economic competition is dependent on the spread of practices which are not innate but may be learned from an indefinite number of social actors. It is for this reason that absent restrictions on competition, socio-economic evolution proceeds at a much faster rate than natural or biological evolution.

From a classical liberal perspective, many existing practices should be challenged precisely because they may not have developed through a process of competitive trial and error but have been imposed in ways which have limited the scope for decentralised learning. In the context of money and finance, for example, central banking institutions and government monopolies on the issuing of currency have often been imposed for political reasons and in particular the desire of governments to raise revenue without resort to direct taxation. As Hayek (1988: 103) points out: 'money has almost from its first appearance been so shamelessly abused by governments that it has become the prime source of disturbance of all self-ordering processes'. Seen in this light, the key to improving financial stability in the market system may reside not in looking for further ways in which governments can regulate the supply of money, but in subjecting the design of regulatory mechanisms to a process of competition in which those institutions that debase the currency can be driven out of business by those who exhibit greater financial discipline.

The idea that societies can function on 'invisible hand' principles of voluntary exchange and competition is, of course, itself a contribution to the 'gene pool' of ideas. Social evolution depends on the battle between competing ideas and can be halted or reversed owing to human error. There is, therefore, no implication that 'whatever is must be efficient'. For much of human history, the prevailing assumption has been that social order can only be maintained by the exercise of deliberate authority. It has been the contribution of the classical liberal tradition to argue that this is not so. Market practices appear to have developed initially out of historical accident, but it was the subsequent recognition of their advantages that led classical liberals such as Smith, Hume and later Hayek to argue proactively for a framework which would remove obstacles to their further growth. The fact that it is often difficult to judge which particular institutions have been imposed from above rather than evolved from below does not undermine the value of this approach. Looking for ways to expose institutions to competitive trial and error may be a more robust method than applying a neo-classical model that assumes away knowledge problems and imperfect motivation.

Recognising the benefits of competitive processes is not to deny a role for institutional design. Rather, the central concern is to create a framework within which evolutionary processes can be harnessed to beneficial effect. Institutions should be judged on the scope they provide to explore new and potentially better solutions to problems and their capacity to facilitate the spread of successful adaptations. At issue is the extent to which institutions provide signals that identify inefficiencies and a selection mechanism that weeds out bad decisions. From a classical liberal perspective, the institution of a market economy with minimal government intervention provides key aspects of such a framework. As Buchanan and Vanberg (2002: 126) show, the distinguishing feature of this environment is the liberty of entry into and exit out of different occupational, locational, behavioural and organisational categories. The normative selection criterion by which classical liberalism judges 'success' and 'failure' is the account of profit and loss resulting from the capacity of consumers to 'exit' from experiments they deem 'failures', and to patronise those they judge 'successes'. Support for 'consumer sovereignty' follows from recognising that in an uncertain world where we do not know 'who knows best', 'exit' increases the chance that people may escape from any errors that occur. In a world where 'experts' disagree amongst themselves and where even the most intelligent actors are largely ignorant of the complexities involved in an advanced economy there is, from a classical liberal view, little reason to favour a paternalistic alternative.[7]

To work effectively markets need a framework of property rights, but the conditions that produce an effective framework cannot be specified in other than the most general form. A focus on the evolutionary nature of markets, therefore, also applies to the institutional rules of the market economy itself. Classical liberalism maintains that the evolutionary learning that occurs within markets should be operative on multiple levels so that people can exit and enter competing and often overlapping institutional designs (Buchanan and Vanberg, 2002). Different constitutional arrangements may be evaluated in terms of the extent to which they constrain the powers of governments by subjecting them to competition from alternative systems of rules. Institutional evolution between markets and the rules that frame them is, however, likely to be less effective than the process of competition within markets, because it lacks a direct equivalent of the signalling and selection mechanism provided by the account of profit and loss. This is, from a classical liberal perspective, one of the most important reasons for limiting the role of states to the relatively few functions that only they may be able to provide. In the final analysis, the precise boundaries between public and private sectors will be decided by political judgement, but the relevant 'lines' will be drawn very differently if this judgement appreciates the role of competition as a 'discovery process' than if policy-makers assume that the knowledge necessary to improve on the 'failures' of the market is 'given' to those who wield political authority.

Politics and the Panglossian Fallacy

Before concluding, it is crucial to distinguish this classical liberal argument for the 'minimal state' from those theoretical approaches that are indeed guilty of a Panglossian outlook. The Chicago school of political economy, in particular, infers efficient outcomes from its commitment to the central assumption of neo-classical economics – that agents are rational utility maximisers. According to this reasoning, whatever institutions and policies currently exist should be assumed efficient because if they were not, rational economising agents would change them accordingly. To suggest that outcomes are inefficient would be to abandon the view that people are in fact rational actors.

Initially, such arguments were invoked against 'market failure' theories. Demsetz (1969), for example, argued that if information and transaction costs are positive then a failure to internalise externalities may not constitute 'market failure', but may reflect real costs that may not be overcome in a more efficient way. Unless it can be shown that some institutional alternative does not face similar costs there is no reason to assume that government intervention will improve on an 'imperfect' market. More recently, however, this argument has been turned on its head by theorists such as Wittman (1995) who challenge the analysis of 'government failure' put forward by the Virginia school of public choice. According to Wittman, public choice accounts are inconsistent with the basic axioms of neo-classical theory. Unless the assumption of rational maximising behaviour is dropped, there is no reason to suppose that existing public policy structures are inefficient. Principal versus agent problems and the phenomenon of rational voter ignorance insofar as they reduce the effectiveness of democratic accountability reflect real costs which it should not be assumed would be overcome by moving towards an alternative institutional structure. As Wittman (1995: 2) puts it: 'Nearly all of the arguments claiming that economic markets are efficient apply equally well to democratic political markets; and conversely, that economic models of political market failure are no more valid than the analogous arguments for economic market failure.'

Taken to their logical conclusion Wittman's arguments imply the abandonment of comparative institutions analysis in order to maintain the consistency of the neo-classical framework. It would, for example, be difficult to see how the efficiency properties of the Soviet Union prior to the collapse of Communism could be challenged. The system persisted for 70 years and the absence of a revolution throughout this period may have reflected that when all costs and benefits were accounted for the Soviet model was more efficient at achieving material prosperity and social equity than any realistic alternative. Similarly, the persistence of policies such as trade protection and various price controls, which many economists consider clear evidence of 'inefficiency', may not be judged inefficient when the costs and benefits associated with alternative forms of wealth redistribution are taken properly into account.

It is, however, the limitations of the neo-classical framework that should indeed be recognised. The robust political economy case for classical liberalism contends that people are not fully rational but that market processes facilitate learning and a higher level of rationality than a regime of political controls. Whether evolutionary forces tend toward more efficient outcomes depends on the institutional context in which they operate.[8] The first and most crucial point to note that distinguishes 'democratic markets' from 'classical liberal markets' is that the former involve higher levels of coercion. When individual voters cannot, save for leaving the country, 'exit' from principal–agent relationships with politicians they are effectively forced into a series of collective action problems and may become trapped in inefficient structures.

In terms of 'knowledge problems', the efficacy of the political process is compromised because relative to markets it lacks the signalling and selection mechanisms that enable people to learn about more efficient methods and practices. It is dubious to speak of efficiency when there is no equivalent of the profit and loss accounting that allows market participants to identify inefficiencies and to alter their behaviour in a more efficient direction. Politicians and civil servants do not sell goods and services directly to their citizens so they are unable to discern the economic value of the goods they provide. In a democratic process, the vote of someone who values a particular good very highly counts for no more than that of someone else who values the same good much less. Although interest group log-rolling enables voters to express their values in a more nuanced way, there is no equivalent of willingness to pay in markets when it comes to revealing the variety and intensity of individual preferences. What is politically efficient in terms of garnering votes may not generate the highest economic value (Mitchell and Simmons, 1994; Boettke et al., 2007).

The scope for learning and discovery in the political process is further undermined by the character of the choices made. Once a government has been elected, citizens cannot actively test alternative policy platforms because opposing politicians and interest groups are prevented from supplying competing service bundles in the period between elections. Individual voters have no means of continuously switching between suppliers in a process governed by majority coalition and politicians have no way of comparing the results of different experiments on other than a consecutive basis (Wholgemuth, 1999).

With respect to incentives, the relative lack of competition in the political process may reduce the pay-offs from searching out inefficiencies. When politicians have the option to garner resources through coercive powers of taxation rather than through efficiency savings then they may opt for the former and not the latter. That taxpayer and consumer groups may not mobilise against such inefficiency should not be taken to imply that no such inefficiency exists, any more than the fact that revolutions against oppressive regimes are rare should be taken as evidence that dictatorships are welfare enhancing. In both of these cases, it may simply be that the losing interests find themselves with a massive collective action problem. Though it may be in the collective interests of the 'losers' to bring about institutional or political change, it may not be individually rational for any one actor to push for reforms given the miniscule chance that their personal contribution will be decisive to the final outcome.

It follows for classical liberalism that while it may not be possible to subject the supply of all goods and services (such as territorial defence and certain environmental goods) to the process of market competition, the deficiencies of politics are such that the process of 'privatisation' and the extension of consensual exchange should proceed wherever possible. Of course, none of this implies that people should be prevented from subscribing to purely democratic forms of decision-making on a voluntary basis, just as there should be nothing to stop people from voluntarily abandoning the institution of private property by opting for the communal arrangements of, say, a kibbutz. What matters is whether there is scope for dissenters to persist with alternative decision-making models so that people can compare the costs and benefits of alternatives on a continuous basis. From a classical liberal standpoint, unless people have opted into a collective choice structure through a non-majoritarian process of voluntary exchange there are strong grounds to question the efficiency properties of such structures.

CONCLUSION

This chapter has sought to defend the robustness of classical liberalism against theories of 'market failure'. It has argued that the efficiency standard set out in the neo-classical model has little relevance to the practical evaluation of market processes relative to systems of political control. When judged against an alternative, evolutionary standard the economic case for liberal markets matches the criteria for a robust political economy more effectively than 'market failure' theories old and new. To defend the economic case for classical liberalism is of course to make the normative assumption that economic criteria should be the motivating force of public policy. Some of the most significant challenges to classical liberalism, however, come from perspectives that challenge the moral rather than the economic implications of classical liberal ideals. It is to these challenges that the subsequent chapters in Part I now turn.

NOTES

1. In agricultural markets such as that for grain, which are often thought to most closely resemble a 'perfectly competitive' structure, it is often not the case that knowledge of the appropriate production and management techniques is 'given'. As O'Driscoll and Rizzo (1996: 109) point out, in the tending of vineyards and even activities such as the growing of feed corn, different production techniques exist literally side by side. It is doubtful, therefore, whether the neo-classical understanding of competition is appropriate even in these markets.
2. Throughout the period 2008–10, governments throughout the major democracies appear to have engaged in precisely such panic measures in response to the financial crisis that followed the so-called 'subprime' mortgage bubble – a bubble arguably precipitated by a ten-year period of an excessively lax monetary policy pursued by central banks. On the one hand, apocalyptic statements from the US Treasury concerning the need for 'unprecedented intervention' in the mortgage market appear to have exacerbated a wider financial panic. And on the other hand, once a critical mass of policy-makers publicly supported this intervention many others followed, apparently for fear of being depicted as favouring a 'do-nothing' approach. It is not possible at this juncture to comment further on the likely effect of these measures, but at the very least the manner in which politicians responded to these events would seem to illustrate that the 'herd instinct' is not confined to markets.
3. This is not to imply that government regulation removes all heterogeneity. In the case of the banking industry, for example, there is evidence that a significant number of institutions sought to avoid the loose lending practices that precipitated the financial crisis, in favour of a more conservative approach (Friedman, 2009: 153–4). The point here is that the scope for such diversity is reduced by statutory regulation. This homogenising effect is most pronounced in the case of regulatory mandates which legally require a particular form of action, but it is also significant in cases where regulation though not mandating a specific behaviour encourages actors to 'follow the herd'. The latter phenomena appears to have been

particularly evident in the credit rating business where the conferment of a privileged position on a small number of rating agencies by financial regulators encouraged a large number of financial institutions to assume that the credit ratings provided by these bodies were beyond doubt (Friedman, 2009; White, 2009).

4. It will not do to argue, as Stiglitz (2009) has, that the financial crisis was facilitated by the dominant influence of 'Conservative ideology' which encouraged a laissez-faire mentality among regulators and a 'free-for-all' in financial markets. On the one hand, it is not the case that financial markets have been 'unregulated'. Rather, the crisis appears to have followed from a combination of 'over-regulation' in some areas, such as the legal protection from competition granted to credit-rating agencies; and 'under-regulation' elsewhere, such as the loosening of controls on lending to low-income households. On the other hand, suppose that ideology was as influential as Stiglitz maintains. There is no reason to believe had regulators been under the influence of an interventionist or 'social democratic' ideology that the possibility of 'systemic failure' would have been lessened. The fundamental problem facing such regulators would be to decide, in the face of uncertainty and imperfect knowledge, which regulatory interventions would have been most effective. In the absence of a competitive process that would allow rival regulatory models to be tested against each other, then the legal enforcement of any one set of regulations would increase the possibility of systemic failure should the wrong model be enforced. The case for 'free markets' is not that there should be no regulation with exchange taking place in an institutional vacuum – but that there should be competition between different regulatory standards. Monopoly control of regulatory design does not reduce the prospect of systemic failure it increases the likelihood of such failure.

5. It should be noted that the free-rider model of market prices is questionable even on its own terms. In order to arrive at the conclusion that uninformed market participants can free-ride on those who have sought out costly data, Grossman and Stiglitz assume that prices adjust instantaneously to full information equilibrium. As Streit (1984: 393–4) points out, however, this is an unrealistic result which assumes that traders cannot profit from their information before it becomes more generally available. It is only through the process of buying at a lower price and selling at a higher price – that is, by realising a profit from 'search' – that the market is alerted to the newly revealed data. In equilibrium, however, by definition there is no scope for any trade to occur (Thomsen, 1992, 38–9).

6. It might be argued that the failure of credit rating agencies in making appropriate risk assessments, and their subsequent role in the financial crisis of 2008, undermines the argument that competition for reputation may help to overcome asymmetric information and adverse selection problems. This would, however, be the wrong conclusion to draw. As noted earlier, the credit ratings agencies have been protected from competition by government mandates which have secured a permanent stream of income for the established ratings firms – irrespective of their performance. It is the legal privileges granted to these firms that has limited entry into the ratings business and has thus undermined the scope for alternative risk assessment models to enter the market and the incentive for existing firms to remain alert to the possibilities arising from rival business models (Friedman, 2009; White, 2009).

7. The latest attempt to justify 'paternalism' has arisen from behavioural economics. According to this school of thought, individual agents are prone to a range of 'irrational behaviours' and 'cognitive biases' stemming from 'weakness of will', and difficulties in processing information that prevent them from achieving their 'true' preferences (see, for example, Jolls and Sunstein, 2006). Such 'irrational' conduct, it is suggested, may be 'corrected' by appropriately designed public policy interventions informed by 'experts'. The fundamental problem with these arguments, however, is that they assume that knowledge of what people's true preferences are and how to 'correct' for cognitive biases without generating unintended negative consequences is 'given' to the relevant policy-makers. This literature also ignores the possibility that the 'experts' who are to be charged with 'nudging' the public in the appropriate direction are not themselves subject to cognitive biases – such as, for example, an overvaluation of their own capacities to correct the errors of others. For a Hayekian-inspired critique of behavioural economics, see the discussion by Rizzo and Whittman (2008). Chapter 6 of this book provides some more detailed discussion of these arguments in the context of the welfare state.

8. This is not an 'institutionalist' argument of the sort associated with the 'historical school of economics'. The latter suggested that the assumptions of economic theory, such as human responsiveness to incentives, are only of relevance in the context of a market capitalist system, with the implication that in non-market institutions actors do not respond to incentives and information in a rational way. The argument here, however, is that people are sensitive to information and incentives whatever the institutional context, but that the context determines both the quality of the information and the structure of the incentives that they face. For more on this distinction, see Boettke et al. (2007).

3. Exit, voice and communicative rationality: the challenge of communitarianism I

INTRODUCTION

The arguments for classical liberalism articulated in the previous chapter are not widely accepted by mainstream economists, but it would be fair to suggest that the economics discipline provides a degree of support for 'privatisation' notable for its relative absence in contemporary political theory. Even authors such as Stiglitz who are critical of classical liberalism are not unsympathetic to at least some of the arguments in favour of markets and competition. One of the reasons for this difference between disciplines derives from the tendency of neo-classical economists to make certain assumptions about human nature, the character of individual action and the purpose of social institutions. These include the view that people are predominantly self-interested and that the primary purpose of institutions is to aggregate individual preferences into an efficient 'social welfare function'.

From the perspective of many political theorists, however, the assumptions of modern economics are highly questionable and support for classical liberal institutions derived from such premises leads to morally questionable outcomes. Building on a broader communitarian critique, it is argued that liberal political economy neglects the 'situated' nature of human beings whose preferences and values are determined in large part by the institutional context of decision-making. According to this view, a greater emphasis should be placed on the communicative processes through which people's preferences are formed and on developing practices that institutionalise a search for the 'common good'. The favoured alternative to the classical liberal principle of 'exit' in this context is a 'voice-based' conception of deliberative democracy.

This chapter addresses the argument in favour of democratic deliberation within communitarian thought. Having outlined the critique of markets and 'exit-based' institutions, the chapter shows that classical liberalism is fully compatible with a situated conception of social actors. On close examination the reasons why classical liberals favour 'exit' over 'voice' have much in common with the foundations of communitarian theory. Although it is reinforced by attention to incentives, the classical liberal emphasis on 'exit' does not rest on assumptions of 'selfishness' but on the knowledge-enhancing properties of 'spontaneous order'. Seen in this light, processes that allow for exit and competition may represent a more robust way of delivering the communicative benefits that communitarians believe can only be achieved within the confines of a social democratic forum.

COMMUNITARIAN POLITICAL THEORY AND DELIBERATIVE DEMOCRACY[1]

The widespread scepticism towards classical liberalism evidenced in contemporary political theory owes much to the communitarian challenge to the basic assumptions of liberalism as a political philosophy that has occurred over the last 30 years. While classical or minimal-state liberals such as Robert Nozick and egalitarian, welfare state liberals such as John Rawls differ markedly in their normative views on the legitimate extent of the state, they are, it is argued, united in subscribing to an ethic that puts the interests of the individual above the moral claims of the community.

For communitarians, liberal theories are based on a faulty understanding of 'the self'. In the accounts offered by Rawls (1971) and Nozick (1974) the individual is thought to be independent of social identity, he or she is free to define and choose his or her own values, and is capable of defining a personalised conception of 'the good'. Society is, therefore, conceived in reductionist terms and amounts to nothing more than an aggregate of individuals who have little in the way of common interests. It is in this context that communitarians such as Taylor (1985) argue that liberalism neglects the fundamentally social nature of human beings. The capacity to engage in reason and to possess values should not, on this interpretation, be seen as a property of isolated individuals but as a product of existence within a historically developed community. Social institutions such as language are shared or intersubjective phenomena which extend the capacity for reason and choice beyond the subjective experience of the individual actor.

Writing in a similar vein, MacIntyre (1981) argues that liberalism reduces questions of morality to one of personal preference in such a way that it becomes an entirely relativistic concept. Insofar as liberals have a conception of the 'common good' this is seen to reflect the aggregate sum of individual preferences. As MacIntyre points out, however, without some overarching sense of morality that transcends the individual actor, principles such as respect for private property themselves become matters of personal preference. Liberal institutions and the assumptions that underlie them may as a consequence exercise a morally corrosive effect on the social order. Society is no longer seen to constitute a 'community united in a shared vision of the good of man' (MacIntyre, 1981: 219–20) but is seen instead to be little more than a 'collection of strangers, each pursuing his or her own interests under minimal constraints' (ibid.: 233). For MacIntyre, in place of this individualist mentality the primary concern of political theory should be with institutions that allow people's preferences to be evaluated and if necessary challenged against a conception of the 'common good' reflective of the community as a whole.

Charges of this nature apply to all variants of liberalism that emphasise the utility-maximising individual as the starting point of political theorising, and they have increasingly been levelled against the economic theory thought to underlie the case for unfettered markets. Economic theory is criticised for advancing a narrow conception of human motivation which, when institutionalised in a market economy, results in the impoverishment of the 'public sphere' and the conditions for a genuinely social process of value formation. Liberalism and economic liberalism in particular are seen to have an excessively 'thin' conception of rationality which reduces to the pursuit of efficiency objectives. According to the critics, what is needed is a richer or more communicative notion of reason which recognises that creativity and argument concerning the appropriate content of people's ends are equally if not more important than solutions to the constrained optimisation problems that concern modern neo-classical economics.

At the forefront of these attacks have been the contributions of Habermas and the 'critical theorists' of the Frankfurt school (for example, Habermas, 1984, 1990, 1996). According to these authors, market institutions encourage an excessively 'instrumental' form of rationality where human action is centred on application of the most efficient means to achieve an established set of ends. Miller (1989: 252), for example, distinguishes between an 'aggregative' and a 'dialogical' model of politics and society. Aggregative institutions are associated with the bargaining relationships reflected in markets and interest group politics. Dialogical institutions, however, involve attempts to persuade people through arguments and to arrive at consensus positions which embody a sense of the 'collective will'. A conception of the common good or collective will is considered of particular importance where incommensurable moral ends are involved and where the aggregation of conflicting values into a 'social welfare function' is impossible. Moral conflicts over resource use should not, on this view, be considered against the utilitarian criterion of willingness to pay, but should instead be dealt with by means of democratic debate and argument. From a Habermasian perspective the 'exit' mechanisms that lie at the core of markets discourage the processes of public argumentation necessary to make people aware of the interests and values of others. The resultant disengagement from civic affairs narrows people's horizons and prevents them from thinking in terms of the 'common good'.

Iris Young (1990, 2000), extends Miller's argument to suggest that a focus on aggregating preferences assumed to be 'given' exogenous to the decision process entrenches various forms of 'oppression' and 'exclusion' that may result from the exercise of these very preferences. Markets and other 'aggregative institutions' are held not to provide the public space in which established stereotypes and prejudices concerning the identities and roles of women, ethnic or religious minorities and other groups that have experienced social exclusion can be challenged and transformed.

In making these points Habermas and his followers share with communitarians the view that the concept of community does not simply reflect the coexistence of actors within a common culture, but requires that people are consciously aware of sharing such a culture – though as emphasised by Young this may also involve challenging aspects of that culture where it is held to marginalise the members of certain social groups. What matters from a communitarian perspective is that the sense of sharing should be reinforced by the character of political institutions. On this interpretation, community fulfils its potential when there is collective deliberation about social goals and collective determination of social choices. This particular understanding owes much to Marx's view that 'true freedom' requires that people act with a unity of social purpose. As Marx (1906, Chapter 1: 92) puts it: 'the life process of society … does not strip off its mystical veil until it is treated as production by freely associated men, and is consciously regulated by them in accordance with a settled plan.'

If markets and the 'exit' principle fail to provide an appropriate context where the constituents of the common good can be articulated, then a process of deliberative democracy is thought best placed to remedy these deficiencies. Classical liberal criticisms of socialist-style central planning are considered outdated because they ignore the possibility of a more decentralised alternative to bureaucratic hierarchies which builds on an extended notion of democratic participation. For 'critical theorists', central planning systems are as guilty as markets of fostering an excessively instrumental form of reason (see, for example, Dryzek, 1990, 2001). Whereas markets privilege the role of individual consumers who are assumed to 'know best', central planning hierarchies privilege the role of 'experts', who are assumed to have perfect knowledge of social needs and values. The alternative to both markets and central planning, therefore, is a system of dialogical social planning where decisions are subject to a process of communicative collective action in which all citizens are empowered to participate in a process oriented to creativity and the discovery of social ends (Adaman and Devine, 1997).

Habermas suggests that in order for the democratic process to foster such a dialogue it must take the form of free and open argumentation where no one can be excluded in principle from the discussion and where all those who are possibly affected by the resultant decisions have equal chances to enter and take part (Habermas, 1996: 305–6). Democratic processes should also be free from forces of internal 'domination' which may compromise the equal participation of all citizens. The latter requires a commitment to greater equality of material resources and thus a removal of many of the inequalities in wealth and status that result from a market economy prior to the allocative public decisions to be made (Young, 1990: 184–5; Habermas, 1996: 306; Young, 2000: 228–35; Brighouse, 2002: 55). Finally, collective deliberations must be concluded by a process of majority decision. Fallible majority opinion is considered a reasonable basis for decision-making until those in the minority position can convince the majority otherwise. In an ideal form of deliberative democracy this process of majority rule should not simply reflect which preferences have the greatest numerical support, but should be determined by the proposals the public believes to have been supported by the 'unforced power of the better argument' (Habermas, 1996: 305–6).[2]

While accepting that these conditions are very onerous, deliberative democrats contend that the 'ideal speech situation' constitutes a critical benchmark or regulative ideal that should be used to judge the relative performance of different institutions and practices. This ideal may not be attainable in practice, but reforms which move closer towards the ideal are to be sought wherever possible. Three sets of arguments are advanced in favour of the deliberative ideal. The first is the epistemic claim that deliberative democracy produces better and more rational decisions than non-deliberative alternatives such as markets. Democratic deliberation, it is argued, offers the prospect of more holistic decision-making where concerned citizens collectively analyse how their choices affect the lives of others in place of the 'anarchy' of market competition. In addition, public deliberation allows actors to widen their horizons through a process of intersubjective learning which alerts people to new analyses and solutions to social problems that might otherwise go unnoticed (Barber, 1984; Smith and Wales, 2000).

A second set of arguments focuses on the mechanisms needed to control the abuse of power and to encourage greater transparency in decision-making. Although deliberative democrats do not focus on incentives in the manner associated with the rational choice/public choice tradition, they are nonetheless concerned to limit instances of corruption and the distortion of public policy decisions by special interests. From a deliberative democratic perspective the requirement that individuals and organisations justify their decision-making power in a public forum will bring unjustifiable power-relations to public attention, prompting calls for their correction. Processes based on exit and bargaining, by contrast, are said to reproduce the prevailing structure of power and inequality.

A third set of arguments develops the ethical or moral contention that decisions arrived at via democratic deliberation reflect fundamental norms of justice more effectively than those resulting from the actions of dispersed individuals and organisations pursuing their own ends. Young (1990, 2000), for example, argues against 'aggregative' institutions such as markets on the grounds that they fail to engage people adequately in considering the needs of 'differently situated others' and do not adequately reflect the notion of 'equal respect'. A deliberative conception of democracy, by contrast, is held to provide a forum in which people listen with respect to the views of others in order to give those who are members of 'excluded' groups, such as ethnic and cultural minorities, an equal voice in public decision-making.

Precisely how far the extension of deliberative democratic procedures should be pushed remains a matter of some dispute. In its more radical variants authors such as Adaman and Devine (1997) advocate a form of 'participatory socialism' and the 'democratisation of economic life' where the control of enterprises is vested in the hands of workers' and citizens' councils. Similarly, for theorists such as Young (1990: 250–51; also Young, 2000), deliberation should be an all-encompassing principle which would require that anyone affected by a socio-economic decision should have the right to participate in the decisions concerned. On this view, all decisions which affect the production and distribution of goods including the good of social status should be subject to public approval in a democratic forum. Habermas (1992) adopts a somewhat more modest tack when arguing that social democratic procedures should be limited to the central 'steering mechanisms' of the political economy which frame the day-to-day actions of private decision-makers, but do not determine the actual content of these decisions themselves. Common to all these theorists, however, is a view that existing liberal democracies fall well short of the deliberative ideal and that any moves to extend the range of voice-centred public deliberation should be welcomed accordingly.

CLASSICAL LIBERALISM, SPONTANEOUS ORDER AND COMMUNICATIVE RATIONALITY

The communitarian critique constitutes a serious challenge to those who defend classical liberal institutions in terms of a model grounded in the view that people are rational, self-interested and unchangeable in terms of the values they wish to pursue. It should be emphasised, however, that these criticisms of rational choice models are equally applicable to 'market-failure' theories such as those of Stiglitz that argue for government intervention from the very same assumptions. Insofar as markets, or any other institutions, are defended exclusively in these terms then the criticisms raised by communitarians are telling. The economic case for classical liberalism defended in the previous chapter, however, does not rely on a rational choice account. Rather than seeing the market economy as a context where people maximise pre-given interests, classical liberalism conceives of markets and other 'spontaneous orders' as complex communicative networks that facilitate the exchange of knowledge, ideas and expectations (see, for example, Wholgemuth, 2005). This conception emphasises the importance of evolutionary processes that allow for learning at multiple different levels. In what follows, the similarities and differences between this evolutionary case for the 'exit principle' and the views of communitarians are outlined. The subsequent sections apply this account to challenge the robustness of voice-based deliberative democracy.

Individualism: True and False

The most immediate similarity between classical liberalism and communitarian thought is evident in Hayek's conception of 'true individualism' (Hayek, 1948b). This perspective is explicit in its recognition that people are 'situated selves', who acquire many of their preferences, values and practices from the social environment and must be distinguished from the 'false individualism' that conceives of society as the rational creation of isolated individuals aiming to design 'optimal' or 'efficient' institutions (Hayek, 1948b: 6). It is the latter tradition that is reflected in neo-classical economics and in contractarian approaches to political theory such as those of Rawls.

According to Hayek, the defining feature of the individual as a 'social being' is his or her incapacity to comprehend more than a tiny fragment of his or her surroundings, owing to the constitutional limits of human intelligence. To recognise that people are a product of their society is not, therefore, to imply that the social environment is itself the deliberate creation of an identifiable group. Rather, the socio-cultural environment often arises from 'spontaneous ordering' processes that are 'the result of human action, but not of human design'. Institutions such as language, respect for possessions and other habits and traditions that constitute individual identity are not 'natural' processes, but neither are they the result of deliberate 'invention'. Such practices may subsequently be codified (as in a dictionary) or in cases such as property law enforced by an organisation such as the state, but the rules and practices themselves are not typically the deliberate creation of any particular actor or organisation (Hayek, 1960: Part 1; Hayek, 1982: Part 1).

A focus on the importance of 'spontaneous order' stems from the view that in a world more complex than can be directly perceived, individuals must 'voluntarily' accept certain culturally transmitted rules, such as those of language, without consciously thinking about them. These rules are themselves part of an evolutionary process that is not the result of conscious reason but nonetheless facilitates reasoned action. Spontaneous orders develop via a complex process of imitative learning. Language, for example, while developing out of the human capacity for communication, emerges as the unintended by-product of multiple communicative acts not directed towards any specific purpose. As new words and combinations spread via a process of imitation and adaptation, their initiators are not consciously aware of how these practices will be used and adapted by others. Similarly, speakers are typically unaware of the multiple nodes that initiated the words and phrases in common usage and the 'reasons' why such symbols have been adopted (Hayek, 1960, Part 1; Hayek, 1982: Part 1). As Hayek puts it:

> The mind is embedded in a traditional impersonal structure of learnt rules, and its capacity to order experience is an acquired replica of cultural patterns which every individual mind finds *given* ... To put it differently, mind can exist only as part of another independently existing distinct structure or order, though that order persists and develops only because millions of minds constantly absorb and modify parts of it. (Hayek, 1982: 157)

According to this interpretation, 'community' involves the relations of shared identification, morals and commitments associated with observance of spontaneously evolving cultural rules, including language and social mores such as respect for property. As in communitarian accounts, therefore, the sense of morality transcends the individual actor and is not equated with personal preferences (Hayek, 1960, 1967b). Nonetheless, while individuals identify themselves through the social practices in which they are embedded, they follow separate goals rather than the conscious pursuit of some 'communal end'. Indeed the 'community', when understood as a spontaneous order or catallaxy, cannot be considered to have ends of its own. To speak of a 'communal end' would require that society operate as an instrumental organisation, a sort of 'super-person' that defines the ends of its citizens. In an 'open society', however, people have communal attachments to shared cultural rules such as language, which order their behaviour, while also having the liberty to experiment in the pursuit of a wider variety of different ends.

Community, Complexity and Spontaneous Order

Understood in these terms, though classical liberalism recognises the culturally situated nature of the individual, its understanding of the implications derived from this view differs from that of communitarians such as MacIntyre. Whereas the latter sees a 'society of strangers' held together by impersonal relationships and unintended social outcomes as a sign of moral decay, from a classical liberal perspective an advanced and complex form of community can only be achieved when it is not based on the conscious pursuit of a 'social purpose'. The type of community advocated by MacIntyre is only appropriate to a tribal type of society which is small enough in number and sufficiently simple in its interrelationships to be comprehensible to its members. If a more complex and advanced form of community is to be sustained, however, then it is not possible for the members of such a society to be consciously aware of the many and diverse factors that contribute to the evolution of different ends and means.

Hayek's conception of society as a dynamic spontaneous order is strikingly similar to that developed by 'critical theorists' such as Young, who are eager to avoid the implication that the content of community is 'fixed' and can be interpreted in terms of a unitary and unchanging conception of the 'common good' (Tebble, 2002). For Young, just as the content of individual preferences should not be seen to reflect an underlying and unchanging 'essence', so the identity of the social groups that constitute the community should not be seen to reflect an identifiable 'group essence' (Young, 1990: 246–7). On the contrary, in the context of contemporary advanced societies where there are many different communal identifications, the boundaries of these identifications may shift and people may find themselves identifying with a wide variety of groups which often have overlapping and cross-cutting memberships. People may, therefore, share identifications on some dimensions but may differ on many others. Personal identity then is never entirely determined by one's membership of a particular social group or community, but is better conceived as a partial identification, which is itself open to a process of constant evolution (for more on this, see Tebble, 2002).

What matters in the above context is the scope that different institutions provide for cultural rules and identities to evolve dynamically, while also providing a basis for order and coordination. It is here that, from a classical liberal perspective, the importance of relying on 'spontaneous orders' comes to the fore. Spontaneous orders offer signposts to individual action and provide for a degree of regularity in people's lives, while allowing room for a decentralised process of incremental experimentation. Since people 'voluntarily' observe the rules of the spontaneous orders into which they are born rather than have them enforced coercively by an external organisation, they are better conceived as 'flexible rules' that are subject to constant revision 'at the margin'. Knowledge concerning potentially successful adaptations to social practices is widely dispersed across the myriad individuals and organisations that make up society and could never be perceived in its entirety by any one group. People are, however, able to draw on the knowledge of widely dispersed agents of whose existence they may be totally unaware, as successful experiments (for example, new words, inventions and cultural mores) ripple out via a process of imitation from dispersed decision-making nodes. According to this view, incremental change via competitive testing of alternate practices facilitates a richer process of social evolution than socialist-style attempts to 'reconstruct' cultural practices in total. For such attempts to be successful would require an organised group to possess all the necessary 'data' needed to understand the functioning of society and to reconstruct it accordingly (Hayek, 1948b, 1960, 1982).

As the previous chapter showed, it is these concepts of spontaneous order and limited rationality that lie at the core of the classical liberal advocacy of markets. The market economy is understood both as a spontaneous coordinating mechanism which facilitates adjustment between the different values of dispersed social actors, and as an evolutionary process in which the content of these values is subject to dynamic change. The coordinating role of markets is manifested in the fluctuating price signals that communicate the changing availability of goods and enable people to adapt their behaviour, without knowing very much about the 'circumstances of time and place' affecting distant others. Markets, however, also perform an evolutionary function where the factors that determine 'which goods are scarce goods' are shaped endogenously by the process of competition. Consumers and producers do not participate in markets on the basis of pre-given preferences and production functions, but are alerted to and acquire previously unforeseen tastes and organisational practices via the market process itself. It is for this reason that the general equilibrium framework of neo-classical economics is rejected. Economic actors do not enter markets with full information, but acquire and communicate knowledge via the rivalrous clash of divergent ideas. It is the winnowing and sifting of competition that encourages the emulation of profitable ventures, and discourages the spread of erroneous ideas in the supply of goods.

Though evolutionary competitive processes take their most advanced form in the context of market institutions, spontaneous orders are also evident in other aspects of a classical liberal framework and in particular the principle of political federalism or interjurisdictional competition. The latter principles are of particular relevance in the context of those collective goods and regulatory procedures that may not be supplied effectively on an individualised basis. From a classical liberal standpoint interjurisdictional competition enables a much greater degree of experimentation in service provision than more monopolistic governance structures, as competition between different packages of collective goods and regulations facilitates open-ended discovery of the most desirable service bundles. As individuals and organisations move from one jurisdiction to another, and thus alter the distribution of tax revenues, a spontaneous adjustment process may be set in motion as the relevant authorities change the pattern of services they provide accordingly. Such processes are not equivalent to the more open competition and constant adjustments to changes in supply and demand facilitated by decentralised market prices, but they are more likely to generate experimentation and to coordinate dispersed knowledge than attempts to secure coordination from a single centre of political control.

Endogenous Preferences and Public Choice

It should be emphasised that none of the arguments sketched so far make any assumptions about individual motivations. They do not, for example, assume that people are or should be self-interested. What distinguishes the account presented here from rational choice theory is the focus on the knowledge-enhancing benefits of spontaneous orders. Rational choice accounts such as those of the Virginia school of public choice focus instead on the incentives that markets and the 'exit' principle provide for people to coordinate with others (for example, Buchanan and Tullock, 1962). A focus on the evolutionary and communicative aspects of rationality need not, however, require the complete abandonment of rational choice concepts. Though not a necessary component of classical liberalism, rational choice insights do provide an important complement to it.

The key point to highlight in the above context is that a rational choice perspective is compatible with a 'situated' view of social actors. The work of Kuran (1995) and Chong (2002), for example, recognises the role played by socialisation in shaping individual identity. What these authors argue is that while people are influenced by their social surroundings, they are not constituted entirely by them. People have the capacity to challenge prevailing social norms 'at the margin' and via such agency can contribute to the development of new cultural forms. Different institutions may thus be evaluated in terms of the incentives or disincentives they provide in this regard. It is at this juncture that Virginia school arguments concerning the merits of exit-based institutions are of relevance. Other things being equal, one would expect that exit-based institutions, and markets in particular, reduce the costs of challenging established norms and values precisely because they do not require approval from large numbers of actors. In markets, for example, consumers can opt for alternative products even if they are in a minority status, and entrepreneurs can supply new product lines without requiring permission from any one hierarchy or majority. Similarly, in a context of interjurisdictional competition, different political authorities can experiment with different packages of social rules without approval from an overarching agency, and citizens can opt out of particular jurisdictions without consulting their neighbours.

If it is conceded that individuals have at least some degree of agency, then it is not unreasonable to ask whether they have incentives to exercise this agency and to examine how different institutions compare in terms of these incentives. To analyse incentives is not necessarily to assume that people are self-interested, but to recognise that however altruistic people are, they are less likely to take actions that have a high opportunity cost. Instrumental rationality must and should, therefore, play a part in any political economy for the simple reason that whether individually or collectively, at some point ends have to be decided on and efficient means chosen. While it may be desirable for people to 'transcend' self-interested motivations, to suggest that it would be equally desirable for them to ignore all cost–benefit calculations is untenable.

EXIT VERSUS VOICE: THE KNOWLEDGE PROBLEM

It should now be clear that classical liberalism does not assume that individuals are immune from communal identifications. Rather, where it challenges communitarian theory is in its normative account of the institutional processes compatible with a 'situated' understanding of 'the self'. In their support of deliberative democratic arrangements, communitarians argue that a more extended and communicative form of rationality is best advanced through debate and argument in a public forum. In making this claim, they imply that the constituents of 'community' may be discerned if all those affected by socio-economic decisions can be brought together to participate in a public dialogue. As the following discussion aims to show, however, there are fundamental problems with deliberative democratic procedures that ignore the requirements of a robust political economy and may cripple the capacity to deliver on the claims advanced in their favour.

Deliberation and the 'Synoptic Delusion'

In order for the elements of a complex community to be consciously coordinated in accordance with the 'common good', a synoptic overview of how all the different components of the relevant community interact would be required. Yet, from a classical liberal perspective it is the very magnitude of the interrelations between the elements that make up complex social wholes that prevents their comprehension by a group of minds engaged in such a process. If social wholes are more complex than the sum of their individual parts then it follows that none of the constituent elements, even when gathered together in a public forum, can comprehend all of the factors that contribute to their advance (Hayek, 1957). This 'synoptic delusion' (Hayek, 1982) may not, as is sometimes suggested (see, for example, Barber, 1984; Notturno, 2006) be resolved by developments in computer technology, because the more such technology develops the more complex are the range of decisions that can be made by each of the decentralised elements that constitute the community. No matter how sophisticated technology becomes, the complexity of the social system at the meta-level will continue to be higher than the cognitive capacities of its constituent elements. Hayek (1952: 185; 1967b, 1967c) makes this point explicit when he notes that:

> Any apparatus of classification must possess a structure of a higher degree of complexity than is possessed by the objects which it classifies ... therefore, the capacity of any explaining agent must be limited to objects with a structure possessing a degree of complexity lower than its own. (Hayek, 1952: 185)

Seen in the above light, the fundamental problem with deliberative democracy is that it places cognitive demands on people that are impossible for them to meet.

The central error that communitarians make here is the claim that people should consciously analyse how their actions affect the 'common good'. From a classical liberal perspective, the central problem of social coordination is to enable people to adjust to circumstances and interests of which they cannot be directly aware. This is not to suggest that 'other-regarding' behaviour is impossible, but that such behaviour will necessarily be confined to a small cognitive sphere encompassing the people and causes with which the relevant actors are personally familiar. The market price system and other spontaneous orders facilitate a complex process of mutual adjustment enabling individuals and organisations acting at the micro-scale to coordinate in spite of their cognitive limitations, by transmitting in a simplified form knowledge that represents the interrelated decisions of many dispersed actors. Classical liberalism does not deny the notion of the 'common good' or reduce such a conception to an aggregation of individual values. On the contrary, shifting relative prices are thought to enable a process of mutual adjustment among actors pursuing a diversity of open-ended and perhaps incommensurable goals – an adjustment that increases the chance that any one of these ends might successfully be achieved (Hayek, 1973: 114–15).

In emphasising the importance of conscious deliberation as the key to societal rationality, communitarians appear to be proposing little more than a form of 'central planning' by debate. Now, this charge may seem extreme in view of the explicit commitment by most communitarians to a specifically localised and 'community-centred' form of deliberation. Young (2000: 45–6), for example, recognises that a unitary model of deliberative democracy based on face-to-face communication is unattainable owing to the scale and complexity of contemporary urban societies. In order to address this problem she proposes a 'decentred' or localised form of politics where the relevant representatives are closer to the citizens and more likely to have knowledge of their needs and values 'on the ground' (see also Adaman and Devine, 1997). This emphasis on the importance of decentralisation is, however, somewhat surprising given that communitarian criticisms of liberalism and markets are directed against the alleged 'atomism' of processes that fail to encourage greater 'unity' in decisions. If decentralisation down to individual 'communities' is to be encouraged then it is not clear why a still more radical decentralisation down to individuals themselves ought not to be encouraged as well. It might be suggested that individuals are always embedded in local communities so that decentralisation down to this level is appropriate, whereas more individualised decision-making is not. Yet, such an argument cuts against the claim that the content of communal identification is no more fixed than that of individual identity. If identity is fluid and cross-cutting then the designation of 'local' community 'boundaries' is essentially arbitrary and closes off the very process of intersubjective (read intercommunity) learning that communitarians claim to favour.

Moreover, if it is conceded that 'no community is an island' then to focus on local deliberation merely begs the question of how the actions and choices of many different 'communities' are to be adjusted to one another at the meta-societal level (Prychitko, 1987; Tebble, 2003). As Hayek puts it:

> Once decentralisation becomes necessary the problem of coordination arises – a coordination which leaves the separate agencies free to adjust their activities to the facts that only they can know and yet brings about a mutual adjustment of their respective plans … this is precisely what the price system does under competition, and what no other system even promises to accomplish. It enables entrepreneurs, by watching the movements of comparatively few prices … to adjust their activities to those of their fellows. (Hayek, 1944: 55–6)

Under complex conditions where millions of intercommunity decisions must be adjusted to one another it would be impossible for local deliberators to comprehend the nature of the interrelationships between all the relevant actors. Absent an equivalent to the price system which reduces the complexity of the decisions that each of the decentralised communities must make, there is no mechanism available to coordinate what might otherwise be a disparate and inconsistent set of agendas. If complex intercommunity relations are not to be coordinated through market price signals – or an equivalent such as the shifting pattern of tax revenues that may occur under competitive federalism – then at some point recourse must be made to a central 'coordinating' authority. It is, however, precisely this form of 'central planning' that is subject to the 'knowledge problems' highlighted by Hayek.

The Problem of Tacit Knowledge

The inability of deliberative democratic processes to facilitate social coordination is further exacerbated by the problem of communicating what Michael

Polanyi (1951) has termed 'tacit knowledge'. The latter encompasses 'on-the-job know-how' or the 'practical knowledge' derived from cultural or organisational 'routines', specialisation in a field of work, or 'experience' of a particular market. It may also include a person's understanding of the values they attach to particular goods, the precise differences in which may not be communicated linguistically. When asked to value the different elements that make up a given basket of goods, an individual may not be able to explicate how much they value one good in relation to another – such knowledge can only be revealed in the act of choosing itself (Buchanan, 1969). As Sowell puts it:

> The real problem is that the knowledge needed is knowledge of subjective patterns of trade-off that are nowhere articulated, not even to the individual himself. I might think that, if faced with the stark prospect of bankruptcy, I would rather sell my automobile than my furniture or sacrifice the refrigerator rather than the stove, but unless and until such a moment comes, I will never know even my own trade-offs, much less anybody else's. (Sowell, 1980: 217–18)

By definition, the tacit data held by dispersed individuals and groups cannot be put into words. Neither can knowledge of this species be 'gathered' and placed at the disposal of a public forum because the participants may not even be aware that they themselves possess it. By privileging linguistic forms of knowledge transmission, therefore, deliberative procedures lack any mechanism that allows tacit knowledge to be put to effective public use. Exit-based institutions, on the other hand are able to communicate tacit knowledge indirectly through the actions of people as they enter into and exit from a variety of competing arrangements. In markets, for example, the prices that emerge from the unintended results of multiple buying and selling decisions are able to transmit the knowledge in individual minds that cannot be expressed verbally. When people make buying and selling decisions as producers (choosing which goods to produce and how to produce them) and as consumers (choosing between a variety of purchasing alternatives), they transmit 'messages' to one another. As Horwitz (1992) explains, what is crucial is that buyers and sellers need not be consciously aware of the knowledge they possess or why they value one course of action in the way that they do. All that is required is for people to act on the basis of their knowledge and the relevant information is fed into the price system. Similarly, under interjurisdictional competition, individuals and corporate bodies need not be able to put into words why they prefer living or working under one jurisdiction rather than another. All they need to do is to act out their preferences in this regard and their knowledge will be communicated through the marginal shift in revenues towards one authority and away from another.

The capacity of institutions that emphasise 'exit' over 'voice' to transmit tacit knowledge is of further significance with respect to the processes that facilitate the discovery and transformation of social values. If individual preferences are shaped endogenously by the social environment, then for communitarians it follows that they should be subject to a process of democratic criticism and debate by the community as a whole. On a classical liberal understanding, however, this conclusion does not hold because the process of value formation is by no means confined to acts of articulate persuasion. The vast majority of the goods that people desire are 'acquired tastes' which they learn to desire by seeing other people enjoying them (Hayek, 1967d). Similarly, the spread of knowledge in markets, the arts and science does not typically proceed by collective deliberation but advances when individuals and groups have a private sphere that secures the freedom to experiment with projects that do not conform to majority opinions. Then, incrementally, through a process of emulation the prevailing wisdom may change over time.

To restrict 'exit' mechanisms in order to arrive at 'consensus' decisions reduces the total number of decisions made and hence limits the range of lived experience from which people may then learn. Competitive processes allow contradictory ideas in countless production and consumption lines to be tested simultaneously without the need for majority approval. Employing the exit option enables actors who dissent from the majority opinion to follow their own ideas without impinging on the ability of the majority to follow theirs (for example, Wholgemuth, 1995, 1999, 2005; Friedman, 2006). Precisely because markets and interjurisdictional competition afford people the space to implement their ideas rather than simply talking about them, people are then able to emulate or avoid such role models as the benefits and costs become visible to a wider set of actors. The emphasis on explicit reasoning and the 'power of the better argument' under deliberative democracy, therefore, far from encouraging the discovery of new values seems more likely to stultify the transformation of attitudes and practices including those that may impede the progress of 'excluded' groups. This argument does not suggest that classical liberal institutions will necessarily lead to an elevation in values, but that a process allowing for decentralised action by minority individuals and groups may be more likely to do so than one bound by majority decisions.

EXIT VERSUS VOICE: TRANSPARENCY AND THE INCENTIVE PROBLEM

The Problem of Rational Ignorance

The arguments raised thus far do not assume that deliberative democratic institutions fail owing to problems of inadequate incentives. On the contrary, they apply even in the 'best-case' scenario where people are other-regarding and where all those affected are able to participate in the manner afforded by an 'ideal speech situation'. Once it is recognised that 'incentives matter', however, then the robustness of deliberative democracy is cast further into doubt. There are strong grounds to believe that people have insufficient incentives to acquire information about politics, and a similar lack of incentive to submit their preferences and values to critical scrutiny in a context of collective choice. In a large-number democracy the chance that any one citizen's contribution will have a decisive effect on the outcome for themselves or for their fellows is vanishingly small. Far from becoming an informed and active citizen, therefore, it may be rational to be 'ignorant' about the content of public deliberations. The larger the number of issues decided by democratic procedures, the more pronounced this problem becomes as the information costs of judging many different political issues rise correspondingly (Somin, 1998: 436–7; Hardin, 2000). Even a civic-minded person may not spend much time checking political information for the sake of casting an informed vote, when the chance of affecting the outcome of an election is so trivial. Such a person may be better directing their energies to activities that can have a decisive effect on a specific outcome, such as, for example, the decision to spend time and money on the charity or cause of their own choosing.

Empirical studies in Europe and the United States confirm that voters, irrespective of educational achievements and social class, tend to be ignorant of even the most basic political information. In the United States, for example, analysis suggests that as many as 70 per cent of voters cannot name either of their state's senators and the vast majority cannot estimate the rate of inflation and unemployment within 5 per cent of their actual levels (Somin, 1998; see also Pincione and Tesson, 2006). That voters exhibit such high levels of ignorance of such basic political information and know so little about matters which are 'high profile' and appear in the public media on a regular basis suggests that they will be even less informed about the effects of the more detailed policies that may pass through legislative and bureaucratic chambers.[3]

It does not appear to be apathy or obstacles to participation that best explain such ignorance, but the lack of incentive to participate in an informed manner. To reply to this suggestion as Barber (1984: 234) has, that people 'will quickly appreciate the need for knowledge' once they are offered 'significant power' to deliberate on public affairs, is to ignore that the opportunity to deliberate may not give them any significant power at all (Somin, 1998). Indeed, relative to a market situation or a regime of competitive federalism, where each person's decision to enter into a particular exchange or jurisdiction is decisive in determining their personal outcome, a transfer of activities into the arena of democratic deliberation is likely to result in a relative disempowerment of most actors. Under markets and competitive federalism, people have much stronger incentives to become informed about their purchasing or location decisions because the costs of failing to be adequately informed are concentrated on them, whereas in a large-scale democracy the costs of failure are spread across the rest of the voting population.

The phenomenon of rational ignorance is likely to impoverish the quality of public deliberation even if one assumes that people are civic-minded in outlook. These problems are magnified, however, if the assumption of other-regarding motivations is relaxed. It is the inadequate incentive for people to monitor the behaviour of political representatives that may enable special interests to capture the decision-process. Supporters of deliberative democracy who recognise that the problem of self-interest needs to be overcome contend that the process of public debate will be sufficient to expose those arguments which are offered out of self-interest rather than the common good (Young, 2000). Under conditions of rational voter ignorance, however, this is precisely what public deliberation will not be able to achieve. Relative to a situation where actors can improve their situation by 'exiting' from those suppliers or jurisdictions that fail to provide what they promise, public deliberation offers few incentives for people to inform themselves about the quality of the decisions made in their name.

From a classical liberal perspective, the information vacuum that results from rational public ignorance will quickly be filled by the representatives of special interest groups. These groups are likely to be of two kinds. On the one hand, they may include producer interests who have a high per capita stake in influencing the results of public deliberation and who, being relatively small in number, face lower transaction costs of organisation and a greater capacity to overcome free-rider problems (Olson, 1965, 1982; Tullock, 1994). On the other hand, they may include representatives of 'cause-based' groups whose members share an expressive commitment to a particular ideology, religion or social identity set. The problem of free-riding is minimised for the latter groups because in such cases political participation, far from being a cost to be avoided, is a benefit to be sought – in much the way that some people enjoy spectator sports owing to the opportunities they provide to display affection or hostility towards particular teams (Brennan and Lomasky, 1993). Either way, the bulk of the population including taxpayer and consumer interests and those who lack a strong identity set of one kind or another are likely to be relatively undermobilised. The knowledge of public affairs that such people receive however, may be disproportionately affected by information from organised special interests – the quality of which the majority of the population will have few incentives to examine.

The Problem of Rational Irrationality

The problem of rational ignorance is reinforced when the incentives to question one's existing values and prevailing understandings of the world are also considered. The costs to the individual of maintaining and expressing false beliefs in the sphere of democratic participation are trivial because the chance that any individual contribution to public debate may affect its result is vanishingly small. As a consequence, there is a tendency towards 'rational irrationality' (Caplan, 2007; see also Brennan and Lomasky, 1993). In a process which removes the 'exit' option, the costs of supporting irrational policies are spread across all other members of society rather than being concentrated on those holding to false beliefs. The rational questioning of personal beliefs and preferences in a democratic setting has collective goods attributes and will, therefore, tend to be 'underproduced'. In a market or market-like context, on the other hand, holding to false beliefs or prejudices has a direct cost to the actor concerned. Thus, the employer who refuses to hire people owing to their race or sexual orientation and the consumer who refuses to buy products made with 'foreign' labour will have to pay higher prices relative to more open-minded market participants because such prejudicial buying reduces the supply of employees or other partners to exchange (see also Becker, 1971).

Collective action problems associated with democratic deliberation are further compounded by the phenomena of 'preference falsification'. Set against the trivial benefits derived from participation there may be high costs to the individual from challenging the prevailing wisdom. Those who wish to defend groups or values that are not appreciated by the general population may fear the social consequences of expressing these beliefs in public (Kuran, 1995). Even when potentially large numbers wish to challenge the relevant beliefs, if there is uncertainty about the level of support then serious collective action problems are likely to ensue. It will be in each actor's interests either to stay quiet or even to support the status quo, avoiding the risk of ostracism in the hope of free-riding on the arguments of others. If sufficient numbers reason accordingly, then far from reflecting a free and honest discussion people may actually voice opinions with which they privately disagree in order to maintain social approval. In these 'lock-in' cases one could envisage a theoretical scenario where state action could facilitate moves towards an alternative set of social practices. These would not, however, be the actions of a state that 'listens to the public' through a process of democratic deliberation. On the contrary, they would be those of a government willing to override the expressed values of the majority, assuming somewhat unrealistically that such a government could actually know which particular set of values to support or to enforce.

Cultural 'lock-in' effects of the type discussed above may also occur within private markets, and the evolution of social values may be correspondingly slow. Similarly, as the phenomena of stock market 'bubbles' and 'depressions' demonstrates so clearly, 'spontaneous orders' are prone to herd-like behaviour and may become 'stuck' in path-dependent processes of upward or downward spiralling which may perpetuate erroneous decisions. Although such problems are pervasive in markets and other exit-based procedures the potential for 'lock-in' may be less severe than under collective democratic alternatives because persuasion costs are relatively lower. In markets, for example, in order to secure support for an unconventional enterprise or practice it is not necessary for entrepreneurs whether in the commercial sector or in civil associations to voice their opinions in a public forum and neither is it necessary for them to secure the support of a majority (Wholgemuth, 1995, 1999, 2005). All that is required when there is 'freedom of entry' into the market is for entrepreneurs to persuade a sufficient number of people to support the enterprise or venture such that it is able to cover its costs. With lower persuasion costs and the possibility for many different minority opinions to be implemented, the costs of dissenting from the status quo are likely to be lower and the chance of becoming 'locked in' to a dominant set of values is correspondingly reduced.

More generally, although people in markets are influenced by the majority opinion they have more scope to challenge mistaken points of view because: (1) they do not require majority support before they enter or exit from a particular relationship; and (2) they may profit personally by dissenting from the status quo. Thus, the most successful stock market traders are typically those who 'beat the market' by selling when the majority of other participants are buying, or buy when the majority are selling. Similarly, entrepreneurs and consumers who do not share the racist or sexist prejudices of their fellows may profit personally by breaking from such prejudices and entering into exchanges with people against the prevailing social norms. It is owing to the greater scope that exit-based institutions provide for such independent action that though not immune from path-dependencies and 'lock-in' effects these may be less evident than under a majoritarian alternative.

EXIT VERSUS VOICE: THE MORAL ARGUMENT

The obstacles that prevent deliberative democracy from delivering the communicative benefits claimed in its name may reflect problems intrinsic to deliberative democratic structures per se. The argument presented thus far is not that deliberative institutions are prevented from working by artificial constraints. Rather, the contention is that the regulative ideal central to deliberative democracy may be incompatible with the goals it seeks to achieve. When compared to exit-based arrangements and markets in particular, attempts to make social institutions more deliberative may reduce the range, quality and complexity of social communication. These failings are of equal relevance in the context of the moral arguments advanced in favour of a greater reliance on democratic voice.

Logistics and Equal Respect

The central moral argument for deliberative democracy is that it is more likely to reflect ethical norms of justice than bargaining in markets or market-like structures because it enables members of 'excluded' groups including the poor and various cultural minorities to have their views registered in a public forum and to be heard with equal respect (Young, 1990, 2000). As the foregoing discussion has shown, however, even in the 'best-case' scenarios a combination of knowledge problems and incentive-based deficiencies will block the process of communicative rationality that deliberative democrats seek to enhance. In practice, 'real-world' examples of deliberation are likely to perform even less impressively than these arguments imply, for it is never suggested that all of the population will actually be involved in the relevant decision-making given the logistical impossibility of providing a forum sufficiently large to meet the requirement that all those affected by a decision should be able to take part.

Any workable form of deliberative democracy will inevitably take a representative rather than a participatory form, and hence will fail to reflect the detailed views and values of the vast majority of the population, irrespective of whether they are members of 'included' or 'excluded' groups. It is not clear, therefore, why communitarians consider deliberative democracy more respectful of the views of the poor and minorities than exit-based alternatives such as markets. While the range of choices open to the poor and the excluded in markets is less than those available to the better-off, the decisions that they can take, such as spotting better-paying job opportunities or sources of cheaper products, may be more likely to have a decisive effect on their lives than reliance on distant representatives and the periodic chance to vote in elections. Markets are not constrained by the limits of a deliberative forum because the views of every individual are fed into the price system through the constant and variegated buying and selling decisions that they make. Moreover, precisely because they do not rely on majority decisions, markets seem much more likely to cater to minority interests and cultural niches. Relative to markets, deliberative democratic structures give both too little and too much power to majorities. They give too little power because the vast bulk of the public has very limited scope to decide the content of the political agenda. They give too much power, however, because once that agenda has been set by the ruling representatives the majority position will be imposed against the wishes of the dissenting minority.

It may, of course, be argued that inequalities in buying power show that classical liberal institutions do not secure people the respect they deserve. Whether equal respect is in fact an appropriate criterion of justice and what is implied by such a concept will be considered in greater detail in Chapter 5. What is at issue for present purposes, however, is that deliberative democratic institutions may be incapable of delivering on the goal of equal respect owing to the obstacles highlighted above. A move away from the principle of competitive exit and towards deliberative democracy is to move away from a position where both rich and poor individuals, 'included' and 'excluded', can exercise a decisive effect over the allocation of resources – though with the rich having a wider range of options – to a situation where the vast majority of people exercise little or no individual influence over the choices made in their name. Greater equality between rich and poor goes hand in hand with greater inequality between the people at large and a limited number of 'representatives' who may wield more power over resource allocation than had previously been exercised by anybody.

Self-representation versus Group Representation

One attempt to rescue the moral argument for deliberation from objections of the above nature is closely associated with the work of Young (2000). Though she recognises that direct representation of diverse interests in a democratic forum is a logistical impossibility, Young contends that the interests of an array of people including those of excluded minorities may be reflected if the understanding of what constitutes appropriate representation is changed accordingly. While it is true that representatives in a democracy cannot literally speak 'as' the people, they may nonetheless speak 'for' them and especially for those suffering various forms of exclusion and oppression. To speak 'as' the people would require that individuals literally 'speak for themselves' or at the very least have common interests and opinions to those of their representatives. To speak 'for' the people, however, simply requires that representatives recognise the diversity of experience in their society. According to this view, one does not have to be poor, female or gay in order to speak up for those who fall into the relevant social groups. Neither is representation necessarily confined to elected politicians, but it may also include the role played by representatives from various civil associations such as women's rights and gay rights organisations. On Young's view, therefore, while deliberative democratic structures are imperfect they offer better prospects to ensure that the interests of the 'excluded' are properly respected than if the latter are left to fend for themselves in markets and other non-deliberative forums.

It is, however, hard to see that Young's 'solution' is adequate to the problems in hand. As Tebble (2003: 205) has argued, if the claim of 'critical theorists' such as Young that communal identifications and interests are no more fixed or 'pre-given' than those of individuals is accepted, then any form of representation is morally problematic. To say that one is speaking 'for' the interests of the 'poor', 'women' or 'gay people' is to presuppose that such groups have an identifiable and common interest. Yet if people's sense of their identity, values and preferences is cross-cutting and in a state of constant flux no such common identity can be held to exist. A person who shares the characteristic 'gay' may differ on many other dimensions with others who happen to share this particular aspect of identity. They may, for example, differ in terms of their income, race, religion and regional or cultural background. More important, the constituents of what it 'means to be gay' may themselves evolve in diverse and unanticipated ways. Democratic representation in such a context will always reflect the very particular understandings of the representatives concerned, and may tend to attribute homogenous and stereotypical viewpoints to the memberships of various 'communities'.

To favour a representative version of deliberation, moreover, is to undermine the claim that democracy facilitates social learning, for when politicians represent others, understanding of their constituents' views precedes deliberative engagement with respect to the content of those views (Ryfe, 2005). And, in the unlikely event that they do actually reflect the perspectives of diverse constituents prior to deliberation, politicians who change their own opinions during the process of debate with other representatives cease to reflect the community from which they are drawn. It is not the constituents themselves who are engaged in the process of argumentation and learning. Insofar as politicians change their perspective as a consequence of deliberation this only serves to widen the knowledge gap between themselves and those they represent.

The above problem is not significantly alleviated when political representatives are the members of civil associations such as women's and gay rights organisations. There is little reason to suppose that the representatives of such groups have anything more than a very partial understanding of the values, needs and identities of their members. That people join such organisations at all – and the vast majority of women and gay people do not – is more a reflection of the character of the democratic process. Indeed those who are sufficiently motivated to join in collective action of this nature may constitute a non-representative sample committed to a very particular interpretation of what a female or gay identity consists of. By contrast, many of those who happen to share the characteristics 'gay' or 'female' but who do not associate with any particular interpretation of this identity are likely to be under-represented. Voting is a relatively crude mechanism which requires that issues are packaged in a simplistic way in order that they may be decided by majority rule. It is in the very nature of such procedures that people will be viewed as homogenous, stereotypical 'communities' rather than in a more nuanced and variegated manner. As Tebble (2003: 206) concludes, 'it is not *how* groups are represented but rather *that* they are represented' that leads one to doubt whether deliberative democracy can deliver on its aim of treating 'differently situated others' with due respect.

On a classical liberal view, a more robust alternative to representation in a deliberative democratic forum is to allow people to speak and, more importantly, to act for themselves through their choices to enter into and exit from relationships with competing commercial organisations, voluntary groups and political jurisdictions. Via such a process of 'self-representation' people may choose those options which best reflect their personal mix of values and identity traits in a more subtle manner than is possible by periodically voting on the results of deliberations by a small group of representatives. In an environment where exit prevails, moreover, the constituents of one's identity may themselves evolve as a wider array of dispersed entrepreneurs and voluntary organisations compete by offering new combinations of goods, services and ideas in an attempt both to cater to existing values and to create new identity configurations. It is significant in this regard that markets in such fields as music and recreation were catering to different conceptions of, for example, 'gayness' long before the democratic process had moved towards greater equality in civil rights (Lavoie and Chamlee-Wright, 2001).

The above argument does not, it must be emphasised, imply that the exit principle may not itself allow various stereotypes and prejudices that exclude people to be reflected. Rather, it is to suggest that relative to deliberative democratic alternatives, exit-based institutions such as markets may provide more scope for people to escape and to challenge such prejudices. There is little reason to believe that state-centric decisions, subject to deliberative procedures or otherwise, are somehow able to avoid the problems that arise from the prejudices of citizens and their representatives. Democratically elected governments have, after all, been responsible for all manner of enforced discriminations ranging from racist zoning regulations to employment laws designed to restrict the opportunities of women (Sowell, 1981). Those who wish to challenge established values may, therefore, be more likely to do so in an environment that emphasises exit over majority rule. For a group such as gays, for example, it may be better to live under a system of competitive federalism where it may be possible to escape from oppression by 'exiting' to a minority jurisdiction which is tolerant in its attitudes, than to have to persuade a national majority of the need for cultural change, before having the scope to exercise ones orientation in public.

Insofar as communitarian supporters of deliberative democracy have responded to this classical liberal analysis, they suggest that the process of public deliberation itself encourages people to exhibit greater respect producing a more inclusive form of decision-making where people transcend their own perspectives and acquire greater appreciation of the situation of others (Young, 2000). Yet, setting aside the logistical problems of bringing together the relevant actors there is little or no reason to suppose that engaging in public dialogue will lead people to respect one another. At the very least, there seems an equal likelihood that the more people become aware of the values held by other individuals and groups the more they may come to disrespect those values (Kukathas, 2003: 157). There is nothing about a specifically deliberative democratic form of decision-making which better equips it to reduce the likelihood of minority oppression. Indeed, from a classical liberal perspective, such procedures are more likely to promote conflict. The extension of democratic control into areas where there is not already widespread agreement on values may result in a power struggle as different groups compete to gain control of the state apparatus in order to impose their own particular version of the common good. Unless the relevant disagreements suddenly disappear, in the final analysis it is the power of majority coalitions and coalitions of a small number of representatives at that, which will determine the actual decisions made.

From a classical liberal perspective, 'agreeing to disagree' and not requiring collective decisions in the first place is an alternative way of promoting greater openness and tolerance. Studies of political behaviour confirm that most people do not agree with communitarians that the existence of value conflict provides sufficient reason to politicise decisions. On the contrary, people tend to want to avoid discussion of controversial moral positions in public forums. In a comprehensive analysis of the structure of political participation, Mutz (2006) has shown that political discussion becomes more frequent as relationships between participants to dialogue become more intimate. People tend to form close relations with others who already share many of their moral attitudes and who feel comfortable discussing these with one another. In less intimate contexts such as the workplace, however, although people are more likely to meet those holding different moral beliefs they are also much less likely to engage in political conversation out of social politeness and a desire to minimise conflict. Insofar as people do discuss political and moral questions in such contexts, moreover, this tends to occur because the discussions do not culminate in binding collective decisions. Broader patterns of civic participation appear to conform to a similar pattern, with participation in voluntary associations oriented to uncontroversial and non-political ends proving more popular than membership of groups pursuing controversial and partisan causes (Mutz, 2006, especially Chapters 2 and 4).

By far the most disturbing element to emerge from the above findings for communitarians is that those who exhibit the open-mindedness and tolerance of others necessary for deliberative democracy to function are precisely the people who avoid active politics (Mutz, 2006: Chapter 5). The more tolerant people are of other viewpoints, the less likely they are to want to engage in activity that will result in coercive collective decisions. The way that most people show 'respect for others' in their everyday lives is either to avoid politics altogether or to keep the company of like-minded people. Those inclined to take the time and trouble to become involved in political activism tend to be drawn from the ranks of 'true believers' who are partisan and often intolerant. People who are the most knowledgeable about politics and who consciously identify themselves with particular causes report minimal social contact with those of alternative political views. Such findings are particularly telling given the inexorable tendency for deliberative democracy to collapse into a representative form. In an echo of Hayek's (1944) discussion of 'Why the Worst Get on Top', they suggest that under deliberative democracy the limited set of actors charged with making complex ethical and moral trade-offs may be the very people who are least likely to exercise tolerance and respect for a diversity of conflicting viewpoints.

Bargaining and Communication

Against all of these arguments communitarians may still maintain that deliberative democracy is ethically superior to the exit principle because it relies on argument rather than bargaining power. The analogy usually invoked in this context is with the process of scientific debate – it is considered inappropriate to decide the merits of competing theories according to willingness to pay and the intensity of individual preferences which are the primary criteria in market-like settings. Likewise, for communitarians, many questions of resource allocation should be determined by the 'power of the better argument' and not by willingness to pay. The problem with this view, however, is that most such decisions involve issues pertaining to scarcity and the complex trade-offs necessitated by competing sets of values, which different individuals and communities may choose to make in different ways. Decisions concerning appropriate levels of expenditure on, for example, transport infrastructure or health care are not akin to matters of scientific 'truth' which can be judged 'right' or 'wrong' on the basis of reasoned argument.

If the importance of disagreement and trade-offs is recognised then the underlying problem is to find a process through which different value judgements and trade-offs can be made, communicated and adjusted to one another. It is at this juncture, however, that the process of democratic deliberation runs into the problems discussed throughout this chapter. Knowledge pertaining to ethical and cultural standards, local conditions of supply and demand, the availability of substitutes and all manner of context-specific factors does not exist as a coherent whole which can be surveyed or gathered by a group of representatives. The dispersed 'bits' of knowledge may, however, be communicated by impersonal signals such as market prices which transmit in codified and simplified form the many different value judgements made by countless individuals and groups. People both inform the price system of their personal judgements through their decisions to enter or exit particular markets or jurisdictions, and are informed indirectly by the price system about the judgements made by distant and unknown others. When resource allocation involves countless dispersed trade-offs the indirect form of communication that results from the generation of market prices may be the only effective form of communication available.

The type of 'bargaining' that occurs in markets and interjurisdictional competition, it must be emphasised, is significantly different from that which often occurs in a strictly majoritarian arena. The defining characteristic of markets and market-like processes is that they involve consensual exchanges. In the process of 'political bargaining', however, the terms of 'exchange' are not consensual because majority coalitions are able to impose costs on minority actors who are not – save from the leaving the country – able to exercise the 'exit' option. It is not clear how 'bargaining' can be entirely avoided under any set of institutions, for if disagreement over social dilemmas persists then in the final analysis it will be the relative power held by different sets of actors that determines the decisions made. The advantage of the exit principle, however, is that those who find themselves in a relatively weaker position may have some scope to avoid unwanted decisions being imposed upon them. Even in the case of what are more explicitly moral questions, reliance on the exit principle may be preferable. Those who find themselves in the minority on whichever side of the abortion debate, for example, may find it better to live under a regime of interjurisdictional competition where they have at least some scope to live under an authority that reflects their own point of view, rather than face a unitary system of moral laws.

Equality, Inequality and Communication

Bargaining in markets and other exit-based institutions is, of course, by no means an egalitarian process. From a classical liberal perspective, however, inequality is not incompatible with the communicative conception of rationality that deliberative democrats are keen to encourage and, indeed, is crucial to the transmission of knowledge. As Hayek (1960: 85) puts it: 'If the results of individual liberty did not demonstrate that some manners of living were more successful than others, much of the case for it would vanish'. In markets, for example, the discovery of profit opportunities sends out a signal to other actors and facilitates the spread of the most successful production and consumption models. Similarly, the location choices of people and the shifting pattern of revenues under competitive federalism may indicate differential responses to innovations in the tax and regulatory choices of local jurisdictions.

Seen in this light, the egalitarian requirements of Habermas's 'ideal speech situation' obscure the fact that knowledge, while dispersed, is not and cannot be equally distributed. Just as the process of scientific advance is characterised by new discoveries and the rise of 'dominant' theories, which then become subject to attack, so, entrepreneurial profits are constantly whittled away as new competitors enter the fray (Polanyi, 1951). From a classical liberal perspective, therefore, equality of mutual influence is not a valid criterion against which institutional performance should ever be judged.

Deliberative democrats themselves appear to concede that 'unequal' influence is not incompatible with the principle of 'equal respect'. Harry Brighouse, for example, argues that:

> inequalities that result from public reason giving seem acceptable. There is nothing disrespectful about offering sincere reasons for one's views and asking those to be considered by others. So the argument (for deliberative democracy) allows those who are better at persuasive public-reason giving to be more influential, as long as their influence is as a consequence of their actual persuasion of others. (Brighouse, 2002: 58)

If inequalities resulting from persuasion are acceptable, however, then it is not clear why communitarians consider to be unacceptable those inequalities that result from the differential success of people who persuade others to purchase goods in the market or to enter a competing political jurisdiction. Deliberative procedures are unlikely to be any more inclusive or egalitarian than institutions that rely on the power of exit. Indeed procedures that rely on the statement of explicit reasons are likely to exclude systematically those individuals who are less able to engage in the articulate persuasion of majorities, but who may still possess valuable knowledge embodied in the exercise of entrepreneurship, a practical skill or the adherence to a particular ethical code. In markets and under competitive federalism, rich and poor, articulate and inarticulate can act on the basis of relatively easy comparisons between prices, qualities of goods and lifestyles across competing products and jurisdictions. Deliberative institutions, by contrast, give special advantage to those skilled in the use of articulate persuasion alone.

Inequalities in market-like arrangements may, of course, be reproduced owing to path-dependent processes. People may, for example, invest in wealthy people or those who have an established reputation simply because they have wealth or reputation, rather than backing a newcomer who actually has the better ideas. Deliberative democratic procedures are, however, also subject to a variant of the 'inheritance effect' and this may be more pronounced than under arrangements based on more competitive principles.

Those who have exercised the 'power of the better argument' will inevitably come to the deliberative forum with a greater stock of social status, in the same way that those who have demonstrated prescient entrepreneurship enter markets with greater buying power. In markets, however, opportunities for newcomers to challenge the status quo are not dependent on the capacity to persuade majorities in a public forum. People may also prove themselves by offering cheaper or better opportunities to others, and potential investors can 'beat the market' by backing promising newcomers with their own money without needing to wait for majority approval.

Relative to markets, therefore, procedures that rely on the exercise of majoritarian voice seem as likely to reinforce inequalities by discriminating against those who lack the skills necessary to persuade majorities via formal argument. Moreover, because democratic procedures tend to encourage a 'group-centred' rather than an individualised form of representation, people may 'inherit' a hearing for their views by mere virtue of their attachment to those groups whose representatives have won out in earlier rounds of public debate. Spokespersons for business associations, trades unions or environmental groups may be invited to participate in a public forum primarily because previous representatives of these groups have offered persuasive arguments. In principle, there seems little difference between such cases and those where a person inherits greater buying power in a market because a family member was a successful entrepreneur.

It may, of course, be argued that the capacity to maintain 'undeserved' influence in a democratic forum depends on the ability of today's representatives to continue offering good arguments. Yet, the same logic may be applied in the case of inherited wealth. In a competitive market the capacity of the wealthy to maintain their relative standing will depend on the extent to which they continue to invest their assets in ways which enhance consumer welfare. Deliberative democrats such as Young argue for wealth redistribution prior to the process of public debate on grounds that private 'money power' exercised within the political process (via campaign contributions and political advertising) may enable the wealthy to manipulate the process in order to entrench established positions (Young, 1990: 184–5). From a classical liberal perspective, however, this is not an argument in favour of redistribution, but an argument for limiting the scope of the political machine that facilitates the exercise of such power. The capacity of the wealthy to maintain their position in ways which diminish consumer welfare is not an intrinsic element of a market economy per se, but may result from the capture of an interventionist state apparatus that distributes favourable regulations, tariffs and subsidies and which shelters the wealthy from the 'creative destruction' characteristic of unfettered markets. If the concern is to limit the power of the wealthy, but without removing those inequalities which reflect superior performance, then the best way of achieving this may be to limit the scope for anticompetitive state intervention, whether conducted in a deliberative democratic manner or otherwise.

CONCLUSION

The introductory chapter of this book set out some principles of 'robust political economy' in the context of comparative institutions analysis. It should now be apparent that the communitarian advocacy of deliberative democracy fails to meet the requirements of institutional robustness in this regard. Communitarians have a well-developed theory of how they would like the democratic process to operate but have failed to explain how any actual political system could come close to fulfilling these ideals. Far from encouraging the communicative processes that communitarians wish to advance, deliberative democracy seems more likely to thwart them. Assuming 'other-regarding' motives, deliberative institutions are unable to reflect the views and knowledge of more than a tiny subset of the population. Relaxing the assumption of 'other-regarding' motivation, deliberative institutions offer little protection against the abuse of power either by political representatives or by special interest organisations.

NOTES

1. The term 'communitarian' is used in this chapter and throughout the book to refer to a particular style of argument rather than to a substantive political position. In political theory, the term 'communitarian' is typically used to describe authors, such as MacIntyre (1981) and Taylor (1985), who challenge the understanding of the individual self and its relationship to notions of reason and justice held by liberals such as Rawls. Many writers who use aspects of these arguments or are influenced by them do not, however, consider themselves to be 'political communitarians'. In this book the term 'communitarian' is used in a somewhat looser sense – referring to a style of argument which emphasises the 'social' aspect of human existence, the endogenous nature of preferences and the claim that collective choice processes and deliberative democracy, in particular, are best placed to facilitate social learning and to build trust. On this usage of the term there are a number of authors who consider themselves to be 'liberals' (for example, Miller, 1989, 1995) or supporters of 'difference' (for example Young, 1990, 2000) but who nonetheless invoke a communitarian 'style of argument' to defend their preference for deliberative democratic institutions.
2. Habermas's arguments have been highly influential. While there are subtle differences between authors about the appropriate conditions for effective deliberation, a wide range of authors invoke variations on a deliberative democratic theme. These include, for example, Benhabib (1996), Bohman (1996), Cohen and Arato (1992), Fraser (1993) Laclau and Mouffe (1985) and Mouffe (1993). Though many deliberative democrats may accurately be described as 'communitarians' a number of those influenced by Habermas locate themselves within the liberal egalitarian tradition – for example Guttman and Thompson (2004).
3. The implication here is not that citizens should actually know everything about politics in order for the democratic process to be effective. In principle, there is no more need for a citizen to know about the mechanics of legislation than there is for a consumer in a market to

know all the details of the production process involved in making the goods they consume. Rather, the argument here is that on those more detailed matters, such as the opportunity cost of legislation, where it would be in the interests of individual citizens to be informed there is in fact little incentive for them to be so – and much less incentive than for an equivalent person making buying and selling decisions in a market.

4. Exit, trust and social capital: the challenge of communitarianism II[1]

INTRODUCTION

Though it is an important theme in the arsenal of communitarian arguments that challenge classical liberalism, the case for deliberative democracy is by no means the only such theme. A related set of concerns focuses on the moral norms necessary to sustain social institutions, and the wider relationships between commerce, democracy and civil society. At issue here are the concepts of trust and social capital.

Contemporary communitarians suggest that an excessive reliance on markets and market-like processes disturbs the 'social capital' essential to the functioning of any society and actually undermines the morals needed to maintain the market economy itself. On the one hand, it is argued that markets 'need' the state if they are to function effectively and that the pursuit of an 'unregulated' or 'free market' system is chimerical. On the other hand, communitarians argue that in order to sustain social capital the commercial ethos should be counterbalanced by institutions based on different operating norms. According to this view, active or enabling government action provides an outlet for more community-centred norms and can help to build the behavioural traits that sustain the social fabric.

This chapter examines the relationship between classical liberalism and social capital. The next section sketches both the negative case against market processes and the positive case for government action in helping to promote or to 'build' trust. The subsequent three sections question the robustness of these arguments in the following vein. First, it will be argued that communitarians misunderstand the type of institutional framework compatible with an advanced economic order. While it is true that markets require some form of 'regulation' it does not follow that all or even most of this regulation need be provided by the state. In addition, the moral norms that are said to be undermined by 'free markets' are often exclusive and are precisely the type of practices that may impede socio-economic development. A cosmopolitan economy requires that people operate in a 'mixed' environment of behavioural norms which combines impersonal contractual relationships or 'bridging social capital', with more intimate ties or 'bonding social capital'. It will then be shown that a classical liberal order constitutes a 'macro-framework' able to sustain an appropriate mix of these behavioural norms. Finally, drawing on the principles of robust political economy, the discussion suggests that elected officials may lack the knowledge to plan successful interventions in civil society and that incentives built into the democratic process may transform social capital into a resource that facilitates predatory rent-seeking over civil endeavour.

TRUST, SOCIAL CAPITAL AND COMMUNITARIAN POLITICS

The concepts of trust and social capital refer to the basic behavioural norms that facilitate processes of social interaction such as those found in the context of commercial exchange, and the willingness of individuals and groups to adhere to these norms without recourse to official sanctions such as fines and imprisonment. Economists analyse how different institutional arrangements affect the transactions costs involved in monitoring social relations and hence the incentive structure that actors face when deciding whether or not to engage in shirking or other forms of opportunism. Where the costs of monitoring those with whom one wishes to cooperate are low, then shirking behaviour is thought less likely to occur than when these costs are higher. Within this context, the presence of strong norms of interpersonal and interorganisational trust is believed by many social scientists to reduce such transaction costs; the more that social actors trust one another to honour agreements and not to 'free ride' in joint endeavours, the less time they will have to spend monitoring each other's performance.

The Historical 'Myth' of the 'Free Market'

At the core of contemporary concerns surrounding social capital are a series of long-standing suspicions about the allegedly 'corrupting' influence of commerce and of the social instability wrought by unregulated markets. Critics of liberal markets maintain that such markets undermine the norms of trust and honest dealing essential to their own functioning and thus raise the transactions costs involved in coordinating everyday life. Plant (1999: 10), for example, argues that: 'In order to work effectively the market requires certain moral attitudes on the part of those involved, and ... there is some danger of these moral underpinnings being disturbed by markets themselves, thereby striking at the roots of their own efficiency and effectiveness.'

This critique of liberal market processes forms a central tenet of contemporary social democratic politics and is also evident in the revival of interest in 'institutionalist' economic theory. Early 'institutionalists' such as those involved in the German 'historical school' were hostile to the universal application of marginalist economics by theorists such as Carl Menger, favouring instead an approach emphasising the cultural specificity of 'economising' behaviour. It is, however, in the writings of Karl Polanyi that contemporary institutionalists find their principal inspiration. Polanyi (1944) argued that the pursuit of a 'free market' system is chimerical. He defined the modern 'market economy' as an economic and social system controlled and directed by markets alone – where land, labour and capital are traded on the basis of relative prices set by the interaction of supply and demand. Historically such an economy did not, argued Polanyi, emerge spontaneously owing to what Adam Smith described as the human propensity to 'truck, barter and exchange', but was the result of political and often coercive imposition by a state heady on the ideology of classical economics. Insofar as 'markets' had existed before this era, these were not based on the pursuit of personal profit, an impersonal rule of contract and the free play of supply and demand, but were embedded in a network of solidaristic obligations 'administered' by community organisations such as churches and the craftsmen's guilds. These obligations were, in turn, enforced by the state.

According to Polanyi, the period of 'laissez-faire' capitalism that arose in the eighteenth and nineteenth centuries was an historical aberration wrought by a sustained period of government intervention and centralised political control. The institutional framework that characterised this era and the individualistic values that went with it were the creation of legislative fiat, such as the repeal of the Corn Laws, the end of public charity and the creation of a 'free' labour market. The result of this great experiment in social engineering, however, was a period of social dislocation resulting from the propensity of the 'market system' to destroy pre-existing relationships built on non-market values such as reciprocity and redistribution. Seen from this perspective, the widespread movement to regulate markets that occurred towards the end of the nineteenth century, and accelerated thereafter with the rise of the welfare state, was a 'protective response' to the social destruction inflicted by an era when market values were allowed free rein. For Polanyi, therefore, the market economy is neither 'free' in its origins and neither can it be left 'free' to function without the protective intervention of the state.

Trust, Social Capital and the Critique of Liberal Markets

Contemporary institutionalists, exemplified by Geoffrey Hodgson, are less hostile to the notion of a market economy per se than was Polanyi, but they maintain that market processes should be subordinated by institutions not characterised by contractual exchange (see, for example, Hodgson, 1998). Unlike many of the authors considered in the previous chapter, Hodgson is fully aware of the coordinative problems central to deliberative democracy. He maintains, however, that while markets are needed to generate price signals reflecting the changing scarcity of different goods, the contractual process which generates such signals depends too heavily on cash incentives. Price-coordinated markets encourage an acquisitive and selfish spirit that undermines trust and respect for contract and property rights. Moral or pro-social behaviour such as the keeping of promises and the observance of contracts is understood to have many of the properties of a collective good: private individuals will tend to underinvest in it because the benefits that accrue are dispersed throughout society, appear only in the long term and are non-excludable (leading to free-rider problems), whereas the costs of respecting basic norms are far more personal and immediate. Markets, therefore, are parasitic on the social capital needed for their maintenance and will always be unstable in the absence of countervailing institutions governed by different operating norms.

Building on this account Hodgson develops a critique of those 'neo-liberals' who wish to extend market competition to all but a very few public-good functions (such as defence and larger-scale issues of environmental pollution) that may define the boundaries of a minimal state. There are, of course, many authors within the neo-classical tradition who see a more ubiquitous set of public goods and instances of 'market failure'. Hodgson's argument against extending markets is not, however, based on practicalities. On the contrary, even if markets can be extended into areas such as health, education and environmental protection (via the assignment of property rights) and where there may appear to be an efficiency case for privatisation, such moves should be resisted on moral grounds. In Hodgson's view there is a large sphere of relationships that should be immune from the rule of contract. Even writers such as Hayek, he notes, do not believe that relationships within families and between friends should be based on market exchange. Such relations are characterised by altruism or reciprocity, and it is the existence of such non-contractual relationships that sustain social capital. For Hodgson, this creates a contradiction in classical liberal thought. Thus:

> The proponents of market individualism cannot have it both ways. To be consistent with their own arguments, all arrangements must be subject to property, markets and trade. They cannot in one breath argue that the market is the best way of ordering all socio-economic activities, and then deny it in another. If they cherish family values then they have to recognise the practical and moral limits of market imperatives and pecuniary exchange (Hodgson, 1998: 84).

The family is not, on this view, the only institution that provides an important source of non-market norms – the modern welfare state also represents an institutional embodiment of resource allocation based on reciprocity and buttresses social capital against the excessive individualism of private markets.

In a further extension of this claim, Hodgson reinforces the communitarian argument that liberal morals are too 'thin' and should be replaced by a view of the individual as a social being whose preferences should be judged against a 'thicker' conception of the common good. Economic liberalism, he contends, is 'atomistic' in maintaining that markets allow for the free expression of preferences, the content of which is fixed independently of social context. Such an approach neglects the capacity for people to widen their horizons and to educate their preferences by a process of social engagement, which is more likely to be encouraged by mechanisms of collective rather than individual choice. For Hodgson, however, it is not only individual preferences that are changed when subject to social democratic procedures, but the very character of the actors concerned and their propensity to engage in competitive (read 'selfish') or cooperative (read 'other-regarding') forms of behaviour. Seen in this light, welfare state institutions act as an exemplar of social norms that encourage cooperation rather than competition and should be maintained in order to preserve social capital and institutional diversity. By contrast:

> The widespread implementation of 'free market' ideas creates a system with a relative degree of structural uniformity dominated by pecuniary relations of contract and trade. This has been discussed by Louis Hartz and Albert Hirschman who saw a problem of the potential or actual stagnation of both a moral and an economic kind, in the type of developed market individualism that is most advanced in the United States of America. (Hodgson, 1998: 82–3)

Social democrats such as Hodgson are not, of course, unique in making such claims. Writing from a conservative communitarian perspective, for example, John Gray (1998) contends that market liberalisation and increasing female labour market participation are contributing to the destruction of family life and to an increase in crime. For conservative communitarians the freeing of markets in recent years has undermined the religious basis of society that was traditionally an important source of common life and shared values.

Trust, Social Capital and the Case for the Enabling State

The preceding arguments make the negative case that markets undermine trust. A corollary of this stance is that state action is required to promote social capital in order that a more robust functioning of markets and democratic institutions can be achieved. One of the most important claims made for social capital in this context is that it has the power to 'make democracy work' (Brehm and Rhan, 1997; Uslaner, 1999; Putnam, 2000). Following Putnam's example, membership of civic associations such as sports clubs, social clubs and other not-for-profit organisations is held to encourage a spirit of collaboration and a wider willingness to participate in collective projects including active participation in democratic politics. According to this view, when the public are generally cooperative, the transaction costs of implementing public policy will be lowered and the quality of the inputs into the political process will be reflective of a more informed and active citizenry.

In light of these insights, an important element of the communitarian strategy to build social capital involves programmes of institutional redesign focused on the involvement of civil associations in the creation and provision of state services. In an argument that builds on the claims of deliberative democracy, the contention here is that 'public participation' in service provision avoids the 'knowledge problem' of 'top-down' bureaucracy by ensuring that planners receive information from multiple actors or stakeholders who have better access to 'on-the-ground' knowledge reflecting the communities concerned (Healey, 1997). Improving the flow of information between service providers and civil society is considered central to a strategy based on building trust because it removes the sense that public policy is something that is 'done to' the community and creates a dynamic where voluntary organisations craft public policies for themselves. The development of trust, it is claimed, will itself improve the quality of state services as both citizens and producers cooperate directly with the government rather than seeking to thwart official objectives. Active participation in politics generates trust, which makes policy delivery more robust, which in turn generates more trust and so on, in a virtuous circle of accumulating social capital.

A second element of communitarian political strategy involves attempts to promote the associations thought to exhibit the appropriate community-centred norms. According to this view, the existence of civil associations increases trust and hence the probability that societies can overcome scenarios where the imperative is to behave in a 'free-riding' vein. It follows, from this view, that governments should provide financial and institutional support for voluntary organisations and 'not-for-profit' associations as a way to encourage the norms of trust that sustain the social fabric (Dowley and Silver, 2002). A related argument offered by Hodgson (1998) suggests that the state should intervene in the economy in order to preserve a diversity of ownership structures to ensure that overly individualistic forms of enterprise, such as the individual shareholder model and the joint stock company, do not dominate the institutional landscape. This could include the promotion of worker cooperatives, public corporations and welfare state agencies and would, argues Hodgson: 'sustain a much greater degree of cultural and behavioural variety than the system advocated by market individualists' (Hodgson, 1998: 65–9).

In short, just as neo-classical analysis of economic 'market failures' brings forth calls for 'corrective' government action to internalise externalities, so communitarian accounts emphasise the 'social' nature of market failures and the need for cultural interventions to ensure that trust and civil association are produced in quantities that would not prevail under laissez-faire.

CLASSICAL LIBERALISM AND SOCIAL CAPITAL

The communitarian critique of classical liberalism rests heavily on the Polanyi-inspired view that markets require state regulation in order to function; that the 'economising behaviour' witnessed in such markets is an artifice of state action; and that further state intervention is required to counteract the disruptive influences that the 'economistic' response to market forces brings about. None of these assertions, however, is adequately supported by the historical evidence and the normative conclusions derived from them are highly questionable.

The Spontaneous Origins of Markets

At the core of Polanyi's account is the claim that prior to the 'imposition' of 'capitalism' by the nineteenth-century state, the world was largely characterised by a 'gain-less economy' where markets barely existed. The historical record, however, reveals ample evidence of profit-seeking behaviour for centuries, if not millennia, prior to the alleged 'creation' of 'economic man' by nineteenth-century liberalism. As Hejeebu and McCloskey (2000) note, from price-sensitive behaviour among the Mayan Indians to the complex trading networks that existed in ancient Mesopotamia the widespread historical evidence of spontaneous economising behaviour contradicts Polanyi's central claims (see also Silver, 1983; Curtin, 1984; Chaduri, 1985; Snell, 1991). In the context of Britain, for example, Postan (1966) and MacFarlane (1976) document the development of sophisticated agricultural and labour markets under the fragmented legal structure of medieval England with 'free' rather than 'administered' prices. To the extent that the eighteenth- and nineteenth-century British state engaged in deliberate attempts to further the development of market institutions, therefore, these efforts did not take place in a cultural vacuum but were to a significant extent the culmination of hundreds of years of incremental change.

While open markets can be imposed by administrative fiat, as they may have been to some extent in post-war Japan, evidence suggests that many market practices have developed precisely where state power has been at its weakest, or in spite of attempts by states to stamp markets out.[2] North (1990), for example, has shown that markets developed largely by accident in those parts of Northern and Western Europe where the power of centralised monarchy was at its weakest and where merchants were able to escape administrative controls (see also Rosenberg and Birdzell, 1986; Pipes, 1999). More recently, twentieth-century evidence confirms that responsiveness to price signals and incentives is evident even in social systems explicitly committed to the eradication of price-sensitive behaviour. At the height of the 'cultural revolution' in China, for example, black markets were still in operation (Huang, 2008), and the clandestine markets that today account for up to 50 per cent of gross domestic product (GDP) in some developing countries suggest that the notion that markets must somehow be 'set up by the state' is groundless (De Soto, 1989; Boettke, 1994).

On a Polanyian understanding, any evidence of state intervention both contemporary or historical is taken as proof positive that markets cannot exist without the visible hand of state action, and that evidence of such action reveals the absurdity of a 'free market' economy operating through a 'self-regulating' invisible hand. From a classical liberal perspective, however, the case for 'laissez-faire' has never been based on the view that it is possible to dispense entirely with the state or 'state-like' entities. On the contrary, following Adam Smith, the concern of classical liberalism has been to distinguish those forms of hierarchical action which impede the potential of societies to develop beneficial self-regulating mechanisms, from those actions which help to make these processes more robust (McCloskey, 2006). Among the most important of the latter is the provision of a legal framework which protects and enforces property rights. A central concern of classical liberalism, therefore, has been to elucidate the conditions under which potentially predatory states can be transformed into agencies which provide the rules within which commercial activity can flourish. At issue here has been the importance of fragmented political power and the role of interjurisdictional competition in checking the potential abuses of state actors.

Though markets may need some form of hierarchical agency to secure the framework within which a 'spontaneous order' may unfold, as Caplan (2007) has pointed out it makes no more sense to say that markets are 'parasitic' on state action because no large-scale economy has ever existed without some such action than it does to say that states are parasitic on markets because no large-scale state has ever existed without relying on an element of market exchange. The former Soviet Union was, for example, famously dependent on a small percentage of privately owned plots to supply the lion's share of its agricultural output (Pipes, 1999). The key question, therefore, is to discern how much state action and what type of state action is compatible with the economic and social benefits that 'invisible hand' processes can bring. Markets do need 'regulation' but it does not follow that this regulation should be 'social democratic' in character.

In a similar vein, classical liberalism has never maintained that narrowly selfish behaviour is all that is required to sustain the social fabric. Commitment to a liberal market does not privilege the commercial ethos per se. Historically, commercial exchange has taken place against many different cultural backgrounds, some of which have been broadly supportive of commerce and others which have been merely tolerant or even hostile towards markets and trade. The issue, therefore, is what balance needs to be struck between the 'self-interested' norms that characterise commercial exchange and the norms appropriate to more communal relationships. These are the questions that underlie the contemporary discussion of social capital and it is to these questions that attention will now turn.

Classical Liberalism and the Importance of Bridging Social Capital

The communitarian critique of liberal markets builds on the view that commercial morality is 'too thin' to support a stable civil order. The logic of this position suggests that if the role of markets is extended, then levels of trust are reduced. From a classical liberal perspective, however, communitarians may be misguided about the type of moral framework necessary to sustain social cooperation on the widest possible scale.

In order to ascertain the relative strength or weakness of the communitarian position, it is important to recognise that while social capital is crucial to the successful functioning of any society, it must also be emphasised that not all forms of social capital are equally suitable in this regard. Putnam, in particular, makes a distinction between bonding (or exclusive) social capital and bridging (or inclusive) social capital (Putnam, 2000: 22–3). Bonding social capital describes the cohesion that exists between small groups of similar people, such as family members, close friends and colleagues and perhaps the members of ethnic or religious groups, while the bridging variety describes the networks of 'generalised trust' that diffuse information and link acquaintances who may be very dissimilar people.

Communitarian critiques of classical liberalism focus on a relative decline in bonding social capital. Concerns about the decline in religion, traditional values and community solidarity fall clearly into this category. Yet from a classical liberal perspective, it is precisely this type of social capital that should be 'kept in its place' if looser and more complex bridging relationships are to form between people who differ in their goals and values. Solidarism in pre-market society was almost exclusively an intragroup phenomenon with intergroup relations characterised by habitual conflict. As Hayek has argued, it was learning to submit to an impersonal ethos that did not require widespread agreement on substantive ends that allowed intergroup relations to become more productive. As links between people increasingly centred on trade, the communitarian ethos of the tribe became confined to small groups such as family, friends and voluntary associations based on face-to-face relations and a common set of ends. Such groupings were, however, embedded in a much wider 'catallactic' order, not governed by any one set of ends, but held together via a nexus of impersonal relations such as contract and respect for property (Hayek, 1988).

Far from being an era of widespread cooperation, it would be better to characterise the pre-industrial era as one ridden with highly exclusive social practices. The guilds, churches and corporatist structures that were enforced by the pre-industrial state – as eulogised by Karl Polanyi – constituted a form of bonding social capital premised on the exclusion of those sections of the population deemed not to conform to prevailing community norms. As Ogilvie has documented in her detailed analyses of the guild system in pre-industrial Germany, not only did the existence of these 'solidaristic' associations and their restrictive practices stifle innovation and economic growth, but they also contributed to the systematic exclusion of women, members of ethnic and religious minorities and other 'outcast' groups. In contrast, the more liberal economies of the Netherlands and England where the state did not enforce the privileges of the guilds were much more successful in the promotion of innovation and growth, and provided superior employment opportunities for women and 'unconventionals' (Ogilvie, 2003, 2004).

Within this context, communitarians appear divided among themselves in understanding the appropriate relationship between 'thick' and 'thin' moral norms. On the one hand, for example, Hodgson (1998) argues that the dynamism of the market economy and the spread of the commercial ethos unsettle established norms of social solidarity and identity. On the other hand, however, he supports the standard communitarian view which recognises that the content of people's preferences and identity should not be seen as fixed and unchanging. As the previous chapter noted, for 'multicultural communitarians' such as Young the environment of an advanced urban economy is one where there are many different identifications open to constant flux. According to this view, such fluidity is to be welcomed because it reflects the capacity of those who have been oppressed by traditional communal norms with respect to religion, gender roles and sexuality to challenge established sources of authority and to create entirely new bases of communal identification. It would seem, therefore, that there is a choice to be made between an emphasis on traditional 'thick' notions of solidarity, which may exclude and oppress certain sections of the population but which have the virtue of stability, and a more dynamic environment where there are opportunities to escape oppressive social norms but where there is a relative lack of solidarity.

From a classical liberal perspective, the development of generalised trust or bridging social capital requires that the moral framework shared between actors is relatively 'thin'. Where people differ in religion, cultural values and other aspects of identity and where the basis of their identity is evolving, it is unlikely that they will agree on a common set of purposes. In such circumstances the use of state power to enforce a shared set of goals is likely to produce conflict as groups will compete to capture the governmental apparatus to impose their own particular vision of the good society (Kukathas, 2003). Attempts to develop greater 'solidarity' may be as likely to fracture society as to 'unite' it. The development of bridging social capital necessarily involves a thin set of morals, such as tolerance of others, the observance of contracts and respect for private property that can be shared by actors with otherwise diverse and perhaps even conflicting moral codes.

As well as minimising conflict between those who differ in cultural values, 'thin' moral rules are required by commerce because most people involved in exchanges are either completely unknown to each other, or known only in a relatively impersonal setting such as the relationship between a buyer and a seller. Where contacts between people are of the 'weak' variety it is not possible to evaluate in detail the 'thicker' moral character of the actors concerned (such as their level of attendance at church or a mosque, or their sexual peccadillos), because the information costs involved are excessively high. In situations of commercial exchange the aspects of a person's character that are most pertinent are relatively minimal or 'thin', including such criteria as their contribution to the account of profit and loss or their willingness to observe contracts.

The necessity to develop a 'thinner' moral framework brought about by the rise of commerce was one of the central themes in the writings of Adam Smith and David Hume. According to Hume, 'sympathy with persons remote from us is much fainter than with persons near and contiguous' (Hume, 1739–40/1985). Smith, meanwhile, described the concentric circles of sympathy that emanated outwards from close family to friends, more distant relatives, acquaintances and finally to strangers. It is not that people act immorally in failing to care for complete strangers as much as family and friends. Rather, from Smith's point of view, intense feelings of sympathy, which include love and friendship (or for that matter hate), are necessarily reserved for those of whom we have detailed personal knowledge, while feelings towards those of whose character we are largely ignorant are 'thinner' in terms of content and intensity.

It follows from this 'knowledge-based' recognition of the limits to 'sympathy' that different levels of morality and expectations about the constituents of appropriate conduct are required in different social contexts. As Otteson (2003) has argued, the norms that Smith's 'impartial spectator' would observe in relations between family, friends and colleagues are different from those approved between strangers.[3] The morals expected in commercial relations which are often between relative strangers or at best acquaintances will tend to be more impersonal, focused on principles such as the observance of contracts, and will be oriented more towards the self-interest of the parties involved rather than the direct benefit of 'others'. It is not, therefore, that commerce corrupts our sense of morals as communitarians are want to imply, but that the context of commercial exchange requires a different sort of morality. Smith was not of the view that the commercial ethos would pervade the family or other intimate ties, and clearly believed that if people behaved in their more intimate relationships in the way that they do in their commercial relationships they would meet with disapproval.

Classical Liberalism and the Spontaneous Generation of Bridging Social Capital

The question remains, of course, whether the cash nexus and the observance of contracts are sufficiently robust to sustain the bridging social capital on which they depend. Smith's answer to the question of how to sustain a commercial society was that virtuous behaviour will arise spontaneously because it is in each individual's interest to cooperate with others. 'Honesty is the best policy' because people are unlikely to enter into contracts with those who possess a reputation for underhand dealing. As a consequence of market competition, even individuals who desire only their own personal advancement are led to behave in what is at least a morally tolerable fashion. The Smithian invisible hand not only guides people towards prosperity, but it also guides them to observe the basic set of morals that sustain the 'weak ties' on which a commercial society depends.

   While Smith's depiction of commercial society anticipated later work suggesting that cooperation can evolve spontaneously among actors pursing their own interests in repeated exchanges and games (for example, Axelrod, 1984; Allison, 1992) his portrayal of eighteenth-century commerce, along with others who inspired 'le doux commerce' thesis,[4] was nonetheless based upon experience of transactions among tradespeople who had at least some direct personal knowledge of each other. Smith was less convinced, however, that market exchanges could spontaneously produce trust when exchanges are more anonymous or not repeated and where actors may profit from opportunistic cheating (Smith, 1776/1982: 538–9). Such a view questions the ability of markets to self-regulate when exchanges are not repeated, and as discussed in Chapter 2 is now reflected in the analysis of information asymmetries put forward by contemporary economists who have sought to re-emphasise the significance of 'market failure' (see Akerlof, 1970; Stiglitz, 1994). According to this perspective, in a market where, owing to consumer ignorance, there is no reward for trustworthy conduct, unscrupulous suppliers drive out the good, unless the state steps in to perform the quality control function.

As Hayek always emphasised, however, market institutions should be seen as 'discovery processes' which evolve in ways that even the most far-sighted economist cannot anticipate (for example, Hayek, 1948d, 1978a, 1978b). Market failure theory predicts that where there are information asymmetries, massive inefficiencies will persist and potentially profitable trades will fail to occur owing to the absence of information and/or trust. What market failure theory has failed to anticipate, however, is how entrepreneurs have innovated to fill the 'trust gap' and to remove impediments to trade. Gains from trade have been exploited by entrepreneurs who specialise in checking the trustworthiness of others and who create social capital by developing a reputation for supplying appropriate levels of assurance. In doing so, entrepreneurial innovations such as the development of brand names and simple reputation-building devices such as 'money-back' guarantees have transformed potentially non-repeated exchange scenarios into examples of repeated or iterated transactions. Thus, empirical analyses of markets hypothesised to exhibit asymmetric information, such as those for used automobiles, offer no support for the theoretical claim that competition leads to declining product standards (see Chapter 2, p. 38 of this volume and the collection of essays in Cowen and Crampton, 2002).

Brand-named goods and franchised stores, in particular, provide an assurance function by reducing information costs and provide an entrepreneurial bridge between otherwise anonymous buyers and sellers. A producer of pharmaceutical goods may, for example, have no contact with the final purchasers of his or her product, but may have repeat dealings and a relationship of trust with a branded pharmacy outlet, which in turn may have repeat dealings and a reputation for excellence with the final consumers of the good concerned. Markets, therefore, constitute a 'division of trust' in the same way that Hayek sees the price system drawing on a 'division of knowledge'. What matters is that each link in the chain may specialise in developing a reputation for good conduct or may acquire information about the trustworthiness of the particular link which is most relevant to them. Just as market participants need know very little about the majority of prices in the economy to engage in 'economising behaviour'– what they need to know about are changes in the price of the final goods that they buy – so there is no need for most people to know very much about the trustworthiness or otherwise of the vast majority of market participants; what they need to know is the reputation of the particular brands on which they rely. Since most people are, however, involved in overlapping reputational networks, the average level of trustworthiness expected from a person picked out at random in a developed market economy will be quite high. The general pressure to maintain one's reputation exerted in a competitive environment will tend to encourage the internalisation of cooperative norms which will 'keep people honest' even in situations where they might benefit from shirking behaviour.

In an international marketplace, brand names are a particularly important means of ensuring that consumers without local knowledge receive a guaranteed quality of service. A person may, for example, stay at a franchise outlet such as a Holiday Inn in any major city of the world and be assured a certain level of cleanliness before he or she has had the opportunity to learn about the reputations of local hotels. In this case, the Holiday Inn brand acts as the assurance that a particular form of quality control has been exercised on behalf of the consumer. The very existence of such reputational brands in turn acts to raise the average standards offered by the local suppliers in their attempt to attract custom.

Retailers and other 'middlemen', then, 'supply' the trust and assurance that is 'demanded' to facilitate successful market transactions. Until consumers are confident that a new good or service will provide what it promises, they are unlikely to purchase it. Trust is a highly valuable asset for which there is a 'demand' and for this reason it is 'supplied' rather than undermined by the market. While the vast majority of participants within an advanced market economy do not engage in face-to-face exchanges, a host of institutions have developed spontaneously to provide the trust necessary to sustain commercial exchange on a vast scale. Thus, empirical analyses of 'generalised social trust' find no evidence that the proportion of people who exhibit trust in others declines with exposure to market forces. On the contrary, research conducted by a dozen anthropologists in the developing world suggests that those who come from societies exhibiting higher levels of market integration are more likely to behave in a cooperative vein than those from subsistence societies that have little contact with the commercial world (Henrich et al., 2005). Similarly, in a cross-country study of over 50 states Berggren and Jordahl (2006) find a strongly positive correlation between the degree of economic freedom in a society (especially the security of property rights) and levels of generalised trust.

That the bridging relationships essential to commercial exchange may themselves develop through a process of 'spontaneous order' is best illustrated in the context of international trade networks. Seen through the lens of 'market failure' analysis international trade should be a particularly unpromising area for there to be any kind of 'order' because there is no formal state or state-like authority at the global level to enforce the terms of international contracts. In these circumstances, potential trading partners might be unwilling to negotiate contracts owing to the high transaction costs and uncertainty involved when enforcing agreements with unknown foreign partners. Benson's work demonstrates, however, that competitive, reputation-based mechanisms can evolve solutions to these problems. In a direct contradiction of the Polanyian thesis that states 'create markets', Benson (1989) shows how historically the *lex mercatoria* or 'law merchant', developed without the coercive power of the state. Merchant communities developed their own courts and legal systems in order to facilitate transactions which transcended the limitations of political boundaries and local protectionism.

More recently, Leeson's (2008) work shows how private arbitration agencies have emerged as an entrepreneurial strategy to facilitate trade across borders. There are currently over 100 international arbitration institutions across the world, including organisations such as the International Chamber of Commerce and the London Court of International Arbitration, and 90 per cent or more of all international trade contracts contain relevant arbitration clauses. Willingness to sign up to private arbitration sends out a signal that the party concerned is unlikely to renege on a deal. Those who refuse to be bound by the terms of private arbitration, meanwhile, are unlikely to find willing partners to trade. According to Leeson, private arbiters frequently settle contractual disputes involving sums of between $1 million and $1 billion. The absence of state structures at the international level does not seem to have prevented the emergence of massive transborder trading networks with the volume of world trade having increased thirteenfold since 1960. Abuses do occur within this system but in a context where there are multiple organisations needing periodically to cooperate with others there are powerful incentives for transboundary actors to develop a reputation for good conduct. This does not rule out the possibility that involvement of state-level agencies may facilitate still more interaction, but it does refute the view that only the state can provide the regulatory environment in which commercial activity can flourish.

CLASSICAL LIBERALISM AND THE MIX BETWEEN 'BONDING' AND 'BRIDGING' SOCIAL CAPITAL

The analysis thus far has highlighted the mechanisms that enable a market economy to maintain bridging social capital spontaneously. It is important to recognise, however, that while a classical liberal framework places less reliance on the 'bonding' social capital associated with stronger, more personal ties it does not eliminate such relationships in favour of a society entirely governed by commerce. On the contrary, market institutions provide a meta-environment in which both bridging and bonding social relationships can coexist, and where practices conducive to wider cooperation may be promoted at the expense of others.

Families, Voluntary Associations and the Mix between Bonding and Bridging Social Capital

Maintaining an appropriate mix between bonding and bridging social capital is crucial because if an advanced society is to function effectively people must learn to live in what might be termed two 'different worlds' (Hayek, 1988: 18). On the one hand they participate in the 'micro-order' of families and family-like groups based on a high degree of personal intimacy and held together by the pursuit of shared ends linked to that very intimacy. On the other hand, however, in order to acquire the goods and services they need to sustain themselves families must participate in a 'macro-order' of more distant if not anonymous relationships with countless other actors who do not share their specific ends.

While the tension between the norms exhibited in families and those required in a commercial context is real, the family[5] acts as a bridge between the 'micro-order' of the small group and the 'macro-order' of the wider society, for it is as children in the context of the family that people first acquire the skills necessary to maintain relationships with others. Within families these skills pertain to intimate contact, but because families are themselves embedded in multiple external relationships characterised by differing degrees of familiarity, they also provide a school for the skills, such as respect for property and possessions, required to maintain one's reputation in more impersonal contexts. These may range from the still relatively personal interactions in schools and voluntary associations to progressively more distant and anonymous business and trade relationships, such as those in firms, where the expectation is that one may judge and be judged on the more unforgiving criteria of contributions to profit and loss (Horwitz, 2005).

Viewed through this lens, there is no substance to communitarian claims that the logic of market liberalism requires the replacement of family-like bonds with a process based entirely on contractual exchange. Reliance on market signals such as the making of profits and losses generated through commercial exchanges is, for example, appropriate where people need to coordinate with many other agents, who do not share their substantive ends, and where reliable mechanisms are required to reduce free-riding or predatory behaviour when actors are not known to one another personally. Family relations, and other groupings based on a shared vocation such as religion or amateur sport, do not typically involve significant coordination problems, as members are usually involved in the pursuit of shared or very similar goals. Insofar as there are free-rider problems in such situations these are more readily overcome without recourse to the discipline of profit and loss accounting, owing to the relative ease of processing information about and monitoring actors with whom one is intimately familiar.

As Horwitz (2005) has argued, there is no more likelihood that a liberal, competitive environment will lead to the elimination of the family than it will lead to the elimination of other institutions such as the firm. Unlike families, firms are organisations that must mobilise cooperation from larger numbers of people who may not share common ends, and may require mechanisms such as performance-related pay to control problems of shirking and free-riding. The internal operations of firms are largely hierarchical and reflect the efficiency advantages that can be gained from replacing the decentralised bargaining of 'spot contracts' and 'piece work' with an internal system of command and control (Coase, 1937). Firms are, however, embedded in a meta-level environment of market competition in which the quality of their governance structures, their reputation for probity and capacity to deliver goods to consumers are tested against those of rivals. Firms, therefore, suppress internal competition, but are subject to external market forces resulting from the decentralised decisions of hundreds and thousands, if not millions, of consumers and investors. Thus, owner-manager firms, joint-stock companies, worker cooperatives and mutual associations all compete for reputation, sales and investment capital.

Just as the boundaries between firms and the wider market are fluid, shifting with developments in technology and changes in individual preferences, so too are the boundaries between families, voluntary associations and the market. This fluidity does not, however, imply that commercial relationships are ever likely to replace the close-knit bonds that people form in families, with friends and to a lesser extent as members of intermediary organisations such as sports clubs. If organisations such as firms (and different firm structures) have advantages in certain domains, then so too do families. Among the most obvious of these is the provision of conditions conducive to the personal intimacy that most people desire. Families or family-like structures provide an environment in which detailed, personal knowledge of the partners' tastes and values can be developed to the mutual advantage of those concerned.

Families may, of course, 'contract out' certain functions to individuals and firms in the wider market rather than perform them 'in-house'. Which goods and services are purchased commercially rather than produced in the household will vary depending on the preferences and opportunity costs of the families concerned. High-income households, for example, may spend proportionately more time working and may purchase childcare, dry-cleaning and eating out rather than perform these tasks themselves. As Horwitz (2005) points out, however, these dynamics do not necessarily imply a decline in intimacy and bonding. In the case of childcare, for example, parents are still in the best position to tailor their choice of provider to the character of their child. Similarly, as the 'economic' functions of the family such as cleaning and food preparation shift to the market, the time saved on these tasks may enable the family to pursue additional 'non-economic' activities with their children such as participation in sports or leisure. Seen in this light, state actors are no more likely to possess the knowledge to determine the appropriate position of the relevant boundaries, any more than they are able to decide effectively which elements of a firm's production should be 'contracted out' or provided 'in-house'.

The theoretical weaknesses of the communitarian critique are mirrored by the empirical evidence concerning the effect of liberal markets on cultural and associational life. There is, for example, little to suggest that when monetary payment for sex is legalised a higher proportion of people consider prostitution a desirable form of sexual relationship (Epstein, 2003: 147–8). Even a cursory glance at the contemporary political economy and culture of the United States offers scant support for Hodgson's claim that more market-oriented societies are characterised by conformity to pecuniary relations. The United States continues to exhibit very high rates of volunteer service compared to European countries (Skcopol, 1996; Beito, 2000), has one of the highest rates of religious observance in the developed world, and exhibits the highest rate of private (as opposed to governmental) aid to developing countries.[6] Similarly, the coexistence of traditional groupings such as the Amish with a modern market economy is hardly suggestive of the motivational conformity that social democratic descriptions of American capitalism portray.

Firms and the Mix between Bonding and Bridging Social Capital

The market economy constitutes a 'macro' environment which sustains a variety of non-commercial bonds at the 'micro' level such as those found in families and voluntary groups. Even commercial relationships, however, also create opportunities to generate bonding social capital of their own. The 'weak' interactions that characterise commercial relationships bring together people from many different social and cultural backgrounds and in so doing may create opportunities for the development of new social bonds and shifting identities. It is precisely because people enter markets in order to pursue commercial gain that they tend, at the margin, to be less concerned with the religious or ethnic origin of their partners to exchange and, as a consequence, expose themselves to the unfamiliar. The development of bridging social capital in this manner may in turn facilitate new forms of bonding social capital as people are alerted to alternative lifestyles and identities through the everyday interactions involved in commercial life. Such processes may include development of cross-cultural friendships, and even deeper bonds such as office romances and marriages between people from different cultures who may have never met were it not for their participation in the 'impersonal' world of work and commercial exchange (Storr, 2008). It is partly for this reason that Hayek (1982) frequently used the Greek term 'catallaxy' to describe the market economy, the original meaning of which was to 'turn from an enemy into a friend'.

In addition, market relationships are often composed of individuals working together within firms who, as Von Mises (1949: 345) put it: 'co-operate in competition and compete in cooperation'. The relative capacity of firms to develop an internal culture conducive to such dynamics as 'team spirit' and loyalty is a key factor in their ability to deliver products in a competitive way. A successful business enterprise needs to strike a delicate balance between the dangers of excessively friendly bonds between workers and managers on the one hand, and the loss of loyalty resulting from excessively distant and impersonal processes on the other.

Consider in this context the spread of Japanese working practices to the US in the 1980s. Prior to this period, American auto-firms had for many years been organised in a hierarchical or 'Taylorist' manner with a strict line of command between senior managers, middle managers and shop floor workers. By the 1980s, however, Taylorist organisations were lagging in productivity and losing money relative to Japanese plants that operated flatter management structures. The latter practices promoted greater levels of trust between workers and management owing to the culture of responsibility engendered on the shop floor and thereby reduced the transaction costs of production. Owing to their greater profitability, Japanese working practices were increasingly imitated by American firms. In this case, open competition and the account of profit and loss stimulated not only significant product improvements but also the spread of management cultures more conducive to workplace cooperation (Fukayama, 2001). Had protectionist policies advocated by comunitarians been in greater evidence, it is doubtful that such cultural learning and the spread of new forms of social capital would have proceeded as quickly, if at all.

Culture, Ethnicity and the Mix between Bonding and Bridging Social Capital

If the competitive position of firms is a function of the ability to strike a balance between bonding and bridging social capital, so in a market environment different social norms prove themselves more or less compatible with the wider social networks necessary for economic success. The experience of different ethnic and immigrant groups is particularly instructive in this regard. Many such groups often find it difficult to access credit and employment opportunities on arrival in a new society because they do not possess the reputational signals, such as credit ratings or a bank account, that are taken for granted by established members of the society concerned. The most successful immigrant communities have been those that have mobilised their own internal bonds to generate the reputational resources necessary to link with the wider community. Korean immigrants to the United States in the 1970s, for example, were often capital-poor and lacked English language skills. The close-knit nature of the Korean community, however, enabled its members to offer low-cost savings and credit services to one another, which facilitated the rapid development of a merchant class specialised in construction, restaurants and the grocery trade. In this instance, the bonds in the Korean community encouraged the accumulation of capital, which in turn allowed the development of reputational links with the wider society, as evidence of property ownership enabled Korean entrepreneurs to obtain bank accounts and credit from formal financial institutions (Landa, 1995; Sowell, 1996; Chamlee-Wright, 2006).

Membership of particular ethnic or religious groupings can also offer other advantages in developing linkages with a broader range of social actors, especially in the context of commercial exchange. Chamlee-Wright (2006), for example, notes the reputation for fair dealing that was associated with Quaker merchants in the eighteenth and nineteenth centuries. In such cases the distinctive manner, dress or speech, maintained internally out of commitment to a religious faith or other cultural norms, may also carry economic benefits by providing the right set of reputational signals to those outside the group. Seen in this context, cultural 'stereotypes' often perform an equivalent function to reputational brands in the marketplace, and in those parts of the developing world where global and even national brands are often absent they may be the primary mechanism that actors use when judging whether or not to enter a particular exchange. In conditions of bounded rationality where actors lack full information, people frequently rely on habits and rules of thumb based on cultural symbolism as a way of reducing the cost of searching for the most trustworthy agents.

It must, however, be recognised that not all bonding social capital is conducive to successful external linkages – indeed some groups may have no interest in exchange relations with others; they may wish to isolate themselves from the wider society and may thus be immune from reputational incentives. Just as there are differences in the quality of the social and behavioural skills transmitted by families in terms of their capacity to link with the macro-social order, so too there are differences between the compatability of various cultural norms and the behaviour necessary to promote cooperation and economic development. The persistence of poverty across several generations among some immigrant groups, compared to the simultaneous rise of others, suggests that not all forms of bonding social capital are well adapted in this regard. While the persistence of immigrant poverty in some contexts may be the product of outright racism in the surrounding society, the rise out of poverty of other groups who have experienced similar racism suggests that this is not always the dominant factor at play.[7] The repeated commercial success of ethnic and religious groups such as the Chinese, Jews, Gujarati Indians, the Ibos of Nigeria and the Lebanese in a variety of different countries would appear to imply that some types of bonding social capital exhibit a competitive advantage relative to others (Sowell, 1996). A competitive market, therefore, while not hostile to bonding social capital per se, may well exhibit selective pressure in favour of those 'cultural brands' that enable the formation of wider social linkages.

ROBUST POLITICAL ECONOMY AND THE EVOLUTION OF SOCIAL CAPITAL

Though the above arguments suggest that classical liberal institutions are able to sustain an appropriate mix of social norms, communitarians maintain that positive government action is needed to 'build' social capital in order to generate wider benefits which may otherwise be 'underproduced'. As with more narrowly economic arguments for government regulation, proposals to intervene in the evolution of civil society must from a classical liberal perspective be scrutinised in terms of robust political economy. The theoretical case for policy interventions to promote social capital must show that policy-makers have the knowledge to intervene in an appropriate manner and that they have adequate incentives to do so.

Government Failure and Social Capital: The Knowledge Problem

A Hayekian perspective suggests that governments may lack the knowledge to intervene effectively in order to promote cooperative social norms. If public funds are allocated to civil associations then politicians and policy-makers will be required either to fund all associations equally – and thus run the risk of subsidising practices that may be inimical to wider cooperation – or to 'pick winners' by offering differential funding according to what they deem the most suitable cultural or associational norms. There is, however, little reason to believe that cultural interventionism of this genre will not be subject to the same 'knowledge problems' as industrial planning. Politicians may be in no better position to predict which associational practices promote social capital than they are of knowing which business ventures to sponsor.

Writing in this context, Chamlee-Wright (2008) discusses the implications that arise from recognising that social capital, like economic capital, is not a homogenous 'stock' which can be manipulated on the basis of aggregate statistics. Neo-classical analysis reflected for example in the work of Solow suggests that capital is a measurable quantity (the number of factories, computers and so on) from which the marginal effect of additional units on the level of economic growth can be ascertained. From a classical liberal perspective, however, capital is a complex and heterogenous structure, which is not open to measurement in terms of aggregate effects. On the one hand, whether a good is considered part of the capital stock or is viewed as a consumption item is, in part at least, dependent on divergent evaluations of the economic environment held by many different individuals and firms. The effect of additional units of capital with respect to economic growth, meanwhile, is largely qualitative rather than quantitative in nature. Recognising the heterogeneity of capital suggests that new and different investments may result in enhanced productivity of the existing stock, thus avoiding the neo-classical conclusion that the growth of capital implies diminishing returns. Similarly, the heterogeneity of capital suggests that any one element will have multiple though limited uses. As Chamlee-Wright (2008) notes: 'a desk-top computer can be used effectively in some production processes, but not in others'. Only some capital combinations will be technically feasible and still fewer will be economically feasible. Economic growth, therefore, is not primarily the result of the aggregate level of capital per se, but depends on the capacity of the economic system to match the 'right' combinations of capital goods. The institutional robustness of the market economy stems precisely from its capacity to facilitate a process of experimentation in capital combinations and to generate decentralised signals (profits and losses) which communicate the relative success or failure of the many different elements at the micro-scale.

Applied in the context of social capital, these insights suggest that not all forms will be appropriate for all tasks and in all situations, and the relative significance of different norms will shift with innovations in both cultural and economic practices. The capacity to achieve successful projects will depend on the ability of social actors to learn which combinations of behavioural norms are required in different situations. An established manufacturing enterprise may, for example, need to combine bonding type sentiments on the shop floor and to promote such relationships via 'team-building' exercises organised around the encouragement of, say, after work sport, while simultaneously relying on a much looser set of bridging relationships with consumers centred on the reputation of the firm's product. The type of social capital utilised by an Internet entrepreneur, on the other hand, may depend more exclusively on the cultivation of a bridging network developed by word of mouth.

Knowledge of how to combine appropriate elements of the social capital structure is widely dispersed across a diversity of individuals and organisations and much of this knowledge may be tacit in nature. Successful entrepreneurs are those who 'read' the existing pattern of social norms in which they find themselves and piece together different elements accordingly. This applies in the context of both voluntary associations focused on 'non-economic' activities such as religious groups or amateur sports clubs, and in the context of a business enterprise. A successful sports club may, for example, have to combine a powerful sense of team spirit with an entrepreneurial capacity to strike bridging relationships with commercial firms that supply catering facilities and kit. A business person, on the other hand, may have to consider how the personal networks established through membership of sports clubs, churches or amateur musical societies may be drawn upon to spread word about a new business venture. How much time should be spent using such face-to-face relationships relative to the more impersonal reputational signals that may be sent out via an advertising campaign? These are the sorts of questions that must be answered via entrepreneurial action. In turn, every entrepreneurial attempt to find appropriate combinations will, 'at the margin', transform the set of social norms that face other actors as the results of successful experiments ripple out from dispersed decision-making nodes via word of mouth, imitation and the account of profit and loss.

If social capital is a heterogenous and evolving 'spontaneous order', then it is unlikely that policy-makers will know enough about the complexities involved in such an order to intervene appropriately. The latter problem is evidenced by Putnam's focus on the alleged decline of social capital reflected in the diminished membership of voluntary associations such as bowling leagues, and the implication that policy-makers should intervene in various ways to rejuvenate civil associations of this type. Putnam's account fails to give sufficient weight to the manner in which social change has prompted new and unexpected forms of social contact. Membership of bowling leagues in the US may well have declined but other groupings not accounted for in his sample such as soccer and football leagues have witnessed massive growth and on some estimates have increased at a faster rate than population growth (Schudson, 1995; Ladd, 1996).

The mixed nature of these findings on the trajectory of social capital is not surprising. Longitudinal studies of voluntary groups may be subject to a variant of the deficiencies associated with central economic planning: in a dynamic social context it may be impossible for any one social scientist or group of social scientists to anticipate the evolution of civil society. Newly emerging groups, reflected for example in the massive growth of online fora, many of which have evolved their own reputation mechanisms (Hardin, 2004; Steckbeck and Bottke, 2004), are often not anticipated by analysts and policy-makers alike. More importantly, policy-makers are unlikely to make adequate judgements about the extent of social capital on the basis of aggregate data that attempt to measure the 'stock' at any given time. Even if the aggregate number of civil associations is in decline this does not necessarily constitute evidence that social capital per se is eroding. Rather, it may simply reflect that particular groupings that were once of value are being rendered obsolete by economic and cultural change. If the state distributes funds to support those sections of civil society that appear to be in decline, then this may divert resources away from new and qualitatively better-adapted forms of association. As Chamlee-Wright (2008) notes, that membership of formal fraternal societies and ladies' auxiliaries has declined in recent years may not be evidence of depleting social capital but may reflect the increasing irrelevance of such groups to women who inhabit dual-earner households and who prefer to organise their social lives around playgroups and other less formal associations.

A similar argument applies against Hodgson's view that the state should intervene to promote organisations such as workers' cooperatives, in order to maintain behavioural and motivational diversity. In many European countries cooperatives have been supported by government intervention, but the results continue to be poor. Even relative successes, such as the Mondragon system in Spain, have seen their achievements confined to non-innovative production lines (such as washing machine manufacture) that had previously been developed by private corporations, and are thus imitating more conventional business enterprises (Hindmoor, 1999). To suggest that the protection of such failing ventures is necessary to preserve motivational diversity is to assume that it is possible for policy-makers to know what particular mix of organisational and cultural norms is appropriate and for which tasks. Hodgson, however, fails to provide any support for this proposition.

An important reply to this line of argument may invoke the notion of 'path-dependency' or cultural 'lock-in' effects. As noted in Chapter 2, economic applications of this concept suggest that competitive processes may lead to the adoption of inferior institutional practices owing to historical accidents and 'network externalities'. Hodgson may have something similar in mind when suggesting that a 'mixed economy' be preserved in order to avoid cultural and organisational conformity. In the final analysis, however, such arguments do not explain how policy-makers are to know 'how much diversity' is required. For better or worse, and owing to network externalities, English has emerged as the preferred language of international commerce, but how exactly would policy-makers know if and for how long they should try to prevent its further spread in preference to, say, Chinese? Unless those who favour a strongly interventionist line are able to answer such questions then it is unclear why a more laissez-faire approach is not to be preferred.

Government Failure and Social Capital: The Incentive Problem

The focus on the role that 'soft' institutional norms have in socio-economic performance is an important theoretical insight often neglected by economists. It does not, however, remove the need to examine how soft norms and conventions interact with the 'hard' institutional rules of society, such as the legal protection of property rights and the formal punishment of acts such as theft and fraud. Trust is more likely to be maintained in an environment where transaction and monitoring costs are themselves lower and hence help to reinforce the propensity towards trustworthy conduct. In other words, trust reduces transaction costs, but placing people into a 'hard' institutional setting where it is more difficult to monitor and to escape the behaviour of those willing to break this trust is unlikely to be a successful strategy in the longer term. The key question, therefore, is whether institutional incentives reinforce trust, or whether they make it more difficult to detect and to punish untrustworthy conduct and thus reduce the incentive to behave in a non-opportunistic vein. It is in this context that classical liberalism points to the manner in which social democratic interventions may act to raise transaction costs and thus lead to a decline in the quality of social capital over time.

At the individual level, incentives for people to develop a reputation for good conduct by adhering to the norms that sustain civil society may be diminished the more that individual welfare becomes separated from the social and behavioural choices that people make. When people must rely for their living on the capacity to find willing partners to voluntary exchange – through, for example, employment contracts – then they may have strong incentives to invest in reputational signals that will help them to secure the necessary employment. When, on the other hand, people receive a significant proportion of their income from tax-financed income transfers then these incentives are likely to be weakened. If those in receipt of the transfers choose to behave opportunistically (by, for example, failing to seek employment) then taxpayers do not have the option of exiting from the relationship without incurring the massive transaction costs of seeking to persuade the political authorities to change tack. Far from reinforcing social capital, therefore, the institutions of the modern welfare state may well discourage individual investments in socially beneficial norms. When the costs of failing to adhere to these norms are not concentrated on those who choose to break them, then one would expect the relevant individuals and families to be more susceptible to dysfunctional behaviour. It may be significant in this regard that studies of European welfare states suggest that as the level of government welfare spending increases, so public perceptions of individual trustworthiness tend to decline (on this finding, see Oorschot and Arts, 2005).

The growth of the welfare state is, from a classical liberal standpoint, by no means the only domain where government intervention may undermine the reputational incentives that sustain social capital. The replacement of private, competitive systems of regulation in areas such as product quality with an increasing reliance on government regulation may also have a similar effect. Nowhere do these processes appear more evident than in the field of money and the regulation of banking.

Prior to the advent of regulatory institutions such as the US Federal Reserve, individual banks and banking associations competed for funds on the basis of reputation and a system of 'private law'. In the absence of state-supported deposit insurance, private lending institutions had to attract depositors by, for example, ensuring the acceptability of the currencies they issued, limiting the potential for 'bank runs' to insolvent institutions, and monitoring the character of lending practices in member associations. Institutions that failed to provide adequate systems of verification found themselves at a competitive disadvantage relative to those that had a reputation for probity and sound judgement. Depositors, meanwhile, had strong incentives to seek out those institutions with the most secure reputation because a failure to invest with a sound bank could risk their entire investment, and the decision to invest time in monitoring the performance of the governance structure was decisive in determining their access to sound financial practices (White, 1984, 1989; Timberlake, 1993). The presence of these incentives was by no means sufficient to eradicate financial crises and panics over institutional solvency, but they did provide a context where the effects of any abuse of trust could be confined to a relatively small sphere.

The advent of a government-regulated banking industry, by contrast, has over time transformed this nexus of incentives. With centralised government institutions assuming more and more responsibility for the integrity of the financial system, individual banks no longer have a positive incentive to develop a reputation for best practice. Instead of competing for depositors on the basis of probity, banking institutions increasingly seek ways to avoid government regulations – safe in the knowledge that should their practices prompt a 'bank run', they will be 'bailed out' by the state (for example, Beenstock, 2009). Government officials, meanwhile, have relatively weak incentives to enforce effective controls because regulators lack property rights in the system such that they cannot profit from effective enforcement and do not suffer the losses from overseeing weak systems of corporate governance. Finally, on the demand side of the equation, the provision of state-financed deposit insurance has reduced the incentive for depositors to seek out the most trustworthy institutions. With the state committed implicitly or explicitly to bailing out banks, there is little reason for people to incur the costs of seeking out best-practice institutions. The fact that 'bank runs' have, until very recently, been virtually eliminated does not therefore constitute evidence that government regulation of banking is effective, but may simply reflect the lack of incentive for depositors to switch between institutions according to their reputation for probity. Neither do people have an incentive to monitor the performance of regulators in their capacity as voters. In a large-number electorate the chance that any one voter's lobbying effort will affect the quality of the regulatory environment under which their funds are administered is vanishingly small. From a classical liberal perspective, it is the legacy of this incentive structure that has pervaded financial markets for much of the last 100 years and increases the possibility of 'systemic failure'. From the deficiencies of the US Federal Reserve system in the 1930s, through to the implosion of the US savings and loan industry in the 1980s, to the global financial crisis of 2008, the competitive mechanisms that help to overcome information asymmetries and reinforce incentives for trustworthy conduct in other markets have been progressively undermined (Hoskins, 1993; O'Driscoll and Hoskins, 2006; Wallison, 2006).

If government action often reduces incentives for individuals and firms to maintain a reputation for good conduct, then so too may it reduce the incentives for civil associations to behave in a manner that advances the common weal. From a classical liberal standpoint, involvement of people in civil associations is broadly positive and can provide a socialising influence that encourages them to maintain a reputation by adhering to basic norms of cooperation. The involvement of civil associations in politics, however, whether to advance the interests of their members with respect to government policy or in seeking financial support from the state, is far from an unalloyed good. To favour the increased participation of organised groups in politics is to neglect the potential impact of these groups on those who are not well placed to engage in collective action.

On the one hand, the interests of individual voters are unlikely to be reflected adequately in a system that emphasises democratic participation over individual choice. Declining participation in democratic processes may not be the product of undue cynicism on behalf of electorates, but may be a rational response to the fact that individual participation in decisions about public policy makes virtually no difference to the services that any particular person will receive (Tullock, 1994; Somin, 1998). Insofar as participation in the electoral process is sustained, this may reflect the civic duty that people feel towards maintaining the democratic process. The cultural attachment to democratic institutions is an important element of social capital, but it is a stock that may not be enhanced by the democratic process itself owing to the deficient incentives and collective action problems that ensue in an environment that removes the option of individual or organisational 'exit'. Democratic participation may be sustained by appeals to civic duty, but even this is likely to decline over time as people come to recognise how ineffectual voting is as a method for acquiring the goods and services that improve their quality of life.

With weak incentives for individual participation in politics, the heightened involvement of civil associations in political activity may enable these organisations to transform in character from a focus on voluntary exchange towards predatory rent-seeking. Trade unions, business and professional associations may, for example, play a useful role when they solicit voluntary contributions and provide services to their members. It is a different matter, however, when these associations enter the realm of organised politics in pursuit of subsidies, restrictions on competition and favourable government regulations at the expense of consumers and taxpayers who, being much larger in number and with a smaller individual stake, may find it relatively more difficult to organise against such behaviour (Olson, 1982).

Seen in this light, communitarian attempts to 'build social capital' by providing government support to civil associations are misguided and are likely to spread the rent-seeking dynamics often associated with producer interest groups, to a broader section of civil society. If community groups, charities and sports clubs come to receive an increasing proportion of their income from government then this may change the incentives the groups face. The defining characteristic of a civil association is that it relies on the consent of its members who can 'exit' by withdrawing their individual financial support at any time. Government funding, however, reduces or removes this voluntary form of accountability by creating collective action problems. In order to express dissatisfaction with particular associations, citizens cannot withdraw their individual financial support for the relevant institutions, but must exercise their collective voice as taxpayers – a voice which they have relatively little individual incentive to raise. Under these conditions it tends to be pre-existing associations with the lowest costs of organisation that are able to capture the state apparatus and to engage in rent-seeking behaviour at the expense of the wider citizenry. In the United Kingdom, for example, this tendency has been particularly pronounced in the field of welfare and housing policy where the involvement of charitable associations in the supply of social services has seen these bodies transformed from self-supporting civil associations into bureaucratic lobby groups deriving over half of their income direct from the state (Whelan, 1996; King, 2006).

It is not only producer groups and pre-existing associations that may be advantaged in the battle for democratic attention, but also those who are easier to mobilise owing to their having a strong sense of internal cohesion and identity. Groups with high levels of 'bonding social capital' such as those focused on a particular religious or ethnic identity may be better placed to overcome collective action problems and thus to secure benefits from the state. Similarly, the groups most likely to mobilise politically may be those with the strongest and least flexible form of group identification (Hardin, 2001). Given the high costs of political participation and the existence of collective action problems, people who do participate are likely to be drawn disproportionately from the ranks of those who enjoy political activity 'for its own sake' or for the expressive benefits derived from venting their feelings in public displays of group identification (Brennan and Lomasky, 1993). By contrast, people with a more fluid and pluralistic identity set, who do not feel any particular sense of group loyalty and whose relationships are built predominantly on the 'weaker' form of 'bridging social capital', may be the least likely to act politically. As a consequence of these asymmetric incentives for political mobilisation the distribution of resources may be skewed in favour of those who exhibit strong identifications at the expense of those who do not. Alternatively, the democratic process may become an arena for conflict between rival identity groups in the struggle for political attention and government largesse. In the latter case, if organisations can rely on the state to supplement their income then they may be less likely to reach out to people beyond their own groups in order to generate income via persuasion and voluntary exchange. The experience of many developing countries is particularly telling in this regard. Far from reducing conflict and increasing interpersonal trust, attempts to encourage democratic participation in the context of ethnic rivalry have often increased social tensions as groups have sought to control the flow of production licences, subsidies and other rent-seeking benefits on the basis of ethnic and religious identification (Young and Turner, 1985; Easterly, 2006).

From a classical liberal perspective, the appropriate relationships between markets, civil society and the state are quite straightforward. Open markets and the interpersonal trust needed for them to function effectively may require the state to secure a framework of 'hard' institutional rules, such as the enforcement of contracts and the prevention of fraud, but they do not require the involvement of the state in the regulation of voluntary exchanges or financial 'support' for civil associations. On the contrary, extending state provision, funding and regulation into those domains where transaction costs are higher than in the private or voluntary sector, and then offering people opportunities to engage in 'democratic participation', may undermine social capital or transform whatever exists into a resource that facilitates rent-seeking rather than production and voluntary exchange.

CONCLUSION

Classical liberalism is often portrayed by its critics as advocating a social order where relationships between people are too shallow to form the basis of a stable civil society. This chapter has shown that the case for open markets is more nuanced than these criticisms imply. What classical liberalism seeks to achieve is a framework that allows people to form 'communitarian' associations at the 'micro-scale', and a capacity to develop thinner norms of cooperation with people who have different and perhaps conflicting associational ties at the 'macro-scale'. The precise mix of behavioural and regulatory norms that can sustain such a 'spontaneous order' is unlikely to be amenable to detailed prediction and manipulation by policy-makers. In the context of an overarching framework which secures property rights and provides incentives for people to signal their trustworthiness to others, however, the relevant mix may be discovered through the decisions of multiple individuals and organisations to exit and enter competing economic and cultural practices.

NOTES

1. This chapter draws on the argument presented in Meadowcroft and Pennington (2007).
2. Fukayama (1995) questions the extent to which market institutions were actually 'imposed' on post-war Japan, arguing instead that many traditional Japanese institutions had already evolved in such a way as to be supportive of private property and trade.
3. In this work Otteson demonstrates convincingly that the so-called 'Adam Smith Problem' – that is, the alleged contradiction between Smith's focus on the capacity of humans to develop norms of empathy and fellow-feeling in *The Theory of Moral Sentiments* and his focus on the primacy of 'self-interest' in *The Wealth of Nations* – is an illusion. As Otteson shows, Smith was attempting to show that different types of social norms and expectations are appropriate in different social contexts.
4. The phrase coined by Montesquieu: Montesquieu, Charles-Louis de Secondat, Marquis de (1748/1961). For a recent and comprehensive statement of the 'doux commerce' thesis see McCloskey (2006).
5. The use of the term 'family' in this context is not confined to the 'nuclear' family and to formal marriages, but may also include other 'family-like' relationships such as those between same-sex couples and close friendships of other sorts.
6. According to findings by the Hudson Institute, US private giving abroad comes close to the total amount of official government aid from all donor countries combined; see the Global Index on Philanthropy, Hudson Institute: New York.
7. According to figures published by the UK Department for Education and Skills and a recent report by the Rowntree Foundation there are massive differences in educational achievement between working-class male children (defined as those who are in receipt of free school meals) across various ethnic and cultural groups, with the 'White British' category exhibiting the worst performance at a mere 17 per cent achieving five or more GCSE grades A*–C. The comparable figure for the Chinese category is close to 70 per cent, for the Indian over 40 per cent, Bangladeshi 38 per cent, Pakistani 32 per cent, Black African 30 per cent and Black Caribbean 19 per cent. Differences of this order within the lower-income category are probably best explained by differences in the cultural emphasis placed on educational achievement between the different groups; see Rowntree Foundation (2007).

5. Equality and social justice: the challenge of egalitarianism

INTRODUCTION

The analysis thus far has sought to rebut some of the economic and moral arguments against classical liberalism. Economic arguments in favour of widespread government action rely on the claim that a laissez-faire approach leads to examples of inefficiency owing to the phenomena of market failure. Moral arguments in favour of a more than minimal state, meanwhile, focus on the contention that 'exit-based' institutions fail to cultivate an environment conducive to ethical learning and that without government regulation such institutions are unstable. Of all the arguments that have been used to thwart the cause of classical liberalism, however, it is the claim that the outcomes generated by minimal state institutions fail to meet appropriate standards of social justice that continues to exert perhaps the greatest influence on public policy debate.

At the forefront of the attacks against the alleged injustices wrought by classical liberalism have been those associated with egalitarianism. Central to these arguments is an attempt to specify the institutional arrangements that are thought to embody the principle of 'equal respect'. For theorists in the liberal egalitarian tradition, the large-scale income inequalities that may be generated by a classical liberal system fail to ensure that all members of society have access to the equal life chances that a commitment to equal respect is said to imply. For contemporary theorists of multiculturalism, meanwhile, inequalities in wealth constitute only one dimension of the failure to show equal respect. According to this view, cultural attitudes towards issues of gender, race and sexual identity may be responsible for non-material forms of 'oppression' which require state action not only to redistribute opportunities for material advancement but also to access social status and esteem.

The purpose of this chapter is to test the relative capacity of classical liberal and egalitarian perspectives on social justice to meet the requirements of a robust political economy. The analysis is divided into four parts. The first part presents the central themes in egalitarian thought that lead to the advocacy of redistributive action by the state. The discussion here, though by no means exhaustive, identifies the broad themes that characterise egalitarian arguments focusing on the claims made by John Rawls, Ronald Dworkin, and Iris Young. The subsequent sections of the chapter proceed to highlight deficiencies in egalitarian conceptions of justice which stem from an inattention to the 'knowledge problem' and a failure to pay sufficient attention to the relationship between ownership and incentives. The purpose of the analysis in each of these sections will be to challenge the supposition that equality of respect should imply support for policies that aim to equalise outcomes or opportunities with regard to wealth or social standing. Instead, the chapter contends that a more robust way to address the questions pertinent to social justice is to have a framework that does not aim to instantiate any one set of distributive norms.

EGALITARIAN POLITICAL THEORY, SOCIAL JUSTICE AND EQUAL RESPECT

Rawls on Social Justice

Classical liberal notions of justice have traditionally focused on securing to individuals a private domain which should be protected from interference by other individuals and by the agencies of the state. Justice, on this understanding, is seen to be done when the principle of 'non-interference' is respected. Following the contributions of John Rawls, these classical liberal conceptions of justice have largely been rejected by mainstream political theorists owing to their alleged failure to grant people the rights they are considered to possess as citizens with equal standing. In *A Theory of Justice*, Rawls argues that classical liberalism, or the 'system of natural liberty', does not meet the requirements of justice because it fails to recognise that distributive shares in such an order are often determined by factors that are 'arbitrary from a moral point of view' (Rawls, 1971: 72). The inheritance of natural advantages such as intelligence, strength and good health and social advantages such as the luck of being born into an educated or cultured family are all factors that may enable people to lead better and more prosperous lives, none of which, however, can be said to be 'deserved' by the actors concerned. It may, of course, be argued that though people do not 'deserve' natural and social advantages derived from accidents of birth, they may nonetheless deserve the differential rewards that flow from their making decisions about how to use and develop their talents and background advantages. Rawls, however, rejects this 'merit'-based view of what constitutes people's 'just deserts' because he argues that character traits that to lead to acts of self-improvement or self-neglect are themselves the product of social factors such as the familial or cultural background in which people find themselves, and thus they too are 'arbitrary from a moral point of view'.

In making these distinctions it is Rawls's intention to frame an account of the principles of justice that can form the basis for a stable social order. Alternative conceptions of justice, such as those based on utilitarian principles for example, are thought unlikely to perform such a task because they allow the possibility that individual rights may be breached if this contributes to the 'happiness of the greatest number'. On Rawls's understanding it is to place excessive 'strains of commitment' on individuals to require that they submit to having their own interests overridden for the sake of 'maximising social utility' (1971: 176–8). In such an order individuals would never know if their rights to property or person are to be sacrificed, and thus would lack the certainty necessary to formulate and implement a plan of life. From a Rawlsian perspective, therefore, justice requires a framework that secures the consent of all members of society rather than a utilitarian calculation where the interests of some are periodically sacrificed owing to the greater gains that might flow to others from the making of such sacrifices.

It is from his recognition that a stable social order requires widespread consent that Rawls derives support for a contractarian approach to the question of justice. According to this view, the just society is one whose institutional rules operate to the mutual benefit of all participants and reflect principles which all actors would willingly support. Rawls's attempt to envisage the circumstances that would produce such agreement results in the theoretical device of the Original Position (OP) where the conditions in which people are to deliberate about the structure of a just social order are specified. In the OP, reasoning occurs behind a 'veil of ignorance' where people do not know their particular position in society, the natural and socio-environmental advantages that they possess, or the particular conception of the good life that they wish to pursue. In addition, Rawls assumes that deliberations occur in a closed society which is not subject to exit and entry. The purpose of making these assumptions is to ensure that the results of the deliberations are likely to be universal and general rather than reflecting the personal interests and biases of the participants. Although it is recognised that people in the OP do not consciously seek to advance the interests of others, the veil of ignorance forces even self-interested agents to reason in such a way that they take the good of others into account when considering their own personal fate.

Rawls concludes that the universal and general rules to emerge from such a discussion would be his two principles of justice. The first of these specifies that: 'Each person affected by an institution is equally entitled to the most extensive sphere of liberty compatible with a like liberty for all.' The second, known as the 'difference principle', states that: 'An inequality is allowed only if the institution that allows it works to the greatest advantage of the least advantaged,' (Rawls, 1971: 302). It is this second principle of justice, alongside a commitment to 'fair equality of opportunity', which is thought to constitute a direct challenge to classical liberal accounts and is widely held to imply support for an expansive and redistributive welfare state.

The logic behind Rawls's derivation of the difference principle is that people in the Original Position would assume that the only distributive rule which all would agree to would be one of equal shares. Equal shares in this context refers to a share of the social product that results from such factors as intelligence, strength, personal character and cultural background that are deemed arbitrary from a moral point of view and which should, according to Rawls, be treated as a commonly held asset which the parties to a social contract consider how to distribute. Rawls does not claim that the distribution of assets in the natural and social lottery is itself unjust, but that the 'basic structure' of society which deals with the results from this lottery should conform to principles of justice that would be agreed upon by all of its members (1971: 102).

Although equal shares is the starting assumption for bargainers operating behind the veil of ignorance, people recognise that the size of the social product can be enlarged if there are differential rewards which encourage people to work harder than they otherwise might. According to Rawls, inequalities would be agreed upon behind the veil of ignorance, if these inequalities operate to raise the position of the least advantaged class in society. In other words, inequalities are justified if and only if a more egalitarian distribution would lower the absolute standard of living of the least advantaged group. The assumption underlying this concern with the fortunes of the least advantaged class is that people choosing principles of justice behind a veil of ignorance are averse to risks, and not knowing what social position they will assume when the veil is removed they will seek to maximise the standard of life available to those who turn out to be least fortunate in the lottery of life.

The Rawlsian account of distributive justice and the difference principle in particular do not specify how much wealth should be redistributed in order to raise the position of the least advantaged, or indeed whether any redistribution is in fact required. Nonetheless, Rawls's principles of justice are taken by many to imply support for the modern welfare state. Rawls himself clearly believes that redistributive mechanisms are required to correct the distribution of income brought about by market forces, in line with the difference principle. At various points, he explicitly criticises the failure of existing liberal democratic regimes for the injustices they do to the poor (for example, Rawls, 1971: 246–7). Similarly, in his account of the institutions of the social and economic arrangements that reflect 'justice as fairness', Rawls suggests that the basic structure of society should promote the equalisation of opportunities through publicly provided or publicly subsidised schooling and the provision of a social minimum. In addition to providing a regulatory framework within which a competitive market is allowed to work, he suggests that there should be a 'transfer' branch of government charged with ensuring that all receive the social minimum and further, that there should exist a 'distributive' branch of government to 'preserve approximate justice in distributive shares by means of taxation and necessary adjustments in the rights of property' (Rawls, 1971: 277).

Dworkin on Social Justice

Rawls describes his account of justice as one based on principles of impartiality and 'fairness', but other writers within the egalitarian tradition, though sharing many aspects of the critique of classical liberalism, question whether the principles that Rawls himself enunciates are in fact 'fair'. Dworkin (2000), for example, agrees with Rawls that a commitment to equal respect or concern should lie at the heart of a just society. Thus:

> No government is legitimate that does not show equal concern for the fate of all those citizens over whom it claims dominion and from whom it claims allegiance … and when a nation's wealth is unequally distributed, as the wealth of even very prosperous nations now is, then its equal concern is suspect. (Dworkin, 2000: 1)

From Dworkin's perspective, however, the Rawlsian scheme fails to recognise adequately the difference between distributions that are the result of 'chance' and those that are the result of 'choice'. According to Dworkin, the Rawlsian difference principle is unfair because it fails to recognise any role that personal responsibility may play in determining distributive outcomes. Since even qualities such as the decision to work hard and perseverance are attributed to social factors such as family and cultural background, on a Rawlsian understanding nobody can rightfully be said to deserve anything. Equally, however, Dworkin believes that while the difference principle is unfair to those who prosper through certain choices that they make, it is also unfair in failing to secure adequate compensation to those who find themselves in the worst-off group through no fault of their own. The difference principle seeks to 'raise the position of the worst-off', but this does not imply that those who suffer from physical or mental disability, for example, will be compensated for being in the least advantaged social groups.

Dworkin's solution to these problems is the distinction between chosen and unchosen inequalities reflected in the concepts of 'option luck' and 'brute luck'. Option luck refers to those risks that people have the opportunity to consider when making certain choices, such as the possibility of profit and loss when deciding to invest in a particular enterprise or other personal project. Also included in this category are advantages and disadvantages that may arise as a result of certain ambitions, and voluntarily acquired values and preferences. Advantages that people acquire as a result of placing themselves in situations which subsequently turn out to be 'lucky' are thought not to be a legitimate target of redistribution. Similarly, if people find themselves worse off because of certain choices that they make then they are not considered to have a just claim to redistributive benefits.

Brute luck, by contrast, refers to those factors affecting an individual's life chances over which they may exercise no personal control, such as their physical or genetic make-up or the family circumstances into which they happen to be born. People who find themselves in a position of social disadvantage are, according to this perspective, entitled to be compensated for being the victims of such misfortune. A corollary of this view is that those who are advantaged by positive examples of 'brute luck' – those fortunate enough to have greater strength or mental abilities, for example – are not entitled to keep all the benefits they may derive from their lucky status. While it is not suggested that examples of 'good' brute luck are to be frowned upon in any way, the assumption underlying Dworkin's commitment to 'equality of resources' requires nonetheless that those who benefit from 'undeserved' resources should compensate those who are relatively disadvantaged in terms of wealth and social position.

In Dworkin's schema, the principle of 'equality of resources' emerges from a hypothetical scenario not dissimilar to the Rawlsian veil of ignorance. In this case a number of shipwreck survivors arrive on an uninhabited island and must decide how to allocate resources. They do not favour an equal distribution of land, natural resources and so on, because different people will value these things differently, but neither do they expect resources to be distributed on an arbitrary basis. The distribution arises instead from an auction where people are allotted an equal number of tokens (clamshells) with which to bid for resources. The resulting distribution of goods will be unequal, as people choose to spend their resources differently – some may, for example, spend on consumption while others may choose to devote a higher proportion of their tokens to investment goods. The inequalities that emerge from such a process will not, however, be considered unjust (they will meet what Dworkin terms the 'envy test') because all started with the same initial endowment.

Dworkin then extends this principle to include natural or genetic endowments which he suggests justice requires are no more distributed on an arbitrary basis than are land and other assets. In the device of the hypothetical insurance market, he assumes that although people know what their talents are and the income structure of their society, they do not know what income these talents will generate. As a consequence, they purchase insurance against being unable to earn a higher income owing to their restricted talents or disabilities. People will not, argues Dworkin, purchase the maximum insurance because if they turn out to be a high earner the ratio of premium to payout will be too small. Based on the average insurance cover that most people will purchase, however, a minimum income is calculated to which people are entitled. It is in this context that Dworkin's proposals are held to imply support for redistributive state action, with the taxes paid by the better-off compensating those who suffer from genetic misfortune.

Young on Social Justice

The Rawlsian and Dworkinian approaches to equality and social justice continue to be important themes in discussion surrounding the moral basis and appropriate extent of redistributive state action. In recent years, however, these have been joined by theorists of the 'politics of difference' who, while broadly supportive of economic redistribution, are critical of the liberal egalitarian tradition for its excessively narrow interpretation of the issues that the welfare state should address. Iris Young, in particular, is critical of what she terms the 'distributive paradigm' in political thought. Liberal egalitarian discourse on social justice, she argues, neglects many of the most important factors which lead to a lack of equal respect owing to its preoccupation with the distribution of material goods. According to Young (1990: 3), therefore: 'instead of focusing on distribution, a conception of justice should begin with the concepts of domination and oppression. Such a shift brings out issues of decision-making, division of labour, and culture that bear on social justice but are often ignored in philosophical discussions.'

What matters from Young's point of view is that although inequalities of access to material goods are one determinant of social justice, they are by no means the only such determinant. Though many inequalities are reflected in a relative lack of buying power, the lack of respect embodied in such inequalities would not necessarily disappear under a more egalitarian distribution of goods. On the contrary, many forms of oppression stem from a broader failure of social structures to give adequate consideration to the perspectives of 'differently situated others'. Seen in this light, ensuring that the material fortunes of the least advantaged class are maximised as Rawls's theory requires would do little or nothing to ensure that the views and perspectives of this particular group are given adequate consideration in the basic decision-making structures of society. Similarly, providing monetary compensation to the disabled as implied by Dworkin's theory would not be sufficient to ensure that the particular perspectives of disabled people are reflected in the decision-making processes that affect them.

From the perspective of the politics of difference, social injustice results in large measure from institutional structures that privilege the perspectives of certain groups, and cultural attitudes that exclude sections of the population deemed not to fit with majority social norms. In the former instance, the centrality of private property to market economies locates decision-making authority in the hands of businesses and corporate bodies – by its very nature private property excludes non-owners from a right to be consulted about decisions that have a direct effect on the background conditions in which less advantaged social groups live their lives, as when companies lay off large numbers of workers or move their operations overseas. Likewise, the hierarchical decision processes involved in the management of business enterprises and in the bureaucratic allocation of resources by government agencies allow more powerful actors to define the social identity and roles of less privileged groups. Thus, business managers through their control of the division of labour have the capacity to determine the skills and occupational characteristics of workers who have correspondingly little direct say over the nature of their employment.

The above forms of 'structural injustice' as Young sees them are also accompanied by 'cultural oppression'. In these instances even when formal political structures ensure equal rights of political participation and non-discrimination, this apparent neutrality disguises the informal pressures that are brought to bear on certain social groups. Dominant cultural groups in particular tend to monopolise decision-making procedures and to encourage the assimilation of cultural minorities that exhibit different behavioural norms based on alternative notions of sexual or religious identity. The pressure to assimilate with mainstream cultural practices, generated by social stereotyping, perpetuates an unspoken lack of respect for the members of cultural minorities and results in the members of such groups exhibiting a sense of self-loathing rather than self-respect.

Although Young sees the state as one of the central perpetrators of social injustice, in common with liberal egalitarians, however, she also sees the state as the primary locus of attempts to secure the rectification of injustice. According to this perspective, the private realm of civil society and the market cannot be left to operate freely because the unintended consequence of decentralised decisions by private individuals and groups is often the creation of inequalities that are subsequently reproduced by the dynamics of social interaction. When, for example, private corporate actors or middle-class residents choose to disinvest in inner urban areas, these decisions may deprive such areas of the skills and tax base needed to support an education system that can equip working-class residents with the capacity to participate in the wider economy. Similarly, when through everyday social interactions dominant cultural groups steer away from religious or ethnic minorities or exhibit forms of conduct that manifest disapproval of the manners or attitudes of such groups, the result is often the continual marginalisation of the least advantaged.

If Young is critical of liberal egalitarians for their overly narrow analysis of the sources of social injustice, then not surprisingly she is similarly critical of classical liberal accounts which emphasise justice as non-interference. Whereas the classical liberal approach rejects state intervention except in those cases where people inflict direct harm on others through acts of theft, fraud or other invasions of private property rights, on Young's account the concept of 'harm' should be extended to include all of the indirect social consequences that result from decentralised decision-making in civil society and which may 'determine the conditions under which other actors are compelled to act' (Young, 1990: 250–51). As an alternative to the classical liberal view, Young proposes a 'modified Millian test' to delineate those areas which should be subject to corrective action by the state. Practically speaking, this requires widespread income redistribution to ensure that there is rough material equality with respect to economic resources. There should, however, also be a much greater role for the state in the fundamental structures of decision-making than found in existing 'welfare capitalist societies'. Specifically, state action is required to undermine inequalities in social recognition. In the workplace, for example, the state should ensure that the internal operations and investment decisions of private companies are subject to a process of participatory democracy where workers determine collectively the conditions under which they are employed, rather than have these determined by a professional managerial class (Young, 1990: 224).

In the cultural realm, meanwhile, the interests and perspectives of minority social groups should be granted due recognition in collective decision processes so that the religious, ethnic or sexual practices of such groups are not treated purely as a private matter to be tolerated by the wider society, but are seen fundamentally as part of the political identity of the actors concerned. People should, on this account, be able to participate in politics as gay people, religious people or black people, and democratic processes should ensure that these aspects of cultural identity are positively affirmed via formal rights of representation which exhibit equal respect for all cultural groups. In addition, where minority cultures face the pressure to assimilate with the wider society, action should be taken to preserve and to promote their sense of identity by providing financial support for their cultural activities and the enactment of affirmative action programmes to achieve a greater representation of disadvantaged groups in positions of power and social prestige.

THE KNOWLEDGE PROBLEM AND SOCIAL JUSTICE I: EGALITARIANISM AS CONSTRUCTIVIST RATIONALISM

Egalitarian arguments, though clearly differing in points of emphasis, represent a serious challenge to the classical liberal ideal of a minimal state. Support for these arguments must however be grounded in a robust understanding of social processes and the way in which these may constrain the choice of political principles. More specifically, a successful theory of justice must recognise the constraints resulting from 'knowledge problems' and the possibility of self-interested behaviour. It is within this context that classical liberalism challenges the egalitarian interpretation of what is required by equal respect. The next two sections examine the 'knowledge problems' that confront social justice theory. The subsequent section questions the capacity of egalitarian accounts to deal effectively with the problem of deficient incentives or excessive 'strains of commitment'.

Rawls as Constructivist Rationalist

The notion that theories of justice must be informed by an appreciation of social constraints is by no means unique to classical liberalism. Rawls, for example, though specifying that bargaining parties behind the veil of ignorance do not know about their own talents, skills or likely status in a way that might bias their deliberations, is careful to specify that they do have access to 'general facts of social theory' in order to inform an impartial choice of just institutions (Rawls, 1971: 142). If these 'general facts' are now taken to include the record of central planning in the twentieth century then it is not unreasonable to argue that successful institutions must facilitate the creation and communication of knowledge rather than assuming that such knowledge can be 'given' to a single actor or agency.[1] One of the major problems with egalitarian theories, however, is that they often assume away the processes of disagreement and social difference through which the knowledge pertinent to questions of justice might actually be discovered and communicated. This tendency is most apparent in concepts such as the Original Position and the Veil of Ignorance that are central to the Rawlsian account. In constructing these theoretical devices Rawls assumes conditions in which people are lacking in any form of social experience.

Though they know little or nothing about themselves people are assumed to have sufficient reasoning capacity to agree what the appropriate standards of justice in society should be. On a classical liberal understanding, however, the need for social rules and institutions, such as private property rights, arises in large part from the fact that people do not have the knowledge to agree on the pursuit of a single conception of 'social justice'. To assume that they do and that the relevant knowledge can be gathered in a single place is to ignore the requirements of a robust political economy and to be guilty of what Hayek (1982: Part 2) describes as 'constructivist rationalism'.

According to Hayek, reason does not exist independent of personal and social experience, but is in part at least a product of the particular personal and cultural contexts in which people find themselves and (if allowed to do so) it evolves as people are exposed to and learn from actors with different experiences. Knowledge of these perspectives and their implications does not exist anywhere as an integrated whole but emerges from the dispersed interactions and mutual adjustments between a multiplicity of individuals and groups, each with their own partial perspectives. Seen in this context, Rawls's impartial reasoner is equivalent to an omniscient social planner who is assumed to have complete knowledge of all the underlying circumstances pertinent to the determination of an ideal set of distributional rules.[2]

The latter point has increasingly been recognised by those who, though sympathetic to egalitarian objectives, question the epistemological basis of much egalitarian theory. Young, in particular, is critical of what she terms the 'view from nowhere' evident in the Rawlsian account of impartial reason. As she explains:

> Impartial reason judges from a point of view outside of the particular perspectives of persons involved in order to totalise these perspectives into a whole or general will ... Because it already takes all perspectives into account, the impartial subject need acknowledge no subjects other than itself, to whose interests, opinions and desires it should attend. (Young, 1990: 100–101)

In the Rawlsian project the possibility that reason might need to be informed by a process of social learning and experience is ruled out by the assumptions of the model. In the Original Position, bargainers are not only assumed to be identical in characteristics but are prevented from listening to the views and opinions of others and of being influenced by them (Rawls, 1971: 131). Similarly, the assumption that bargaining behind the veil of ignorance takes place in a 'closed society' precludes the possibility that people might learn from and be influenced by the experiences of those outside their own particular context. It is, however, precisely through variations in the experience of social actors – including differences in personal talents, cultural and historical background and attitudes to distribution that people may come to learn what justice may require. These experiential factors are, however, assumed away in the Rawlsian thought experiment because they are deemed 'arbitrary from a moral point of view'.

In light of the 'knowledge problem', rather than assuming that political institutions should aim at a particular distributive pattern, a theory of social justice which meets the requirements of robust political economy must consider what sort of institutional arrangements facilitate the evolution and communication of the appropriate moral principles. Attention should, in other words, shift from a preoccupation with 'static' or 'end-state' theories to ones which focus on the dynamic processes within which principles of justice may be discovered and disseminated.

In order to clarify the above point it should be noted that there is a striking similarity between the Rawlsian method and the general equilibrium analysis of neo-classical economics discussed in Chapter 2. In the latter, it is the assumptions of equilibrium theory (of perfectly rational and informed economic agents) that leads to the conclusion that markets can produce an optimal allocation of resources – and with departures from these assumptions in the 'real world' taken as evidence of 'market failure'. As Chapter 2 argued, however, such models assume away the very social processes that are in need of explanation. In equilibrium theory no attempt is made to explain how market actors acquire the information necessary to coordinate with their fellows or how, in the absence of such information, government planners could know what action is needed to remedy instances of market failure. When the premises of a theorist's model assume away what needs to be explained, then institutions become irrelevant. In 'real-world' situations, however, questions of institutional choice are fundamental to the issue of how social actors are to coordinate and learn from one another in conditions that depart radically from theoretical abstractions. In the specific case of market institutions based on the dispersed ownership of private property, their superiority over socialist systems of central planning derives from a greater capacity to mobilise knowledge which, as Hayek (1948a: 77–8) explains: 'never exists in concentrated or integrated form but solely as the dispersed bits of incomplete and frequently contradictory knowledge that all the separate individuals possess'.

In markets, it is the clash of competing ideas and practices dispersed across different property owners that enables trial and error learning. Differences in prices, profits and losses communicate information and prompt changes in people's behaviour as knowledge concerning the relative success and failure of competing ventures ripples out from a multiplicity of decision-making nodes.

Applied in the context of distributive norms, the different talents that people have, and cultural attitudes towards those talents, inform their reasoning on social justice. Those who emanate from a 'meritocratic' culture may not, for example, believe that it is fair that a large proportion of the income derived from their employing such skills should be transferred to 'the worst-off group' irrespective of the reason why people find themselves in such a position. On the other hand, people who come from a cultural background that favours social solidarity and downplays the value of material progress may not consider it a worthy principle of justice that allows inequalities between individuals for the sake of increasing the standard of living. People who subscribe to religious beliefs, meanwhile, may have views on the distribution of income and life chances that are conditioned by their adherence to a particular faith. More importantly, as people with diverse skills, abilities and views on social justice are continually exposed to other actors who have different experiences, their initial conceptions of justice and fairness may change as a consequence of this interaction. In the same manner that market participants may be alerted to new and better opportunities than they had previously conceived by observing the different terms offered by competing entrepreneurs, so in the context of moral reflection people may change their view of what constitute 'fair terms of cooperation' by observing the results of novel social norms and by opting for those arrangements that they judge to be better. Just as no central mind or agency can be aware of all the factors that determine the content of prices in a market, so from a classical liberal standpoint no such mind can be aware of and synthesise all of the factors that contribute to appropriate rules of distribution.

Dworkin as Constructivist Rationalist

The tendency towards constructivist rationalism and the assumption of 'given' knowledge evident in Rawlsian theory may also count against Dworkin's version of egalitarianism. 'Real-world' questions of distributive justice typically arise where people with different histories, cultures and social attachments come into contact with one another. In terms of a robust political economy, therefore, 'equality of resources' is unlikely to be a viable principle of social justice, in part because people with different social experiences may not agree on what are to count as the 'resources' which should be the subject of distribution. Dworkin's model assumes that resources should be given a marketable price in order that all participants begin with an equivalent bundle, the value of which can be measured against a common metric. Some societies, however (Aborigines, for example), consider it inappropriate that the value of land and other natural resources should be measured against a monetary scale. Yet, Dworkin's theory would require that such assets are 'sold off' in order that the proceeds might be redistributed (Kukathas, 2003: 224–5). A similar difficulty arises with arguments for the redistribution of genetic endowments. On Dworkin's model, people who do not value high monetary rewards but are 'more advantaged' in terms of their genetic make-up would have to work to pay for the high insurance premiums which reflect the value that other social actors place on their talents. 'Less advantaged' people who have a similar preference for leisure, however, would not be required to pay such a premium. There is, therefore, an implicit 'productivist' bias in Dworkin's approach which assumes that resources, be they natural or genetic, should be put to marketable uses (Miller, 1990). With its emphasis on the advantages of markets, classical liberalism does not object to resources acquiring a market price, but neither does it insist that people should participate in market relationships if their particular goals and cultural values place limits on what should be bought or sold.

It is not only views about the appropriate subject of distribution that are socially and culturally varied, but also categories such as natural 'advantages' and 'disadvantages'. If people do not value a level of production significantly above subsistence level then it may not constitute an advantage to have talents and abilities that might lead to the generation of a larger surplus. Physical strength or beauty may be highly prized resources in certain cultural circumstances, while elsewhere mental dexterity may be judged of greater value. Even concepts such as 'disability' are to a significant extent specific to particular cultural and economic contexts. In an advanced economy, for example, people with limited physical mobility may still be able to perform jobs that can earn them a significant income, whereas in a less developed economy the same 'disability' would render them entirely dependent on others for their subsistence. Furthermore, a person's knowledge of their talents and abilities is itself highly uncertain and may be 'discovered' as those concerned pursue particular paths of action and are alerted to alternative possibilities through the process of social and cultural interchange. A person's knowledge of what their own talents are or might be and the incomes they may receive evolves as they come into contact with those from different cultural and economic backgrounds. To take a simple example, conceptions of one's relative 'beauty' may be transformed (for better or worse) by contacts with a culture that values different physical characteristics. Where people with divergent views concerning the appropriate subjects of distribution interact, and where people from various cultural contexts place competing values on talents and abilities, the concepts of 'resources' and advantages and disadvantages are highly fluid and unsuited to a static 'equality of resources'. The latter presupposes that knowledge about the relevant 'resources' can be 'given' to a particular organisation charged with the implementation of social justice.

The difficulties that arise from Dworkin's version of the 'given' knowledge fallacy are encapsulated in the device of the hypothetical insurance market. Under Dworkin's scheme the 'prices' attached to the physical and genetic resources that are to be equalised result from a 'simulated' market – a sort of 'one-off auction' – and not from a genuine and ongoing market process. From a classical liberal perspective, therefore, the prices determined by this simulation will fail to reflect the dynamic 'real-world' factors – technological innovations, new discoveries and changes in cultural tastes – that will prompt constant shifts in the value of the relevant assets. Knowledge of these factors and their implications for resource distribution cannot be centralised in a single place but may only be revealed through the actual buying and selling decisions of multitudinous decentralised agents.

Young as Constructivist Rationalist

With its focus on disagreement and difference Young's approach to social justice may be considered less susceptible to the 'given' knowledge fallacy and the charge of constructivist rationalism. In contrast to Rawls's and Dworkin's attempts to justify their favoured distributional ideals, Young redirects attention to the institutional processes that allow for the discovery and communication of different moral values. This apparent sensitivity to the 'knowledge problem' is, however, called into question by Young's emphasis on 'equality of outcome' not only in terms of material resources, but also with regard to social status and esteem – requiring that the cultural attitudes of 'disadvantaged' and 'minority' groups should be positively affirmed. For all her critique of the 'view from nowhere' central to liberal egalitarianism, it is hard to see how Young's supposedly more open-ended understanding of social justice can be squared with a precommitment to the view that particular interests and values must be publicly supported. The values of disadvantaged and minority groups may prove themselves worthy of equal if not more respect than those of a prevailing culture, just as the ideas of scientific and industrial entrepreneurs that are often publicly ridiculed may subsequently prove their worth in the intellectual and economic marketplace. Many scientific and entrepreneurial ideas are however, indeed devoid of merit and this may also be the case with respect to cultural and distributional practices. It is precisely by discriminating against such practices that people are able to express commitment to an alternative, and may signal to those from whom they wish to dissociate that there may be better ways of organising their affairs. For classical liberals it follows that while cultural or religious minorities should have the liberty to engage in potentially unwelcome practices – such as, for example, employment discrimination on grounds of gender or sexual orientation – people who reject such prejudices should have the liberty to dissociate from those who subscribe to them in order to signal their disrespect for the relevant values.

It is inevitable in a process of evolutionary discovery that the status and esteem of individuals and groups will be fluid. As people choose to associate with some actors and to dissociate with others on a range of different terms, and as individuals and groups adapt to these choices, the resources and status of the relevant actors will shift accordingly. Within this context, unequal outcomes are an unavoidable manifestation of cultural and economic fluidity and may be necessary to promote the process of cross-cultural interchange and learning that Young claims to favour. Suppose, for example, that a firm or cultural group that discourages sexual discrimination in employment practices proves itself more productive than a group which holds to notions of male superiority. In this case, it is the very existence of inequality between the relevant 'cultures' that may be best placed to prompt a challenge to potentially oppressive social norms. Seen through this lens, there is no more reason to grant support to those associations and groups that suffer losses of resources and members, and who may feel 'undervalued' or 'disrespected' as a consequence of social interaction, than there is to support business ventures that prove unable to retain customers on a voluntary basis.

From the standpoint of classical liberalism, it is not only Young's precommitment to equality of outcome that reflects a lingering 'constructivist' mindset, but her support for democratic deliberation as the most appropriate mechanism to determine the constituents of social justice. As argued in Chapter 3, the central deficiency of deliberative democracy is that it places cognitive demands on people that are impossible for them to meet. In the specific case of social justice, the knowledge pertinent to appropriate principles of distribution cannot be centralised in a public forum and the complexity of the factors that contribute to the formulation of distributional rules cannot be grasped by a group of minds engaged in a deliberative exercise. Rather, such dispersed and complex knowledge may only be reflected in the unintended patterns that emerge spontaneously from the interaction of a multiplicity of individuals and groups.

Justice, Impartiality and the Knowledge Problem

If it is recognised that understandings of social justice must take on a more dynamic and disaggregated form, then it is implausible to maintain that the appropriate content of distributional norms can be 'given' in its totality to any particular individual or group or to an agency such as the state. Government officials – democratically elected or otherwise – are not omniscient and their views on social justice will be conditioned by their own personal and cultural experiences. From a classical liberal perspective, therefore, any attempt to enforce a particular distributional ideal at the societal level will reflect only the very partial perspectives of the actors empowered to engage in such enforcement. It follows that if they are to draw on a wider pool of experiences, traditions and perspectives, social institutions should not seek to instantiate any particular distributive pattern but should allow competing principles of justice to exist in parallel. It is differences in results – that is, inequalities – that enable decentralised agents to learn about the merits and demerits of alternatives, and for these results to be disseminated across the overlapping perspectives of countless actors none of whom may be aware, individually or collectively, how their particular choices contribute to the evolution of distributional norms.

Insofar as equality is of relevance in such a context, then this may only apply to the equal enforcement of the rules necessary to enable rival distributive norms to coexist. For classical liberalism, this is precisely the reason why the principle of equal respect should be confined to the enforcement of 'negative' rights of 'non-interference' such as the protection of persons and property, rather than implying support for 'positive' rights to particular social outcomes. These 'negative rights' should not be seen as 'rules of justice' per se, but are better thought of as basic norms of interaction, or Humean 'conventions', which may be necessary for people who hold to different conceptions of social justice to coexist without permanent conflict (on this, see for example Barry, 2004). On a classical liberal understanding robust political institutions are not those which aim to secure justice, but are those that reduce conflict and maintain the peace in conditions where there may be no basis for agreement on what justice requires.

In view of this analysis it is worth reconsidering what the requirements for a genuinely 'impartial' choice of social institutions might be. Insofar as the notion of impartial reason is not to be guilty of 'constructivist rationalism', it must refrain from making arbitrary and ad hoc assumptions about the information that social participants possess. It must not, for example, assume à la Rawls, that people are 'risk-averse' and that they know themselves to be considering distributive rules for a 'closed society'.[3] If the choice of social institutions takes place behind a veil of genuine ignorance, then it seems highly unlikely that people would opt with certainty for any particular distributive rule – such as the Rawlsian 'difference principle'. If people are genuinely ignorant, not only of their talents and social position, but also about the values and beliefs they will possess, their knowledge, attitudes to risk and how these are likely to change in light of experience, then it seems more plausible that they might opt for a 'basic structure' that would enable them to learn about and to choose between competing distributive standards. In other words, one might expect people to favour an 'open society' that allows different individuals and groups to enter and exit from a variety of cross-cutting arrangements provided by families, firms, neighbourhood associations and the panoply of cultural and civil institutions that distribute money, goods and social status. The processes of interpersonal and intercultural learning and adjustment that would occur in such a framework, though offering no guarantees that the 'right' principles might be discovered, would nonetheless increase the chance that any person or group picked out at random would have the opportunity to find the 'right' set of distributional rules.

Now, it might be objected that the charge of constructivist rationalism levied against egalitarianism throughout this section completely misses the point of what normative political theorising is supposed to be about. For, at least in the case of Rawls, the entire purpose of his theory is to prescribe and to advocate a particular set of values – that is, 'justice as fairness' – rather than to describe a process that might elicit the often erroneous (from Rawls's viewpoint) values and standards of justice that people currently happen to have. Devices such as the veil of ignorance are designed with the explicit purpose of ruling out non-impartial ethical theories and values. To claim that Rawls ignores the existence of value diversity and disagreement, therefore, mis-understands the nature of his project, which is precisely to reduce value diversity by screening out unjust values and to show which ones – such as, for example, those of Nazis – are unjustifiable. Seen in this regard, the evolutionary reasoning set out here is in danger of collapsing into a purely descriptive account of value diversity, and of justifying an 'anything goes' approach to matters of right and wrong.

The line of criticism sketched above has some merit in the sense that classical liberalism, as it is understood in this book, advocates a relatively 'thin' conception of 'justice' rather than committing itself to a more substantive ethical framework. This does not, however, imply the existence of an 'anything goes' mindset. What the classical liberal perspective aims to achieve is a more robust understanding of what impartiality requires, given the constraints that face all human agents – including normative theorists. In a sense, all political theories are 'constructivist' insofar as they advocate any particular set of institutional arrangements. For classical liberals, however, this constructivist element is confined to the process of 'using reason to understand the limits of reason' (Hayek, 1957). Before determining the nature of what is right and wrong, a robust account of impartiality must recognise the nature of the constraints set by the limits of human cognition. Insofar as normative theory is engaged in the process of prescribing institutions, therefore, these prescriptions must be relatively thin in order to grant scope for learning and evolution in conditions of limited rationality. In the context of theories of justice this results in the recognition of a 'meta-level' norm – toleration – which gives the maximum rein to individuals and groups to use knowledge derived from the results of their own practical experiences in crafting responses to the distributive problems that they face. Toleration is the prescribed ethical principle that emerges from recognising the limited reasoning capacity and differentiated knowledge that people possess, and the empirical fact that they disagree about matters of distributive justice. This focus on toleration does not imply that people should be required to show respect for the ethical values of others with whom they disagree, but it does imply the institutionalisation of a framework that allows for the peaceful coexistence of rival value systems by securing a realm of non-interference. Nazism and other forms of totalitarianism, insofar as they are based on the violent suppression of others, are indeed ruled out by such a framework.[4]

Rawls, it should be noted, seems only too aware of the problems that complexity and differentiated knowledge might imply for the robustness of his particular theory. The assumption that all agents behind the veil of ignorance have identical knowledge and conceptions of their interests is designed to ensure that the relevant actors 'have no basis for bargaining in the usual sense' (Rawls, 1971: 139), and 'we can view the choice in the original position from the standpoint of one person selected at random' (ibid.). This assumption:

makes possible a unanimous choice of a particular conception of justice. Without these limitations on knowledge the bargaining position in the original position would be hopelessly complicated. Even if theoretically a solution were to exist we would not, at present anyway, be able to determine it. (Rawls, 1971: 140)

For classical liberalism, however, there is an alternative method of dealing with the inherent complexity of distributive justice. Instead of implying that people who do not accept the difference principle are somehow morally suspect, we can accept the reality that they differ in their knowledge endowments and enable solutions to the 'hopelessly complicated bargaining problem' to emerge by securing people a protected domain and allowing them to enter into and exit from competing 'social contracts' (on this, see Palmer, 2007).

In order for a classical liberal framework to match such requirements, there need be no assumption that decisions to 'exit' and 'enter' particular arrangements should be costless. Critics of classical liberalism contend that 'exit costs' within the market and civil society are often 'excessive' and compromise the value of the exit principle (for example, Barry 1995, 2001). The latter perspective reflects the hyper-rationalism evident in neo-classical economics where departures from 'perfect competition' – that is, the supply of identical commodities by multiple producers, none of whom can affect the prices charged – are seen as 'market failures'. As argued in Chapter 2, however, this approach is incompatible with the notion of markets as evolutionary 'discovery processes' which alert people to different and changing options. Market competition is often of the 'price-making' variety where firms innovate by introducing new products and processes that have not been thought of by their rivals, and where there are profits to be made before the latter are able to adapt to the relevant innovations. 'Bargaining power' and 'costs of exit' are always present in such a context. People are rarely able to secure products which meet all of their individual requirements on every dimension. If a firm offers an imperfect product from the consumer's view, but one which is still superior to those offered by competitors, then the costs of exit for that consumer are by definition 'excessive'. Indeed, any situation where people deem that the benefits of an option are exceeded by the costs would count as an 'excessive cost' (Kukathas, 2002, 2003). For markets to work effectively, what is required is not 'perfect competition' where people are indifferent to an identical set of options before them, but that incumbents are open to challenge from new entrants offering different and better opportunities than currently available.

Similarly, in the realm of distributional and cultural norms, people will rarely find arrangements that match all of their needs and values, so 'exit costs' are bound to exist. Nonetheless, an environment that allows for competition between norms of distribution may allow new entrant associations to offer 'better principles of justice' than those currently on offer. A framework that emphasises competition and freedom of association, though 'imperfect', may be more robust than an alternative which involves not more competition but the empowerment of a single authority to determine and enforce what it considers to be the 'right' set of distributive norms. From a classical liberal perspective, there is no more case for assuming that the state is in a position to define what counts as an 'excessive cost' of exit than there is to assume that governments can know the 'right price' for commodities when competition departs from 'perfect' conditions. It is precisely what constitutes the 'right price' or an 'excessive cost' that needs to be discovered. The bargaining terms that would emerge from a competitive process cannot be simulated or replicated by a system of central regulation but may only be discovered through a process of actual competition, however 'imperfect' it may be.

THE KNOWLEDGE PROBLEM AND SOCIAL JUSTICE II: TRADE-OFFS AND THE MIRAGE OF SOCIAL JUSTICE

Classical liberalism, then, is sceptical of the case for putting any particular distributional principle at the centre of social justice theory, but it is not at all clear whether egalitarians are themselves committed to social justice as an absolute concept.

The Indeterminacy of Egalitarian Justice

Both Rawls and Dworkin concede that equality might be traded off against other objectives, and in the process their theories lose commitment to any determinate distributive outcome. In the former instance, Rawls retreats from the implications of his 'difference principle', which taken to its logical conclusion would require that billions of pounds or dollars should be taken from the better-off, even if the benefits to the worst-off from such a transfer would be little more than a few pennies per capita. Rawls proceeds to note that 'the difference principle is not intended to apply to such abstract possibilities' (Rawls, 1971: 157), and thus concedes that the principle should not be pushed 'too far', that is, that there may be legitimate trade-offs between the difference principle and other valued outcomes.

Dworkin (1981: 322), meanwhile, concedes that the abstract principle of 'equality of resources' may be traded off with other objectives. In the case of those who suffer from severe physical and mental disability, for example, no amount of compensation could make up for the disabilities at hand – even if all resources were devoted to such cases, the 'compensation' would be insufficient and in the process nothing would be left over to provide for the needs and wants of the able-bodied. Although the severely disabled constitute an extreme case, the same problem may apply, albeit to a reduced extent, with less severe disadvantages. Dworkin, therefore, is eager to avoid a 'slavery of the talented' and suggests that redistribution via his hypothetical insurance scheme should provide 'adequate' incomes for the disadvantaged rather than equal incomes.

That Rawls and Dworkin are unwilling to pursue egalitarian objectives at all costs should be recognised as a virtue of their respective theories, because the alternative would constitute what Badhwar (2006) describes as a mono-maniacal approach to equality – that is, one which refuses to recognise that there are a variety of values to be pursued within a good society. Thus, while the relief of poverty is a worthy goal to pursue and one which may rank very highly in the value scale of some people, the world offers a range of other similarly worthy goals. These may include a higher average standard of living, the pursuit of intellectual or artistic excellence, or a desire to protect the natural environment. More importantly, the pursuit of such ends may conflict with 'social justice'. In the case of living standards, for example, one of the most important functions of a competitive market is to shift resources away from actors who fail to maximise value towards those who prove better at doing so. It is the resultant inequality in control over capital goods that raises the average level of wealth. Greater material equality or satisfying the require-ments of the difference principle may, therefore, come at a price that people are unwilling to pay. Similarly, in the case of environmental protection, even small improvements in the material position of the worst-off may require losses of valuable landscape or additions in pollution which people may not wish to tolerate. Although it may be uncomfortable to think in such terms, people make implicit trade-offs in this manner on a regular basis. They can and do, for example, spend money on university libraries and high art that could be devoted to the most disadvantaged social groups.

Recognising the importance of trade-offs in the above regard downgrades the relative status of equality because there are so many legitimate reasons to break with egalitarianism that it ceases to look like a moral absolute (see, for example, Kekes, 2003: Chapter 5). If the possibility of making trade-offs between rival objectives and social justice is recognised, then it is difficult to see why the pursuit of egalitarian justice should be considered the 'first virtue of social institutions' (Rawls) or the 'sovereign virtue' of governments (Dworkin).

A further and significant implication of recognising the centrality of trade-offs is that people may wish to make them differently, and when their values conflict it is doubtful that an agreed blueprint can be found to determine how much inequality is acceptable and how 'social' decisions should be made. Young's insistence that material inequalities between cultural groups must be reduced as a condition of empowerment, while insisting on the freedom of groups to pursue their own modes of life, is particularly puzzling in this regard. Egalitarian objectives cannot easily be squared with cultural self-determination if for no other reason than that different cultural norms and their associated trade-offs produce different material and economic consequences. People who opt for 'socialist' principles of distribution are, for example, unlikely to generate the same wealth as those who favour more competitive forms of resource allocation. Similarly, groups that reject technological innovations, as do many of today's radical or 'deep' greens, are unlikely to generate the same opportunities for material advancement as people who embrace technological progress. This is not to suggest that existing inequalities are wholly attributable to spontaneous cultural differences, as opposed to historical acts of violence or theft, which run counter to the non-interference principle.[5] Rather, the point is that even in the absence of these factors inequality may result from the coexistence of different social norms, and there is no single trade-off to determine how much inequality is in fact 'acceptable'.

It might, of course, be argued that there are some needs such as minimal nutritional requirements that may be established 'objectively' and which are more readily identifiable than an 'optimum' level of inequality (Gamble, 1996: 49). Yet, there are several problems with even this stance. First, it is not self-evident that matters such as adequate standards of nutrition can be identified in a strictly objective manner. The definition of appropriate nutritional standards in one time period and culture may be considered grossly inadequate in other contexts where expectations of longevity are much higher. Second, the identification of those actors to whom an enforceable commitment to nutrition is owed may not be identified objectively. Will the standard be applicable within a particular socio-economic context, or will it apply to all human beings irrespective of their history and cultural milieu? In a context of cross-cultural fluidity and interchange there is unlikely to be agreement on which specific individuals and groups are to be eligible to benefit from the minimal standard. Finally, in the unlikely event that people agree on the content of the social minima and believe that all actors should in principle be eligible to receive it, this would not imply agreement on the extent to which achieving the standard should be pursued at the expense of other goals. People may not, for example, concur that it is worth providing an open-ended commitment to keep alive every starving child in the developing world, if the cost of doing so diverts resources away from other worthwhile objectives, such as the funding of research and investment which may improve average living standards for people in generations to come.[6]

Justice, Responsibility and Spontaneous Order

If the legitimacy of trading off distributive principles with other objectives is recognised, and if it is further admitted that people may choose to make these trade-offs in different and changing ways, then the pursuit of 'distributive justice' at the macro-societal level may be equivalent to chasing a 'mirage' (Hayek, 1982: Part 2). In an 'open society' where people with different goals and values interact, there is no one agency responsible for the distribution of income and the macro-distributive pattern is not the deliberate intention of participants either at the micro or at the macro scale. Markets, for example, do not distribute resources according to any particular conception of merit (how hard people try, for example). Rather, rival firms within markets adopt different criteria to determine pay scales and the requirements for 'merit-based' promotion. In addition, the overall pattern of distribution is as likely to be affected by personal relationships, gifts and charitable donations as it is by payments for services supplied on a contractual basis. More importantly, while those who work and/or save hard may do well in markets, the rewards that people receive may also be determined by chance discoveries and other random events such as a shift in the demand for a particular skill or resource. In such an order there is no one standard or set of trade-offs against which the results of 'the market' may be judged, and neither is there a person or group who could be held to have acted justly or unjustly in this regard. People both affect and are affected by the decisions made by countless dispersed actors, none of whom is able to determine the justice of any particular distribution and none of whom may be aware how their own particular standards and choices have contributed to that distribution.[7]

Now, it might be argued that though the outcomes that emerge from a 'spontaneous order' are not the deliberate intention of any one actor, people are nonetheless responsible for how they react to the relevant outcomes (Lukes, 1997; see also Plant, 1994). According to this view, a failure to react in an appropriate way to excessive inequality may rightly be condemned as unjust. The problem with this argument, however, is that it avoids the question of what an appropriate response would be. It is only meaningful to say that people are failing in their responsibilities to 'social justice' if they are in a position to know how much poverty or inequality is acceptable, and fail to act accordingly. People may, of course, seek to correct a particular distributive outcome according to their personal or group-based view of the trade-offs involved, but in no way can such actions be said to increase the level of distributive justice across society as a whole. The most that could be claimed in such a context is that people have made distributive choices that accord with their own particular scale of trade-offs. In an 'open society', however, there is no one 'social standard' against which the fortunes of different individuals can be judged or ranked. Egalitarians are not in a strong position to reject this analysis, for as noted above, writers such as Rawls and Dworkin are unable to offer a determinate account of 'how much' inequality is in fact acceptable.

A further and still more significant aspect of the 'knowledge problem' should also be emphasised at this juncture. In the unlikely event that there is in fact widespread agreement on how to trade off a particular distributive norm, such as the 'difference principle' or 'equality of resources' with competing objectives, people will nonetheless lack the capacity to know how they should act to bring about the desired level of inequality. To suggest that a particular decision increases or decreases social justice, the relevant actor, whether a private individual (through charitable action) or a government department (through tax and spending decisions) would need answers to the following kinds of questions, among many others. Will the recipients of transfer payments engage in activities and spend the relevant money in ways which increase or decrease their earning power in the labour market? To what extent might transfer recipients spend on a consumption bundle that increases the demand for unskilled labour, and thus reduces income inequality relative to spending, which raises the demand for already higher-paid occupations and thus may increase inequality? People would also need to know how their decisions to switch a given level of expenditure away from consumption or investment and towards redistribution will affect overall outcomes. Will, for example, firms in industries that previously supplied consumption items to the relatively rich, lay off workers who may suffer a period of unemployment as a consequence? What will be the economic implications for the suppliers of these companies? How easy will it be for the relevant workers to find jobs in response to the new pattern of expenditure by the disadvantaged, and how might this affect inequality? And, will redistribution reduce the availability of capital to those organisations best placed to increase the supply of better-paying jobs to the disadvantaged in the future?

In order to answer such questions and to be held responsible for their actions it would be necessary for people to anticipate the choices and thus effectively to 'read the minds' of countless other individuals and organisations. In the absence of this capacity then the decisions that people take to exchange goods and services or to give resources and time to others will continually transform the distribution of income in unanticipated ways. If freedom of action is upheld, knowledge of 'who should give what to whom' in order to produce any particular level of inequality (desirable or otherwise) cannot be 'given' either to individuals themselves or to a collective forum such as that provided by the state. Where people have freedom of action, therefore, it makes no sense to speak of them acting 'justly' or 'unjustly' with respect to any particular macro-distributive pattern. This conclusion does not reflect the potential selfishness or opportunism of the relevant actors in avoiding their responsibilities to social justice. On the contrary, it is based on the recognition that however well motivated people may be to achieve a particular distributive pattern, in a complex society where their decisions must dovetail with those of millions of others they simply cannot know what the appropriate action should be.

It will not suffice to reply that holding people responsible for their actions refers not to every specific exchange or act of giving, but to the willingness of people to uphold a 'basic structure' of society which provides the background opportunities and resources, commensurate with an 'acceptable' level of inequality. The difficulty is precisely that knowledge of which opportunities and resource allocations constitute the relevant 'structure' can never be made available either individually or to a collective institution such as the state. In the case of rates of taxation, for example, a tax rate that secures a given level of inequality at a particular point in time may not be commensurate with such inequality at a subsequent point, because ongoing changes in technology, tastes, spending and employment patterns will continually alter the distribution that results from that level of taxation in countless unanticipated ways. In these circumstances it would be impossible for those charged with implementing the relevant tax to know in what direction to change it in response to the myriad factors that affect the distribution of income.

Consider further in the above context the implications of Young's approach to the prevention of 'structural injustice', and in particular the requirements of her 'modified Millian test'. The latter states that:

> Agents, whether individual or collective, have the right to sole authority over their actions only if the actions and their consequences a) do not harm others, b) do not inhibit the ability of individuals to develop their capacities within the limits of mutual respect and toleration, and c) do not determine the conditions under which other agents are compelled to act. (Young, 1990: 250–51)

From a classical liberal standpoint, there is simply no way that knowledge pertinent to each of these conditions could ever be accessible to a public authority – including one subject to processes of democratic participation. Every decision at the micro-scale – to buy or sell, to invest or to disinvest, to adopt a particular cultural practice or to eschew another – will both affect the 'structural conditions' that face other social participants and simultaneously be affected by those conditions. In order to determine whether the overall structure of decisions 'harms others' (by reducing or increasing their income or sense of esteem, for example) or 'determines the conditions under which they are compelled to act' (by reducing or increasing the range of available opportunities, given their talents and skills), it would be necessary to know how any of the actions that take place within that structure dovetails with all of the other decisions simultaneously made by countless individuals and groups. It is, however, precisely the inability to centralise the knowledge concerning the effect of all these decisions that precludes the public 'justification' of any particular distributive outcome.

Oppression and Egalitarian Justice

If freedom of action produces unanticipated results then the tendency for egalitarians is to favour measures that limit such freedom and compel people to behave in particular ways. This tendency is clearly evident in Young's proposals for mandatory 'worker participation'. According to Young, in order to guarantee a right to 'meaningful and satisfying work' employees must be granted the right to participate in the management and investment decisions of the businesses that employ them (Young, 1990: 250–51). In advancing these proposals, Young does not appear to recognise that there may be a trade-off between 'meaningful work' and the generation of wealth. If, as the disappointing record of worker cooperatives demonstrates (see, for example, Hindmoor, 1999), a specialised division of labour with gradations of skill and expertise is better at generating prosperity, then many workers may wish to opt for higher economic rewards over a right to 'meaningful work'. It is not clear, however, that Young would allow workers to choose employment in organisations that offered such arrangements because on her account this may result in their capacity to 'determine the conditions' of others. Specifically, if a minority of workers choose the inegalitarian option and if such organisations prove more efficient, are favoured by consumers, and generate higher revenues, then it may become more difficult to raise capital for investment in 'participatory' management forms as an increasing number of people may seek to copy conventional corporate practices.

The logical implication of Young's argument would appear to be that the state should prohibit employment in traditional capitalist enterprises.[8] Indeed, in order to secure the material equality she desires, Young's proposals would need to go even further. The right of workers in individual enterprises to make their own decisions would have to be strictly limited because if workers in some firms prove more enterprising and successful then they may drive their less enterprising counterparts out of business. In order to 'liberate' people from the 'structural injustice' brought about by other people's choices, therefore, Young's approach would require the creation of a massive, not to mention an inegalitarian, structure of compulsion in which it will be agents of the state that 'determine the conditions under which others are compelled to act'. That such agents may be subjected to a process of democratic deliberation does not disguise the inegalitarian nature of such a process. As was shown in Chapter 3, the transfer of decision-making authority away from millions of individuals in the market and civil society centralises power in the hands of a tiny number of political representatives who will lack the knowledge to reflect the values and interests of those they are supposed to 'represent'.

THE INCENTIVE PROBLEM AND SOCIAL JUSTICE

The analysis thus far has focused on the 'knowledge problem' and how this may limit the robustness of egalitarian principles relative to the classical liberal alternative. A further set of issues that must be addressed by a robust political economy, however, relates to the importance of incentives. Rawls's theory in particular is explicit in recognising that the social framework should not place excessive 'strains of commitment' on people. The recognition that only a 'world of saints' would be willing to face excessive personal burdens may thus be seen as an endorsement of the view that 'incentives matter'. From a classical liberal perspective, however, it is a failure to take seriously the issue of providing adequate incentives that may further limit the applicability of egalitarian theories of justice.

Incentives and the Separateness of Persons

One of the most important aspects in which egalitarian ethics appear not to give sufficient weight to incentives surrounds questions of ownership, and in particular the ownership of talents and other advantages specific to particular persons. The assumption that personal talents should be considered as part of a 'common asset' the distribution of which should be decided according to the application of the 'difference principle' (Rawls) or that genetic resources should be redistributed equally following their valuation in a hypothetical insurance market (Dworkin), fails to give sufficient weight to the idea of 'self-ownership'. A similar argument may also be raised against Young's modified Millian test, which prohibits people from benefiting from the use of resources, talents and abilities if this in any way can be said to 'determine the conditions under which other people act'.

This is not, of course, the intention of egalitarians, for especially in the case of Rawls the entire purpose of his contractarian thought experiment is to overcome the inattention to the 'separateness of persons' that characterises utilitarianism. From Rawls's perspective the latter is guilty of treating people merely as means for the achievement of various 'social' ends. In their daily lives, people make personal cost versus benefit calculations all the time – when deciding to take one job over another, for example. Utilitarianism, however, extends the principle of making trade-offs within a person's life to the making of trade-offs between lives, and thus fails to respect the discreteness of individual agents. More specifically, large-scale inequalities of income are sometimes considered a 'price worth paying' in order to increase the average level of societal wealth. According to Rawls, this approach places excessive burdens on the 'worst-off' social groups and the 'difference principle' is proposed as a more just alternative compatible with a view of society as a 'cooperative venture for mutual advantage'. What Rawls does not seem to recognise, however, is that the 'difference principle' may itself place excessive burdens on people, and in particular on those who are better endowed in terms of genetics, personality and social background. Application of the difference principle implies that the attributes of the better-off are to be used merely as instruments for maximising the position of the worst off. Insofar as the better-off are to be awarded higher incomes in exchange for the use of their talents, they are only to be granted such incomes if doing so raises the position of the least advantaged class (see, for example, Nozick, 1974; Lomasky, 2005; Schmidtz, 2005).

Rawls, of course, does not conceive the issue in this way because from his perspective the distribution of talents and other endowments is 'arbitrary from a moral point of view'. Support for the 'difference principle' as a corrective to the 'natural lottery' arises from the contention that: 'It may be expedient, but it is not just that some should have less in order that others may prosper' (Rawls, 1971: 15). As Rawls continues: 'When society is conceived as a system of cooperation designed to advance the good of its members, it seems quite incredible that some citizens should be expected, on the basis of political principles, to accept lower prospects of life for the sake of others' (Rawls, 1971: 178).

Now, one may agree with Rawls that people do not 'deserve' the talents and other characteristics that they are born with and that the accidental distribution of advantages and disadvantages is neither 'just nor unjust' (Rawls, 1971: 102). It does not follow, however, that such distributions should be subject to some sort of 'corrective' process in the manner that Rawls implies. As Schmidtz (2005: 165) has argued, no human being fixes the result of the natural lottery so that 'some have less in order for others to prosper', or to 'accept lower prospects of life for the sake of others'. Thus: 'When a baby is born with a damaged spinal cord, it is not so that healthy babies may prosper. When the next baby is born needing no special care, this does not come at the first baby's expense. The natural lottery is not zero-sum' (Schmidtz, 2005: 167).

The implication of Rawls's statements, by contrast, appears to be that it might somehow be better for those who are less well endowed by the natural lottery if no one was born with the talents and abilities conducive to prosperity. If the intention was to distribute talents so that 'others may prosper', however, then one would distribute more talent to people and not less (Schmidtz, 2005: 166). The mere presence of talents and abilities in some people already raises the prospects of those who are less well endowed by generating opportunities for mutually advantageous exchange. What Rawls's theory implies is that those who find themselves in the least advantaged class should benefit twice: first from the higher standard of living in a society that may arise where there are at least some talented people who choose to use their abilities; and second from the application of the 'difference principle', which entitles them to an additional share in the relevant prosperity.

When viewed in these terms, though people may have done nothing to 'deserve' their natural endowments, to suggest that decisions concerning how they deploy such talents are also 'arbitrary from a moral point of view' is to disrespect the separateness of persons and may discourage people from developing their talents in a productive direction. In effect, the Rawlsian approach treats people's abilities as a fixed asset to be consumed according to the maximum advantage of the least well-off. As with other resources which are held in a 'common pool' or 'open access' condition, however, such an approach may fail to 'internalise externalities' and may encourage a propensity toward 'free-riding'. Why would people choose to develop their abilities, if they cannot prevent others from appropriating the benefits of their investments?

From a classical liberal perspective, talents and abilities are not equivalent to a 'manna from heaven' resource which people must decide how to consume. Rather, such abilities are what people bring to the negotiating table, and their decision to develop them is a net contribution to the social product which requires an environment of appropriate personal incentives (Schmidtz, 2005: 171–2). Insofar as Rawls is willing to encourage producers by allowing for inequalities that raise the absolute position of the least advantaged, the provision of such 'incentives' is seen as a concession to the better-off. Yet it is precisely because it treats the abilities of the better-off as part of a common pool from which they are not entitled to benefit that Rawls's approach is unlikely to encourage their full participation in what is supposed to be a cooperative social venture.[9]

Similar problems arise in the case of other accounts that conceive of personal endowments as part of a collective pool. Dworkin's proposal to compensate for the effects of bad brute luck by taxing the talented in order to secure equality of resources would, for example, seem to provide relatively little in the way of incentives for people to reveal themselves as the possessors of talents and abilities. Dworkin, unlike Rawls, does not believe that decisions to work hard or apply one's talents are 'arbitrary', but his determination to treat genetic endowments as a collective resource from which the talented must effectively 'buy back' the right to a higher income is unlikely to encourage their willing participation. This is especially so given the enormous difficulty of judging how much of a person's achievements are due to their personal choices to actively develop or discover whatever talents they may have, from those that are merely the result of innate ability. As noted earlier (p. 124) the knowledge that people have of their own talents and endowments is not 'given' to them in advance of the actions they take, but is discovered through the particular actions and choices that they pursue in their lives.

Whether one is the beneficiary of 'brute luck', therefore, cannot be separated from the 'option luck' involved in the proactive discovery of one's talents. From the perspective of classical liberalism, the reluctance of people to reveal their true level of 'resources' in such a context would not necessarily reflect a moral failure on their behalf but may stem from the fact that Dworkin's scheme treats the assets of the talented as a means for the benefit of the less able, rather than a discoverable contribution to the social product which is due recognition in its own right.

Young's modified Millian test fairs no better with respect to the provision of incentives. On Young's account the acquisition of wealth by the talented would constitute an action which 'determines the conditions under which other agents are compelled to act'. If, for example, someone was to develop entrepreneurial skills which enabled them to acquire control over a larger share of resources than the average person, then the mere exercise of these skills could be said to preclude the less talented from acquiring an equivalent position of status and authority. Control over the relevant assets would thus become subject to participatory democratic procedures. In a similar vein, if a person with athletic ability chooses to develop their sporting prowess to the fullest extent then this may constitute action which discourages the less athletic from engaging in competitive sport owing to their minimal prospects of attaining equivalent status and esteem. While it is not clear from Young's account how much redistributive action would be deemed appropriate in such contexts, what is clear is that virtually any action that people might take that secures them a relatively advantageous position would open them up to potential political interference. As a consequence, people would lack certainty about the resources they would be allowed to retain and would have little incentive to invest in activities that might distinguish themselves in any significant way.

Incentives and Ownership

The lack of incentive for individuals to contribute as producers which may result when personal assets are treated as part of a collective pool is also reflected in the manner that egalitarian theories treat the acquisition of external resources and parts of the natural world. In theories such as Dworkin's, for example, the equal shares assumption stems from the character of thought experiments which conceive of people arriving in a specific place simultaneously and having to decide how to allocate the available 'unowned' resources between the relevant parties. Classical liberalism does not challenge the view that 'equal shares' may be an appropriate assumption to make in such circumstances. What it questions is the applicability and the robustness of such a principle in most 'real-world' situations where people do not arrive simultaneously in the same place and where resources are typically already owned by people with different histories and attachments. Put simply, there will be no incentive for people to use and develop resources in a productive manner if the results of their endeavours are subsequently to be treated as part of a common asset, ripe for redistribution. As Schmidtz (2006: 152–7) has argued, when people arrive at different times and in different places, a more appropriate principle to adopt is that of 'first possession'. The latter rule gives those who are the first to use a previously 'unowned' resource the security to invest in expanding its productive potential, safe in the knowledge that they will be able to reap the benefits from doing so. Property rules of this kind induce people to discover resources, encourage productivity and may help to minimise disputes by providing a clear set of expectations.

Egalitarian theorists have tended to reject the first-possession principle on the grounds that it violates the so-called 'Lockean proviso' which states that the private appropriation of natural resources is only legitimate if the relevant appropriators leave 'enough and as good for others'. Kymlicka (1990: 115–17), for example, argues that acts of private appropriation narrow the range of options facing those who are not in a position to appropriate resources, and that people's life chances should not be determined by 'the arbitrariness of the first come first served doctrine'. In Kymlicka's view, therefore, the principle of equal shares may constitute a fairer procedure because it equalises chances to shape ones own life. At the very least, he maintains that alternative forms of ownership, including various mixes of collective and common ownership, should be considered as a viable alternative to unrestricted private appropriation. Presumably theorists such as Young would agree with this approach on the grounds that private appropriation of property may 'determine the conditions under which others are compelled to act'.

It is not, however, clear that these arguments count so decisively against the 'first come, first served' principle. On the one hand, while it is true that 'latecomers' do not receive an equal share to the beneficiaries of the first-possession rule, it is not the case that those who are unable to appropriate resources have their options narrowed in the way that Kymlicka suggests. As Schmidtz (2006: 150–57) explains, in conditions of resource scarcity the fulfilment of the Lockean proviso may require private appropriation. Disallowing private appropriation of assets and maintaining an 'open access' regime reduces people's options, because in the absence of clear ownership rights incentives to conserve or to enlarge the stock of resources are impaired owing to the capacity of others to act as 'free-riders'. In general, latecomers are much better off and have more options available to them because of the actions of those who are able to appropriate property (Schmidtz, 2006: 156). The wealth of today is due in large part to the fact that previous generations undertook the investments conducive to prosperity. It is the fact that people have security of possession that encourages them to act in ways which expand the subsequent range of options for those who are not in a position to secure initial acquisition (see also Feser, 2005: 77). If people are prevented from keeping the benefits of their efforts, then rather than seeing newcomers and immigrants as potential partners in a cooperative venture they may start to perceive such people as a predatory threat to be avoided wherever possible.

The second difficulty with arguments such as Kymlicka's is that they are open to precisely the sort of problems alleged to characterise the case for private appropriation. Specifically, proposals for mixed or semi-common ownership that Kymlicka advances may themselves require a first-possession rule if they are to be effective. The case for first possession does not assume that those who acquire property are atomised individuals devoid of social relationships. People may acquire property collectively as members of social groups and they may devise different combinations of private and communal ownership and different rules of distribution as the most appropriate way to solve the problems of resource allocation that they face. The key point is that different groups of people arrive at different points in time, and in order for any type of ownership structure to work effectively those who have developed a resource, whether individually or communally, must be able to exclude those who did not participate in the original venture (Feser, 2005: 68). People will be reluctant to expand the available supply of resources if other individuals and groups may subsequently arrive and claim a portion of their wealth. The first-possession rule, therefore, may be as important to cases of common or group ownership as it is to more individualised property structures.[10]

Of course, it might be argued that some people do not wish to benefit from an expanded stock of resources, preferring a life without significant material possessions. Seen from this perspective, the desire to exploit natural resources in order to expand production of capital and other goods may not constitute legitimate grounds to warrant appropriation of property on a first-possession basis. Two points need, however, to be noted in this context. First, the existence of material inequalities between individuals and groups that are the focus of egalitarian theory does not seem to be the real issue in such cases, because the relevant people do not value opportunities for material advancement and presumably would not object to being 'left behind' – though they may well dislike being surrounded by others with more materialistic values. Second, insofar as some people wish to maintain the existing stock of resources rather than use them to create capital, they too would benefit from the adoption of a first possession rule. The alternative would be to keep resources in an 'unowned' state. This would, however, provide no more security for conservation-minded actors than it would for anybody else, because in the absence of clear rules delimiting who owns what, those who do wish to use resources for greater material consumption would be free to engage in acts of unrestricted plunder (Stroup, 2005).

What is untenable from the perspective of institutional robustness, therefore, is not the case for 'common ownership' in the sense of a structure designed to fulfil a particular production or conservation goal, but the view that resources as a whole should be treated as the 'common assets of humanity' with all people, by mere fact of their existence, granted an equal right to a particular share. In such circumstances the very idea of ownership and the benefits associated with it ceases to have any content. As Feser (2005: 62) emphasises, it is not clear how one can be said to 'own' something if no one is in principle excluded from making a claim on it. When everyone owns a resource, then no one owns it and all of the benefits from internalising costs that ownership usually brings are lost. Irrespective of whether people are pursuing conservation or production goals, the inability to exclude others and to benefit from one's own decisions removes the incentive for people to take responsibility for their own actions. None of this is to deny that there are genuine problems surrounding what is to constitute 'first possession': do people need to use a resource in a particular way in order to claim a recognisable title, or is the mere presence of people in a certain area sufficient to meet the first-possession requirement? Rather, the point is that first-possession-type rules may provide people with greater security and incentives to take responsibility for their actions in a way that rules which assume some form of universal common ownership may not.

It should be noted in the above context that the limits of universal common ownership have increasingly been recognised by some within the egalitarian tradition itself. In his later work, Rawls in particular suggests that the application of the difference principle is not appropriate when considering relationships at the international scale (Rawls, 1999). According to Rawls, 'justice as fairness' is appropriate in situations where people 'agree to share one another's fate' (Rawls, 1971: 102). In other words, when people have deep and ongoing relationships with others then it may be possible for them to subscribe to strong moral principles governing matters of resource distribution. When the relationships between social actors are fewer and more superficial, however, then it may be to break the 'strains of commitment' to expect them to adhere to common distributive rules.[11] Rawls, therefore, is at odds with those of his followers who insist that a consistent application of egalitarian principles requires redistributive policies with a cosmopolitan and even global reach (for example, Pogge, 2002).

From the perspective of robust political economy, it is indeed implausible to maintain that differences in wealth between nations should be evaluated against a common distributive principle. In a world characterised by cultural and political diversity it may be unreasonable to require that people should be held responsible for the distributive pattern that emerges from the actions of others with whom they may have little or no personal contact, and who may exercise a different set of social and cultural priorities arising from different historical experience. Why, for example, should people in societies that have embraced norms conducive to the generation of wealth be required as a matter of justice to transfer funds to people in cultural contexts that may not them-selves be conducive to such prosperity? One may, of course, wish to encour-age giving to less prosperous parts of the world in order to relieve human suffering, but it does not follow that any specified amount of giving should be enforced as a requirement of justice. Were such a requirement to be intro-duced, there may be fewer incentives for people to rise above the average level of wealth because this would render their assets an immediate target for redis-tribution. There may, in the meantime, be little incentive for those who fall below the average level to modify cultural and political practices that discour-age wealth generation if they are to be supplied with additional resources as a matter of political right.

Insofar as common norms of justice are able to find support from people with widely differing cultural and historical backgrounds, this support will most likely be confined to largely 'negative' norms such as prohibitions against violence and theft, rather than 'positive' commitments to specific distributive outcomes. The argument here, then, is analogous to the discussion of social capital that occupied the previous chapter. When people differ in terms of culture, religion and other aspects of identity it is unlikely that they will find agreement on distributive norms. In such circumstances, in order to minimise the possibility of conflict and to encourage the development of 'bridging' relationships a 'thinner' set of moral norms is required, such as tolerance of others and a willingness to observe contracts, which can be respected by people with otherwise diverse and perhaps conflicting moral codes.

To recognise that the requirements of justice in situations where people have fewer contacts and lesser knowledge of the parties concerned will be 'thinner' is clearly of relevance when the concerns are international in scope. Crucially, however, similar considerations also apply within the context of the contemporary nation state. In most cases the relationships that people have with their countrymen in advanced societies are no more personal and affec-tive than they are with those who occupy more geographically distant parts of the world. In the highly mobile and multicultural mass societies that charac-terise most of the developed world, it is far-fetched to suggest that people who are strangers should agree to 'share the fate' of others by committing to a common set of distributive norms (Lomasky, 2005, 2007). Egalitarian critics of Rawls are thus right to highlight the inconsistency between advocating the difference principle within national boundaries while rejecting its applicabil-ity on the international stage. Where such critics err, however, is in their deter-mination to develop common norms of justice at the global level. From a classical liberal perspective a more robust way of resolving the inconsistency in the Rawlsian position is to recognise that there should be no commitment to a specific distributive outcome whether nationally or globally (see, for example, Kukathas, 2006). Attempts to enforce distributive outcomes at the macrosocietal level are likely to promote conflict and to transform potentially positive-sum relationships between relative strangers into zero- or even negative-sum games.

CONCLUSION

Egalitarian arguments constitute perhaps the most important theoretical challenge to classical liberal political economy, and in a practical sense continue to provide the most widely cited rationale for the redistributive measures undertaken by contemporary states. Notwithstanding the frequency with which these arguments are heard, it is the contention of this chapter that classical liberal institutions may be better placed to deal with the dilemmas that surround questions of social justice. A framework of minimal government sustained by the principle of 'non-interference' may facilitate a process of ethical learning between competing sets of distributive norms; it may allow individuals and communities to approach the trade-offs pertinent to issues of distributive justice in a variety of ways; and it may avoid the creation of an inegalitarian power structure in which any one actor or group of actors is able to impose adherence to a particular distributive ideal. Furthermore, such a framework may provide the incentives that are necessary to hold individuals and voluntary associations properly accountable for the distributive norms that they choose to follow. By contrast, egalitarian theories assume that knowledge of what justice requires is or can be 'given' to a single actor or group and they pay insufficient attention to the role of incentives. When compared to classical liberalism, therefore, the institutions proposed by egalitarians fail to meet the requirements of a robust political economy.

NOTES

1. Rawls claims that: 'there is no essential tie between the use of free markets and private ownership of the instruments of production' (1971: 271); that theories of justice are neutral between questions of public and individual ownership; and that 'market socialism' is a viable system. In view of the epistemic arguments examined in Chapter 2, however, and the record of socialist regimes in the twentieth century, the relevant 'general facts' must now include recognition that the use of 'free markets' is dependent on the private ownership of property. The knowledge necessary for social coordination cannot be generated effectively when there is a single owner of property (that is, state socialism). Neither can it be generated when the extent of decentralisation is determined by a superior 'public

owner' (that is, market socialism), rather than through a bottom-up process of competition between a diversity of private owners.

2. The equivalent in economic theory is the Walrasian auctioneer in the neo-classical general equilibrium model.

3. As Schmidtz (2005: 223) points out, in making the assumption that the choice of distributive principles occurs in a 'closed society', the conditions Rawls specifies behind the 'veil of ignorance' amount to a case of misinformation, since people acting in many 'real-world' situations do have the option of leaving one society in preference for another.

4. What constitutes violent oppression in this context is of course a difficult issue to define in the context of children and their interests. Whether practices such as child circumcision or the participation of children in contact sports should be prohibited within a tolerationist framework is difficult to resolve; on these problems see the debate between Barry (2001) and Kukathas (2002).

5. The most appropriate principle of justice to apply in this context would appear to be the Nozickian idea of 'justice as rectification', which requires that those who breach the non-interference principle compensate those whose domain they have transgressed; see Nozick (1974). There are, however, significant problems in applying even this notion given the difficulty – with the passage of time – of assessing how much of the relevant inequality is due to acts of theft and exploitation, and how much is due to differences in culture, choice and differential responses to market signals. For a Hayekian inspired analysis of such problems, see Tebble (2001).

6. Hayek appears confused about the logical implications that follow from this analysis. Thus, while rejecting that social justice is a meaningful goal to pursue in a context where there is no agreed standard to evaluate outcomes, he proceeds to offer support for the state provision of a minimal safety net (for example Hayek, 1982: 87). What Hayek advocates here is a more threadbare version of enforced redistribution aimed at securing those unable to earn a living in the market a basic minimum of food and shelter, as opposed to the more extensive measures envisaged by egalitarian supporters of the welfare state. Nonetheless, Hayek offers no reason to believe that there is any more basis for agreement on what this 'safety net' should consist of than there is to determine the 'justice' or 'injustice' of any particular 'gap' between the 'rich' and the 'poor' (Tebble, 2009).

    It might be argued here that Hayek's advocacy of a 'safety net' is not designed to secure 'social justice', but the more modest goal of relieving suffering – in much the same way that most people's decisions to offer aid to the victims of natural disasters such as the Asian tsunami of 2005 did not seem to be motivated by concerns over a particular 'gap' between the rich and poor, but on the desire to address an immediate human need. Hayek's advocacy of government action in this regard, rather than relying exclusively on private charitable supply, may stem from the belief that poverty relief – or disaster relief programmes – constitute a form of collective good that may be 'undersupplied' owing to the high transaction costs of organising purely voluntary contributions. In this case, Hayek's argument constitutes an efficiency and effectiveness case for government action rather than one based on a notion of justice. This argument is not inconsistent with Hayek's wider political economy, which while sceptical of most 'market failure' arguments (see Chapter 2 of this volume) does not entirely discount the possibility of genuine market failures. The question of whether 'poverty relief' should indeed be treated as a collective good is considered in Chapter 6.

7. Hayek does recognise that concepts of justice and injustice are appropriate within specific organisations operating according to a unitary goal or purpose. Within a firm, for example, if contracts lay out a particular set of procedures with respect to pay scales and the promotion of staff, but management proceeds to break these contracts or to change the arrangements on an arbitrary basis, then on Hayek's account such examples would constitute cases of injustice. His point is that the notion of distributive justice is inappropriate at the macro-societal level, because an 'open society' is not a single organisation based on the pursuit of agreed goals and purposes. Rather, it is a nexus or 'catallaxy' containing many different individuals and organisations each with their own separate purposes and standards of value. There are, for example, many different firms with different pay scales and promotion procedures which people may choose to 'exit' or 'enter' according to their particular values, trade-

offs and circumstances. Hayek's point is that the overall 'social' distribution that results from the interaction of these various actors cannot be attributed to any one actor or group and neither can it be judged against any one scale of values.

8. This is, of course, the essence of the point made by Nozick (1974) when noting that social-ist schemes of distribution, while claiming to 'empower' workers, would have to 'forbid capitalist acts between consenting adults'.

9. It should be recognised that Rawls's willingness to make this 'concession' is a relative merit of his theory and compares favourably with the more extreme egalitarianism of theorists such as Cohen (1995). According to Cohen, the recognition that people may require personal incentives if they are to act in ways which raise the standard of living amounts in effect to a form of institutionalised immorality. For Cohen, anything less than strictly equal shares is incompatible with people 'undergoing the fullest possible realisation of their natures' (Cohen, 1995: 396).

10. The hundreds of case studies of 'common property regimes' conducted by Elinor Ostrom and her colleagues suggest that while agreement on distributive norms within groups (such as performance-related pay or resource allocation lotteries) may enable them to overcome collective action problems, large-scale redistribution conducted at the national level often promotes a zero-sum or negative-sum process of between-group conflict owing to the absence of shared norms of fairness (see, for example, Ostrom, 1990, 2006).

11. For a full discussion of Rawls's views on this point, see Lomasky (2005).

PART II

Classical liberalism and the future of public policy

6. Poverty relief and public services: welfare state or minimal state?

INTRODUCTION

Part I of this book applied the principles of robust political economy to consider and rebut some of the major objections to classical liberalism arising from economics and political theory. Part II now turns to the practical implications of this analysis in three domains that have shown themselves most resistant to the classical liberal case. These are the welfare state, international development and environmental protection. The first of the chapters in Part II explores these issues in the context of the welfare state.

The relief of poverty in developed economies and the supply of 'public services' have come to be viewed as essential functions of elected governments. For critics of classical liberalism, this movement away from the principle of non-interference in civil society has been a thoroughly progressive development. Within this context, proposals to extend voluntary action and private markets are criticised on economic and moral grounds. Economists point to 'market failures' associated with collective-good dynamics and information asymmetries held to prevent the effective operation of markets in areas such as education and health care. Political theorists, meanwhile, contend that even if an efficiency-oriented case for classical liberalism can be sustained, such an approach would strain the social fabric owing to its failure to address issues of social solidarity and distributive justice.

Drawing on the principles of robust political economy this chapter tests the classical liberal alternative to the modern welfare state against its rivals. Focusing on 'knowledge problems' and incentive-compatibility issues, the analysis challenges both the economic and moral case for welfare state institutions. It first sets out the core principles which inform classical liberal views concerning appropriate arrangements with respect to poverty alleviation and the supply of education and health care. The subsequent three sections construct a defence of the classical liberal perspective against objections raised from 'market failure' economics and both communitarian and egalitarian variants of political theory.

POVERTY RELIEF AND PUBLIC SERVICES: A CLASSICAL LIBERAL VIEW

Classical Liberalism and Poverty Relief

Arguments in favour of the welfare state are often couched in terms of the need for a redistributive apparatus to reduce the incidence of poverty. Classical liberalism contends, however, that the surest way to eradicate poverty may be to maintain a framework which encourages high levels of economic growth and in the process generates better-paying forms of employment for all sections of society – a framework that may be threatened by an excessive focus on redistributive intervention by the state. While recognising that some individuals and groups may be willing to trade off the benefits of economic growth for social equity,[1] classical liberalism insists that such a trade-off does in fact exist. At the heart of this trade-off are the 'knowledge problem' and incentive compatibility issues which informed the framework of robust political economy applied in Part I.

From the perspective of classical liberalism, one of the most important functions of a competitive market is to transfer resources to those who are most likely to add value. Knowledge of which individuals or groups are in the best position to generate additional wealth is not, however, 'given' to a central agency, but emerges through the process of competition as the buying and selling decisions of many dispersed actors continually alter the distribution of capital and social positions. Resources may, of course, be obtained through chance discoveries and people may have valuable skills owing to a particular social or cultural inheritance rather than to any 'effort' exercised on their behalf. What matters, however, is that those who are better placed to add value, for whatever reason, are able to secure a greater share of resources in order that the overall standard of living may be raised. Insofar as income redistribution alters this pattern, then it may lower performance by transferring assets to economically less competent agents. This is not to imply that redistribution fails to contribute in an immediate way to the living standards of the poorest. Rather, the point is that there is a price to be paid in terms of lost opportunities for longer-term sustainable growth. The standard of living for all strata in the future is likely to be lower than it would have been in the absence of actions which reduce the current capital stock held by the successful.

Though economic growth is fundamental to poverty alleviation, this does not imply that there is no room for deliberate efforts that relieve specific instances of hardship. Even in a successful economy, people may find themselves in need of assistance owing to the loss of employment, old age, illness or disability. Classical liberalism contends, however, that a more robust way of addressing these problems may be through voluntary collective action rather than enforced programmes of tax-financed 'welfare'. Historically, one of the most important mechanisms for poverty relief was the development of mutual aid associations. 'Friendly societies', credit unions and insurance cooperatives were self-governing entities founded by the working poor and financed by small-scale contributions from the poor themselves to provide a safety net in case of hard times (Green 1993: 30). Entitlement to draw 'benefit' from a mutual aid association was derived from a contribution to a collective fund which could be drawn upon should the individual or family concerned experience misfortune. Though membership was by no means universal, the majority of low-income people were not left to 'fend for themselves' in the era before the welfare state, but relied on voluntary collective action to secure unemployment relief and provision for old age. In the context of the United Kingdom, for example, Green (1993: 87) reports that of the 12 million covered by the National Insurance Act of 1911 at least 9 million were already members of friendly societies or insurance cooperatives (see also Davies, 1997; and in the US context, Beito, 1997).

Though the potential for mutual aid constitutes an important element in the classical liberal approach to poverty alleviation, so too does a role for philanthropic endeavour. Again, the historical record suggests that many services currently supplied via tax-funded agencies have previously been performed by voluntary associations. In the context of British housing, for example, philanthropic supply by organisations such as the Peabody Trust and the Improved Industrial Dwellings Company were responsible for the provision of thousands of residential units to those on the very lowest incomes. These were joined by other organisations such as the Salvation Army and Dr Barnados which catered to the needs of children and the very poorest. Indeed, it was often innovations in the work conducted by these voluntary bodies that pioneered 'welfare' professions such as social work – long before the provision of state services (Whelan, 2008; see also Husock, 1997, in the US context).

Classical liberalism, then, questions a 'universal' system of poverty relief in favour of a welfare 'mosaic' combining variations of mutual aid and private charity alongside a framework which secures a general rise in prosperity. At the core of classical liberalism is recognition that 'solutions' to social problems are not 'given' to a single agency. In the context of welfare and poverty relief this applies with respect to the appropriate principles of distributive justice that might determine questions of absolute or relative poverty, and also the mechanisms that might best deliver any particular understanding of what such justice requires. From the standpoint of institutional robustness a critical advantage of a liberal, pluralistic system is that it would allow competing visions of distributive justice and methods of poverty relief to coexist, and would facilitate emulative learning as different models could be tested via trial and error competition. The greater the scope for alternative methods of poverty relief to be implemented, the greater the chance of discovering and disseminating the most successful principles. By their very nature, government systems of universal provision reduce the scope for experimentation and stifle the 'discovery processes' required to ascertain which 'solutions' to poverty may actually work (Husock, 1997).

A second advantage of a voluntaristic form of collective action pertains to the issue of incentives, and in particular the problem of 'moral hazard'. A system combining mutual aid with charitable supply, though not immune from such problems, may be less susceptible to them. The supply of funds from a mutual aid association would be conditional on the individual concerned having made a financial contribution to the association rather than reflecting a state-guaranteed 'right' to support. As a consequence, there would be strong incentives for people to secure employment and to build up a record of contributions in order to qualify for relief should they lose the ability to work. In the context of charitable supply, meanwhile, the absence of a state-financed guarantee would encourage recipients to find employment owing to the possibility that relief might be removed. The provision of a guaranteed minimum income by the state, by contrast, may reduce the incentive for people to participate in the world of work and commercial exchange – and especially for those who have limited earning power owing to lack of relevant skills (Schmidtz, 1998; Bergh, 2006; Shapiro, 2007).[2]

Evidence on Poverty Relief

Evidence on the effectiveness of government 'anti-poverty' programmes compared to more liberal alternatives is relatively sketchy, but there is sufficient experience to confirm that state-sponsored income redistribution is not a necessary condition for the eradication of poverty. The recent success of societies such as Hong Kong, for example, has taken place in the context of little or no income redistribution. From a position where the vast majority of the population were classified as poor in the 1950s, Hong Kong has moved to a position where income levels are comparable to those prevailing in 'developed' countries with much more extensive systems of income transfer (Cowen, 2002). Within the category of longer-established developed countries, meanwhile, poverty levels in Switzerland are not dissimilar to those found in Sweden even though the latter has a far more generous system of state-provided welfare. Government expenditures as a share of gross domestic product (GDP) in Sweden have averaged between 15 and 20 per cent higher than those in Switzerland, yet poverty levels in the respective countries are very similar (Curzon-Price, 2004: 32). France, meanwhile, spends a similar amount on income transfers as Sweden, yet experiences higher levels of poverty. Though not conclusive, these cases question whether existing welfare states constitute value for money in terms of poverty reduction.

With respect to economic growth it is difficult to ascertain the precise effect of redistribution because a significant proportion of government expenditure is not targeted directly at the poor but consists of benefits and services paid out to middle-class groups. It is also possible that certain government expenditures such as those on infrastructural provisions may have a positive effect on growth rates.[3] Nonetheless, cross-country analysis conducted by Barro (1991) confirms that high levels of non-infrastructural government spending do indeed correlate with lower levels of economic growth (see also Folster and Henrekson, 1999, 2006; Gordon and Wang, 2004). More individualised studies reveal a similar pattern. In the early 1960s, for example, Sweden had lower levels of taxation and higher levels of income inequality than the United States, but ranked in the top two or three nations in terms of per capita income (Lindbeck, 1997). In the intervening years, however, Swedish taxes have risen to be among the highest in the developed world and the income distribution has become one of the most egalitarian – but in terms of per capita income, Sweden has fallen 10–15 places in the equivalent ranking. Some recent improvements in Swedish economic performance have corresponded with an attempt, albeit limited, to reduce the rate of taxation (Lindbeck, 1997; Bergh, 2006; Johanssen, 2008).[4] Though annual differences in growth rates induced by these variations in government expenditures are small in percentage terms, the compound effect is far from trivial. As Cowen (2002: 45) has noted, if the annual growth rate of US GDP had been just 1 per cent lower in the period between 1870 and 1990, America in the 1990s would have been no better off than a country such as Mexico in the equivalent year (see also Gwartney and Lawson, 2004; Vedder, 2004).

Turning to evidence on private forms of poverty relief, the historical record reveals the diversity of responses that may arise in the context of a greater role for civil society. In nineteenth-century Britain and in the United States, mutual aid associations and friendly societies coexisted with a wide array of civil associations including church groups, temperance societies, self-help clubs and Masonic lodges, all of which, as well as providing support to those in need, placed a value on 'character-building' and socialisation into practices perceived conducive to a life free of the need for public relief (Davies, 1997; Beito, 1997, 2000). The results of these efforts, when judged against the criteria of the associations themselves, appear to have been impressive. As Davies notes, the heyday of UK mutual aid associations between 1850 and 1900 corresponded with a marked decline in crime, illegitimacy and drunkenness and a sharp increase in private saving (Davies, 1997: 60; see also Fukayama, 2001: Chapter 16). These improvements in the material and social conditions of the poor contrast favourably with social trends characteristic of the post-war welfare state. While rising crime, alcohol and drug addiction and a collapse in private saving may also reflect social trends that have little relationship to the growth of government welfare, it is difficult to maintain that these programmes have had no effect on such trends. Market-induced deindustrialisation, the relative decline in male manual labour and the increasing feminisation of work in service industries may also have contributed to these trends (see, for example, Gray, 1998). The disruptive social effects of market forces were, however, probably much more dramatic in the mid- to late nineteenth century – rapid industrialisation, the unprecedented growth of towns and the decline of agricultural and rural ways of life being far more pronounced than recent shifts wrought by 'globalisation'. Yet, far from being an era of decline in the economic and social status of the poor, this was a period of steady improvement. Though living conditions for the poorest 10 per cent were miserable by contemporary standards, this was due to the relative poverty of the day and these conditions would have been ameliorated with further economic growth (Davies, 1997; see also Hayek, 1949).

Classical Liberalism on Education and Health Care

Just as classical liberalism questions the robustness of government welfare provision, so too it challenges the view that 'public services' such as education and health care should be financed and provided by the state. Seen through this lens, there would be substantial benefits from transferring these services into the commercial market and other forms of voluntary provision.

The primary reason for such a move would be to introduce appropriate signalling mechanisms to indicate the quantity and quality of the education and health care that people desire. In the absence of price signals reflecting the relative willingness of people to purchase different bundles of services, consumers are left with no effective mechanism to indicate their preferences with respect to these goods. Accountability is also blunted when people cannot exit on an individual basis from those suppliers with whom they are dissatisfied, and where they are subject to a monopoly with the coercive power to raise revenue via taxation. From a classical liberal perspective, the voting mechanism or participation in consumer councils are poor substitutes for the capacity of people to enter and exit a range of contractual arrangements with their own money. The latter provides better incentives for people to be informed about their choices, allows for a more fine-grained expression of preferences, and offers a more immediate and direct way of holding suppliers to account. Outcomes under a classical liberal model would be unequal, but the relevant inequalities would operate to raise the overall standard of provision. Those who are wealthier, better educated and more informed are likely to secure superior services in the short term by exercising the exit option, but competition for the money of the 'marginal consumer' who exercises this freedom will over time also raise the standard and efficiency of provision even for those who lack such resources. The service models that secure greater profits are likely to be copied, thus spreading best practice to a wider group of consumers, and those that make losses can be taken over by the more successful suppliers or by those seeking to mimic them. Less-educated consumers also have the option of imitating the choices of those who are better informed by drawing on reputation devices such as brand names. Equivalent mechanisms operate far less effectively in the political process, because marginal voters – including the better-educated – have much less incentive to be informed about public policy decisions, given the miniscule chance that their personal decision to acquire more information will affect the result of an election.

In the context of education, a classical liberal model would allow the content of the curriculum and the form of provision to be decided by the choice of individual parents to enter into or exit from relationships with a diversity of suppliers. These may include conventional 'schools' providing a set curriculum on a specialist educational site. Alternatively, they may include a diversity of specialist teachers or institutes providing tuition in a particular subject from which parents would select their own customised bundle. In the latter context, education would not consist of 'schooling' in the usual sense of attendance at a specific institution, but may involve student participation in a mix of different and cross-cutting educational settings. Taking this analysis further, there is no necessity for education to be associated with the formal relationships that exist in a teacher–pupil context. On the contrary, the broader social environment may also include alternative contexts for learning that may be of equal if not more significance to the learning process. Thus, reading groups, religious associations, sports teams, newspapers and Internet-based social networks might all compete in the provision of educational opportunities, as might the potential for people to acquire skills via employment and vocational training.

In the case of health care, a laissez-faire model would see the finance and delivery of services take place in the private and voluntary sectors, whether through direct payment or participation in insurance schemes. Standard-setting and quality control would be determined through a process of competition for reputation between alternative providers. In such a model, competing accreditation agencies would replace government licensing operations to determine the qualifications necessary to engage in medical practice. Doctors, hospitals and insurance providers would compete freely for reputation and accreditation agencies would themselves compete in terms of developing a reputation for reliable advice with respect to the health care market. As well as learning from their own experience with alternative providers, consumers would also be able to learn from their fellows as news of the different experiences with various parts of the health care industry would be spread via word of mouth and increasingly in an age of internet communications, perhaps the use of online networks. The process for approving pharmaceutical products would, from this perspective, also be dealt with by reputation-based mechanisms that would induce the sellers of drugs and medical devices to protect themselves from fraud and product liability actions through the offer of appropriate product guarantees and similar trust-building devices.

Evidence on Education and Health Care

In view of the overwhelming role that governments now play in the finance and delivery of education and health services, it is difficult to offer clear-cut evidence in favour of the classical liberal alternative. There is, however, sufficient historical and contemporary experience which provides some tentative support for the analysis set out above. Evidence on the benefits of 'full privatisation' is most compelling in the case of education. Historical data confirm that prior to large-scale government involvement, literacy rates were high and access to educational opportunities was widespread. There have been numerous attempts to discredit the work of E.G. West (1994, 1970) which is most closely associated with these claims in the context of Victorian Britain, but as Tooley (1996: 31–48) has shown, when adjusting appropriately for the poverty of the Victorian era, West's case remains robust (see also Tooley, 1995). Mitch (1992), for example, found that private schools in the Victorian era were at least as effective as those sponsored by way of government subsidies, and delivered these results on two-thirds of the expenditure in state-subsidised institutions. More generally, the relatively laissez-faire educational system that prevailed in the UK prior to 1870 generated far higher rates of literacy than the highly centralised and state-driven system in France, and similar levels of literacy to those in Germany. Coulson (1999) documents equivalent evidence in the context of nineteenth-century America, where literacy rates were already high before the advent of state education.

Though the historical evidence offers support for the classical liberal position, the strongest pointers are, however, more contemporary. Coleman and Hoffer's (1987) analysis of the US educational system, for example, found that when adjusting for socio-economic status and school selection bias, private schools consistently outperformed state schools in developing students' cognitive abilities. Similarly, Chubb and Moe (1990) examined a national sample of US public and private schools and found that when adjusting for socio-economic status, private schools delivered superior results to public sector equivalents. Other studies indicate that the superior performance of private suppliers is achieved for half the cost of that witnessed in state schools.

Coulson's (2004) analysis of studies conducted in both developed and developing nations found that of 50 comparisons that could be made on criteria such as cost-effectiveness, 41 of these indicated a clear advantage for private provision (see also Wenders, 2005).

In the context of the developing world, meanwhile, a host of studies have shown a consistent pattern of the private sector yielding superior results in language skills and mathematics with lower levels of resource inputs. Thus, research in the Philippines found private schools delivering 1.2 times the level of achievement per unit of pupil expenditure than equivalent state schools, and in Thailand almost seven times the achievement per unit of input (Jimenz et al., 1991). These findings have been replicated by Tooley et al. in a massive comparative study of private and state education for low-income groups in countries including India, Nigeria and Ghana (see Tooley et al., 2005; Tooley and Dixon, 2006; Tooley et al., 2007). The results show that the majority of education for the poor in these countries is provided by the private sector, and that poor parents prefer to send their children to private schools even when 'free' state education is provided in the respective locality. With respect to quality and effectiveness, in the worst-case scenarios students fare no worse than in government equivalents, and in the majority of cases they perform considerably better even though expenditure on teacher salaries and infrastructural inputs is as much as half that in the state sector.

Turning to health care, historically there is good evidence to suggest that the absence of government provision was not an obstacle to widespread availability including to those in low-income groups. Beito (2000), for example, reports that in early twentieth-century America, annual health care was covered via friendly societies and mutual aid groups for the equivalent of a day's wage for a typical labourer. In Britain, meanwhile, Green (1985) has shown that the vast majority of the population had access to care through either the direct payment of fees, insurance and mutual aid societies, or charitable supply through the voluntary hospitals movement. Whether private medical provision resulted in a higher standard of care is difficult to judge, in part because of the need to make appropriate adjustments for the relative poverty of the day and also because of the absence of government-provided facilities against which to make direct comparisons. Nonetheless, that doctors were often the primary agents lobbying for greater government regulation of the industry via the adoption of occupational licensing laws and the introduction of compulsory price fixing boards – often against the wishes of consumer groups – is at least suggestive that state intervention was not necessarily the best mechanism for improving the quantity and quality of care (Green, 1993).

Contemporary evidence on health care provision offers only tentative pointers about the relative performance of more and less market-oriented systems because the state has come to play such a dominant role in all the major developed nations. Even in the United States where the private sector plays a relatively larger role, government-funded services such as Medicare and Medicaid, a complex system of centrally determined regulation for private medical insurance, and tax inducements favouring third-party insurance over direct payment highlight that the US in no way equates to a 'free market' model (Herzlinger, 2007; Shapiro, 2007: Chapter 3). To the extent that comparative data are available with respect to the effect of alternative funding systems, these offer little in the way of systematic trends. This difficulty stems from the fact that health 'outputs' are affected by a host of 'input' variables such as lifestyle, dietary habits and genetic variations which affect outcomes independently of the system concerned. Southern European and some East Asian societies, for example, show consistently longer life expectancy irrespective of the health system in play.

Of the few studies that examine the quality of health inputs relative to outputs, these tend to show that where health care has the potential to make a difference, privatised forms of provision perform relatively well. Singapore, for example, has probably the most market-oriented system in the world with almost 70 per cent of expenditure channelled through private health suppliers. It has life expectancy data equivalent to other Asian economies yet achieves these results for only 3.5 per cent of its GDP – lower than in equivalent Asian countries with greater state intervention and between half and a quarter less than the state-driven systems of Canada and Western Europe (Bessard, 2008: 18–19). That the United States exhibits very high levels of health expenditure as a percentage of GDP but delivers no better results in terms of life expectancy is popularly taken to imply the relative inefficiency of its 'mixed system' of private and public funding. When looking at how well US medical care deals with ill-health, however, the picture is somewhat different. Though the incidence of conditions such as prostrate cancer, breast cancer and heart disease is higher in America than in many developed nations – arguably owing to lifestyle and dietary choices – actual mortality rates for patients with these diseases are below the average for developed nations as a whole, suggesting that the quality of care in the US is relatively high (Goodman et al., 2004). With respect to efficiency, one of the few direct attempts to compare per capita costs and quality between systems also shows US health care in a more favourable light. Thus, Feacham et al. (2003) found that for a per capita cost of just $200 more per year, the large California-based provider Kaiser Permanante supplied two and half times as many paediatricians, twice as many obstetricians and gynaecologists, and three times as many cardiologists per enrolee as the British National Health Service.

The American health care system also performs better on more qualitative variables and in particular its responsiveness to patient wishes. In part this seems to reflect the willingness of market-sensitive suppliers to offer treatments which, though adding little to life expectancy, reduce pain and improve a range of quality of life indices throughout the period of ill health (Goodman et al., 2004). Where the US system fairs poorly in international comparisons, however, is with respect to inequalities in access to care. Cross-country comparisons published by organisations such as the World Health Organization (WHO) use composite indicators, many of which are heavily skewed towards 'fairness' criteria, with low scores given to those systems where there is inequality of access on the basis of income or ethnic status – irrespective of the absolute level of care available to any one group.[5] As the previous chapter argued, from a classical liberal perspective there is in fact little reason to suppose that people will agree on the extent to which equality should be traded off against other values, such as higher average standards. To some extent, therefore, the low scores given to the US system may be taken to reflect a very particular interpretation of 'fairness' by the WHO.

'MARKET-FAILURE' OBJECTIONS

The classical liberal account sketched above stresses that poverty reduction and 'public service' provision may take place within a framework of minimal government action. Both the reduction of poverty and the supply of education and health care are, however, deemed by market-failure analysis to be plagued with collective-good problems resulting in their relative 'undersupply', thus questioning the robustness of the classical liberal approach.

In the case of redistributive action to address poverty, it is argued that citizens may fail to contribute sufficiently on a voluntary basis to poverty reduction measures. No single contribution will make a significant impact on the condition of the poor overall and the benefits – such as fewer homeless people and potentially less crime – will 'spill over' for 'consumption' by people irrespective of their personal contribution. In accordance with the standard account of incentives for 'free-riding', therefore, people will not bear the personal costs of reducing poverty unless the government uses its tax raising powers to mandate contributions from others (Buchanan, 1984; Barr, 1992).

Variations on these 'external benefits' arguments are also applied in the context of education and health care. Although these may seem like private services, from the critic's perspective the benefits to individuals from being well educated or healthy are not captured solely by the individual concerned. Education in particular is said to generate positive externalities such as higher economic growth, the creation of a more engaged population, greater democratic participation and lower levels of crime – benefits which cannot be captured via personal investment decisions. Economic growth, for example, may be higher in a society where people are better educated, but the personal returns from education represented by a higher income may not reflect additional benefits – such as increases in the demand for labour stimulated by innovations and technical improvements – that education may bring about. A similar argument is often made in the context of health care where a personal decision to inoculate against disease may also reduce the potential exposure of others who do not themselves inoculate.

Owing to the expertise necessary to determine appropriate provision, asymmetric information problems are considered to impair the robustness of education and health markets (Arrow, 1963). Given the inability of relatively 'ignorant' consumers to offer differential rewards for the highest levels of service, it is suggested that markets will tend to supply relatively poor-quality products. Alternatively, given the high value that many people place on education and health care, producers may exploit their informational advantage and supply 'unnecessary' treatments or 'overpriced' services to unsuspecting clients. Either way, from a market-failure perspective there is little reason to believe that the interaction of supply and demand in these markets will result in welfare-enhancing results without government regulation and/or direct provision.

In the specific case of health care markets, where payment may take the form of insurance contracts, an additional 'market failure' may result from 'adverse selection'. If the sellers of health insurance lack the information to determine the health status of prospective clients then they may counteract the possibility of accepting too many high risks by charging higher prices – a process that squeezes out lower-risk actors who may find it difficult to secure coverage at an appropriate price. Insofar as insurers attempt to deal with such problems, their lack of detailed information on health risks may result in the supply of policies that are not adequately tailored to the needs of individual clients. People may, for example, be charged or excluded according to their membership of various group 'stereotypes' such as those pertaining to age, race or genetic profile, irrespective of whether their personal health status diverges from the relevant group characteristics (Akerlof, 2002).

A third and final 'market failure' analysis draws on 'behavioural economics' and what has come to be known as 'libertarian paternalism'. According to this perspective, the need for intervention arises not from deficiencies in individual preferences – a failure to place sufficient importance on education and health, for example (as more traditional forms of paternalism might suggest) – but from a range of cognitive and psychological biases that prevent people from achieving their own stated objectives. At issue here are 'weakness of will' and 'incomplete information' on risks that may lead people to make 'suboptimal' or 'non-rational' decisions (Sunstein and Thaler, 2003; Jolls and Sunstein, 2006). In the context of voluntary solutions to social security and poverty relief, for example, people may know that making regular contributions to a mutual aid association will secure protection against misfortune or old age but may lack the 'willpower' to sacrifice short-term consumption benefits over those accruing in the distant future. Left to their own devices, individuals may spend too much and save too little. In a health care context, meanwhile, people may be overoptimistic and underestimate the dangers associated with certain lifestyle choices or the risks of being left without insurance. Decisions over health care may also take place at a time when people are in a state of relative distress and are thus unable to make appropriately rational decisions.

From the perspective of behavioural economics governments can and should intervene in welfare-related markets in order to ensure that people make 'more rational' choices. This intervention may take the form of compulsory enrolment in private or state-run savings and social security schemes; the introduction of taxes and subsidies to discourage risky or unhealthy behaviour; and stricter regulation of choices to enter into contracts, such as those governing risk and insurance that may have long-term consequences.

Is Poverty Relief a Collective Good?

The above analyses have proven remarkably tenacious in debates on the welfare state, but from the standpoint of classical liberalism close inspection reveals significant weaknesses in each of the 'market-failure' claims. Nowhere are these weaknesses more apparent than in the notion that poverty alleviation is a collective good. An important characteristic of such goods is that no individual can make a significant difference to their supply. A personal decision to drive less frequently, for example, will not have a significant impact on the collective good of urban air quality. Irrespective of how others behave, the optimal strategy for the individual may be to carry on driving and polluting. If his or her fellow citizens are polluting, then any decision not to pollute will make no impact on the overall problem. If, on the other hand his or her fellow citizens cease to pollute, then the decision to drive and pollute will be equally indecisive. In the case of poverty relief, however, the only way to sustain this analogy is to treat poverty as a 'national' problem or a problem faced by large classes of people which cannot adequately be addressed by any one actor or group. Yet, in most cases it is far from evident that poverty should be conceived in this way. An individual decision to give money or other assistance to a particular person or family in poverty can have a decisive impact on that person's condition in a way that deciding to stop driving cannot affect urban air quality either at the micro- or at the macro-scale. If poverty alleviation measures are directed at specific individuals or targeted groups then they should not be considered as collective goods (for example Friedman, 1990).

Conceiving the issue in this vein reveals two dimensions where market-failure analysis does not meet the requirements of a robust political economy.

First, even if poverty 'as a whole' has collective-good attributes, knowledge of how to solve individual cases is not collectively held. On the contrary, it is widely dispersed among different individuals and groups, each of whom is likely to possess unique information about particular people facing poverty, including knowledge of why those concerned are in need of assistance and what, if any, measures are best tailored to address their problems. A voluntarist approach combining mutual aid, one-to-one assistance and donations to charitable bodies would enable a plurality of actors, each with specialised knowledge, to tailor their poverty alleviation efforts to specific individual contexts. Insofar as government funding deprives such individuals and voluntary bodies of resources and centralises 'welfare' in a bureaucratic apparatus, it may reduce the capacity of people with local knowledge to respond to problems where they could have a decisive effect and transfer resources to actors who may lack the knowledge to do so.

The second problem with the collective-good argument is that to treat poverty alleviation in this way actually creates collective-good dynamics of its own. Placing all poverty alleviation resources into a single 'pot' reduces the capacity for any individual voter to have direct control over the manner in which their own contribution is spent. Indeed, if poverty relief is a collective good it is difficult to see why in a democracy the institutions of the welfare state would not themselves result in an 'undersupply' of poverty alleviation. If poverty is a 'national' rather than a local or individualised problem, then there is no reason why people should be thought more likely to vote for appropriate welfare measures than they would be to give voluntarily to civil associations. Just as the decision of a single individual or group to offer voluntary aid to the poor will not make a significant impact on the problem of poverty as a whole, then so too the decision of any one person to vote for more government spending on welfare provision will be irrelevant to the actual level provided – the latter will be determined by how the rest of the electorate votes. It is possible that people may campaign for poverty reduction measures to secure private expressive benefits – such as the social approval from being seen to 'care about poverty' (Brennan and Lomasky, 1993) – but this is not a decisive argument in favour of public supply because similar benefits could be obtained by individuals advertising their own private acts of giving.

Overall, government action seems likely to reduce the robustness of institutions and to exacerbate collective-good problems because removing the 'exit' option prevents individuals from judging how their personal contributions affect outcomes. When taxpayers who fund failing programmes cannot exit with their own money, then the only form of accountability left is that of democratic voice. Yet, given the minuscule chance of affecting the result of a large-number election it is rational for voters to remain ignorant about the relative effectiveness of specific programmes. It is precisely this ignorance that may allow opportunistic behaviour to go unchecked. This opportunism may refer to those recipients who fail to take adequate measures to get themselves out of poverty. Or it may refer to the poor performance of those responsible for discharging the relevant schemes. Disincentives in controlling poor performance may apply not only with respect to employees charged with administration of welfare, but also to those who demand the necessary taxpayer funding. The pursuit of expressive benefits by those seeking social approval by demanding greater 'concern for the poor' may also perpetuate ineffective policies. If the costs of failure are not concentrated on those who demand additional funding, then the latter are likely to demand a higher level of support than may be warranted. Whereas voluntary donors pay personally for failing welfare programmes, in a collective-choice scenario the financial cost of failure is spread across the electorate as a whole. And, when the decision to reconsider support for a particular welfare programme is unlikely to affect either the future of that programme or the size of one's own contribution to it, there are few incentives to ponder alternatives (Brennan and Lomasky, 1993; see also Caplan, 2007).

Dealing with poverty by way of mutual aid or charitable donations, by contrast, enables the problem to be approached on a smaller scale and may generate a more direct connection between personal contributions and specific results, which at least to some degree circumvents collective-good dynamics. This connection is, of course, most pronounced in the context of one-to-one giving where the donor can observe directly the results of the aid on the specific individual who is the target of concern. The connection is less apparent when donations are given to charitable organisations catering to the needs of larger numbers. Even in this context, however, the capacity of a donor to exit from one charity to give to another determines the manner in which his or her own resources will be spent. From a classical liberal perspective, mutual aid and charitable provision may also provide better incentives to discourage shirking and opportunism. In the case of mutual aid and friendly societies, for example, the decision of an individual to join an association and to make contributions determines whether or not they will be eligible for subsequent benefits. With the financial sustenance of mutuals dependent on there being a pool of economically active members, the latter have stronger incentives – either through themselves, or via a management board – to ensure that successful programmes are put in place to limit dependency and fraud. In the case of charitable giving, meanwhile, the spending decisions of donors are tied to identifiable outcomes. Organisations that fail to deliver an effective programme of relief can be penalised as dissatisfied members 'exit' in favour of those demonstrating a superior record (Shapiro, 2007: Chapter 6).

Public Services and External Benefits

If collective-good arguments fail to sustain a robust political economy/
comparative institutions case for government action on poverty relief, these
arguments are equally misguided in the context of education and health care.
The claim that 'public services' will be 'underproduced' without intervention
ignores Buchanan and Stubblebine's (1962) crucial, but often neglected
distinction between policy-relevant externalities and those that are policy-
irrelevant. The former occur where the 'supply' of a positive external effect is
determined by the ability to charge for the relevant units, whereas a policy-
irrelevant externality is supplied irrespective of the capacity to exclude non-
payers. A 'landscape entrepreneur' may not, for example, invest in
constructing a public park if he or she is unable to profit by charging for access
to the grounds. The decision of a householder to provide a rose garden for his
or her personal enjoyment, on the other hand, may not be affected by the
capacity to charge onlookers for 'viewing rights'. The distinction between
policy relevance and irrelevance here depends on whether the externalities are
inframarginal. The latter refers to externalities that exist, as in the case of the
rose garden, but where interventions would not produce marginal improvements in the level of supply. Thus, if the government subsidises gardeners to
increase the production of roses, the externality is inframarginal when the
subsidy exceeds any value placed on the additional roses by passing members
of the public who may not register the existence of a few extra flowers. In
other words, the externality is inframarginal because for purely private
purposes the gardener is already taking into account (albeit unintentionally)
the interests of external beneficiaries.[6]

Buchanan and Stubblebine's analysis suggests that, owing to the social
nature of life, externalities are ubiquitous but most of them are irrelevant from
a policy perspective. Purely private decisions to adopt a rigorous skin care
regime or to attend fitness classes to maintain the interest of one's spouse may,
for example, generate positive externalities for others who appreciate the
beauty of the human form. It is unlikely, however, that a more satisfactory
level of supply could be induced by government encouraging people to spend
additional resources on their appearance. Indeed, to do so might be to transfer
resources away from what are potentially more valued uses.

From a classical liberal perspective, there is little reason to suppose that
education and health care generate policy-relevant external effects. First, it is
not clear that benefits generated by private decisions are uncompensated or
that they might not readily be internalised via private mechanisms. In the case
of education, for example, the fact that an educated person may raise the
productivity of others with whom they interact is likely to be reflected in that
person commanding a higher wage or salary than a less educated person. One

would expect profit-seeking firms to pay more for workers who raise the productivity of their co-workers. In the case of health care, meanwhile, private organisations such as firms would, in the absence of government action, have an interest in the 'public health' of their workers and thus have strong incentives to ensure that all those working for the organisation concerned have inoculations against disease (requesting inoculation certificates as a condition of employment, for example) in order to avoid productivity losses. In the case of some highly infectious diseases it may well be that the transaction costs involved in monitoring whether people have been appropriately vaccinated are too great for individual firms or private associations to undertake, but such cases are few and far between and it is not obvious that the nation state is the optimum level of hierarchy through which to internalise the relevant externality – though this cannot be ruled out as a possibility.

Second, insofar as decisions over education and health do generate uncompensated effects these seem likely to be inframarginal and thus policy-irrelevant. Given that people have private inducements to invest in basic literacy, numeracy and health care – such as the greater likelihood of finding a job – it is not clear why governmental efforts to encourage additional investment would be worthwhile. A similar analysis applies to private decisions to invest in more sophisticated training. In general, the expectation of commanding a higher wage or salary will itself be sufficient to induce the supply of any relevant spillovers, irrespective of whether these are compensated directly.

The market-failure case looks weaker still when considering the massive 'knowledge problem' that governments would face. Since inframarginal externalities are ubiquitous, it is difficult to see how government agents would know where to intervene. In the case of education, for example, positive external effects are not simply generated by formal acts of schooling but by a host of other 'educational' activities – such as private book reading, newspapers, membership of amateur musical and historical societies, on-the-job training, watching television and use of the Internet. Similarly, in the context of health care there are all manner of factors ranging from diet and exercise through to marital status that may be said to generate wider 'public health benefits'.[7] Successful intervention would require that policy-makers know which, if any, of these activities are worthy of assistance and, more importantly, the relative contribution of each activity to the external benefit concerned. The absence of profit and loss signals for those intervening, however, removes the possibility to discover the marginal contribution of any particular intervention.

As decisions over the finance and delivery of education and health care become the preserve of government agencies, consumers are also subjected to increased collective-action problems. As people lose the capacity individually to determine how much of their resources to spend on education and health and which forms of provision to support, the incentive for them to make informed choices will diminish owing to the phenomenon of rational voter ignorance. It follows that even if there are any positive external effects generated by education and health expenditure, these are unlikely to be generated by a system of government supply owing to the incentives for consumer ignorance and producer capture and inefficiency that such systems may create.

Asymmetric Information and the Welfare State

There can be no doubt that markets in education and health care are constrained by problems associated with information asymmetries. From a classical liberal perspective, however, there is little reason to suppose that government action will be more robust than a non-interventionist approach, for just as markets test rival products and production processes so too they allow different methods of managing information asymmetry and adverse selection problems to compete with each other. If the inadequacy of information creates the potential for opportunistic action then there will be competitive scope for organisations to attract custom by developing mechanisms which demonstrate a commitment not to abuse any informational advantage. In the same way that brand names, franchise operations and money-back guarantees constitute entrepreneurial innovations to overcome asymmetric information in markets such as those for used cars, so in the context of education and health care one would expect an unfettered market to generate equivalent institutional innovations. Tooley's work on private education in the developing world confirms this expectation with the emergence of small entrepreneurial 'chain schools' in even some of the poorest communities. Despite the relative 'ignorance' of consumers, the quality of the education provided in these establishments is not equivalent to that in a 'lemons market' but is typically superior to that found in the state sector (Tooley and Dixon, 2006; Tooley et al., 2007).

Markets also allow for alternative ownership models to deal with incentive compatibility issues. In retail markets, for example, consumer cooperatives have often emerged as owners of supply operations to deal with food quality and safety (Ricketts, 2000). Where consumers find themselves negotiating with suppliers in conditions of relative ignorance then it may be advantageous to form a club which owns the supply chain in order to reduce the possibility of exploitation. Whether the benefits to consumer co-ops from administering supply chains outweighs the costs, depends on the scale of the information asymmetry at hand. In the context of health care, prior to widespread government action cooperative arrangements were indeed developed by mutual associations and friendly societies in order to overcome the bargaining disadvantages facing those seeking medical care – arrangements that proved so successful in containing costs that it was the medical profession that lobbied for government regulation in these markets on the grounds of 'excessive' competition and low salaries for doctors and other health workers (Green, 1985).

It should be noted in the above context that many depictions of 'market failure' in education and health care refer to practices that should properly be seen as entrepreneurial successes in overcoming the causes of such failure. In the context of adverse selection, for example, the propensity of health insurers to charge premiums according to membership of classes such as those based on age or other group-based criteria may simply be an adaptation to the excessive cost of tailoring products to more individualised requirements. Though older people vary considerably in their state of health, elderly people or those with pre-existing conditions require, on average, larger expenditures than do other groups. Although in an 'ideal world' it may be preferable to tailor products directly to individual circumstances, from the perspective of robust political economy the information costs associated with such efforts would be massive. Faced with the potential for adverse selection it would be evidence of 'market failure' if there was no effort to charge people according to the probability of their requiring treatment (Smith, 2007: Chapter 5). This is, of course, precisely the situation under 'single-payer' systems which supply services according to government-determined criteria of 'need'.

None of the above disguises that choices in education and health markets may be difficult. Where long-term investments are involved, as is often the case in education, then the decision to switch between suppliers may be very costly. Similarly, in the context of health insurance markets, it may be that one only discovers the quality of the cover in the case of serious illness – an event which the consumer would hope occurs so infrequently that comparisons between alternatives are not desired. Consumers do, however, receive direct feedback that links their decision to opt for a particular supplier to the quality of the service they receive. Competitive forces operate, as people can transmit information to one another about their experiences, as consumers seek to learn from relatives, friends and colleagues and as suppliers compete for reputation and approval from accreditation agencies that pool information from a wider range of experiences. What matters from the standpoint of robust political economy is that although these markets are 'imperfect', they provide a context where rival models are tested competitively and where consumers and producers have incentives to reduce information asymmetries. In the consumer's case, the individual retains control over which suppliers receive his or her funds, and the decision to acquire more information before purchase is decisive in determining the service he or she actually receives. In the producer's case, meanwhile, profits can be made by devising management and organisational structures that bridge information asymmetries and secure a reputation for good conduct.

In contrast to the classical liberal model, government regulation and/or provision tends to exacerbate incentive compatibility problems, which are readily illustrated in the context of American health care. A free market in health care would allow consumers to choose between payment methods ranging from 'out-of-pocket' expenses to cover routine health costs, through to individual or employer-provided insurance. The insurance market itself would see open competition between basic plans covering catastrophic events such as the threat of life-threatening disease or disabling conditions, and more comprehensive options where a large number of routine conditions are covered via third-party payment. In the American context, however, tax incentives have encouraged reliance on employer-provided insurance which is especially prone to information asymmetries, and regulatory mandates requiring that routine procedures are covered by insurance plans have reduced competition between more and less comprehensive schemes (Herzlinger, 2007; Shapiro, 2007: Chapter 3).

Each of these interventions increases incentive compatibility problems over cost and quality control. Out-of pocket payments provide consumers with strong incentives to reduce information asymmetries because they face the up-front costs of the care they demand and can make relatively easy cost, quality and reputation comparisons between different suppliers. Tax distortions in favour of employer-provided insurance are, therefore, particularly damaging. As people come to rely on third parties to pay for their treatment, the incentive to make cost-sensitive decisions is reduced. This 'moral hazard' applies in the context of individual insurance plans, but is especially pronounced with employer-provided schemes where the cost of the policy is borne by the employer. The employee does not typically see what the relevant health care package costs – wages are lower than they otherwise might be, but employees are not directly aware of the wage they would have received were employers not to provide payment via health benefits. As a consequence, employers have relatively limited incentives to seek the best-value plans, and since the costs fall on employees as a whole, individual workers have similarly limited incentives to consider the cost of the care they demand. A reliance on insurance is probably the most desirable way of financing the treatment of catastrophic conditions, but individually purchased plans which are discouraged by the tax system give people more information and better incentives to consider the costs of care. Similarly, regulatory mandates remove the possibility for consumers to see the cost differentials between less-comprehensive (cheaper) and comprehensive (more expensive) schemes, so the balance between out-of-pocket payment and insurance is distorted in favour of the latter.

If US-style interventions in the health care industry have increased information asymmetries, then this problem is, however, even more pronounced in so called 'single-payer' systems such as the British National Health Service.

In this context both the finance and delivery of care are controlled by the state, with the price system almost entirely eliminated from the patient–supplier relationship. As a consequence, consumers have no scope to compare the costs and benefits of rival models of supply – and indeed are left in a state of almost total ignorance with respect to the costs of the treatments they receive. In the absence of any price signals acting as spontaneous constraints on consumer demand, the only source of cost and quality control is derived from professional providers who ration care according to government-determined criteria of patient 'need'. Whether there are ethical advantages to such a system in relation to a free market model is a question that will be returned to in due course, but it is mistaken to advocate a system which will reduce the availability of cost information as a solution to alleged 'market failures' that result from consumer 'ignorance'. Similarly, whether it is appropriate on ethical or egalitarian grounds to charge groups such as the elderly higher insurance premiums must remain open to question, but it is erroneous to see a system which deliberately detaches the cost of care from the person receiving it as superior on efficiency grounds.

Cognitive Bias and the Welfare State

Welfare state arrangements are not best placed to address information asymmetries and neither are they in a strong position to cope with the cognitive biases emphasised by behavioural economics. People rarely make choices on the basis of full information or perfect rationality, but it does not follow that intervention by government agents will make their decisions any more rational. On the one hand, there is no reason to suppose that administrative experts will not themselves exhibit behavioural biases – such as, for example, a tendency to overestimate the value of expert knowledge. More importantly, however, while behavioural scientists in general may have better knowledge about the biases that limit the rationality of people's choices, the specific knowledge needed to cope with particular instances of irrational conduct is not 'given' to any single group of experts (Rizzo and Whittman, 2008). On the contrary, different behavioural experts have different views on the appropriate response to particular cognitive biases. And, detailed knowledge of the reasons why people make the particular choices that they do, whether rational or otherwise, is more likely to reside with those who actually make the relevant choices.

What the above analysis implies is the need for competition between different strategies to overcome cognitive bias. An environment characterised by freedom of association and disassociation provides numerous ways in which decision-making problems of this nature may be addressed. People may, for example, join clubs and voluntary associations which exert different forms of social and peer-group pressure to steer them in one direction or another. Religious associations have, of course, long discouraged alcohol consumption and have favoured abstinence in various aspects of life. As noted earlier, many of the nineteenth-century mutual aid associations modelled themselves explicitly as 'character-building' enterprises that encouraged thrift and an independent spirit. In the contemporary world, the various reward schemes offered by health insurers to encourage personal fitness, devices such as minimum-term gym memberships, and penalty charges for early withdrawal from investment accounts are all examples of privately generated strategies to cope with 'weakness of will' and 'short-sightedness'.

The classical liberal approach, then, does not claim that people are fully rational but it does suggest that individuals are more likely to be aware of their own character traits than distant experts, however technically skilled in behavioural economics. Someone who is, for example, prone to 'weakness of will' may find it advantageous to join an organisation that instils discipline, such as the army, a martial arts or amateur boxing club – a life choice which may be entirely inappropriate for an individual who already exhibits strength of character. Of course, it may be objected that people may lack the knowledge and/or determination to avail themselves of such strategies. If people are as lacking in motivation to address their character problems as this analysis would imply, however, then there would seem no more reason to believe that the same people would vote for a government proposing to subject them to 'libertarian paternalism'.

In contrast to the flexibility of the classical liberal approach, the imposition of centrally determined mandates and taxes is chronically insensitive to individual and cultural differences. Interventions requiring compulsory health insurance or mandatory registration in savings schemes, for example, discriminate against those who prefer the flexibility of 'out-of-pocket' forms of health payment and those who have a genuine preference for present over future consumption. Unless, therefore, behavioural economics is to collapse back into more conventional forms of paternalism, not to mention authoritarianism – which claim to know what preferences people should have – then it is imperative that the chosen interventions are able to distinguish choices which result from 'weakness of will' or 'short-sightedness' and those that reflect genuine unbiased preferences. Centrally imposed regulations and taxes are, however, not well placed to identify such differences.

COMMUNITARIAN OBJECTIONS

The 'market-failure' case against classical liberalism considered above focuses on the alleged inefficiency of civil society and the market. From a communitarian perspective, however, it is the values promoted by these arrangements that are inappropriate to the nature of the issues with which the welfare state is charged. The centrality of the 'exit' principle under classical liberalism is thought to assume that all goods should be treated as commodities and to ignore the possibility that market relationships may undermine values such as reciprocity and solidarity. There are several dimensions to these arguments advanced in the specific context of the welfare state.

A frequent charge levied against classical liberalism is that the introduction of a commercial dimension into areas such as social security, education and health care replaces relationships built on professional trust, with narrow contractual principles where people are concerned primarily with their own interests rather than an 'ethic of care' towards other parties. This argument is encapsulated in the claim that markets undermine the 'public service' ethos. In contexts where information asymmetries are thought to be pronounced, profit-seeking behaviour unconstrained by an ethos of service to fellow citizens will, it is argued, result in the exploitation of those who lack the information to make appropriate choices. This is, from a communitarian perspective, but one example of the need to 'keep markets in their place' in order to maintain the basic values of other-regarding action on which markets rely, but which they do not themselves supply (Hodgson, 1998).

A second and related argument maintains that monetary exchange and the exit principle undermine social relations based on affection and fellow feeling. The bonds reflected in families and friendships would, for example, be destroyed if the parties adopted a 'cost-counting' mentality where one expected to be paid for the giving of time and gifts. The essence of such relationships is that they are long-term commitments where realisation of the good requires a more expansive understanding of oneself to include the good of those to whom one is attached. The persons to whom the good refers are not isolated individuals but people who see each other as members of a committed union. The impersonality of the exit principle found in markets is said to undermine relationships of this nature, for in contexts such as marriage and friendship it is a commitment not to exit at the first sign of dissatisfaction or stress that is the key to success (Anderson, 1990). What is required is a willingness to take the time to listen to and understand the perspective of the other person and to engage in dialogue in order to work through shared problems. From a communitarian perspective, the successful provision of social security, education and health care is similarly dependent on long-term commitments such as those between the donors and recipients of welfare, old and young, teacher and student, and doctor and patient. Seen through this lens, these common bonds of citizenship and identity will only be sustained if people are required to engage in a democratic dialogue with one another rather than being able to exit from contractual relationships in the search for a 'better deal'.

Underlying the above objections is a belief that not all goods should be considered as marketable commodities, and that when the value of a good cannot be reflected through market exchange, alternative arrangements emphasising a different set of ethical norms should be preferred. More specifically, values such as friendship, solidarity, educational enlightenment or good health are not 'use values' which can be bought or sold. The process of assigning a monetary price would be to damage the values concerned. To assign a weighting of say £50 000 to the receipt of a rounded education and say £100 000 to the maintenance of good health would be to miss the essence of what are inherently non-commodifiable goods (Sunstein, 2003: 88). Within this context, social democratic procedures are held to reflect better the values embodied in welfare, education and health care. Instead of allocating resources according to ability or willingness to pay, decisions should reflect the reasoned judgements of people about the status of the particular ideals embodied in the goods concerned. In the case of education, for example, while a market system would allow parents to exit from those schools that do not suit their taste, from a communitarian standpoint the advantage of a system of public supply is that it provides a forum where people must attempt to persuade others of the reasons underlying their particular conception of educational values. Seen in this light, a state system in which goods are provided on a universal, non-exclusive basis and where exit is prohibited encourages people to engage in a social process of reason-giving. It is precisely this process of giving reasons for one's decisions that constitutes respect for one's fellows and reinforces common bonds of citizenship (Anderson, 1990: 201–2).

Classical Liberalism and the 'Public Service Ethos'

At the core of communitarian arguments is the assumption that a classical liberal framework privileges relationships based on the pursuit of narrow self-interest. This assumption, which is central to the communitarian critique, is however false. Support for a liberal market implies that individuals and organisations should be able to enter into and exit from relationships with others as and when they see fit – but it says nothing about the substantive commitments and values that may be reflected through the relevant entry and exit decisions. Many organisations with different internal cultures and value systems coexist in markets: not-for-profits, cooperatives, mutual associations and partnerships may, for example, attempt to develop an internal ethos and service culture that differs from those in owner-managed firms and joint-stock companies. Even the latter frequently attempt to inculcate a particular set of values or organisational culture in order to secure a particular market niche. Seen in this light, there is no basis to the claim that a classical liberal alternative would undermine 'professional values' in welfare services. There are numerous walks of life where financial transactions are compatible with an 'ethic of care' towards one's clients – personal services such as those provided by lawyers being an obvious case in point. Professional associations and standard-setting bodies can and do operate in markets performing equivalent functions to franchise operations and brand-name capital with competition for reputation between different codes of conduct. There is, as a consequence, every reason to believe that demonstrating a commitment to 'public service' values would be a very significant dimension on which the providers of these services may seek to attract custom.

Far from supporting competition on professional or ethical dimensions, government provision and or regulation often acts to discourage it. Ricketts (2000), for example, has shown how regulation of the financial services industry in the UK may have accelerated the trend away from mutual ownership structures such as those formerly provided by building societies. With detailed regulation of lending now conducted by government bodies (such as the Financial Services Authority in the UK), financial institutions no longer have much reason to compete on grounds of reputation and ethos. While rates of return may have been less than those found with conventional banks, people often preferred building societies and mutuals on grounds of lower risk and the values embedded in their governance structures. With the governance of finance now centrally regulated, however, there is little reason for consumers to favour a mutual or not-for-profit bank over conventional investor-owned enterprises which tend to compete more on grounds of price. In the context of the welfare state this process of centrally induced standardisation may well have proceeded even further. Where education and health services are largely controlled by tax-financed agencies there is little or no scope for suppliers to compete on either price or ethos. In such contexts, suppliers cannot differentiate their product in terms of price or values, and neither can they receive a direct financial signal from people indicating which particular weightings of price and ethical considerations are favoured.

Classical Liberalism and Reciprocity

If a classical liberal regime is not antithetical to professional values, neither is it hostile to reciprocity. That people are at liberty to exit and enter different relationships does not preclude the development of personalised ties. While it is true that a 'cost-counting' mentality in the context of personal bonds would undermine their basis, it does not follow that the consideration of costs is or should be entirely absent, or that the liberty of people to terminate such relationships is inherently destabilising. In the context of friendship, for example, someone who is always willing to receive gifts and favours but who never offers a gift or favour is unlikely to remain one's friend in the longer term.

Where the communitarian critique may be on stronger ground is with respect to the impersonality of many market relationships. To the extent that this observation is accurate, however, it is far from obvious that the impersonality is due to monetary exchange per se. How can the relations that pertain between most people in large-scale and highly mobile societies be anything but impersonal? Values such as reciprocity can only be robust in contexts where one has a specific history with another person or group, and where one has detailed knowledge of the contribution made by a friend, neighbour or colleague. Reciprocity is a value that can be cultivated in contexts where people have specific histories with one another, but it makes little sense to speak of this value in relationships with abstract groupings such as 'citizens', 'the community' or 'society', which consist of people who are, for the most part, complete strangers (for example, Schmidtz, 2006: 91–3). How would one know which particular 'bit' of 'society' to reciprocate with, and more importantly whether the relevant actors are actually worthy of such an action when compared to other potential recipients of one's attention? Within this context, it is implausible to suggest that the welfare state is somehow the institutional embodiment of reciprocity and fellow feeling. The delivery of social security, education and health care by large, impersonal bureaucracies hardly meets the level of reciprocal intimacy found in families or between friends and colleagues. It is precisely in these more impersonal contexts of bureaucratic supply that problems of shirking, free-riding and predatory rent-seeking may emerge if competition and the scope for exit are restricted.

Though impersonality may be an inevitable feature of a mass society, the classical liberal alternative provides at least some scope for people to craft forms of provision which may develop longer-term bonds reflecting elements of reciprocity or community values at the micro-scale. In a liberal market system people may favour impersonal business contracts to secure provision for old age, health care and education, but they also have the scope to secure these services by joining mutual aid groups, friendly societies or cooperatives. While it may not be possible to generate the same intensity of feeling found in more familial settings, at the very least people have the opportunity to attach themselves to a particular set of ideals and can build a historical relationship with a distinct group of people by participating voluntarily in a form of collective responsibility. Voluntary financing is crucial to the robustness of such ventures because people must make a personal contribution in order to qualify for any benefits. This is, from a classical liberal standpoint, a profoundly socialising influence because individuals must engage directly with others and learn to take responsibility for their actions and the consequences they may have for the group as a whole. Such voluntary forms of collective endeavour may provide a context where people can develop a sense of fraternity precisely because they contribute out of choice.

It is not, therefore, the principles of freedom of association and disassociation that are more likely to 'atomise' people, but the coercive nature of a tax-financed welfare state. There is little or no opportunity to develop fraternal feelings between taxpayers and the recipients of welfare state services, most of whom are complete strangers and who have no reason to engage with one another directly (Schmidtz, 1998: 76). Far from encouraging reciprocity, such arrangements may simply encourage people to externalise responsibility for their actions onto others of whom they have little or no personal knowledge. Indeed, from the perspective of many egalitarians the delinking of individual fortunes from dependence on family background and cultural ties is one of the primary advantages of the welfare state. While it would be unfair to blame communitarians for the resulting impersonality, the latter do seem culpable in maintaining that government agencies are somehow repositories of the fraternal spirit.[8]

It is significant in the above light that the welfare states often considered successful by communitarians – and especially those of the Nordic countries – are small-scale, often culturally homogenous societies not dissimilar in character to, say, provincial towns in more diverse societies such as Britain and the United States. To some extent this homogeneity and relatively small scale may counteract the problem of impersonal supply. The only way to maintain the relevant 'community cohesion', however, in the face of the 'atomising' effect of the welfare state may be to 'keep strangers out'. Denmark has, for example, adopted some of the strictest immigration controls in Europe, and after years of pursuing a liberal immigration regime, Sweden has moved in a similar direction.[9] Elsewhere, the more generous welfare state provisions found in continental Europe have gone hand in hand with a more restrictive approach to immigration than has been the case in the United States, where welfare payments are typically lower (Miller, 1995).

Communities, Trade-offs and the Welfare State

Communitarians are correct to emphasise that social security, educational enlightenment or good health are not marketable commodities akin to say ice cream or breakfast cereal. Again, however, recognition of this truth does not discredit the case for freedom of association and market exchange as a more robust alternative to the welfare state. The case for 'privatisation' does not imply that the value of all goods can be 'measured' against a common monetary scale. Money is a medium of exchange, not a 'measure' of 'social value' in the way, for example, assumed by economists who advocate 'social cost–benefit analysis' to determine education and health expenditures. All that matters from a classical liberal perspective is that people value goods differently, and it is these differences that create the opportunities for exchange.

People may not be able to 'put a price' on 'enlightenment' or the 'value of life', but they may nonetheless disagree on how much they are willing to spend on education and health care relative to alternative uses of their resources (on this point, see Gaus, 2003). It is these differences that may give rise to market prices – the latter tending to reflect what the marginal buyer is willing to give up to secure the good concerned. Prices themselves, however, cannot be said to represent the 'total value' of a good to any particular individual or group – and there is no implication from classical liberalism that they do. In a similar vein, it should be recognised that though values such as 'good health' are not 'commodities', the means to acquire these goods are not unlimited resources which should be immune from pricing or from a competitive system where different forms of supply are subjected to the account of profit and loss.

If there is no agreement on how to value services such as education and health care then there seems no reason to suppose that a common identity can be manufactured by requiring that they are provided by a tax-financed government monopoly – albeit one subject to deliberative democratic procedures. In cosmopolitan societies such as Britain and the United States there are all manner of individual and cultural differences based on cross-cutting identities so it is difficult to see why these variations should not be played out in a pluralistic welfare system. It is the scope that a classical liberal system affords for people to act out their differences, rather than simply talking about them, that allows for innovation and which facilitates learning across identity sets as people can witness various interpretations of 'community' as expressed by different individuals and groups.

Now, communitarians are keen to emphasise that they do not favour a monolithic 'nationalised' welfare state where the content of services is determined by central bureaucracies unresponsive to local knowledge and citizens' preferences. Anderson (1990: 200–201), for example, claims that voice-based mechanisms of local democratic participation need not impose a 'bland uniformity of provision', but can provide greater possibilities for citizens to 'realise their preferences as reasoned ideals rather than as merely private tastes'. In the final analysis, however, irrespective of whether people act on 'reasoned ideals' or 'merely private tastes', a majoritarian system will reduce the scope for experimentation. If decentralisation down to 'local communities' is necessary to avoid a 'bland uniformity of provision', then there would seem to be no case against a still more radical decentralisation that allows minority individuals and groups the freedom to enter or exit from competing welfare services, and in the process to define and redefine the contours of 'community' for themselves.

EGALITARIAN OBJECTIONS

The communitarian challenge to classical liberal welfare arrangements focuses on 'community' and 'reciprocity'. From the perspective of egalitarians, however, the primary inadequacy of classical liberalism is its failure to address adequately, if at all, issues of social or distributive justice.

For those in the liberal egalitarian tradition, social justice requires that life chances should not be unduly affected by factors beyond the responsibility of the individuals concerned. In its Rawlsian variant, egalitarianism maintains that little of what individuals receive is the result of choices for which they can be held personally responsible. It is not only the distribution of natural talents and social background that are determined by the lottery of birth, but also the capacity of people to make the best of whatever assets they may have. According to this view, insofar as they are justified at all, inequalities in income may only be compatible with justice if they operate to raise the absolute position of the 'worst-off'. For Dworkin, however, egalitarian justice recognises a greater role for the choices that individuals make. 'Equality of resources' requires that people are not unduly advantaged or disadvantaged by 'brute luck' – the latter referring to factors such as physical or genetic make-up and economic inheritance over which people exercise no personal control. Justice requires that differences in income arise from the choices individuals make, and not from inequalities in their initial resource endowment.

Whichever of these views is taken, a classical liberal alternative to the welfare state would produce results that depart from distributive justice. Rawlsians, for example, question whether the focus on mutual aid and charitable giving would secure to the worst-off an income sufficient to make up for unchosen disadvantages. Since the membership of mutual associations would be drawn from the ranks of the poor, the level of protection against unemployment and security in old age might be substantially less than that afforded by the more affluent. Charitable organisations, meanwhile, may be in a position to stipulate conditions of eligibility for poverty relief – such as requirements that recipients are seeking work or conforming to some other behavioural norm. From a Rawlsian perspective, however, a minimum of income is required as a matter of distributive justice and should be provided unconditionally (Van Parjis, 1995). For Dworkin's followers, meanwhile, the voluntary nature of poverty relief in the classical liberal system would allow the beneficiaries of brute luck to refrain from transferring resources to those who are unfairly disadvantaged in the natural and social lottery (Rakowski, 1991). Seen in this light, there may be no substitute for coercive intervention and the provision of government-guaranteed welfare to secure the disadvantaged the resources they are due.

With respect to education and health care, Rawlsians view these services as 'primary social goods' that determine life chances, and maintain that the classical liberal model would fail to provide them in a manner that secures 'fair equality of opportunity'. In the case of education, for example, a free market system may result in people with similar natural talents receiving unequal levels of provision owing to differences in parental income (Brighouse, 2000). In health care markets, meanwhile, the capacity for people who may have similar congenital health risks to secure high-quality care may be affected by differing capacities to purchase health insurance (Daniels et al., 1997). Social justice requires either that the state uses its coercive powers to supply these goods universally, or alternatively while maintaining an element of competitive provision, reduces the effects of inequalities in purchasing power via redistributive taxation to fund the less fortunate.

For Dworkinians, on the other hand, access to education and health care must address unchosen inequalities, and in particular those genetic advantages and disadvantages that make some people more or less talented and susceptible to ill-health. In the case of education, a state system might be considered best placed to ensure that resources are targeted on those who lack natural abilities. Insofar as markets in education are to be permitted, participation must be equalised to take into account natural disadvantages – which may, for example, require additional resources for those lacking in talents so that they may compete on more equal terms. With respect to health care, Dworkin favours a system of state-supplied universal health insurance in order to secure access on more equal terms for the disabled and others with a genetic disposition towards serious forms of ill-health. Again, to the extent that markets in health services are to be permitted, the disadvantaged must be subsidised in order to compensate for their relevant misfortunes (Dworkin, 1993).

These egalitarian critiques are taken a stage further by the 'politics of difference'. For authors such as Young, classical liberalism neglects the manner in which civil society and the market reproduce 'structured inequalities' in status, reflected in the attitudes expressed towards groups differentiated by economic class, ethnic origin or cultural values (Young, 1990, 2000). In the case of poverty relief, for example, while mutual aid may be welcomed as a form of group solidarity, a reliance on voluntary welfare provision would be to ignore that incomes of the poorest social groups reflect their position in employment hierarchies determined by conceptions of 'merit' and 'worth' held by business managers and other dominant social interests. Similarly, charitable support for the poor will tend to reproduce the behavioural values favoured by higher-status groups who control the supply of funds. The demands of social justice, therefore, require not only a redistribution of income as favoured by liberal egalitarians, but a redistribution of social status so that those in less privileged groups may exercise greater control over the decisions that affect the conditions in which they act. From the standpoint of the politics of difference, only government funding and coordination of services has the power to undermine inequalities of income and social status. This should involve a radical democratisation of provision including special representation and affirmation of the perspectives of less privileged groups. All decisions pertaining to income distribution, education and health care should be subject to a process of collective democratic control limiting the scope for private actors to reproduce 'structured inequalities'.

Equality, Trade-offs and the Welfare State

Notwithstanding the priority that egalitarians place on distributional equity, reasonable people can and do disagree over matters of social justice. When people with different histories and cultural values interact it is questionable whether equality should in fact be accorded priority. As the previous chapter argued, rather than assuming the validity of a particular distributive ideal, robust institutional practices are those that facilitate learning and discovery about different principles and which hold people accountable for the distributive norms they opt to follow. From a classical liberal perspective, therefore, much of the egalitarian case in favour of the welfare state merely begs the question of whether there should in fact be a society-wide attempt to enforce a particular distributive norm. The absence of agreement over social justice points towards institutions that enable people to enter and exit institutions governed by different distributive principles – and this is what the mosaic of voluntary arrangements in the classical liberal model would permit.

Egalitarian ethics, then, are open to challenge, but even if one grants that they are of some merit, egalitarian support for the welfare state is puzzling on its own terms. In the unlikely event that there is agreement on a principle of social justice, people may nonetheless be unwilling to pursue such a principle at the expense of all other values that contribute to their conception of a desirable life. They may not, for example, be willing to reduce crime to a minimum because the opportunity costs in terms of less material goods, health care and education may be judged excessive. Similarly, people who support the 'difference principle' or 'equality of resources' may be unwilling to spend all of their resources on maximising the position of the worst-off or compensating unchosen disadvantages if these objectives conflict with other values such as economic growth, educational excellence and higher average standards in health services. As noted earlier in this chapter (pp. 152–4), there is a sufficient body of evidence to confirm that high levels of income redistribution do indeed reduce economic growth and hence the total number and quality of opportunities available in society at large. Similarly, state control over the finance and delivery of education and health care may lower standards of provision – including that for the poor.

Given the inevitability of such trade-offs it is plausible to assume that inequalities in education and health services may reflect trade-offs between equality and other values, so it is not clear why inequalities under the classical liberal model should necessarily be thought unjust. In the case of health care, for example, inequality may be a necessary requirement of a higher average standard because the latest techniques cannot be instantly accessible to all. The most advanced medicines and treatments may be extremely costly and it may not be possible to provide them to more than a relatively small number of patients. It is only the possibility that a small number may have initial access to such care that may allow cheaper and better methods to be spread more widely in the future (Hayek, 1960: Part 1). Within this context, one of the reasons why health care costs in the Unites States are relatively high by international standards is that the United States invests large sums in the search for and trial of new drugs and treatments which subsequently become available to the world at large for a much cheaper price (on this, see Cowen, 2006; Herzlinger, 2007).

To the extent that egalitarians recognise such trade-offs, they claim that a society based on equal respect requires that they should be considered in a public forum and manifested through the collective decisions of the welfare state. From a classical liberal perspective, however, it is not clear why this conclusion follows. People may vary in the extent that they are willing to trade off egalitarian criteria against other objectives, and knowledge about these values cannot be 'given' to a single centre charged with an appropriate allocation of resources. Under a classical liberal model inequalities in access will reflect a host of factors including individual effort, accidents of birth and cultural background, and the caprice of supply and demand. Under a more state-centric model, by contrast, those who are to benefit from any necessary inequalities in access to education and health care will have to be chosen according to criteria determined by politicians. What the argument for the welfare state amounts to, therefore, is the belief that the holders of political power should substitute their own view of the appropriate trade-offs for those reflected in the choices of millions of individuals and civil associations. There is, however, nothing egalitarian about an arrangement that concentrates the power to allocate resources in a political elite that may lack the knowledge and incentives to 'respect' the values of those it is supposed to 'represent'.

Competition, Spontaneous Order and Egalitarian Justice

Disagreements over trade-offs between egalitarian objectives and other values raise questions about the desirability of a unitary system of welfare provision. Additional challenges arise, however, even if there is agreement on the extent to which the 'difference principle' or 'equality of resources' should be the focus of concern. From the perspective of robust political economy, to recognise that people may share such abstract aims does not imply that there is agreement on how to pursue them, or that knowledge of how to achieve the desired pattern is accessible to the agencies of the welfare state.

Insofar as it is possible or desirable to achieve them, therefore, it may be that a more robust method of securing the aims of social justice would be to rely on a process of competitive experimentation. Consider the Rawlsian difference principle. As the comparison between Sweden and Switzerland illustrated earlier, some countries are able to reduce the incidence of poverty for a much smaller share of taxpayers' money than others. There are, it would seem, many unanswered questions about how to raise the position of the worst-off. Does redistribution raise the absolute standard of living for the poor? Should redistribution be conditional on behavioural changes, and should it be supplied via cash payments or the provision of 'free' services such as education and health care? Rather than assuming that answers to these questions are 'given' to the administrative arm of government, the 'basic structure of society' must facilitate the discovery and communication of 'who should give what to whom'.

No individual or group may have the knowledge to construct the society-wide pattern of resource allocation that accords with the difference principle. Individuals may, however, act on the basis of knowledge concerning resource availability, and solutions to specific instances of poverty of which only they may be aware. Is a person best placed to help the disadvantaged by starting a new enterprise and employing poorer sections of the population? Would it be better for someone to take a high-paying job and contribute part of their income to a charitable association? Does a person have an aptitude for charitable work? If charitable activity is indeed the best way for a person to help the disadvantaged, should this take the form of monetary contributions or spending time directly with the less well-off in order to provide education, advice on health care or the transmission of values conducive to prosperity? Every such attempt to answer the requirements of the difference principle at the micro-scale will affect, and will be affected by, the actions of countless distant and unknown agents informed by knowledge of their own particular circumstances. In the context of this 'division of knowledge' coordination may best be achieved by spontaneous adjustments where adaptations to decentralised actions ripple out from a multitude of decision-making nodes via word of mouth, imitation and the signals provided by the price system.[10] In conditions of complexity and dispersed knowledge there can be no 'guarantee' that the requirements of the 'difference principle' will be achieved, and neither can individuals be said to know whether their own actions contribute to the overall achievement of the principle. The problem here is compounded by the absence of a clear test of success and failure in catering to the interests of the worst-off equivalent to the profit and loss system in a context of competitive market exchange. The absence of such direct signals will slow the process through which best practice can be discovered and disseminated. Nonetheless, without a framework that allows for a process of competition and emulative learning, the prospects of 'maximising the position of the worst-off' may be even more remote.

To some extent, of course, the relevant process of discovery may be facilitated by comparing the relative efficiency of different welfare states within their particular territorial domain. Yet, in terms of institutional robustness there is little or no reason to privilege the nation state as the primary unit of experimentation. The structures of competitive federalism may, as in the case of Switzerland, allow for a more decentralised system of provision that allows for the simultaneous testing and comparison of rival welfare models, rather than relying on a central agency which may only try out single experiments on a consecutive basis. Furthermore, if the logic of the evolutionary case for decentralisation is recognised then there seems no reason why a still more radical decentralisation of decisions to individuals and voluntary associations acting through the mosaic of institutions that constitute the market and civil society might not deliver more effectively on this promise. What should be clear is that once the assumption of 'given' knowledge is abandoned there is no obvious reason why support for a universal welfare state should follow even on egalitarian grounds.

Similar arguments apply with respect to Dworkin's 'equality of resources'. Egalitarians are divided when it comes to deciding what counts as 'option luck' or 'brute luck' (Arneson, 1996). In the case of education, for example, some wish to compensate those who lack natural abilities and intelligence. Others maintain, however, that intelligent people who may require high levels of educational inputs in order to achieve personal fulfilment do not 'choose' to have 'expensive tastes', but are victims of brute luck. The difficulties of assigning the categories of brute luck and option luck are further illustrated in the context of health care. It is not obvious that it is unjust to charge higher insurance premiums to those with genetic dispositions to illness. So long as health is not wholly determined by genetic factors, the provision of price signals may provide incentives and information that encourage behavioural changes (for example, in diet) and may thus improve a person's health prospects. In this case, price signals may enable people to make better choices – and hence to enter the realm of 'option luck', whereas the absence of such financial inducements to behavioural change may reinforce the prevalence of 'bad brute luck' (Shapiro, 2007: Chapter 3). Gender differences also offer some insights into the difficulties of determining the constituents of brute luck in this regard. Women might be considered undue beneficiaries because female life expectancy is typically several years longer than that of men

(Kekes, 1997). On the other hand, since men may have benefited from patri-archal social values and tend to secure higher incomes, the provision of compensatory payments might be thought inappropriate and the 'rate of exchange' between these varieties of luck may be subject to uncertainty.

The above examples reveal a still further complexity. Put simply, if social justice is to be achieved it is necessary to compensate individuals and to not to focus on categories such as 'men', 'women', 'the poor' or 'the disabled'. The members of these 'groups' do not benefit or suffer universally from 'injustice' (Kekes, 1997). Some men are poor and some women are rich – so on egali-tarian grounds it would be an injustice not to compensate individual poor men for their lower life expectancy simply because they belong to a group that has on average a higher income. Similarly, some of the poor may be the benefi-ciaries of intelligence, good looks and a sunny disposition, while others born into wealthy families lack intelligence, are physically unattractive and suffer from depression – so it would be an injustice to take resources from the latter for the benefit of the former. In other words, to focus on a single dimension of unchosen inequality while neglecting other dimensions would be to replace one form of injustice with another. 'Equality of resources' requires that all of the unchosen factors that contribute to a person's initial endowment are assigned a value against which compensatory payments should be made.

It should be evident that given the multiple dimensions that contribute to a person's endowment the pursuit of equality would be a fiendishly complex task. This complexity is magnified when considering that the unfolding choices made by different individuals and groups continually alter the value of the resources that a person holds. Shifts in technology and the demand for particular skills will for example, alter the value of the unchosen 'talents' that different actors possess. Similarly, exposure to different educational models may reveal 'unchosen' talents that people were not previously aware they had. And, innovations in health care will alter the level of resources needed to treat genetically determined conditions. In light of this complexity, it is hard to envisage how knowledge of the factors that contribute to a person's resource endowment can be made available to a government agency charged with implementing an egalitarian social insurance plan.

Now, it might be suggested that the above argument does not count deci-sively against the welfare state, for the same reasons that this chapter chal-lenged the 'market-failure' analysis of private insurance. That private insurers are not able to tailor their products according to the personal characteristics of individual consumers, but tend to rely on group-based classifications, is not evidence of 'market failure' if the costs of customising policies are excessive. Likewise, it may be conjectured that the failure of a state-financed social insur-ance scheme to compensate perfectly for all unchosen inequalities does not count against the robustness of such a scheme when considering the difficulty of the task in hand. The intention of the argument presented here, though, has not been to suggest that it is possible, let alone desirable, to correct perfectly for unchosen inequalities. Rather, the claim is that given disagreements over what counts as 'option luck' or 'brute luck' and because the factors specific to individual circumstances are inaccessible to distant bureaucracies, the combination of one-to-one giving, philanthropy, mutual aid and the competitive supply of insurance under the classical liberal model may be better attuned to address the complexities in hand. Equality of resources will not be achieved under classical liberalism, but compelling people to finance a universal welfare state seems particularly ill-suited to the complex and ever-changing causes of 'injustice' in this regard.[11]

Oppression and the Welfare State

Even if the welfare state is unlikely to 'maximise the position of the worst-off' or to secure 'equality of resources' it might still be argued that it is better placed to undermine the 'structured inequalities' of income and cultural status that concern the 'politics of difference'. The latter argument presupposes that the relevant inequalities are in fact 'reproduced' via decentralised choices in civil society and the market. On closer analysis, however, much of the relevant inequality is not 'structured' in the manner suggested. In the case of income, for example, even some of the more pessimistic studies on social mobility in the United States confirm that while mobility between income groups is 'imperfect',[12] within a typical decade more than 50 per cent of those in the lowest category move up the income distribution – and the effects of parental income on that of descendants are effectively wiped out over two generations (Rose, 1991; Solon, 1992; see also the discussions by Choi, 1999, 2002; Reynolds, 2006: Chapter 8).

A second misreading of structural inequality in this context pertains to the issue of status and merit. Young (1990), for example, maintains that inequalities of income and status in markets reflect the merit attached to different jobs by business owners and other elite groups. While this may be true at the level of individual enterprises, the wages and other sources of income that flow to different groups are not determined by any one set of actors and neither do they reflect any particular notion of 'desert'. In a market economy incomes reflect the relative scarcity of particular talents and assets, and these values are determined by the buying and selling decisions of countless different people. The massive incomes that accrue to sports stars, pop musicians and various 'celebrities' are not determined by notions of 'desert' held by corporate bosses, and neither are the incomes of other more 'mundane' occupations. For better or worse, they reflect what people are, at the margin, willing to pay to secure the relevant services and products. While high incomes may correspond with popular notions of merit and desert, they may also flow to people who are not considered particularly meritorious – but who happen to benefit from a shift in demand and supply or a particular social fad. Conversely, many groups that are often held in high esteem by some sections of the public – such as health care workers – may not receive a correspondingly high level of income. What matters from a classical liberal standpoint is that there is no one standard against which the fortunes of individuals can be judged or ranked. Beyond those with whom people are intimately familiar, they may not be in a position to judge on the 'just deserts' of others.

Classical liberalism, then, cannot secure equality of status, but the dispersal of decision-making authority to millions of individuals and organisations reduces the power of some to judge on the merits of others – and to a greater extent than would be possible under Young's 'group-differentiated democracy'. The latter presupposes that there are in fact 'group-based' perspectives that represent 'working-class' interests or those of other groups such as women and cultural minorities. In the absence of unity within the relevant 'groups', however, democratic representation of the 'disadvantaged' and the power to block socio-economic changes that affect their standing would introduce a new hierarchy that privileges political actors charged with defining what the 'group' perspective is supposed to be.

Consider the question of how to respond to the changes in the distribution of income and status that have been ongoing in many developed nations. It is widely accepted that rising income inequality has followed upward shifts in the demand for jobs requiring high levels of human capital-raising differentials between low- and higher-skilled employment. The combination of increased demand for high-skilled jobs and increasing female employment may further be accentuating inequalities owing to a disproportionate growth in the number of dual-earner households at the upper end of the income distribution. These shifts are exacerbated by technological and social changes displacing traditional 'male' manual jobs with service industries that employ higher proportions of women.[13] Within this context, what does a 'working-class' or 'female' perspective consist of? Does 'working class' refer to those who lack natural talents and who may see a diminution of their relative income and social standing owing to these changes? Should it include poor people who may be willing to tolerate a decline in relative income or status in exchange for a higher absolute income? Does 'working class' refer to those currently on low incomes but who have the ability to seize the now increased opportunities to move into higher-paying jobs – and who may not wish to see the potential gains taxed away? Should it refer to those in male-dominated manual professions or encompass those in the more female-oriented service industries? Will the 'female' perspective reflect those who wish to see equal employment status with men, or will it include those who prefer not to work but who may witness a decline in non-paid sources of esteem owing to shifting cultural attitudes concerning the 'appropriate' role of women? One could, of course, list numerous other dimensions on which there may be differences within the respective 'groups'[14] over not only the division of labour and income, but also the allocation of resources on health care, education or other 'primary social goods'.

In light of the above questions, the central coordination of income and social investments proposed in Young's 'group-differentiated welfare state' seems totally out of place with the complexities at hand. Relocating decisions away from markets and civil society elevates the status of politicians in deciding who is to count as 'disadvantaged' and what they are to require. Similarly, institutionalising a majoritarian form of decision-making seems unlikely to 'liberate' minorities who may wish to act in ways contrary to those favoured by the majority either in society at large, or with respect to their designated 'group'. Seen through this lens, the greatest source of 'disadvantage' may be the assumption that needs and interests must be centrally determined by democratic 'group representatives' rather than allowing people at all levels of society to define their own needs and interests by entering and exiting relationships with a mix of commercial and civil associations.

CONCLUSION

Rhetoric over the importance of low taxes and the need to inject competitive discipline into 'public services' aside, government funding and supply continues to dominate the fields of poverty relief, education and health care across most developed countries. The resilience of the welfare state in this regard is perhaps best explained by the unfamiliarity of electorates – most of whom have never experienced the non-governmental supply of welfare services – with the mechanisms through which a classical liberal model might operate. The analysis presented in this chapter suggests that the political strength of the welfare state cannot be explained by the robustness of the intellectual arguments cited in its defence. Though some of the points advanced by 'market-failure' theories have merit, they are of limited relevance when set against a refusal to offer coherent explanations of why welfare state institutions are not subject to similar if not more serious sources of 'failure'. Communitarian and egalitarian arguments, meanwhile, continue to ignore the requirements of a robust political economy. They assume that the contents of community and social justice can be placed at the disposal of welfare state institutions, with little or no attempt to explain how this knowledge can be achieved and how the mechanisms proposed can deliver the desired objectives.

NOTES

1. For a recent example of the view that while equality may not necessarily deliver in terms of increasing prosperity it tends to promote other aspects of a good society, such as lower crime, better mental health and greater happiness, see Wilkinson and Pickett (2009). For a point by point critique of the evidence on which this view draws and for an argument that there is little if any correlation between equality and these variables see Snowdon (2010).

2. For a detailed analysis of the disincentive effects of government welfare in the context of the Swedish welfare state, see Bergh (2006).

3. This is not to imply that infrastructure can only be provided by government action – there are many mechanisms that can allow for effective provision via private voluntary action; see, for example, Beito (2000), Klein (2002) and Arne (2002).

4. Bergh (2006) offers a detailed critique of the argument advanced by Lindert (2004) that the Swedish welfare state is in many respects a 'free lunch'.

5. On the WHO analysis of health care systems over 60 per cent of the points awarded are for egalitarian criteria such as 'financial fairness'. The latter awards higher scores to systems where the poor do not have to spend a higher percentage of their income on health care costs, relative to the rich. Such criteria are bound to discriminate against any market-driven system and to bias the results in favour of government-funded or heavily redistributive schemes, since it is almost inevitable that in a market system those on low incomes will pay a higher percentage of their overall income on essentials such as health care (and also food and housing) than will those who have a higher disposable income. This does not, however, say anything about the actual quality of the care that those on low incomes receive. On the WHO fairness criteria a health system with extensive inequality of access, but where everyone has access to good care, would rate lower than a system in which the overall standard of care was poor, but where the gap between the quality of that received by the rich and poor was comparatively small. For an analysis of this and other biases in the WHO data, see Whittman (2006).

6. The best way of conceiving this issue may be as follows. Suppose a person living in an isolated cottage spends a great deal of time and effort creating a beautiful garden for their personal enjoyment. They do so with no regard whatsoever to any wider public interest, because there is no public presence in this location. Suppose, then, that a group of ramblers discovers a new route that passes by the cottage and they derive pleasure from observing the garden. The gardener's decisions do not suddenly become 'suboptimal' because he or she has not been able to charge the ramblers for the pleasure of witnessing the garden. In this case, how could a subsidy to encourage additional provision 'improve' the allocation of resources? If a government subsidy was introduced, would the ramblers notice or value, say, an extra row in the herbaceous border?

7. For a discussion of evidence on the contribution of marriage to 'happiness and health', see for example Ormerod and Johns (2007).

8. For an interesting description of the asocial, 'hyper-individualism' that welfare state institutions may generate, see Tragardh's (1990) account of the cultural effects of the Swedish welfare system. In this paper, Tragardh notes that the provision of professionalized services in such realms as child care, education and care of the elderly has effectively 'liberated' the individual from the ties of family and local community that were previously the primary sources of social support. Tragardh appears to view this as a positive set of developments, but it is hard to see how such a view could be endorsed on communitarian grounds. Bergh (2006) provides an analysis of the disincentive effects brought about by the Swedish welfare system; see also Johanssen (2008).

9. For more on this relationship, see Tebble (2006). It should be noted that societies which have historically been relatively homogenous from an ethnic or cultural point of view may be able to resist the potentially fracturing effects of immigration for longer than those societies which have always been more internally heterogenous. In the former instance there are likely to be much stronger pressures on immigrants to conform to prevailing community norms than in societies which are relatively lacking in a sense of common identity. The latter

phenomenon may well explain why a society such as Sweden has been able to absorb quite a high number of migrants without – until relatively recently – straining the sense of common identity.

10. Consider in this light the comparative response of bureaucratic agencies and private actors to the aftermath of Hurricane Katrina in the United States. The victims of this disaster were clearly among the 'worst-off' social groups and yet a web of bureaucratic procedures and controls by organisations such as the Federal Emergency Management Agency (FEMA) prevented a response properly attuned to the situation on the ground. By contrast, private agents such as Walmart – the supermarket chain – and various local churches were supplying water and other essentials to people in New Orleans within hours. For a discussion of these events, see Sobel and Leeson (2007).

11. In other words, the effects of 'luck' cannot be removed by appropriately tailored policies, if for no other reason that in the absence of the knowledge necessary to determine what should be compensated and how much, many individuals will find themselves in the 'unlucky' position of living under a regime which, from their point of view, compensates for the 'wrong kind of luck'.

12. 'Perfect' mobility would be achieved if the chance of those at the bottom of the income distribution rising to the top was equal to the chance of those at the top, falling to the bottom. The absence of 'perfect mobility', it should be emphasised, is not necessarily evidence of 'injustice' – even on egalitarian grounds – because at least some of those at the higher end of the income scale may suffer from various dimensions of 'bad brute luck' for which inherited wealth might constitute 'compensation'.

13. For a detailed discussion of these trends, see Deere and Welch (2002).

14. Consider, for example, the effect of immigration. Economic analysis of the recent wave of immigration into the United States from Mexico and Latin America confirms that this has been one of the major factors behind increases in income inequality – with the influx of numerous low-skilled workers depressing wage growth at the lower end of the US income distribution. The increase of inequality within the US, however, has been matched by a decrease in intercountry inequality between workers. Those who have moved from Mexico to the United States are receiving higher pay and better conditions than when they were at 'home', thus reducing the size of the 'gap' between themselves and higher earners both in Mexico and in the United States. In this instance, who is to decide the boundaries of the 'group perspective' for the 'low-paid'? Is it to represent the interests of 'native-born' low-wage workers who may oppose immigration, or is to include potential immigrants who may have most to gain from a more liberal immigration regime?

7. Institutions and international development: global governance or the minimal state?

INTRODUCTION

Recent discussions concerning classical liberalism have been dominated by competing approaches to international development. At issue have been the questions of which institutions are more likely to promote progress in the developing world, and what kind of responses are required from the already developed nations to bring these institutions about. While it is fairly well accepted that an expansion of international trade supported by domestic institutions hospitable to markets is essential, the 'development' literature maintains that such institutions cannot function effectively without widespread government action and the creation of new 'governance' structures at the global scale. On the one hand, it is argued that 'market failures' that block potentially successful paths out of poverty require concerted government intervention at both the national and at the international scale. On the other hand, it is maintained that a laissez-faire approach would destroy communitarian relationships and perpetuate inequalities of income and well-being that are fundamentally at odds with social justice.

This chapter sets out to test the classical liberal analysis of development issues and those of its rivals against the principles of robust political economy that have run throughout this book. It uses theory and evidence to argue that the institutions of private property, open markets and a limited government are a necessary condition for economic and social progress. The process through which these institutions may arise must however be sensitive to the 'knowledge problems' and incentive-based constraints that lie at the core of the robust political economy framework. For classical liberals, there are grounds to be sceptical of attempts to promote institutional change through the creation of a global governance apparatus. Global structures are unlikely to have access to sufficient knowledge and/or the appropriate incentives to implement effective programmes of institutional change. The latter are more likely to arise as an unintended consequence of an evolutionary environment that facilitates institutional competition. The next section of the chapter outlines the specific elements of the classical liberal approach in this regard. The subsequent three sections address potential criticisms that may arise on both economic and moral grounds.

ROBUST POLITICAL ECONOMY, INSTITUTIONS AND DEVELOPMENT: A CLASSICAL LIBERAL VIEW

Why Institutions Matter

Central to the framework of robust political economy is recognition that institutions matter (Boettke et al., 2005). 'Institutions' are the 'rules of the game' that structure the interactions of social actors (North, 1990). These include 'formal' rules pertaining to property rights and the legal security of these rights. Formal rules are crucial because these 'hard' constraints determine the scope which individuals and organisations have to engage in the economic and technological innovations central to the developmental process. Although a necessary condition for economic development, however, such rules are unlikely to deliver if the informal or 'soft' norms of cultural interaction which define the boundaries of socially acceptable conduct discourage economic and technological change. The 'ideal' environment for development, therefore, is one where the hard institutional structure provides scope for economic and technological innovation and where this is reinforced by cultural norms that also embody behavioural traits conducive to growth (North, 1990; Eggertsson, 2005).

Though it seems a trite observation, the recognition that 'institutions matter' is a relatively recent phenomenon in the mainstream literature of 'development economics'. For many years, the dominant neo-classical tradition has downplayed, if it is has not disregarded entirely, the significance of institutional factors. Equilibrium models, in particular, depict economic development as a function of exogenously determined variables such as the availability of capital, access to natural resources, the supply of labour and technology – all of which are held to determine an equilibrium level of economic output (Solow, 1956; Swan, 1956). Although more recent attempts have been made to 'endogenise' the process of growth by focusing on factors such as investment in education and the quality of 'human capital' (for example, Romer, 1994), these models say relatively little about the fundamental question of why some countries are rich and others poor. They do not, for example, explain how it is that some countries are able to accumulate capital more effectively than others, and why some countries utilise available technologies and human capital effectively while others fail to do so.

Institutions and Entrepreneurship

From the standpoint of robust political economy, by contrast, institutions determine whether a society is able to overcome the knowledge problems and incentive-based constraints that characterise the human condition. At issue is how institutions channel the entrepreneurial actions of individuals and organisations. Entrepreneurship is critical because development is largely a product of people discovering and implementing new and better ways of doing things. Seen in this light, equilibrium models are unsuited to understanding the developmental process because they depict the behaviour of economic agents as little more than that of calculating machines responding to a 'given' set of cost and benefit constraints. Human action, however, takes place in a world of uncertainty and imperfect knowledge where the 'data' concerning the relevant costs and benefits are never 'given', but must be continually created through a process of evolutionary growth.

For classical liberalism, private property provides a more robust context for economic evolution because it secures a protected domain where people may experiment in pursuit of their personal plans without requiring the permission of large numbers of other agents. Private property rights tend to expand the scope for entrepreneurial action, and as a consequence increase the possibility that previously unknown solutions to socio-economic problems may be created and spread by a process of emulation (Hayek, 1960; Buchanan and Vanberg, 2002). Competition between property owners is fundamental because it is the capacity to enter markets and to challenge established ways of doing things that alerts social actors to alternative problem solutions. In a market environment of secure property rights the feedback derived from the profit and loss account also facilitates coordination at the macro-societal level as the structure of relative prices emergent from trial and error competition enables people to adapt their production and consumption decisions to evolving shifts in the pattern of supply and demand. Furthermore, the existence of secure property rights tends to direct entrepreneurial endeavour towards positive- rather than zero-sum interactions. When transactions are voluntary they will not take place unless all of the relevant parties expect to benefit *ex ante*. Property rights, therefore, provide incentives for agents to use resources to benefit their fellows by ensuring that they are rewarded for actions which add value and are penalised for those that do not (Buchanan, 1986).

Institutions and Uncertainty

Owing to the imperfect and dispersed nature of knowledge, decision-making always takes place under uncertainty, but from the perspective of robust political economy the extent of this uncertainty is affected by the institutional context of choice. For classical liberalism, private property institutions are more robust because they enable people to cope with uncertainty by reducing the prospect of systemic error. Compared to regimes where decisions are taken at the centre, the dispersal of ownership in a market order tends to confine the effects of any errors to a relatively smaller sphere and provides decision-makers with greater scope to respond to changing circumstances as they face them. Although uncertainty cannot be eradicated, the existence of a 'hard' environment characterised by secure property rights, a stable monetary system and 'rule of law' procedures reduces the range of uncertainty that decision-makers face. Where property rights are insecure, where the value of money is unstable and where rules pertaining to the acquisition and transfer of property are subject to constant and arbitrary shifts, then additional elements of uncertainty are injected into the decision-making environment (Boettke et al., 2005). Actors are unsure what scope they have to take autonomous decisions, and the extent to which they will face the costs and benefits of decisions that they do actually take.

If stability in the 'hard' or formal institutional framework is a prerequisite for development then so too is stability in the informal cultural norms that govern perceptions of acceptable and unacceptable behaviour. Just as secure property rights reduce uncertainty by providing people with clear expectations about the decision-making environment, so stability in cultural norms also smoothes social coordination. Adherence to informal norms, including modes of speech, dress and ways of doing business, reduces transaction costs by enabling people to go about the process of making exchanges without having constantly to re-establish norms that facilitate mutually beneficial interaction (Pejovich, 2003; Eggertsson, 2005).

To recognise that a stable framework is necessary for social progress is not, however, to imply that institutions should be immune from criticism and change. Given imperfect knowledge it is always likely that new and better ways of structuring institutions can be found (Hayek, 1960; Harper, 2003). What matters is that any changes should be subject to trial and error evolution. It is precisely because of the need for institutional flexibility that from a classical liberal standpoint, the coordinating function of 'hard' law should be limited to the maintenance of general 'rules of conduct' via dispute resolution and the enforcement of contracts and property rights. Because changes in formal law require the consent of potentially large numbers of social actors they are often subject to severe collective action problems and are less open to competitive testing, so the process of institutional change may lack the desired flexibility. The greater the extent to which social coordination is achieved through formal commands and regulations, the less scope there will be for decentralised evolution. Seen in this context, one of the great advantages of a classical liberal framework is that it may allow relatively more scope for people to coordinate on the basis of the 'soft' institutional habits that may emerge from a 'spontaneous ordering' process of decentralised trial and error. Cultural conventions and habits are typically enforced through reputation mechanisms and ostracism rather than direct coercion. Those who feel strongly enough about the need to challenge a rule and who may be willing to face social opprobrium can 'break' the relevant convention without needing legal approval. If successful, they may provide role models and experiments in living that may then be copied and absorbed into the wider cultural fabric (Hayek, 1960; Harper, 2003; Pejovich, 2003; Eggertsson, 2005).

Competition: Domestic and International

For classical liberalism, it follows that the role of government in the domestic arena should, wherever possible, be confined to the supervision of a legal framework that protects property rights and secures an environment in which market processes and other 'spontaneous orders' may unfold. This does not necessarily rule out the possibility of government involvement in the supply of collective goods such as transport infrastructure, but it does require that sufficient scope is provided for private forms of supply to evolve as and when it becomes possible for them to do so. Moreover, to the extent that there is government involvement in production this should be conducted on a decentralised basis that allows for territorial competition between different governmental units. Interjurisdictional competition may increase the scope for experimentation in the supply of collective goods and may enable people to exit and enter different territories according to the most favourable bundle of services relative to taxes paid (Harper, 2003).

If domestic competition is a prerequisite of economic progress, then so too can competition in the international arena extend the benefits from domestically market-oriented policies. The latter principle applies to the free movement of goods, services and capital, but also to the free movement of labour. The competitive entry of overseas producers into domestic markets enables consumers to gain access to the lowest-cost forms of production and simultaneously ensures that domestic capital is reallocated towards those sectors where it possesses a genuine comparative advantage. In addition, the free movement of labour and capital enables both individuals and enterprises to exit from regimes which impose excessive regulatory or redistributive burdens, and from social norms and conventions inimical to economic progress (Bauer, 1993; Sally, 1998, 2008).

The resultant gains, it must be emphasised, go well beyond those depicted in the so-called 'static' case by neo-classical economists. Though competition tends toward the most efficient use of resources, it also facilitates a wider process of entrepreneurial innovation in which new knowledge of potentially profitable factor combinations and ideas about what constitutes a productive 'resource' is continually created. The benefits of free trade, therefore, extend entrepreneurial discovery to the international dimension by exposing producers and consumers to previously unforeseen opportunities. Crucially, this includes not only exposure to new products, production processes and modes of organisation, but also increased exposure to people who exhibit different tastes, social norms and cultural conventions. For classical liberals, therefore, free trade is as much a process of cultural interchange as it is one of commercial exchange. Protectionist barriers to competition not only act as impediments to economic progress, but also stultify the process of cross-cultural learning which may alert people to new and potentially better modes of life (Bauer, 1993; Sally, 1998, 2008).

Evidence on Institutions and Development

The developmental advantages of a minimal-state, classical liberal framework find support from a variety of historical and contemporary sources. Although no states have completely adhered to classical liberal principles in domestic and international policy, there is a robust body of evidence which suggests that those forms of government that have come closer to the classical liberal ideal have the most impressive records with respect to economic development.

Historically, economic development has occurred in those parts of the world where political authority has been relatively fractured and where institutional competition has ensured the maintenance of a large private sphere in which innovation has been able to flower. Thus, the emergence of the Italian city states of the Renaissance and the rise of the Northern Netherlands in the seventeenth century were accompanied by a legal framework that secured property rights and facilitated the accumulation of capital (Acemolgu et al., 2000).

The significance of territorial and institutional competition is further emphasised in the work of Weingast (1995), who suggests that over the last 300 years the nations that have led the way in terms of economic growth have been characterised by a form of political economy conforming to the principles of 'market-preserving federalism'. The booming Dutch republic in the early seventeenth century was distinctive on the European continent for its decentralised political system, secure property rights and religious freedom. In eighteenth- and nineteenth-century England, meanwhile, although there was no formal constitution to enshrine territorial competition, prior to and during the industrial revolution entrepreneurs who found the regulatory regime in Southern England stifling could move to the North where the regulatory environment was more supportive (Weingast, 1995; Eggertsson, 2005). In Britain as a whole, the industrial revolution was preceded by the creation of legal and institutional conditions that secured greater protection of property rights and facilitated the free flow of capital across different lines of business to a much greater extent than was possible in most of continental Europe. This framework itself emerged from a fracturing of the political structure that led to limits on the powers exercised by centralised government (North and Weingast, 1989; Weingast, 1997). In the cases of the Netherlands and Britain, access to emerging profits from Atlantic trade facilitated the rise of a large merchant class which, faced with a relatively weak monarchy, exerted pressure in favour of institutions that facilitated private enterprise.

Elsewhere, the massive growth of the United States of America corresponded with a formal constitution that put few restraints on private property, emphasised reliance on market forces as the primary coordinating procedure and decentralised political power through the creation of territorial competition. Although the United States pursued an external policy that was often highly protectionist, the existence of strong market-oriented institutions within the territorial borders of the Union combined with a decentralised system of political administration created an enormous internal zone in which the free movement of goods, labour and capital enabled gains from trade to be realised across a massive territorial area (Rosenberg and Birdzell, 1986). More recently, the rise of Southern China since the 1970s took place against a backdrop where subnational governments had achieved considerable decision-making autonomy from Beijing following the chaos wrought by the 'Great Leap Forward' and the 'Cultural Revolution'. Local officials in the South were able to use their subsequent bargaining power to push for liberalising measures first in agriculture and then in manufacturing, and these were subsequently copied and diffused (Quian, 2000).

With respect to more systematic evidence on economic performance, cross-country comparisons of 'economic freedom' with growth rates offer further support for the view that a market-friendly institutional environment is strongly correlated with overall levels of growth. Although there are difficulties in attempting to measure the components of these 'economic freedom indices' and in assigning relative weightings to the elements involved[1] (for a discussion see Harper, 2003), the consistency of the results is sufficient to offer more than tentative confirmation that a relatively open economic environment and strong protection of property rights are essential prerequisites of economic progress. Haan and Sturm (2000), for example, find that measures of economic freedom are strongly correlated with higher economic growth, while Torstensson (1994) provides empirical support for the view that insecure property rights reduce prosperity. Svensson (1998) uses cross-country regression analysis to show that insecure property rights adversely affect growth when security of property is measured against indices of corruption and uncertainty. In a cross-country study of 82 states covering the period 1980–95, meanwhile, Gwartney et al. (1999) find that an institutional environment that supports economic freedom is the key factor explaining variations in the rate of growth (see also King and Levine, 1993; Gwartney et al., 2006; Dawson, 2007). The direction of causality is also very marked, with increases in measures of economic freedom generating higher levels of subsequent economic growth – but with increases in growth rates not necessarily leading to increases in the economic freedom indices (Easton and Walker, 1997; De Haan and Sierman, 1998; see also Dawson, 2003).

By contrast, alternative explanations of economic development which rely on factors such as climate, geography and natural resources, or the extent of participation in international trade networks, find little in the way of empirical support. Rodrik et al. (2002), for example, conclude that geography, resources and trade have a relatively minimal impact on incomes, whereas institutional factors such as the presence of secure property rights have a very strong impact. That participation in international trade networks appears to be a relatively minor factor in promoting growth does not, it must be emphasised, undermine the classical liberal view concerning the importance of free trade. From a classical liberal perspective, strong domestic institutions – and secure property rights in particular – are essential prerequisites of progress without which trade will provide at most marginal benefits.[2] The classical liberal position is not that international trade is the 'engine of growth' per se, but that participation in international markets offers an extension of the benefits derived from domestic market-oriented policies – an extension which is particularly important for smaller countries that have very limited scope for internal trade and the attendant division of labour.

That a domestic environment which emphasises competition and security of property is the key ingredient to economic development is confirmed by more in-depth qualitative studies of individual countries and their political and institutional trajectory. In a study of 21 countries covering the period 1950–85, Lal and Myint (1996) found that while few of these could be described as 'pure' market economies, those that instituted domestic reforms which increased competition, restrained pressures for large-scale income redistribution and secured property rights saw the highest savings ratios and witnessed the best returns in terms of economic growth.

Development and the Path to Classical Liberalism

If it is relatively clear which institutions facilitate economic development, it is much less clear what sort of measures might be necessary to bring them about. This is especially so because in many cases the most successful policies and institutions that emerged historically to protect property rights and to secure a competitive market order did not arise as a deliberate consequence of agents seeking to pursue this particular goal. On the contrary, they often arose as an accidental by-product of power struggles between rival factions who were unaware of the systemic consequences emergent from the legal rules and institutions subsequently put in place (Weingast, 1995).

That successful institutions often arise in spite of the ignorance of most social actors, and that successful accidents tend to have occurred where power structures have been fractured, suggests the epistemological and incentive-based constraints that inform the robust political economy case for private property and open markets may be as relevant to the question of how these institutions arise. It is in this context that classical liberalism is sceptical of attempts to use external governance structures and programmes of international 'development assistance' to 'speed up' the process of institutional change. While the characteristics of development friendly institutions may be known in general outline, external agents are unlikely to have sufficient knowledge to implement a specific programme with respect to both the 'hard' institutional environment of property rights and the 'softer' institutional setting of cultural norms. Though a movement towards private property in general may be desirable, it does not follow that the particular form that this institution takes or the way it should evolve must replicate the legal structure found in existing developed nations. While individualistic models of property ownership may have evolved successfully in 'the West', it is also possible that alternative forms of private ownership centred around familial or tribal or communal groups may provide the best route towards the establishment of a market economy in contexts where individualistic values are culturally alien. Indeed, as the example of many Native American groups demonstrates, attempts to introduce Western forms of ownership too rapidly may retard development by breaking down indigenous models of social organisation which, though not hostile to the idea of property ownership per se, do not always recognise individualised forms of property (for example, Anderson et al., 2006).

In addition to these 'knowledge problems' external action may also suffer from the incentive-based constraints analysed by the Virginia school of public choice. When development aid is provided by way of enforced tax contributions, citizens in donor nations may face severe principal versus agent and collective-action problems in ensuring that the resources concerned are spent in ways that achieve development objectives. The supply of external assistance, moreover, may create a 'moral hazard' *within* the recipient nations. If such nations know that they will receive a constant stream of externally generated finance, they may have little internal incentive to engage in the potentially painful process of institutional reform (Easterly, 2001; Gibson et al., 2005).

Unless, therefore, the process of hard institutional reform goes hand in hand with a gradual evolution of soft norms and conventions, then the process of development is unlikely to occur. Co-evolution of institutions appears to have been a significant factor in the growth of Western Europe and the United States where a market economy arose unintentionally from the dynamics of power struggles and did so against a cultural backdrop where notions such as the rule of law, respect for possessions and the observance of contracts emerged incrementally over hundreds of years. Such conditions are unlikely to be recreated by acts of external intervention. From a classical liberal perspective, it follows that the best the developed nations may be able to do with respect to their less developed counterparts is to pursue a policy of 'do no harm'. The latter may entail a domestic policy of unilateral trade liberalisation and open borders in the developed nations. These policies may promote greater contacts with the developing world, and may facilitate a gradualist process of institutional and cultural imitation as exposure to both business practices and political institutions in liberal market economies may lead to demands for the adoption of culturally sensitive liberalisations in developing economies themselves. Open borders and capital markets may also constitute a disciplinary check on the predatory actions of governments by providing an exit route for overtaxed capital and individuals fleeing various forms of social prejudice.

'MARKET FAILURE' OBJECTIONS TO INTERNATIONAL CLASSICAL LIBERALISM

Notwithstanding the classical liberal arguments set out above, the dominant stream of thought in development theory continues to be premised on a 'market failure' perspective. This approach is itself advanced in terms of theoretical and empirical analysis of development dilemmas.

The theoretical case against classical liberalism relies heavily on notions of 'path-dependency' and the existence of various institutional 'blockages' and 'lock-ins' that were discussed initially by thinkers such as Myrdal (1957) and Rosenstein-Rodan (1957). A 'vicious circle of poverty' is held to prevent the internal formation of the capital required to trigger the process of economic growth. According to this view, incomes in many developing nations are so low that people are not able to save enough to fund the investment in the capital equipment required for the process of industrialisation to occur. People remain poor, in other words, because they are poor and they cannot escape such 'poverty traps' without external development assistance. 'Savings gap' models of this nature have played a major part in justifying support for the massive aid programmes channelled to poorer countries over the last half-century, and especially to those on the African continent (for a discussion of these see Easterly, 2001).

The above models have also been reinforced by path-dependency theories which posit cultural-economic barriers to investment in developing countries. According to this view, if a country or region has not experienced high levels of investment historically then entrepreneurs are unlikely to change their perceptions of the relevant area in the future and will continue to 'underinvest'. The willingness of entrepreneurs to invest in new plant and equipment is often conditioned by the historical pattern of investment in the countries concerned. Such perceptions are held to play a critical role in the developmental process because they determine whether or not the coordinated investment that may be necessary to trigger economic growth is likely to take place. More specifically, 'coordination failures' may occur when investment in one sector or industry is dependent on the existence of investment in another complementary industry or sector (Rosenstein-Rodan, 1957; Adsera and Ray, 1999; Hoff, 2000).[3] If local entrepreneurs know that people will invest in other business ventures that complement investment in their own particular plants, then they are likely to invest; but if they lack confidence that complementary investment will be forthcoming then they will fail to do so. In effect, these arguments are a macro-based variant of the 'lock-in' thesis discussed in Chapter 2. Just as random consumer choices can 'lock' people into relatively poor products, so a combination of random cultural and economic factors can lock them into an inefficient set of cultural and economic norms. Unless people can be sure that all other actors will simultaneously shift to an alternate set of norms and investment patterns, then a collective-action problem will ensue in which it is in no individual's interest to break from the status quo. Governments can, it is argued, provide the coordinated investment that can change the perception of economic opportunities through a 'big push' strategy helping backward regions and countries to break out of path-dependent stagnation (Sachs, 2005). Such arguments have been used to reinforce traditional 'infant industries' arguments for 'import substitution' policies which claim that developing countries will become 'locked' into low-value sectors unless domestic industries are protected from external competition, and especially from firms in those countries which are technologically more advanced.

These theoretical arguments against a 'free-market' development model have been reinforced by empirically oriented contributions that show poor results where more liberal policy approaches have been pursued, and that point to high levels of state intervention in those societies that have broken out of poverty.

On the one hand, critics point to the performance of developing countries that adopted the so-called Washington Consensus model initiated by international institutions such as the World Bank and the International Monetary Fund. These programmes followed the 'debt crisis' of the early 1980s and included support for the privatisation of state-owned industries, price liberalisation and the lowering of tariffs and industrial subsidies. In return for demonstrating a commitment to such reforms, developing countries, but especially those in Latin America and much of Africa, received a combination of further development assistance and the rescheduling or even cancellation of debts accumulated over the previous 30 years when a more interventionist direction had been common. From the critics' perspective, evidence from the period of market-oriented reforms counts against economic liberalisation. Although the rate of economic growth across much of Africa was disappointing in the post-World War II era it compares favourably with the position experienced by many African countries since the 1980s. Throughout this period many countries have seen a reduction in the rate of economic growth, and indeed large parts of the continent have seen an absolute decline in overall living standards. A similar picture is discernible across Latin America, where growth rates in countries that implemented structural adjustment programmes have typically been lower than the average experienced when policies of import substitution and external protection were pursued.

Evidence of the relative economic failure of the Washington Consensus has also been combined with a reinterpretation of experiences in those nations, and especially those in East Asia, that have managed to achieve sustained economic growth (for example, Stiglitz and Yusuf, 2001). The performance of these countries, far from confirming the case for economic liberalism, is said to offer support for a more state-centric and interventionist approach which directs the market process in accordance with centrally determined objectives. According to Wade (1990), for example, the growth 'miracles' that occurred in Japan, South Korea and Taiwan were accompanied by high levels of government intervention and protection. A significant degree of government control over the allocation of capital was evident, with a relatively high reliance on state-sponsored industrial planning agencies rather than the competitive trial and error generated by the entry and exit of private capital owners. In the case of China, meanwhile, Stiglitz (2001) points to the role played by township and village enterprises (TVEs) which he claims are publicly owned but which simulate the effects of market competition owing to their being controlled by lower tiers of government. This structure of local government ownership combined with a continuing and significant role for higher tiers of government in the financial sector and an active industrial policy are, according to Stiglitz, what lies behind China's industrial success, and not the 'neo-liberal' prescription of private ownership, secure property rights and financial liberalisation. Even in countries such as Hong Kong, which are often highlighted as paragon 'free-market economies', authors such as Wade point to significant areas of government intervention in sectors such as housing which suggest that economic liberalism is not the predominant factor in explaining superior performance.

'Lock-in' and Development

The concept of path-dependency or 'lock-in' lies at the heart of contemporary development theory, but as noted in Chapter 2, there is in fact little empirical evidence to support the view that these tendencies are at all widespread. In the context of technological lock-in, although powerful network effects do exist in areas such as computer software and telecommunications, these are not sufficient to eliminate competition. On the contrary, rival networks can and do exist in these sectors, and the possibility for individuals or groups of individuals or organisations to exit from less satisfactory networks is maintained. Switching from one technology to another is not, therefore, an all-or-nothing move which requires large-scale collective action (Leibowtiz and Margolis, 1995). Such evidence is of equal relevance in the context of the alleged social and cultural 'lock-ins' that underlie the case for 'big push' and protectionist development initiatives. Relatively small but significant differences in the cultural and economic practices of various groups do exist and these differences provide behavioural nodes that can be imitated by others who are willing to adapt accordingly. Although people are to a significant degree the product of their socio-cultural environment, given an institutional context of secure property rights they do have the capacity to break from such norms at the margin and to secure an incremental advantage by engaging in acts of economic and cultural entrepreneurship.

In his many contributions Peter Bauer was keen to point out that people in developing countries are not locked into a homogenous set of socio-cultural norms which prevent scope for individual or organisational agency (for example, Bauer, 1971). Historically, a range of cultural groups such as Gujarati Indians, ethnic Chinese, the Ibos of Nigeria and the Lebanese have participated in extensive commercial and trading networks in many countries and have established a standard of living well above the average of the countries in which they trade. What matters is whether the institutional environment protects such entrepreneurial minorities from persecution and provides incentives for their behavioural modes to be imitated by others. Centralised government action and external action in particular is unlikely to be a robust way of advancing the necessary process of cultural adaptation. Apart from governmental actors lacking the knowledge concerning which particular combination of social norms are conducive to growth in a specific case, state action may undermine incentives to modify growth-constraining norms. If people can rely on states or international governance structures to supplement their income then they may be less likely to challenge their own exclusionary prejudices in order to develop relationships based on voluntary exchange.

More generally, big push models misconceive the manner in which successful development occurs. Instead of requiring large-scale savings or injections of international aid to fund a sudden transition to an industrialised economic structure, the process of development typically occurs through many small incremental adjustments which may mirror the dynamics of cultural evolution. Agricultural development and small-scale manufacturing, for example, do not typically require large-scale savings. Rather, they depend on access to local trading networks and markets so that through a gradual process of exchange, division of labour and specialisation, a small surplus can be generated in order to fund subsequent investments which may then become the subject of further incremental growth. If 'vicious circle of poverty' models are accurate it is difficult to see how the process of development could ever have taken place anywhere. Since most people have been poor throughout the course of human history, the only way in which these models can account for development is to invoke exogenous shocks and resource windfalls, or the forced extraction of investment surpluses from some groups by others, usually in the form of slavery or colonial exploitation.

Exogenous shocks such as famines and disease can indeed break up ineffi-cient institutional structures and may have been significant in fracturing power structures in feudal Europe (North and Thomas, 1973) – but the conditions for successful shocks are unlikely to be 'recreated' by deliberate external inter-ventions. Resource windfall accounts of development are similarly implausi-ble, many successful economies such as Hong Kong and Japan having developed with little in the way of natural resources. 'Exploitation' theories, meanwhile, are contradicted by the sequencing of the contact between devel-oped and developing nations. The nations of the developed world were already significantly wealthier and had access to internally generated capital and tech-nology, prior to any imperialist contacts with the developing world – evidence of which is broadly accepted even by those who are critical of classical liberal views on development theory (see, for example, Pomerantz, 2002).

If the process of development is better conceived as arising from a series of incremental and evolutionary steps rather than a sudden 'leap' out of poverty, then arguments in favour of large-scale government planning to 'coordinate' investment patterns are called further into doubt. Knowledge of which partic-ular investment combinations are appropriate is not 'given', but must be discovered through a process of trial and error learning where there are clear feedback signals in the form of prices, profits and losses, which can commu-nicate the relative success and failure of different projects. In Hong Kong, for example, the developmental process was dominated initially by small manu-facturing plants using unsophisticated technology in areas such as clothing, footwear and plastic toys that shifted incrementally up the value chain to more expensive clothes, fashion items and then technologically advanced lines such as electronics (Lal, 1994). What mattered was the ability of entrepreneurs to move quickly in and out of different production lines and to respond to shifting opportunities and constraints, as and when they arose. Huang (2008) documents a similar story in rural China in the 1980s where rapid economic growth in the wake of agricultural privatisation was led by peasant entrepreneurs who then moved into food processing, small-scale manufacturing and construction. In direct contradiction to Myrdal-style path-dependency models, some of the fastest rates of growth in this period took place in the poorest and most rural parts of the country which were often lacking in public infrastructure and transport links. Insofar as any 'path-dependent' forces were undermined, this was achieved not via central planning, but by removing the crippling regulatory restrictions that characterised the Maoist era.

Notwithstanding these remarks, classical liberalism does not deny that hierarchical action may sometimes be required to solve coordination problems or to break out of path-dependent dynamics. It maintains, however, that the desired extent of such 'coordinated' efforts may emerge through voluntary entrepreneurial actions in the same manner that the desired amount of 'planning' by firms continually evolves through the competitive process of mergers and demergers in markets (Beaulier and Subrick, 2006). The development of large industrial concentrations such as the *keiretsu* in Japan, though they did not emerge in an entirely laissez-faire environment, indicates that there is ample scope within a market economy for 'centralised experiments' in resource allocation to be conducted in a decentralised way (Matsuyama, 1996, quoted in Beaulier and Subrick, 2006). Similarly, the provision of large-scale capital investment by foreign firms as occurred in Singapore provides another route to solving any coordination problems rather than resort to industrial planning by governments. Although large-scale foreign investment may not be a viable alternative in more geographically isolated areas such as sub-Saharan Africa, it is difficult to see how 'big push' planning schemes could work in such contexts either. Massive public investment in providing transport infrastructure to connect such areas to the global market is, for example, unlikely to have much effect when the skills and cultural aptitudes of tribal peoples may not be suited to the uptake of any resulting opportunities. As Bauer (1971) has argued, public infrastructural development is not typically the cause of economic growth, but tends to be an effect of incremental changes in the economic and cultural development of different individuals and groups.

Does Structural Adjustment Discredit Classical Liberalism?

If the theoretical case in favour of 'big push' planning is weak, this weakness is mirrored in the interpretation of the evidence on the relative performance of more and less liberal institutional regimes. From a classical liberal perspective the poor record of structural adjustment is readily explainable in terms of the principles set out in the first part of this chapter. Critics of the Washington

Consensus confuse the rhetoric from politicians and international development agencies concerning 'deregulation', 'liberalisation' and 'privatisation' with the reality of policy implementation on the ground. Although it is true that some measure of liberalisation especially in the realm of external trade and the privatisation of key industries has occurred, its extent is often grossly exaggerated and indeed frequently ignores many aspects which have moved away from liberal principles.

In a comprehensive cross-country analysis of policy change on the African continent, Van de Walle (2001) documents just how little reform has taken place. In the case of tariff reform, for example, Africa was the only region of the world where measures of openness did not increase substantially during the 1980s and 1990s (ibid.: 80) – with protection across the continent averaging four times that found in other non-Organisation for Economic Co-operation and Development (OECD) countries. Since the new millennium, trade liberalisation has proceeded somewhat more speedily in line with worldwide trends, but as recently as 2004 tariffs were still well above those found in the developed world (Sally, 2008: 61).

A similar pattern of limited reform has been evident in the realm of government expenditures, with state expenditure as a proportion of gross domestic product (GDP) actually increasing marginally across most of Africa throughout the 1980s and 1990s. If anything, such data on domestic government spending underestimate the role of the state in the economy because they do not include the huge expenditure from development assistance that has continued to flow into the coffers of African governments. Between the late 1970s and the late 1990s aid as a share of GDP increased from an average of under 5 per cent to well over 10 per cent, and since the vast majority of this occurred by way of goods and services provided directly to states, the size of government expenditure relative to the private economy actually grew throughout the period when structural adjustment policies were introduced (Van de Walle, 2001: 94–6). Although levels of government expenditure in Africa are relatively modest by international standards, they are considerably higher than was the case when the now wealthy nations were at a comparable level of development (Yeager, 1999). More important, it is not so much the size of the African state that is damaging to development prospects, but the character of the actions that these states undertake. Although spending on social services is relatively low, African governments engage in a complex web of predatory regulation through price fixing and state marketing boards which hamper the development of the rural sector and in many instances confine people to a regime of subsistence production. More generally, countries throughout the continent continue to experience weak or non-existent protection of property rights, with periodic 'looting' of private capital by ruling elites and chronic insecurity of persons and property owing to war and interethnic conflict. When judged against a basket of economic freedom indices, therefore, African nations continue to rank as among the 'least free' anywhere in the world (Ayittey, 2008).

In the Latin American context, liberalisation measures have been pushed further than in Africa with more substantial reductions in trade protection and a concerted attempt to place nationalised industries in sectors such as utilities into the private market. Significantly, however, in countries such as Argentina which was held up by the World Bank as a 'model reformer' during the 1990s, there was little evidence of an overall decline in the role of the state. On the contrary, government expenditure as a share of GDP has been maintained or even increased as the proceeds from the various privatisations were used to boost public spending and not to pay off debt (Edwards, 2010). Insofar as reforms have been carried out across the wider continent, these have by no means conformed to classical liberal principles. This is especially so in the case of privatisation where 'reform' has resulted in the creation of legally protected private monopolies, or a process of contracting out to private sector firms where many of the relevant contracts have been captured by rent-seeking interests close to or coterminous with ruling political elites (Vargos Llosa, 2005; Edwards, 2010). The one exception to this pattern has been the case of Chile, where the privatisation process resulted in the creation of more open and competitive markets and where far-reaching reforms to the pensions system have resulted in a wide diffusion of property ownership. Significantly, Chilean growth rates have far outstripped the Latin American average, but the reform process has not for the most part been the subject of international development assistance (Easterly, 2006; Edwards, 2010).

What matters is that these results, far from contradicting classical liberal accounts, confirm that externally financed efforts to promote reform are fraught with epistemological and incentive-compatibility issues. This is not to suggest that reforms must conform to some blueprint of classical liberal purity in order to stand a chance of success. Errors in policy implementation owing to knowledge problems and elements of corruption are probably inevitable during any period of policy change. Crucially, however, the institutional context may increase or decrease the severity of such problems. It is in this sense that the attempt to introduce more development-friendly institutions via internationally financed structural adjustment programmes – whether these are inspired by the Washington Consensus or any other development strategy – is misguided.

On the one hand, tax-financed development programmes such as those of the World Bank are unlikely to be attuned to cultural and economic circumstances on the ground. Coyne (2006), for example, notes the deleterious consequences of development aid in Kenya where studies have suggested that donor assistance has failed to appreciate the significance of ethnic and tribal rivalries and has often intensified these very rivalries. A similar story could be told with respect to the catalogue of failed development projects right across Africa, where access to political power has largely been distributed on tribal and ethnic lines and where the distribution and control of development assistance has become a focal point for often violent conflict (Easterly, 2006).

On the other hand, the supply of development aid may provide little in the way of incentives for either the agencies that procure the relevant funds or the states that receive them to ensure that reforms are implemented effectively. Evidence from a host of development projects in Africa has shown that large-scale funding frequently continues decades after the relevant projects have failed to achieve their stated objectives (Gibson et al., 2005). Similarly, in the Latin American context there is evidence that structural adjustment programmes did not actually involve much in the way of 'adjustment'. The World Bank, in particular, continued to pay out adjustment loans even when there was little evidence of the spending cuts that were supposed to accompany the loans (Easterly, 2001; Edwards, 2010).

Elsewhere, the provision of external development aid may act to reinforce incentive structures that encourage predatory rent-seeking rather than positive-sum instances of voluntary exchange. If ruling elites can secure further resources by accessing international development aid, then this may act to reduce internal pressures for institutional reforms that could lead to a self-sustaining process of growth. Again, the African experience is particularly telling. Notwithstanding trillions of dollars in development assistance over the post-war period, the fact that most of the continent is lacking appropriate institutions is indicative of the 'moral hazard' that large-scale development assistance may create. Far from undermining any path-dependent forces that thwart economic growth, external attempts to promote change appear equally if not more likely to reinforce collective action problems and path-dependencies that undermine movements towards development-friendly institutions.

That the widespread involvement of international development agencies is not the key to success is further illustrated by the example of those states that do appear to be achieving sustained growth. The major success stories in this regard have been Chile post-1983, China post-1979 and, more recently, India post-1991, all of which have far surpassed the average economic performance across the developing world as a whole and in their respective regions. In the Chilean case, market-oriented reforms were initiated under the 'right-wing' dictatorship of Pinocet, but were continued under subsequent democratically elected governments. In China, a nominally Communist dictatorship has remained in power throughout, but has introduced market-oriented reforms and now has tariff barriers well below the developing-world average (Sally, 2008). India, by contrast, has maintained almost uninterrupted democratic rule in the post-independence era, but began a gradualist process of economic liberalisation in 1991. Notwithstanding these differences, what unites these experiences is the minimal or non-existent role of international development assistance in the process of economic reform. Chile, China and India all conducted a unilateral approach to economic liberalisation which has not been 'supported' by way of large-scale aid programmes from the international community. The context and extent of these reforms has, of course, varied – Chile having the most market-driven economy, China moving partially away from central planning and state ownership, and India making relatively more modest steps towards liberalisation in services and some manufactured goods, but not in agriculture. From a classical liberal perspective, however, these cases support the view that a non-interventionist strategy at the international scale is more likely to result in reforms that are appropriately adapted to specific political and economic circumstances and where those who implement the relevant reforms have incentives to make them work (on these examples see Easterly, 2006; Sally, 2008).

Does the East Asian Model Contradict Classical Liberalism?

The success of China and India over recent years has been matched by the continued strong performance of many East Asian economies whose growth has exceeded the world average since 1960 and whose strategies have also received relatively little in the way of development assistance. What, though, of the claim that these instances of unilateral progress owe more to a highly interventionist approach than to the principles of classical liberalism?

The first point to make is that classical liberalism does not claim that countries can move overnight from having a command economy or a highly protected one to an entirely market-driven system operating in a context of complete free trade. Similarly, no amount of liberalisation will secure prosperity in a context where basic institutions such as secure property rights are lacking. As noted earlier, the particular route towards the creation of effective markets will vary depending on the political and cultural context concerned – there is no 'blueprint' via which the process of liberalisation should proceed. Rather, the argument is that a general but clear movement towards domestic and internationally market-oriented policies will produce benefits in the medium to long term. Studies which, like those of Wade (1990), aim to show that the East Asian economies have succeeded with significant elements of government intervention are thus largely beside the point. What matters is the relative performance of states with more or less in the way of government planning and regulation, and the direction of travel in countries over time. When judged against these criteria the evidence does not contradict the classical liberal view. South Korea and Taiwan, for example, had protectionist policies in certain sectors and their growth rates from the 1960s onwards were often impressive. Hong Kong and Singapore, however, operated almost complete free trade and their growth rates were even higher (Choi, 2000). Growth in South Korea and Taiwan meanwhile was itself more impressive following the abandonment of import substitution policies and the adoption of a more neutral though not laissez-faire trade regime in the late 1960s (Lal, 1994, 2002; Powell, 2005). More recently, it is significant that the countries with more liberal financial regimes, such as Hong Kong and Singapore, were the ones to recover most rapidly from the financial crisis of the late 1990s. Elsewhere in East Asia, government action appears to have exacerbated the crisis and to have slowed recovery from it. More specifically, interventionist regimes have shown a willingness to bail out failing banks and financial institutions and thus have created 'moral hazard' incentives for these actors to engage in excessively risky lending practices (Choi, 2000).

Cases such as Hong Kong and Singapore may be 'written off' as 'small-country' exceptions, but the experience of China provides a further and telling counter to the 'market governance' perspective. Stiglitz bases his interventionist interpretation of Chinese development on the notion that so called TVEs (township and village enterprises) are publicly owned entities (for example, Stiglitz and Yusuf, 2001). In a comprehensive empirical analysis of ownership structures across China however, Huang (2008: 68–81) shows that of the 12 million recorded TVEs over 10.5 million are in fact privately owned or in a position of de facto private ownership. Many of these enterprises arose following the programme of rural privatisation that took place from 1979 to 1989 and were responsible for the rapid process of rural development in this period. They were developed largely with capital supplied by small-scale peasant farmers who, while not enjoying the degree of security of ownership found in most developed nations, were granted de facto protection of their property by local government structures and considerably more security than had been the case under the disastrous collectivisation during the 'Great Leap Forward' and the 'Cultural Revolution'.[4]

Significantly, as Huang shows, the expansion and diversification of these enterprises has been stifled since the early 1990s, as post-Tiananmen Square the Chinese government has adopted an increasingly urban-focused and interventionist approach based on attracting foreign direct investment through tax breaks and selective exemption from regulations unavailable to indigenous entrepreneurs. Rural entrepreneurs who could have formed the basis for an indigenous private sector have been unable to expand owing to their lack of access to financial markets, and have increasingly witnessed an erosion of their property rights as the Chinese state has sought to limit the growth of potential centres of political opposition. Although overall growth has been maintained in recent years, unlike the period prior to 1989 when growth was broad-based, most recent development has been fuelled by foreign investment and is heavily biased towards urban centres such as Shanghai. As a consequence, the domestic private sector in China has remained chronically underdeveloped.[5] Moreover, insofar as the Chinese appear to have created successful industrial companies of their own, such as Lenovo (which recently purchased the manufacturing division of IBM), these are Chinese in name alone. Nearly all such companies although operating within China are formally owned and registered in Hong Kong, where they have access to one of the most liberal capital markets in the world. Far from China's system of industrial and financial planning being the cause of their success – as Stiglitz maintains – it has been the ability of entrepreneurial start-ups to exit from the Chinese system of industrial and financial controls and to re-enter China on the more liberal terms granted to 'foreign investors' that has been the critical ingredient. This option is not, of course, available to the vast majority of rural domestic enterprises which remain mired in a growing complex of regulatory restrictions (see Huang, 2008: Chapter 1). Neither is it an option for other parts of the developing world that do not have a Hong Kong as their immediate neighbour.

It must be emphasised in the above context that there is no economy in the world that adheres completely to 'free-market' principles either in the domestic or in the international arena. As Powell (2005) points out, what matters about the East Asian experience overall is that when ranked against a basket of comparative indices the East Asian countries are among the most economically liberal in the world – and much more so than the average for the developing world as a whole (see also Lal, 2002). More specifically, the policies pursued in East Asia, though not 'laissez-faire', were more liberal and market-oriented in the post-colonial era than was the case in the poorly performing regions of Latin America and Africa. Hong Kong and Singapore, in particular, have consistently ranked in the top five most liberal economies. Japan was in the top ten most liberal for over half of the period between 1970 and 1990, and even the more interventionist examples of South Korea and Taiwan have consistently ranked in the top 20 per cent of countries with respect to the various economic freedom indices (Powell, 2005, 315–18). While none of these economies constitute 'pure' market economies, it is difficult to maintain, as authors such as Wade do, that their success has been caused by high levels of state intervention. In the case of Hong Kong, for example, despite there being no state controls over imports, foreign exchange, foreign investment, wages and prices and despite some of the lowest tax revenues to GDP ratios anywhere in the world, Wade claims that superior economic performance cannot be attributed to the presence of market-oriented policies owing to the existence of large-scale public housing provision, land use planning and immigration controls (Wade, 1990: 331–2). If Wade is serious in holding that Hong Kong is not in fact a relatively open market economy, then it is hard to envisage what country is, and whether there is any counterfactual to evaluate the view that interventionist regimes outperform more market-oriented systems.

COMMUNITARIAN OBJECTIONS TO INTERNATIONAL CLASSICAL LIBERALISM

Economic objections to liberal markets have dominated the development literature, but they have increasingly been joined by 'communitarian' contributions which suggest the need for greater political or collective control over the process of cultural and economic interchange. Though there are important differences within the communitarian perspective in terms of the political implications that follow from a global environment of cultural and economic fluidity, what unites this perspective is a suspicion of classical liberalism.

An important strain of communitarian argument advanced by both conservatives and social democrats contends that the spread of market relations at the international level contributes to cultural homogeneity and the eradication of traditions incompatible with the dynamics of global capitalism. Gray (1998), for example, argues that international trade is contributing to the destruction of the social capital characteristic of the 'East Asian' model, and its replacement with a monolithic form of Anglo-American individualism. According to this view, restrictions on trade and capital flows should be implemented in an attempt to preserve such social capital from the effects of market forces.

Gray's concern about cultural homogenisation under open markets emanates from a conservative preoccupation with the need to maintain long-standing local and national traditions, but similar concerns are raised by those on the social democratic left. Miller (1995), for example, argues that democratic institutions cannot function without a shared political identity and culture operating within the territorial boundaries provided by the modern nation state. According to this perspective, while markets have a role to play in the organisation of society, these markets must be embedded within a strong framework of democratic citizenship where people can engage in a dialogue over the constituents of the common good, and where a sense of trust enables people to transcend differences.

The communitarianism of Gray and Miller leads to the stance that collective decision-making should play a significant role in regulating the operation of markets at the national level and where necessary, whether in developed or in developing nations, the implementation of policies that swim against the tide of international markets and their attendant structures. This 'national communitarianism' must, however, be contrasted with a more 'cosmopolitan' variety which argues that global capitalist institutions have already progressed too far to be controlled effectively by the actions of nation states. According to this view, nation states are no longer able to steer an independent trajectory because international market forces disperse the economic and social consequences of decisions made by individuals and corporate actors across a variety of territorial scales. What is required, therefore, is an extension of the bonds of democratic citizenship outwards from the nation state to encompass communities affected by socio-economic forces irrespective of their geographical location.

Cosmopolitan communitarians such as Iris Young (1990, 2000) are critical of what they see as the insularity and inconsistency of the 'nationalist' position. The latter emphasises the capacity of democratic institutions to engage people in a process where preferences are scrutinised for their effects on society as a whole, and where a consensus on the common good can be reached via democratic dialogue. From a cosmopolitan perspective, however, if communicative rationality can occur within nation states there is no reason why such dialogical learning cannot be extended outward to the international and, where necessary, the global realm. This is particularly important given that actions taken by developed countries often impinge directly on the economic and cultural life of those in developing nations who may be disadvantaged by trade and investment decisions taken elsewhere, and who may feel 'dominated' by the hegemony of a 'Westernised' capitalist culture. Young aspires, therefore, to have the 'global division of labour' and the investment decisions of corporations subjected to democratic deliberation at the supranational level. The principle in operation here is a version of the 'modified Millian test' discussed in Chapter 5. This test states that all agents affected by an action should participate in deciding such actions and the conditions that give rise to them. For Young, it follows from this principle that the direction of travel should be towards the greatest possible extension of social democratic processes at the global scale.

Does Classical Liberalism Produce Cultural Homogeneity?

Though they differ on whether collective control over markets should be conducted at a national or cosmopolitan level, communitarians concur that such control is essential to protect cultural diversity. From a classical liberal perspective, however, the claim that international commerce leads to cultural homogeneity is largely groundless. An open international market offers competitive niches to a wide variety of ethno-cultural types, each of which may exercise a comparative advantage in a particular economic domain. Certain cultural norms, such as those emphasising team spirit, may for example prevail in sectors requiring large-scale capital outlays and joint production (such as automobile manufacture), while in other industries a competitive advantage may be exercised by a culture which allows greater room for individual flair (such as textiles and fashion). Historically, Japanese culture has thrived in the former context, whereas the sole proprietor model of entrepreneurship associated with the Chinese has performed better in the latter (Lavoie and Chamlee-Wright, 2001).

More generally, when discussing the effects of international markets on cultural diversity it is crucial to recognise the difference between diversity within countries and diversity across countries (Caplan and Cowen, 2004). In terms of consumption patterns, markets and trade tend to increase the former while reducing the latter. Trade between the UK and Chile, for example, brings products that were previously available only in Chile to consumers in Britain, and vice versa. In this case both the UK and Chile become internally more diverse, with a greater range of choices for their citizens, but the differences between the respective countries become less marked as a direct consequence of trade. On the production side, however, increasing returns to specialisation may operate to intensify regional distinctiveness. As the size of the international market expands, different regions of the world can increase their income by specialising in particular production lines. These specialisations may reinforce the cultural distinctiveness of the regions and communities concerned. In a competitive market, even cultural practices which exhibit no absolute advantage in their contribution towards production or entrepreneurial ingenuity are unlikely to be eradicated owing to the law of comparative advantage. In the context of global trade, the international product can be enlarged if different cultural types specialise in those lines where they have the lowest opportunity cost of production. Even the most inefficient producers and cultures have a comparative advantage in some markets, though they may lack any absolute advantages.

Trade, Communicative Rationality and Social Capital

The analysis set out above does not imply that cultural standardisation at the global level is insignificant – the spread of English as the language of international commerce, for example, presents a clear and obvious case of increasing cultural homogeneity. Rather, from a classical liberal perspective, subscription to common norms and practices on some dimensions may be a prerequisite for the evolution of a more diverse set of cultural forms elsewhere. Crucially, however, the number of dimensions where standardisation may be necessary or beneficial is relatively few. Adherence to a relatively 'thin' set of norms such as a willingness to observe contracts and to speak a common language of trade enables people who may otherwise have very different interests and values to cooperate, whereas attempts to forge a more substantive commitment to a shared set of ends are likely to produce conflict. From a classical liberal standpoint, it is precisely because of their relative impersonality that people in markets tend to be less concerned with the religious or ethnic origin of those with whom they exchange, and as a consequence expose themselves to alternative lifestyles, identities and ways of doing things.

Seen in this context, communitarians fail to recognise that attempts to institutionalise a common identity through the state are likely to close off the very process of social communication they claim to favour. The 'nationalist' version is especially problematic in the context of developing countries where the boundaries of nation states often encompass a wide range of ethno-cultural groups and where there is a lack of interethnic trust. In many developing countries, ethnic and religious identifications form the basis of market transactions; in the absence of secure property rights and formal reputational devices such as credit ratings, people confine their dealings to extended family members in order to overcome a lack of generalised trust. The consequence of such exclusionary action in the market is to limit competition and the gains from trade. State action, however, tends to entrench these exclusionary practices because those that prove successful in capturing the political machine can use the governmental apparatus to enforce exclusionary norms via formal bureaucratic regulation. Protectionist policies based on import substitution and controls on the foreign ownership of enterprises are particularly damaging in this regard. They enrich the dominant familial and ethnic groups that benefit from the restriction of competition and in doing so tend to encourage interethnic conflict over the relevant distributional gains. And, by reducing the penetration of the local market by global brands and management practices they stifle the exposure of local cultures to a different set of social norms that could lead to the spread of more outward-looking practices (Van de Walle, 2001; Easterly, 2006).

To return to the terminology used in Chapter 4, what is required if development is to spread more widely is not the 'bonding' social capital emphasised by 'nationalist' communitarians, but the thinner 'bridging' social capital required and encouraged by greater commercial contacts. The pronounced scepticism towards trade evinced by those who advocate greater 'communicative rationality' at the domestic level is, therefore, particularly surprising. Why restrict trade and communication between different communities in an attempt to preserve a particular social identity at the expense of greater cross cultural fluidity? Of course, some groups may wish to isolate themselves from cosmopolitan forces, but there is no reason to suppose that this isolation should be enforced on others who may be eager to escape the exclusionary prejudices that may occur within the confines of nation states.

Against Global Deliberation

With their emphasis on internationalism the arguments of cosmopolitan communitarians are somewhat closer to classical liberalism. Where classical liberalism differs radically from cosmopolitanism, however, is with respect to the emphasis on developing democratic structures of governance at the supranational scale. Unlike their 'nationalist' counterparts, cosmopolitans, though wanting to respect and to affirm cultural diversity, wish to create a 'thicker' sense of community at the global level and to do so by subjecting a greater number of decisions to collective democratic control. From a classical liberal perspective, however, a more robust way of reducing conflict at the global level would be to minimise the number of decisions taken by such structures.

In a context of cultural diversity there may be even less prospect of achieving agreement on a common set of ends at the global level than there is within the nation state. The empowerment of global political institutions is likely to promote conflict as rival coalitions may vie for control of the massive new source of political power that would reside in such structures. For classical liberals, relationships based on 'exit' such as those in markets or interjurisdictional competition are more likely to empower both individual and organisational actors than collectivist procedures based on democratic 'voice'. The essence of entrepreneurship is to break with the majority position and to lead by demonstration, creating novel solutions to problems which may subsequently be copied and spread. If no innovation may proceed until there is majority support, then social learning is thwarted in favour of the existing majority view. In a global governance context, the limitations on freedom of action here apply not only to the freedom of individuals and corporate bodies, but also to the actions of nation states. As noted earlier, the major success stories of China and India have been based on unilateral institutional reforms, and unilateral liberalisation in particular. It is difficult to see how such reforms could ever have been initiated if approval had first been required from a multilateral structure including representatives of developed nations – who might be threatened by the prospect of competition from rival development models. Even within existing global structures such as the World Bank and the General Agreement on Tariffs and Trade, Europe and the United States have, for example, already been at the forefront of attempts to limit the inflow of cheap imports from China on the grounds of supposedly 'inadequate' labour and environmental standards (Sally, 2008).

Given the complex interconnections between people and places in a global economy, deliberative democratic control over trade and investment of the sort proposed by cosmopolitans such as Young would fail to recognise the constraints emphasised by robust political economy. Implementing the 'modified Millian test' would require that any decision to enter or exit a particular market be approved by a deliberative body consisting of all whose livelihood or cultural practices might be affected by such a decision. Presumably, it would also require that any decision to enter or leave a particular jurisdiction should be subject to the approval of such a body. Young herself, it should be recognised, does not see the issue in these terms, arguing that global delibera-tive structures should provide a 'general framework' of rules within which the 'broad outline' of investment patterns, migration and social standards are determined while allowing space for these rules to be adapted to local contexts by subsidiary deliberative bodies (Young, 2000: 266–71). The incoherence of this stance should, however, be readily apparent. If deliberative control is to function effectively, then those who determine the 'broad outline' must have the power to compel local actors to adhere to the relevant plan when they intend to diverge from it. Yet, it is precisely this sort of 'central planning' which confronts the Hayekian 'knowledge problem'. With the impossibility of consulting the millions of actors involved in countless different industries and jurisdictions, deliberative determination of the 'broad outline' could never account for the knowledge of the myriad of actors affected by this outline, but would be based instead on the perceptions and values of a tiny subset of polit-ical 'representatives'. Instead of trade and investment patterns driven by competition between thousands of companies for the patronage of millions of investors, workers and consumers who represent themselves, they would have to be fixed by a small number of professional deliberators. The latter could not possibly be aware of all the local circumstances pertinent to the individuals and organisations they purport to represent, and would not be subject to effec-tive institutional constraints should they abuse the enormous powers that would be at their disposal. In the context of existing supranational structures such as the European Union, citizens face massive principal versus agent prob-lems in controlling the actions of representatives who are prone to engage in rent-seeking behaviour. The creation of still higher levels of political author-ity at the global level would simply magnify these dynamics.

EGALITARIAN OBJECTIONS TO INTERNATIONAL CLASSICAL LIBERALISM

The arguments advanced by cosmopolitans are mirrored by those who chal-lenge international classical liberalism on egalitarian grounds. Seen in this light, the concerns of social justice theory which focus on the internal arrange-ments of nation states need to be modified to take on board social ties that tran-scend national borders, and to address structural inequalities rooted in the systemic operation of global institutions. The most recent and influential of the arguments made in this context is reflected in Thomas Pogge's attempt to extend Rawlsian egalitarianism to encompass the global dimension.

According to Pogge (2002), the global nature of contemporary socio-economic relations requires universal rules of justice rather than those based on national differences. The dynamics of the global economy require a unitary system of law concerning trade and property rights, and these rules must be justified in terms of a principle capable of universal acceptance. The particular principle that Pogge has in mind is the Rawlsian difference principle. Rawls's own view is that because the difference principle would require that some nations pay the costs of distributive decisions made elsewhere, it should not be applied outside the confines of national jurisdictions. For Pogge, however, there is no more reason not to apply the difference principle externally than there is not to apply it internally (Pogge, 2002: 106). If variations in the distributive norms subscribed to by voluntary associations and local jurisdictions within the nation state – which require that some actors bear the costs of decisions made by others – are not sufficient to disqualify the difference principle, then variations in the policies of nation states do not disqualify its application at the global scale either. Indeed, in Pogge's view it is morally imperative that the difference principle is applied internationally so that the position of the global poor can be maximised.

Building on this analysis, Pogge maintains that there is in effect a global 'basic structure' of rules and practices governing the distribution of resources, but that these practices are fundamentally 'unjust'. Far from advancing the interests of the 'worst-off' in a manner that might be agreed behind a 'veil of ignorance', institutions which structure relations of trade between developed and developing nations operate to the disproportionate benefit of the global rich. The solution to this injustice is the creation of a new set of rules for global governance which restructure the relations between developed and developing nations in favour of the latter. The primary mechanism proposed in this context is in effect the creation of a globally administered welfare state via a 'Global Resources Dividend' (Pogge, 2002: 206–7). This structure would redistribute income from developed to developing nations and would attempt to secure institutional reforms in the recipient nations that would contribute maximally to the eradication of poverty.

Although Pogge's arguments are couched in explicitly Rawlsian terms, it is not difficult to see how these arguments might also be applied within a Dworkinian framework focused on the desire to eliminate the effects of 'brute luck' arising from differences in natural resources, climate, and the various social and cultural endowments that differ between nation states. On this view, since there is radical inequality of access to resources between nations, and since this inequality is often not the result of deliberate choice, then those who lack resources or who confront chances that have been affected for the worse by decisions made elsewhere should be compensated accordingly (for an example of this reasoning, see Beitz, 1979). Resource-rich nations, whether they are rich in natural or in cultural resources, should be taxed in order to fund a more equal set of opportunities for those who are resource-poor. A Dworkinian variant of the global resources dividend would, therefore, act as a form of international insurance scheme for those nations and peoples unfortunate enough to have lost out in the natural and cultural lottery.

These cosmopolitan variants of Rawlsian and 'luck' egalitarianism are magnified in their ambitions by a globalised 'politics of difference'. According to this view, while a fundamental redistribution of resources from richer to poorer nations is an essential element of global justice, it would by no means be sufficient to secure such justice. As noted in the discussion on communitarianism, for theorists such as Young the creation of supranational structures is essential in order to subject international capitalism and the values it promotes to critical scrutiny. Seen in this light, it may be inappropriate to require that developing nations adopt institutional and social reforms that simply reflect the dominant cultural values of the developed world as a precondition for receipt of income transfers. Rather, a globalised politics of difference should aim to ensure that the cultural values of those who 'lose' in the global marketplace are given a more positive identity – instead of being interpreted as 'deviant' practices that should be 'reformed' by dominant economic and cultural groups within the international order.

Is There a Global Distributive System?

Though these various stripes of egalitarian argument have been influential in shaping the contemporary development agenda, from a classical liberal perspective they fail to meet the requirements of a robust political economy. On the one hand, there is no basis for agreement on what 'social justice' requires, and on the other, there are all manner of deleterious consequences that might follow in terms of creating new power structures and deficient incentive structures from attempts to implement such a principle at the global scale (see, for example, Lomasky, 2005; Kukathas, 2006). In short, it may be as mistaken to pursue social justice globally as previous chapters have suggested it may be to pursue social justice within the confines of the nation state.

Consider Pogge's claim that given conditions of interdependence a universal principle of justice is required to govern relationships not only between individuals but also between nation states. Even a cursory glance at the contemporary international scene reveals that there are no commonly accepted standards of distributive justice in operation. Rather, there are a variety of principles even within those countries that have broadly 'market-oriented' or 'capitalist' economies. In the Scandinavian countries, for example, there is support for a high level of income redistribution coupled with severe restrictions on those deemed eligible to benefit from the relevant wealth transfers. Thus, in Denmark recent administrations have sought to halt immigration in order to maintain the integrity of the welfare system as they see it (Tebble, 2006). In the United States, however, a generally more liberal immigration regime goes hand in hand with large-scale public opposition to income redistribution (Choi, 2002). This variety in distributive norms is much greater when considering that many nations – such as, for example, those in the Islamic world – subscribe to distributive principles conditioned by religious beliefs, and elsewhere states such as Venezuela and Bolivia profess a belief in 'socialist' principles of distribution (Kukathas, 2006). From a classical liberal perspective this diversity is a reflection of the trade-offs that exist between helping the worst-off and other conflicting values – such as a desire for higher average standards of living or a preference for greater cultural heterogeneity – and the fact that different associations of people may wish to make these trade-offs in different ways.

Several points follow from the above understanding. First, there is no global 'basic structure' of economic and social relations in the contemporary world. Rather, the global economy consists of a series of interactions between a variety of individuals and groups who reside under a range of competing and overlapping institutional arrangements with respect to the production and distribution of goods. To put the argument differently, it is not at all apparent that a system of 'global capitalism' actually exists. Instead there are economic interactions that take place between individuals and organisations that hail from more or less market-oriented environments, and with some who continue to adhere to more or less state-directed systems. There is, as a consequence, little or no reason to support Pogge's claim that poverty in the developing world is the result of a 'system of rules' rigged in favour of the developed nations.

What Pogge appears to have in mind is that developed nations often impose trade barriers against developing nations while simultaneously urging that developing nations abandon equivalent policies. Yet, it is not the case that developed nations benefit from protectionist policies. While producers in the protected industries do benefit from restrictions on competition, consumers across the developed world pay more for goods and services than they would if such protection were not in place, and their economies as a whole are poorer overall owing to a failure to reallocate domestic capital to those lines where it has a genuine comparative advantage. The available evidence suggests that the developing nations that have the greatest contacts with the developed world and that participate most in the global economy are the ones that have witnessed the most significant improvements in living standards. While these improvements might be greater were there to be a universal abandonment of protectionist measures, it is false to maintain that the primary source of protection stems from the developed world. On the contrary, protection in some of the poorest parts of the world is several multiples of the world average (Bhagwati, 2004: 232). More generally, to suggest that the fate of the world's poor is determined by global structures ignores that the most significant reductions in poverty have been due to the internal policies of market liberalisation pursued by states such as China and India.

If it is recognised that conditions in developing countries can be shaped by autonomous actions within such nations – at least by ruling elites – then it is implausible to maintain that international differences in wealth should be judged against a common distributive principle. It is, for example, far from obvious that justice requires developed nations to compensate the 'worst-off' nation states, many of which – Egypt, Libya, North Korea, Tanzania, Zambia and Zimbabwe, to name but a few – have pursued explicitly socialist development paths. Similarly, it is hard to see why states such as China and India which have undergone a process of institutional restructuring in recent years should, as soon as they pass the average level of global wealth, become the subject of redistributive schemes to aid those who have not engaged in such reforms. Of course, some global inequalities can be explained by the legacy of colonial exploitation and domination, but the huge variation in fortunes between formerly colonised nations suggests this is not the dominant factor at play. Far from supporting Marxist-inspired 'dependency theories', evidence suggests that the income gap between nations that have engaged in internal reforms and the developed world is declining rapidly – notably Chile, China post-1979 and India post-1991 – whereas the income gap with non-reforming nations, many of which impose protectionist measures against each other (as well as against the developed world), continues to grow (Lal, 2006).[6]

To apply the Rawlsian difference principle globally would deny the responsibility that national governments have for the policies and institutions that they adopt, and would entitle the 'least-well-off' nations to transfer payments irrespective of the policies they pursue. It would in effect treat the resources of the entire world as a 'common pool' which would then become ripe for 'free-riding' behaviour. To be fair to Pogge, he does propose incentive mechanisms to encourage poverty-reducing policies in the developing world, and thus appears to want to instantiate some form of responsibility for decisions taken following the creation of the Global Resources Dividend. The problem for Pogge, however, is that he provides no reason to believe that the relevant 'incentives' would be any more robust than those introduced under existing international aid schemes. If trillions of dollars in development assistance and attempts by agencies such as the World Bank to make this conditional on socio-economic reform have failed, then why will the transfer of still more resources and the creation of yet more development agencies do any better (on this see Kukathas, 2006)? From a classical liberal perspective it may be that the best incentives for development would result from a dismantling of the entire apparatus of taxpayer-funded international aid. If citizens in developed nations were able individually to 'exit' from financing failed development projects – and cease to be forced to 'cooperate' with often oppressive regimes

– this would provide the relevant agencies with better incentives to fund only those projects that have a record of success. Similarly, if ruling elites in developing nations cease to have access to external aid then they may have better incentives to abandon institutions and policies that impede economic progress (on this, see Easterly, 2006).

Given the problems with the Rawlsian framework, the Dworkinian or 'luck egalitarian' approach might seem more promising. The problem with this approach, however, is that owing to the 'knowledge problem' there is no basis for agreeing which of today's inequalities between nations are due to 'unchosen' inequalities in access to resources. Consider the cases of Hong Kong and Japan. Although they are among the richest nations in the world, they have developed with little in the way of natural resources. One could argue, therefore, on 'luck egalitarian' grounds that they should not be taxed to fund redistributive programmes to nations such as Bolivia and Venezuela which, though mired in poverty, have access to considerably more natural assets. The problem here, however, is that the very lack of resources in Hong Kong and Japan may have helped to create cultural aptitudes such as a strong savings ethos which are conducive to the generation of wealth. Since those born into such societies today have done nothing to 'deserve' their cultural background, it may equally be argued they should be taxed to compensate people in countries where cultural values are less suited to wealth generation and where the absence of such values may result from access to an abundant resource base. This argument is not as far-fetched as it may seem when considering that it is often suggested that some of the world's poorest countries are afflicted with a 'natural resource curse' that fosters a 'wealth-grabbing' or rent-seeking ethos rather than a wealth-creating one (for example, Sachs and Warner, 2001). None of this is to deny that there is a genuine difference between outcomes that are the result of 'choice' and those that result from 'chance'. The point is simply to emphasise that the distinction between those outcomes that result from choice and those which derive from chance is so uncertain that it cannot provide the basis for a globally agreed principle of distribution.

Flawed though it may be in practice, the virtue of the luck egalitarian approach is that it recognises an element of responsibility and individual agency in global distributive outcomes. The attempt to hold the governments of less developed nations to account, however, is less apparent in Young's global 'politics of difference', which seeks not only a redistribution of wealth from the developed to the developing world but in seeking positive affirmation of 'cultural difference' would place relatively little in the way of conditionality on any such transfers. Although she recognises that poverty in the developing world is sometimes the result of the policies pursued by internal elites, Young (2000: 271–5) is keen to ensure that in order to secure 'non-domination' of cultural minorities by 'external forces' the actions of international development agencies are appropriately 'democratised'. The mechanism she proposes in this context is a greater role for developing nations in international bodies such as the United Nations. Unfortunately, what this approach seems likely to achieve in practice is greater access to the stream of development aid by ruling elites in those countries, many of whose internal policies have contributed most to the problem of poverty in the first place. There is little reason to suppose that such structures would be of any benefit to the poor of the developing world – even if it is developing countries themselves that come to dominate the relevant international bodies – for it is precisely those nations that have become progressively more enmeshed in the system of international development assistance that have some of the worst economic records (Easterly, 2006). Access to the international aid system often subsidises malfunctioning economic and social systems and reduces incentives for ruling elites to engage in internal reform. Far from reducing 'domination', Young's solution to the problem of poverty and injustice would allow these very elites access to an additional stream of funding which could then be used to maintain relations of 'domination' over their own domestic populations.

Against The Globalisation of Social Justice

It should be evident that from a classical liberal perspective there is no global system of resource distribution, and neither should there be an attempt to create such a system. Though there are economic and social interconnections between peoples in different parts of the world, it does not follow that there is any need for universal principles of distributive justice. On the contrary, a global 'spontaneous order' requires general 'rules of conduct' that enable people who differ in their conceptions of what is just to engage in peaceful forms of cooperation (Lomasky, 2007: 208–13). Rules of this nature are typically 'negative' or 'thin' in character and are reflected in norms of nonviolence, respect for property, a willingness to observe contracts and the principle of freedom of association and disassociation. While there should be nothing to stop voluntary associations from devising 'positive' or 'thicker' rules that provide internally for a particular pattern of distribution, in an environment of economic and cultural diversity it is unlikely that these standards would, or should, become widespread. When there is disagreement over what constitutes a just pattern of distribution, the creation of global institutions will thwart cross-cultural learning and simply enable those who secure power in these institutions to impose their own particular distributive ideals (Kukathas, 2006: 20–25).

From a classical liberal perspective, many of the obstacles to a more effective system of international cooperation at present stem from internal state structures which breach the 'non-interference' principle and forcibly prevent people from cooperating across the globe on the basis of a thinner set of moral rules. Domestic trade protection as practiced within both developed and developing nations, for example, represents a coercive attempt to block communication across borders between potentially willing partners to trade. Similarly, controls on immigration designed to preserve the integrity of the domestic welfare state are premised on the view that there are greater commonalities of interest and culture between people who happen to live within particular national jurisdictions, when in a world of cultural and economic fluidity people may have no more affective relationships with many of their fellow citizens than they do with individuals overseas. Indeed in some situations they may have more affective contacts with subsets of individuals in other countries than they do with most inhabitants of their own particular countries. Seen through this lens, the best way of advancing institutions that foster international cooperation and economic development may be to abandon attempts to enforce a unitary set of distributive norms whether at the national or at the global scale.

CONCLUSION

There can be little doubt that problems of acute poverty across large parts of the world constitute one of the most pressing challenges for political economy and public policy. To recognise the significance of such problems, however, should not lead analysts to depart from the principles of institutional robustness that are the central concern of this book. In an age when it is difficult to escape the rhetoric of 'globalisation' it is all too easy for analysts and policymakers to conclude that a 'globalisation of government' constitutes the most appropriate way of addressing the economic and moral challenges of the day. The analysis presented in this chapter suggests much greater attention to 'knowledge problems' and incentive-based constraints when considering the appropriateness of the responses that can be applied by both developed and developing nations. Insofar as the economic and moral dilemmas arising from global poverty are capable of resolution, the most robust route to change may involve minimal government intervention both at home and abroad.

NOTES

1. These indices typically include measures pertaining to security of property, openness to trade, extent of private ownership, labour market regulation, financial regulation and government spending.
2. It is important in this context not to confuse the growth of 'trade' per se with movements

toward 'free trade'. The volume of global trade may well increase for all manner of reasons that have little to do with domestic support for a 'free-trade' regime. Reductions in transport costs may, for example, result in increases in the volume of trade between societies whose internal institutions are socialist in orientation. In this case, though the volume of trade may be rising, the structure of trade will be determined by a domestic policy of central planning which will decide what can be produced and what should be traded. This is from a classical liberal perspective, a further reason why 'trade' per se is unlikely to be a sufficient ingredient to promote sustained growth. Unless the structure of trade emerges from a domestic context which is supportive of competitive markets, then any benefits are likely to be minimal.

3. The example proffered by Rosenstein-Rodan is that of a shoe factory. In this instance, the entrepreneur will not invest in setting up a new shoe-making plant until he or she knows that there will be sufficient investment in other industries – such as food and clothes, for example – to generate a sufficient demand from consumers for the products of the shoe-making enterprise.

4. Stiglitz appears to have made this mistake by equating the fact that TVEs are registered by local communes with formal ownership of the relevant enterprises and their assets. As Huang (2008: 68–81) shows, however, the communes with which the TVEs are registered are locational entities rather than ownership entities, and the vast majority of the capital deployed in these enterprises is derived from private sources.

5. This is not an argument against policies supportive of foreign investment, but against a policy that deliberately favours foreign investment and urban centres over the rural sector. The deleterious effects of hostility to foreign investment were all too evident in India in the period prior to 1991 when the foreign ownership of enterprises in sectors such as manufacturing was all but banned. With India now liberalising its approach to foreign investment but maintaining many regulatory restrictions in rural areas and the agricultural sector, Chinese and Indian experience may be converging.

6. Contrary to Pogge's assumptions, there is reason to believe that the process of international trade liberalisation since 1960 has resulted in a substantial reduction in global inequality. Many studies which suggest an increase in inequality over this period compare the per capita income of the richest 20 countries and the poorest 20 countries in one time period with those in a later period. World Bank studies conducted along these lines, for example, report an increase in the ratio of inequality between the highest- and lowest-income countries from 23 in 1960 to 36 in 2000 (Lal, 2006: 135).

   The most significant problem with these studies, however, is that they ignore the changing composition of the countries in the relevant categories, and in particular they neglect that some of the states that counted amongst the poorest in 1960, but which no longer do so, are those with by far and away the largest populations. Many Asian countries used to count amongst the lowest-income category, but rapid growth over recent years has seen these countries – and their hundreds of millions of people – exit the bottom group. Most of the states that fall into the lowest-income category today are typically found in Africa and have very low populations. Comparing the difference between the top and bottom countries in one time period relative to another is not, therefore, comparing like with like. In order to do so one has to compare the fortunes of the same set of countries over time. Far from showing an increase in inequality, the latter studies indicate a very substantial fall, due in large part to economic liberalisation in China and India. Comparing the fortunes of the same set of countries in 1960 and 2000 sees the 'gap' fall from the rich having 23 times the per capita income of the poorest in 1960, to just 9.5 times the per capita income of the poorest in 2000. When comparing the income and consumption of all the worlds' individuals – as opposed to countries – the Gini coefficients which measure inequality (with 0 representing complete equality and 1 representing complete inequality) all indicate a decline in inequality since 1980. For a detailed discussion of these and related issues, see Bhalla (2002) and Lal (2006: Chapter 5).

8. Environmental protection: green leviathan or the minimal state?

INTRODUCTION

If poverty relief and the delivery of 'social justice' both at home and abroad are considered by many to illustrate the limitations of a classical liberal agenda, then these obstacles are thought minuscule when compared to the imminent threat of environmental breakdown. To focus on the superiority of 'spontaneous orders' in an era when concerns have shifted to the potentially calamitous environmental 'disorder' wrought by markets may seem misguided, and to illustrate the irrelevance of classical liberalism to the most pressing issues on the contemporary public policy stage.

Notwithstanding such an unfavourable background, this chapter argues that a classical liberal framework may be best placed to meet the challenges represented by the demands of environmental protection. Specifically, a focus on issues of knowledge generation and incentives points towards decentralised solutions to collective-good problems as the most robust way of addressing issues of resource depletion. Markets and private property rights have an important role to play in facilitating the discovery of solutions to environmental problems and in providing the incentives necessary to deliver environmental improvements, and may be better placed to do so than command and control regulations and centrally determined pricing schemes. Moreover, where rules and regulations are required to counteract 'market failures', they may be better adapted to the problems in hand if allowed to emerge via a 'bottom-up' process of evolutionary competition. Where this is not possible owing to the global nature of environmental dilemmas then even in this 'worst case' for classical liberalism there may still be little reason to favour the development of a 'green leviathan' either on economic grounds or on those of social justice.

In order to make and to defend the case sketched above, the chapter is divided into four sections. The next section sets out the classical liberal case for a property rights approach to environmental protection issues. The subsequent three sections counter potential objections to this approach arising from 'market failure', communitarian and egalitarian perspectives respectively.

226

CLASSICAL LIBERALISM, PROPERTY RIGHTS AND ENVIRONMENTAL PROTECTION

The widespread mistrust of classical liberalism in the environmental domain owes much to the 'market-failure' perspective of neo-classical welfare economics. In well-functioning markets, prices act as indicators of scarcity which signal to producers and consumers the shifting availability of resources and provide incentives for people to economise in response to underlying conditions of supply and demand. From the perspective of neo-classical economics, however, environmental resources are subject to a variety of 'common-pool', externality and collective-good problems which prevent the generation of a robust set of price signals.

The Market-failure Argument

Common-pool problems typically occur when resources are 'unowned' or are in an 'open access' state. In cases such as the management of fisheries, for example, individual fishermen may have little incentive to conserve stocks because without the capacity to exclude others, the immediate sacrifice of reducing their personal catch in the short term will not sufficiently benefit the actor concerned in the longer term. On the contrary, in an open access fishery the decision of any one fisherman to conserve will simply leave more fish for others to take. Though the collective interest of all would be in greater conservation, no individual fisherman has an incentive to engage in the necessary measures – the optimum strategy is to 'free-ride' and to continue fishing up to the point where stocks are exhausted.

Common-pool problems are closely related to the general issue of externalities, where individuals are unable to reap the full benefits and to face the full costs of decisions that have environmental consequences. When a factory owner emits pollutants into the atmosphere, for example, his or her decision may be influenced by the fact that he or she does not pay a price reflective of the negative external cost that this imposes on those living in the vicinity. Similarly, those who consume products that involve pollution may do so in part because they are not required to pay a price reflective of the damage inflicted on third parties during the production process. Externalities may, of course, also be positive in nature. A farmer may generate benefits for third parties via the adoption of agricultural methods which contribute to the creation of an attractive landscape. The inability of the farmer to demand compensation for the provision of such benefits, however, may give him or her insufficient incentive to supply them in line with the underlying structure of public demand. In the case of both positive and negative externalities, therefore, it is the divergence between the private and social costs of environmental actions that constitute examples of 'market failure'.

Related to the concept of externalities are two qualities characteristic of many environmental goods: non-excludability and non-rivalrous consumption. Non-excludability occurs when the producer of a good is unable to keep non-payers from its consumption; non-rivalrous consumption, when the marginal cost to a seller of providing a good to an additional consumer is zero. Goods exhibiting both these characteristics are known as collective goods, and according to neo-classical welfare economics may be 'underproduced' in an unregulated market. Scenic views are an example – it is difficult to exclude non-payers from the benefits of such a view, and up to the point were crowding occurs,[1] one person's consumption of the view does not detract from the consumption of others. Public goods, on the other hand, exhibit non-rivalrous consumption but the exclusion of non-payers is possible. From the perspective of neo-classical economics, the operation of a profit-induced market may result in the inefficient exclusion of potential consumers. Environmental goods such as nature reserves and public parks will not, according to this view, be supplied in adequate quantities in unregulated markets.

If market failures lie at the heart of environmental problems then the solution to such problems is thought to reside in well-designed government interventions to 'correct' these failures. Such interventions may take on a 'command and control' format or they may involve 'price-based' incentives. In the former instance, public regulators mandate an appropriate form of behaviour. This may involve the imposition of quotas specifying the maximum rate of extraction from a resource such as a fishery, and in more extreme cases the introduction of bans and prohibitions on use. Elsewhere, governments may respond by banning the most noxious forms of pollution, by imposing quantitative limits on the level of emissions, or by mandating the use of centrally approved production technologies. Where the aim is to ensure the provision of goods with positive externality attributes, governments may also commandeer resources to ensure that the goods are supplied in the appropriate quantities.

'Price-based' forms of intervention, on the other hand, do not attempt to mandate a particular environmental outcome, but seek to induce behavioural changes on the part of producers and consumers by using both positive and negative incentives through centrally imposed modifications to the price system. Typically these take the form of pollution taxes and charges to discourage negative externalities, and the provision of subsidies to encourage the supply of public goods.

Market Failure or Government Failure?

Classical liberalism does not question the view that environmental problems arise when private actors are unaccountable for their actions. What it does question is the supposition that political intervention, whether of the 'command and control' or 'price-based' variety, is the best way of 'internalising' the relevant externalities. There are two dimensions to this account which reflect the focus on the conditions required for a robust political economy of institutions and decisions.

The first line of analysis draws on the Hayekian understanding of the 'knowledge problem'. Seen from this perspective, neo-classical approaches to environmental policy repeat the error committed by Lange and Lerner in the socialist calculation debates by assuming that the knowledge necessary to correct for 'market failures' is somehow 'given' to policy-makers (Chapter 2). In an environmental context, the assumption is that trade-offs between environmental and other objectives are known and fixed. The role of policy, therefore, is one of designing the appropriate incentives to ensure that given these underlying constraints, resources are allocated in the most efficient way. Insofar as there is a debate to be had, this centres on the efficacy of the relevant 'incentives'. 'Command and control' measures are deemed appropriate where the objective is not to discourage the use of a particular resource, but as in the case of certain highly toxic substances to prevent their usage altogether. Or, where the aim is to ensure that producers adopt known techniques that can improve such dimensions as air quality, to mandate implementation of these methods. 'Price-based' measures, on the other hand, are advocated where the aim is not to eliminate a particular behaviour or to mandate a specific outcome, but to encourage actors to economise on a resource by treating externalities as a cost of production which can be reduced through substitution and to promote experimentation in finding ways to economise on the relevant margins.

Viewed through a Hayekian lens both command and control and price-based mechanisms are variations of central planning and may be inappropriate because the primary environmental problem is typically not one of giving people the right incentives to act on the basis of 'known' environmental values, but of discovering what the relevant values are. Knowledge of these values is fundamentally dispersed throughout society and evolves in light of the changing ideas of individuals and organisations as they interact with each other and the natural world. The costs and benefits associated with environmental externalities may only be discovered through the decisions that people make when confronted with a range of competing alternatives, and where there are profit and loss signals or equivalents to signal the content of the relevant choices (Cordato, 2005). Just as a process of central economic planning is incapable of generating and accessing sufficient information to set other prices in the economy at a 'socially optimal' level, so environmental planners lack the capacity to set environmental taxes and subsidies at the appropriate rate or to choose the best balance between regulatory or price-based policy tools.

The second dimension of the classical liberal analysis turns to the question of incentives. While misaligned incentives that enable individuals and groups to externalise costs are an important source of 'market failure', it cannot be assumed that the policy process will result in an appropriate realignment of private and social costs. Indeed, from a public choice perspective the collective action problems that can lead to examples of market failure also occur within the political process where producer groups often find it easier to organise collectively and to overcome internal free-riding problems than the consumers and taxpayers who frequently pay the costs of the policies supported by organised 'polluter interests'. These processes may best account for widespread 'democratic failures' such as the persistence of environmentally damaging subsidies in agriculture, logging, coal mining and the construction of subsidised dams and roadways. From a classical liberal perspective it is hard to see why policy-makers should be trusted to correct 'market failures' when the incentives they face often lead to the introduction of inappropriate regulations and to distortions in market prices which generate environmental costs (Anderson and Leal, 2001).[2]

The Case for Private Property

If a system of private property exchange provides the most robust way of discovering values and of coordinating dispersed knowledge, the first principle of sound environmental policy should be to extend the range of private property rights over environmental assets rather than rely on command and control regulations or government pricing schemes. A system of private property rights would allow for a process of competitive experimentation between resource owners, and through the bottom-up generation of price signals would communicate knowledge concerning which of these experiments might be copied and those that might be avoided. In addition, the establishment of exclusive property rights would align incentives in such a way that enables individuals and organisations to profit from those actions that benefit their fellows while ensuring that they pay the cost of those that do not. In the case of common-pool or open access resources such as fisheries, for example, the establishment of exclusion rights to resources would incentivise conservation owing to the capacity of owners to charge for access to the fishery, or alternatively to realise the value of conserving assets by selling to a subsequent owner (for example, De Alessi, 1998).[3] Similarly, the introduction of exclusion technologies to collective goods would enable resource owners to limit free-riding and provide incentives for supply, given the ability of owners to charge a price for access.[4] More generally, the establishment of property rights would help to internalise externalities with violations of these rights via non-consensual acts of pollution subject to punishment in the courts, as with other property rights violations such as theft and fraud (see, for example, Anderson and Leal, 2001).

There are, from a classical liberal perspective, many environmental assets currently held under 'open access' conditions or subject to government ownership and/or regulation that could in fact be 'privatised' and brought within the realm of a competitive market system. These include land-based assets, such as forests, minerals and wildlife, which can be subject to various 'fencing' technologies; stationary resources such as oyster beds; and water-based assets such as rivers and inshore fisheries that are also relatively excludable with existing technology. Empirical studies of such assets under open access, government ownership and private ownership offer strong support for the view that tradable private property rights promote more sustainable management practices (for a summary of this evidence, see De Alessi, 2003).

At a wider level, the theoretical importance of markets in encouraging the adjustments necessary to promote resource conservation is supported by evidence on the comparative impact of different economic systems. According to Bernstram (1995), for example, by the late 1980s, the emission of air pollutants from transport and stationary sources per unit of GDP in the former socialist countries was between 250 and 580 per cent higher than in developed market economies. Cross-country studies of more- and less-regulated market economies are hard to come by, so their conclusions must be treated with circumspection. Of the available studies, however, there is evidence that secure property rights and market prices are significant factors in improving environmental performance. Norton (1998), for example, finds systematic correlations between measures of environmental conservation including forest cover and water quality, and those pertaining to property rights. Similarly, in their analysis of developing economies Bate and Montgomery (2006) find that energy efficiency is consistently lower in heavily regulated countries compared to those where prices fluctuate more freely.

Tackling the Tougher Problems: Property Rights and Institutional Entrepreneurship

The Coasian tradition in political economy has long argued for a property rights approach to environmental management. According to this perspective, if an individual or group owns an environmental asset and someone else wishes to pollute, then the latter may attempt to purchase the relevant rights. Alternatively, if someone owns the 'right to pollute', then those seeking to avoid the relevant costs may compensate the polluter in return for a reduction in emissions (Coase, 1960). In this manner, price signals representing the trade-offs between environmental and competing objectives may be generated spontaneously via a process of decentralised exchange.

Though widely recognised, the property rights perspective is often dismissed by critics because simplistic interpretations assume zero transaction costs in the enforcement of ownership rights and thus are thought of relevance to only a small category of environmental goods where exclusion technologies can easily be applied (for example, Jacobs, 1992; Turner et al., 1994). As was noted in Chapter 2, however, Coase's adoption of the zero-transaction-cost model was meant to show that in such a world the question of appropriate policy institutions becomes redundant (Coase, 1989). In a zero-transaction-cost setting, the prices generated through the costless exchange of property rights would be the same as those imposed from the centre by an omniscient environmental planner. When transactions costs are positive, however, as they invariably are, the question of institutional choice becomes fundamental because different arrangements are more or less capable of identifying and reducing such costs (Dahlman, 1979; Anderson and Leal, 2001).

Restated in Hayekian terms, the property rights or 'free-market environmentalist' position recognises that the ability to internalise externalities is dependent on institutions, but that knowledge of which particular arrangements are best placed to perform such a function is not known in advance. Rather, it must be discovered via a process of competitive experimentation in institutional design. By contrast, the theory of externalities and collective goods is usually presented in terms of neo-classical equilibrium theory where the circumstances that determine such conditions as 'non-excludability' are assumed to be 'given'. The property rights perspective, on the other hand, recognises that the ability to internalise externalities is often a product of institutional entrepreneurship. If markets allow innovators to create new ideas and products, they also enable entrepreneurs to capture the gains from converting collective goods into excludable goods (Anderson and Leal, 2001).

The collective-action problems that underlie many environmental dilemmas arise wherever people need to cooperate with others. Groups of shareholders, for example, face 'free-rider' problems in controlling the appointed managers of the companies they own. From a classical liberal perspective, however, competitive orders may be better placed to discover institutional solutions to such problems. In markets, a variety of institutional designs compete on their capacity to limit free-riding and to build trust between actors. Thus, joint-stock companies compete with manager-owned enterprises, worker cooperatives, consumer cooperatives and mutual associations, each of which adopt different rules of governance that may prove more or less effective. As actors exit and enter different institutional designs, the signals generated by such decisions facilitate a process of institutional learning which ripples through the system as a whole (Ricketts, 2000).

Crucially, institutional pluralism of the above nature may also be suited to the management of environmental collective goods. Very few such goods are completely indivisible in supply – most are territorial and their supply can differ within countries, and between regions and much smaller localities. In principle, therefore, such goods are suited to a process of 'parallel adaptation', where a variety of institutional designs compete simultaneously. Within this context, Ostrom's detailed studies of the management of common-pool resources including forests, irrigation systems and coastal fisheries suggest that institutional diversity is the key to sustainability (Ostrom, 1990, 2006). Where technological advance allows for evolution in 'fencing' technologies then models of individual private ownership may prove effective, but these may coexist with alternative structures based on variations of cooperative or shared ownership between an identified set of resources users. What matters in all of these cases is that resources are converted from an 'open access' state to one where some form of exclusion is introduced at the relevant jurisdictional level.

The capacity to discover new ways of configuring property rights may be of particular relevance to environmental problems that transcend the boundaries of a single property owner and may be a prominent feature of an approach to environmental protection that draws on the principle of competitive spontaneous order. One important example of institutional entrepreneurship in this vein is the system of 'land-lease planning' advocated by MacCallum (1970). In this system, individual property owners contract into a 'proprietary community' that limits the rights of all those who 'enter' the community concerned. Communities are either co-owned by residents in a cooperative or witness a division of property rights between a 'freeholder' or 'plan-lord' who lays down the contractual conditions agreed to by the leaseholders. By submitting to common regulations, for example on development rights and requiring contributions to collective goods such as parks, woodland, roads and street lighting, owners may increase the value of their holdings relative to those that do not enter into such a contractual structure. Communities of this nature now account for the majority of new house-building in the United States and range in size from those covering a few streets or blocks to those encompassing entire towns (Nelson, 2002). In the city of Wuhan in China, meanwhile, over two-thirds of the 500 000 population reside in private residential 'clubs' which provide all infrastructure such as roads, public parks and also manage a contractual system of land use planning (Webster and Lai, 2003).

In the context of such proprietary environmental planning, competition takes place on at least two different levels. On the one hand, individual owners of houses compete with others in the community concerned on those dimensions where they retain strictly private or individual rights. Over questions such as interior design, for example, home-owners may compete to ensure that their particular property is more attractive to prospective buyers than that of their neighbours. On the other hand, however, competition takes place at the level of the proprietary structure as institutional entrepreneurs, whether individual or collective, compete to attract people into their community rather than others by offering different packages of contractual restrictions and obligations (Nelson, 2002; Pennington, 2002). In proprietary communities, rather than have large numbers of individuals trying to negotiate environmental standards with one another – a situation which may well be prone to high transaction and monitoring costs – the creation of a unified management structure which can 'impose' standards, but which is entered on a voluntary basis, constitutes one way of economising on these very costs. Within such structures, institutional entrepreneurs may experiment with a combination of 'command and control' and 'price-based' measures to secure specific environmental goods in the most effective manner. At the same time, however, these attempts at institutional design and 'planning' will be 'priced' spontaneously in a wider environment of open competition as individuals and organisations exit and enter different institutional regimes.

While the principle of proprietary governance might be thought relevant only to localised environmental problems, there is no reason why this principle could not also be applied to larger-scale collective goods. Just as individual property owners may contract into a proprietary system of regulation, so these collective structures may themselves enter into a meta-system of rules governing intercommunity external costs. Indeed the formation of contractual communities to supply localised collective goods may also lower the costs of coping with translocal problems where there are larger numbers of affected parties because the formation of such structures reduces the number of contracting parties (Ostrom, 1990, 2006; Pennington, 2002). Ostrom's work, for example, confirms that regional collective action problems such as the management of river catchments are more likely to be solved when the necessary institutions are arrived at via the creation of 'nested' or 'federated' structures 'from below' rather than have these imposed 'from above' (Ostrom, 2006). Networks or 'leagues' of communities may develop common standards for collective goods and there may be strong incentives for organisations to join such groupings. Few people would purchase property in a community that insisted its members drive on a different side of the street to those of neighbouring communities, just as few purchase mobile phones from providers who do not recognise calls from rival networks. Likewise, it seems unlikely that individuals or organisations would join those groupings that refused to cooperate in solving the collective-good problems that have a direct bearing on their quality of life. As such, the competition and pluralism central to classical liberalism are not incompatible with the emergence of common norms and standards. What matters is that these standards are arrived at by consent rather than enforced coordination and where there is the possibility for dissenters to 'exit' at some level and subscribe to a different set of practices.

The classical liberal approach to environmental protection does not rest on the assumption of 'atomistic' competition. Neither does it rest on a simplistic form of 'privatisation' where resources are simply parcelled out to individual owners. Rather, the primary argument for classical liberalism is that it is a framework of competitive regulation characterised by freedom of contract. It is within such a framework that people may enter into organisational structures that restrict their own behaviour in order to engage in acts of cooperation that can secure a particular collective good. What matters in terms of institutional robustness is that there is scope for experimentation with different bundles and combinations of property rights, in order to discover which structures help to lower the transaction costs of internalising externalities and the relative value placed on collective goods themselves. Equally importantly, there should not be any one owner at the meta-level with the capacity to determine the content of the institutional rules that other social actors must adhere to.

It is for the above reasons that the robustness of state-centric models of property ownership is questioned. Under such models either the state assumes the sole responsibility for determining the manner in which collective-good problems should be addressed – for example by nationalising assets or subjecting their management to a unitary system of regulation. Alternatively, the state determines from the centre how much autonomy more decentralised units of administration may have to experiment with alternative models of collective-good provision. Either way, the scope for the 'bottom-up' emergence of solutions to collective-good problems may be stifled. Should there be only one rule-making body, then any errors tend to be systemic and the capacity to innovate and adapt to local circumstances is impeded by the need to secure the support of an overarching authority or majority. According to Ostrom (2006), where states have nationalised assets and subjected all common-pool resources to a unitary structure, collective-action problems have often intensified. In the case of the management of river catchments and water basins, for example, even local and regional governments have often underestimated the capacity for more decentralised units to devise rules that can internalise costs. As well as reducing the scope for experimentation in environmental rules, the creation of centralised management structures intensifies principal versus agent problems. Other things being equal, the larger the jurisdictional unit and the more agents encompassed by it, the less scope there is for exit and the less the incentive for individual agents to monitor the performance of the superior authority. In these circumstances, it is the groups with the lowest costs of organisation who may engage in 'rent-seeking' behaviour, distorting the rule-making process and externalising costs onto more diffuse constituencies who are unable to 'exit' from the regime but are equally unable to mobilise against the predatory action of organised rent-seekers.

'MARKET-FAILURE' OBJECTIONS TO CLASSICAL LIBERAL ENVIRONMENTALISM

As in other policy domains, the classical liberal approach to environmental protection is based on minimising if not eradicating the coercive role of the state. Yet, in the specific case of environmental protection it is often argued that this approach is incoherent. Economic analysis, in particular, highlights a number of reasons why an extensive role for the state may be required in order to sustain the classical liberal approach itself, let alone any environmental benefits it may deliver.

The property rights approach relies in large part on the introduction of bargaining relationships in order to generate price signals and incentives to balance the environmental costs and benefits of individual and organisational decisions. One of the most commonly raised and important objections to the claim that this approach can dispense with systems of government regulation, however, is that widespread state intervention would be necessary to assign the relevant property rights before any such bargaining can occur. According to this perspective, the act of establishing and enforcing property rights may itself require a form of 'central planning' in assigning the relevant rights, and such a role would not be dissimilar to that involved in the administration of the 'command and control' and 'price-based' forms of environmental policy of which classical liberalism tends to be so critical (Jacobs, 1992).

An additional reason to question the internal coherence of the classical liberal approach centres on its purported commitment to competition and pluralism. It might be suggested that processes that allow for the emergence of private regulatory standards in the classical liberal system would threaten that system from within. If actors can cooperate to solve common environmental problems, would not the same actors also have the capacity to form cartels and monopolies that would undermine the capacity of individuals and organisations to exit from undesirable arrangements (Cowen, 1992)? In the final analysis, without the commitment to the maintenance of democratic state structures that can control and if necessary break up private concentrations of power, the benefits of greater experimentation and accountability proffered by classical liberalism are largely theoretical (Mulberg, 1992).

Notwithstanding the significance of the forgoing objections, perhaps the most serious challenge to the robustness of the property rights approach from an economic perspective is that however much scope there may be for institutional entrepreneurs to solve free-rider problems, there will always remain a large class of 'market failures' which cannot be solved without an extensive and indeed expanded role for coercive government action. Some of the most pressing environmental problems such as the effects of anthropogenic climate change are global in their dimensions. The very idea of competition may thus be thought to be misplaced because the global magnitude of such issues requires a unitary approach which eliminates the exit option. Far from reducing the role of the state, it may be imperative to create 'state-like' structures at the international scale in order to eliminate 'free-riding' behaviour by individual nation states and even regional groupings of such states. The only way that the relevant transactions costs can be overcome is through the creation of more centralised structures that have the power to coerce individual and corporate actors to achieve the required environmental objectives.

Do Environmental Property Rights Require the State?

Each of the above criticisms is widely cited in the environmental policy literature, but they do not succeed in undermining the robustness of the classical liberal position. With regard to the assignment and enforcement of property rights it is obvious that where states are the current owners of environmental assets, any act of 'privatisation' will require some form of government action. A similar situation may prevail where resources are currently in an 'open access' condition and where the state may be required to apportion property rights to the resource concerned. The Japanese government, for example, has effectively 'privatised' inshore fisheries by assigning rights to fishing cooperatives (De Alessi, 1998). In such cases, 'privatisation' may involve auctioning off property rights or may take the form of 'giving away' the relevant assets to private individuals and groups. To the extent that the political authorities are able to attach centrally determined conditions to the subsequent use of such assets, as is the case with marketable quota schemes for example, then it is indeed the case that many of the objections raised against the imposition of 'command and control' or 'price-based' forms of government regulation by classical liberals may also afflict the process of 'privatisation' (Hill, 2005). That said, this hardly undermines the rationale for the property rights approach per se. The process of institutional reform may well be imperfect, but if it facilitates movement in the direction of greater experimentation and realigns incentives, it is probably preferable to the status quo. It seems, for example, untenable to hold that because the process of privatising agricultural land in China has been afflicted by corruption and manipulation by local elites, the resulting property rights arrangement has not resulted in significant improvements when compared to the situation under Mao's programme of forced collectivisation (on the latter, see Huang, 2008).

Although political action is clearly required where a transfer of state property into the private sector is involved, the more general claim that the classical liberal focus on removing government control is incoherent because state action is always required in order to define and enforce environmental property rights does not hold. Put simply, it is not true that market-based systems of private contract depend on widespread state action to function effectively. While it must be recognised that certain forms of political authority may help to sustain a system of private property rights and commercial exchange, it does not follow that there is any necessary connection between the two. On the contrary, both the definition and the enforcement of property rights may occur via a process of competitive spontaneous order and without any form of central, hierarchical control (Ellickson, 1991; Anderson and Hill, 2004; Hill, 2005).

With regard to the definition of property rights, a primary implication of the Hayekian analysis is that in a dynamic world where the nature of socio-economic problems and their related externalities is constantly evolving, it may not be possible for the state to know which externalities to establish rights over. Private parties should, therefore, be allowed the maximum scope to craft and to sculpt their own contractual bargains, and in the process define and redefine on a voluntary basis the precise character of the appropriate set of rights. Thus, the systems of proprietary planning discussed earlier represent a private attempt to overcome collective goods and free-rider problems by assigning a particular set of environmental rights and responsibilities to those who enter the relevant institutional regimes. They are in effect systems of private, competitive environmental law and are similar in principle to other private systems of regulation such as those reflected in groupings such as sports leagues. In these cases the 'rules of the game' which set the parameters within which both competitive and cooperative action may take place are designed on a private basis and without the intervention of external political authority (Pennington, 2008).

It might, of course, be objected that the capacity of private agents and associations to design their own rules is nonetheless dependent on the state to enforce whatever rights and contractual terms happen to be agreed by the parties concerned. As was noted in Chapter 4, however, there is ample evidence to suggest that the enforcement of property rights may itself occur through a decentralised process. Historically, the international law of commerce or *lex mercatoria* has proceeded on this basis and is a prime illustration of the emergence of a legal, regulatory institution without the supervision of a unitary central state (Benson, 1989; Leeson, 2008). Potential trading partners name private arbitration agencies to resolve any disputes that may arise with respect to the performance of their contractual terms. Failure to agree to the involvement of such an independent third party or to submit to an arbiter's decision (such as payment of a fine), limits the potential gains from trade. Just as sports clubs which do not abide by the rules of their particular league soon find themselves without playing partners, so in the case of the *lex mercatoria* merchants who fail to be bound by arbitration soon find themselves in the equivalent of 'outlaw' status. Enforcement, therefore, occurs through the process of multilateral boycott – those who lack a reputation for fair dealing or those who fail to exhibit evidence of having obeyed the terms of independent arbitration are less well placed to find trading partners relative to those who do.

Though it is evident that the definition and enforcement of property rights has no necessary connection with state action, the classical liberal perspective cannot and does not rule out the possibility that states or 'state-like' actors may have a role to play in the process (Hill, 2005). Just as individuals and organisations may contract into structures that help to overcome collective action problems, so too may states and even supranational bodies. Classical liberalism does not simply advocate 'leaving it to the market', as usually understood by this phrase. Rather, it maintains that actors should be able to enter and exit alternative institutional designs (Buchanan and Vanberg, 2002). These institutional designs may result from government action, and states and groupings of states may have a role to play when their boundaries accord with the territorial or geographical dimensions of a particular collective-good problem. Where there are 'open access' resources, for example, then states may need to be involved in creating systems of rules to govern the process whereby property rights might be established and enforced. This may be of particular significance when determining the rules of access to international commons such as the oceans or parts of the atmosphere. Agreements and treaties between states or groupings of states may help lower the transaction costs of solving environmental problems by setting out general rules under which actors can 'stake' and register a new 'claim' should the cost of technology and the benefits of 'enclosure' make such actions worthwhile (Anderson and Leal, 2001). Alternatively, in the absence of property rights solutions to facilitate enclosure, states may agree to systems of rules that limit access to common-pool resources that are subject to a severe scarcity constraint.

Though the classical liberal approach recognises a potential role for state-like structures in managing specific environmental problems this does not, however, imply uncritical support for existing states and supranational organisations. Many of these have sought to eliminate institutional competition and may have intensified collective-good problems by imposing unitary structures of control at an inappropriate jurisdictional level. Consider the case of fishing rights in European waters. Technologies such as sonar monitoring now exist that might allow for the effective privatisation of inshore and even some offshore fisheries, but further investment in the development and application of these technologies has been limited by institutions such as the European Union Common Fisheries Policy that insist on treating oceanic resources as a non-excludable asset (De Alessi, 1998). The argument that only European-wide structures are capable of managing fish stocks owing to the migratory nature of these stocks is questionable. The maritime boundaries of individual nation states do not accord with the migration routes of many species, but neither do the boundaries of the European Union. It is far from evident, therefore, that European institutions are best placed to internalise the relevant environmental costs. Effective management of North Sea fisheries may require cooperation between North-West European states but this is of doubtful relevance to Greece or Italy. Indeed, allowing states which are not directly affected to participate in designing the relevant rules is likely to lead to the externalisation of costs. Similar issues arise in the case of agriculture. The European Union Common Agricultural Policy is generally held to have subsidised environmental damage on a massive scale, and may have created collective goods and externality problems that previously did not exist or were at worst of only national or, more likely, local concern (for example, Bowers and Cheshire, 1983).

It may be significant in the above regard that some of the most innovative environmental measures in fisheries and agriculture have been devised by states that are not party to supranational structures, and thus have greater freedom to innovate and to internalise costs. Iceland and New Zealand, for example, have moved towards a successful system of marketable quotas in fisheries, and the latter has abolished agricultural subsidies on a unilateral basis. While there are clearly some issues that may only be dealt with by larger-scale jurisdictions, in a world of subsidised grain mountains and wine lakes, at the very least, one should be wary of granting additional powers to such entities.

Does Environmental Cooperation Lead to Monopoly Power?

If problems of monopoly power and limits on the exit option exist under current structures, what of the argument that the classical liberal approach would itself lead to examples of monopoly power? As one moves up from institutions that address more localised collective-good problems to much larger-scale issues such as regional air pollution, it is certainly true that the intensity of competition and the range of exit options will necessarily be reduced (for example, Anderson and Hill, 2004). This should not, however, be taken to imply that competition will be ineffective when compared to the status quo. The key issue is whether higher-level institutions are imposed from above or whether they are allowed to emerge via a process of 'federalism from below' where higher-level entities develop through a process of voluntary exchange and institutional entrepreneurship. When, for example, centralised political structures such as the British state, which have imposed systems of control that limit the scope for internal exit, then choose to enter into European-level structures which further reduce the scope for decentralised solutions, concerns about monopoly power are very real. If the process of building 'nested' institutional structures to deal with transboundary problems arises through a bottom-up process of voluntary exchange which requires the consent of the lowest-level units, however, then these concerns are likely to be less pronounced (Ostrom, 1990, 2006).

In a classical liberal order, higher-level institutions which may be needed for environmental rules covering large geographical areas would most likely be confined in their powers to the relatively few dimensions where common standards are required across a larger territorial scale. Coordination on such standards, as in a proprietary community or federation of such communities, will not, however, necessarily enable wider practices of collusion. The appropriate analogy here is with so-called network industries such as telecommunications, where the value of the relevant network rises with the number of subscribers to a particular standard. Attempts to extend membership requirements of such networks to include anticompetitive practices would reduce the potential market for the network concerned. So long as the relevant network is not imposed via coercive measures, dissenting actors at whatever level could set up a rival network exhibiting common standards on those dimensions where cooperation is desirable, but without limiting internal competition on matters which could be dealt with at a lower jurisdictional scale (Leibowitz and Margolis, 1995; Stringham, 2006). If a requirement of subscribing to the grammatical standards of the English language also included an enforceable commitment not to engage in price competition with other speakers, then the popularity of this particular network would soon diminish. Likewise, one can conjecture that proprietary organisations that sought to regulate behaviour beyond genuine environmental externalities would lose out to those that did not. From a classical liberal perspective, that existing states and supranational structures stray well beyond such minimalism is evidence that more often than not, these structures have their origins in acts of coercion rather than being built up from the consent of individuals, firms and voluntary associations.

The Dilemma of Climate Change

While monopoly in general is thought to be undesirable by the majority of economists, in the case of global environmental dilemmas such as anthropogenic climate change it may be argued that competition in environmental standards is undesirable given that the relevant territorial unit at which to internalise costs is the globe itself. It does not necessarily follow, however, that the most effective response to such problems is to empower global-level institutions to enforce environmental controls. A strong theoretical argument may be advanced in favour of a global minimal state with the power to introduce a carbon tax or a programme of tradable emissions quotas. This would provide individuals, firms and higher-level jurisdictions such as national governments with a financial signal to reduce carbon emissions, while allowing a process of decentralised experimentation to deliver on the relevant reductions. These measures might also be reinforced with command and control-style regulations such as mandatory technologies where there are known procedures that might contribute to lowering the rate of emissions without excessive cost (see, for example, Sunstein, 2005).

To offer unequivocal support for the above action, however, would require the validity of some highly implausible assumptions. The first such assumption is that global policy-makers have the knowledge to manage climatic patterns via adjustments to emissions and that they could, in the face of diverse international incomes, preferences and attitudes to risk, agree on the parameters necessary to determine an appropriate rate of reductions. It seems highly unlikely that agreement could be reached on some sort of global cost–benefit analysis because depending on which particular climate simulation model proves accurate, significant parts of the globe may be net beneficiaries from climate change.[5] Centrally determined pricing and quota schemes are, therefore, unlikely to be set at a 'socially optimal' rate and cannot be considered to be 'correct' for 'global market failure'. Attempts to create an optimal set of carbon taxes may be arbitrary, reflecting the particular values of policy-makers or the differential political power of various global actors.

The second difficulty with the argument for a global authority to tackle climate change is the assumption that the creation of such a structure would somehow solve the collective-action problems that underlie the problem of uncontrolled CO_2 emissions. While it is true that large-scale environmental issues, of which CO_2-induced climate change is the most important, are unlikely to bring forth voluntary solutions owing to the difficulty of identifying individual 'polluters', these collective-action problems would not be eradicated with the creation of a global authority. On the one hand, such an authority would face massive monitoring costs in seeking to discover whether its own regulations were being enforced. Equally, however, there would be an enormous principal–agent problem in holding the authority itself to account. Arguably, the most serious collective-action dilemma of all is that involved in holding to account an elected government, and nowhere would this be more problematic than in the case of global-level environmental institutions, however democratic in character. Given the infinitesimal chance of any voter or even an individual state affecting the decisions of a global authority, there would be few incentives to monitor and even less capacity to affect its performance.

Such problems would not be eliminated under the nested, proprietary structures pointed to by the classical liberal approach as a way of managing smaller-scale territorial goods. As one travels further away from outright individual ownership to the nested, federated structures necessary to internalise larger-scale externalities, so potential free-rider dynamics and principal–agent problems within these structures multiply. Nonetheless, an advantage of a bottom-up, competitive system of environmental governance is that by preserving the scope for exit it may reduce the relative significance of collective action per se. Just as shareholders who face free-rider or principal–agent problems in controlling the management of companies are protected by the option of selling shares in poor performers, so the capacity of both individual and corporate actors to exit from poor institutions may provide a check against abuses by the relevant hierarchies. At some point, however, the extent of the monitoring problem facing lower-level actors, combined with the loss of exit that arises when jurisdictional units exceed a certain scale, may result in the potential for the abuse of power. Depending on the scope for such abuse it may be that it is not worth the risk of creating transboundary institutions beyond a certain scale, even if this means that the underlying environmental externality remains unresolved. The creation of a global minimal state to tackle climate change may well exceed such a threshold. Such a state would need to be granted unprecedented regulatory authority, while those under its jurisdiction would have little or no scope for redress should it abuse the power at its disposal.

In light of the above, a not unreasonable case can be made in favour of decentralised adaptation to climate change. Imposing costs now could reduce economic growth, and with it the capacity to deal with whatever climatic changes are likely to occur. The 1 per cent of gross domestic product (GDP) estimated by the recent Stern report on the economics of climate change to be the annual cost of reducing carbon dioxide emissions seems remarkably optimistic in view of the recommendation that cuts in emissions per unit of output need to reach the order of 80 per cent by 2050 (Stern, 2007). Given the notorious difficulties that even national governments have in estimating accurately the costs of relatively simple public infrastructure projects, the odds on the estimated costs of a plan to reduce carbon emissions on such a scale being accurate, seem very low indeed.[6] In addition, individuals, proprietary organisations and nation states may have a better chance of influencing their capacity to avoid the worst effects of climate change by, for example, investing in flood protection, than they would of exercising influence over a global governance structure.

It should now be evident that in the case of global-level environmental problems classical liberalism cannot offer any clear-cut 'answers' or 'solutions'. What should be equally evident, however, is that 'market-failure' analysis is of limited utility in attempting to design appropriate environmental interventions at the global scale because it pays little if any attention to the 'knowledge problems' and incentive-based constraints that must be addressed by a robust political economy.

COMMUNITARIAN OBJECTIONS TO CLASSICAL LIBERAL ENVIRONMENTALISM[7]

Where economic objections to classical liberalism focus on the logistical obstacles to environmental markets, a further set of critics develop a moral argument against 'privatisation'. Theorists in the communitarian tradition do not dispute that at least some environmental goods could be supplied via markets or market-like processes, but they reject nonetheless the view that these goods should be supplied in such a way.

At the core of communitarian objections to the extension of environmental markets is the belief that the individualistic and selfish attitudes that such markets are held to breed are inimical to the goal of a sustainable society. According to this view, if environmental problems are to be addressed at root this requires a fundamental reorientation of moral attitudes away from a 'consumerist' ethos and towards one centred on norms of democratic 'citizenship'. This line of thought has several dimensions which draw on some of the wider philosophical objections to classical liberalism considered in Chapter 3 of this book.

First, it is argued that environmental problems are 'systemic' and therefore cannot be dealt with effectively by approaches such as the definition of property rights that treat individual issues in isolation from others. Ecological systems are complex interrelated wholes where decisions affecting one dimension (such as land management) inevitably ripple out to other aspects of the socio-environmental system (such as water management). Because 'green' thinkers apply to ecological processes the notion that 'the whole is greater than the sum of its individual parts', they regard it as imperative that environmental decisions are based on more collective, 'system-level' processes where concerned citizens analyse consciously how their lifestyle choices impinge on the lives and environment of others (for example, Dryzek, 1987; Barry, 1999; Smith, 2003).

A second and related argument against the emphasis on property rights stems from what many greens see as a preoccupation of classical liberals with 'incentives'. Seen in this light, property rights approaches emphasise the concrete personal gains to be realised from environmental protection rather then encouraging people to reflect on the moral virtue of ecologically sensitive behaviour (Dryzek, 1987; Barry, 1999). The focus on individual incentives in cases where markets can supply environmental goods is said to intensify prisoner's dilemma and collective-good-type problems in cases where markets may not deliver such goods owing to the culture of selfishness that these institutions perpetuate. These problems are, it is suggested, likely to be reinforced in a commercial context where the power of advertising privileges individualistic values oriented around material consumption relative to collective goods such as the maintenance of environmental quality. Collective deliberation, it is argued, provides a context in which the value of such goods can be better articulated to balance the commercial pressure for material growth. Similarly, command and control regulations are judged more likely to inculcate 'other-regarding' behaviour by enforcing a communal conception of what is morally right or wrong in the environmental domain.

A third and final communitarian complaint against the classical liberal approach is that individual willingness to pay is not a valid criterion for a large number of goods deemed to reflect moral and ethical values that cannot, or should not, be bought or sold. According to this view, the classical liberal perspective treats individual preferences as fixed, and thus neglects the possibility that people can be educated to an appreciation of alternative lifestyles when exposed to a moral and institutional context that encourages debate and argument over the gratification of consumer preferences. Within this context, the moral component of a commitment to environmental objectives is deemed as unsuitable for inclusion in a trade-off with 'economic' ends. Moral conflicts over incommensurable ends cannot be captured by the common denominator of money prices and should instead be dealt with via democratic debate – where the value of environmental goods is determined by the 'power of the better argument' rather than willingness to pay (Sagoff, 1988).

The overall essence of the communitarian perspective is captured in the distinction that Sagoff (1988) draws between 'consumer' and 'citizen' preferences. When asking a group of students if they would visit a new ski resort proposed for construction in a national park, Sagoff noted that the majority would gladly visit the resort to benefit from the recreational opportunities. When asking the same group whether the resort should in fact be constructed, however, the majority responded in the negative. For Sagoff, the difference between these responses reflects the distinction between consumer and citizen preferences. As participants in a market for amoral consumer goods, people welcomed the opportunity for new recreational facilities, but in their capacity as critical moral citizens, they were opposed to the destruction of wilderness which they considered to be of value to their community as a whole. From Sagoff's perspective the implications of these findings are clear. If we do not want to live in a degraded environment, we should tend to opt for processes based on collective deliberation rather than on individual consumer choice.

Property Rights, Environmental Markets and the Common Good

Much of the communitarian critique sketched above centres on the purported 'individualism' of classical liberalism and its focus on 'incentives'. With its emphasis on meeting the requirements of a robust political economy it is certainly true that elements of the property rights approach highlight the incentives necessary for resource conservation. Yet, it is not the case that the classical liberal argument for 'privatisation' is dependent on such arguments. As noted throughout this book, the Hayekian or knowledge-based argument in favour of markets and the 'exit' principle makes no assumptions about individual motivations. Rather, it contends that markets are needed to coordinate resource use when underlying conditions are of such complexity that people can never be directly aware of the knowledge needed to adjust their behaviour in a manner consistent with the interests of others.

In view of the 'knowledge problem' the normative relevance of distinguishing between 'other-regarding citizenship' and 'selfish consumerism' that lies at the core of the communitarian critique is called into question. Consider the example provided by Sagoff, where it is argued that 'consumer' action to satisfy recreational 'wants' would favour the construction of a ski resort in a National Park, whereas 'citizen' action may oppose the destruction of unspoilt wilderness considered of value to the community as a whole. This seems to illustrate the merits of the motivational distinction between consumer-oriented and more civic behaviour, but on closer inspection the example fails to justify the conclusion that Sagoff derives. Sagoff himself recognises that most environmental decisions are not matters of moral absolutism, and that goods such as clean air and workplace safety have opportunity costs where at some point additional amounts of cleanliness or safety may be disproportionate to the goods and services that must be foregone in order to pay for them (Sagoff, 1988: 80).

Applying Sagoff's own analysis to the case of ski resorts it may not be that people have a community-centred objection to resorts per se, but that they are opposed to the construction of such a venture in a particular wilderness area – that is, where the costs are deemed too high. It follows that the underlying problem is to find a mechanism to decide where new ski resorts should proceed and how many there should be. For Sagoff, such decisions should be made through a deliberative democratic process based on compromise and debate. It is precisely at this juncture, however, that democratic deliberation faces the knowledge problem highlighted by Hayek. Democratic representatives can never access or process the complex of factors to adjust the demand for ski resorts accordingly. Information pertaining to ethics, local conditions, pressures on land use, and so on, does not exist as an integrated whole and nor can it be gathered into a deliberative forum. Where property rights to land and other assets are defined, however, the dispersed 'bits' of information may be communicated via a nexus of market exchanges transmitting context-specific factors in coded form across the overlapping perspectives of many different actors – shifting demand for ski resorts away from more environmentally valued and hence relatively more expensive sites.

To clarify this analysis, it is useful to compare the Hayekian argument for a property rights approach to the problem of 'open access' resources from those focusing exclusively on motivational concerns. According to the latter, establishing private property rights over resources such as water or fish stocks is crucial in helping to change the incentives that actors face, internalising costs and hence overcoming the 'free-rider' problem (see, for example, Baden and Stroup, 1979). Now, suppose an individual has no intention of 'free-riding' but is motivated as a concerned 'citizen' to reduce his or her water consumption to 'socially responsible' levels. In the absence of property rights and the resultant market prices for water there may be no way for the individual concerned to know what their 'socially responsible' level of consumption is. They may, of course, choose to arrive by 'guesswork' at some level of consumption below their 'normal' rate, but in the absence of prices indicating the most important margins for conservation they would have no idea whether such actions were actually worthwhile. In these circumstances even the most altruistically inclined person is likely to consume as much water as he or she personally requires, because at least she knows what that amount is, whereas the 'socially responsible' level of consumption is shrouded in a fog of ignorance (Steele, 1992: 205). Such problems will, of course, be multiplied indefinitely when taken to include the vast array of production and consumption possibilities that make up an advanced economy, and the complex environmental consequences arising from these possibilities. In short, irrespective of whether people are acting in 'consumer' or 'citizen' vein, without a set of relative prices to guide their actions people will be unable to know how urgent their respective demands on environmental resources may be.

Property Rights and the Evolution of Environmental Preferences

An equally questionable aspect of the distinction between environmental 'citizenship' and 'consumerism' arises in the context of the educative advantages attributed to social democratic procedures. If individual preferences are not fixed exogenously, then for communitarians it follows that these values should be subject to a process of democratic criticism and debate where their virtue, or lack thereof, can be examined by the community as a whole. Classical liberalism, however, does not question the endogeneity of preferences. Rather, it contends that 'exit'-based institutions are more robust in facilitating the discovery of previously unforeseen production and consumption values that may prove to have environmental benefits. According to this view, the spread of knowledge is enhanced when actors are secured a private sphere that enables them to experiment with projects and modes of life that do not accord with majority values.

Private property rights allow a greater range of decisions to be made and hence increase the scope for both minorities and majorities to be exposed to practices from which they may subsequently learn. The vast bulk of the goods that people desire and the techniques of production they employ are things that they learn to desire or employ because they see other people acting in a particular way. In the specific case of 'green' consumption, for example, it is doubtful whether the massive growth in the organic food market that has occurred over recent years would ever have developed if production decisions in the agricultural sector had been entirely the subject of collectivist or majoritarian procedures. For years, organic food was perceived to be the concern of an eccentric 'fringe'. It is, however, precisely because private property affords minorities the space to try out experimental ideas, the merits of which may be indiscernible (rather than simply talking about them), that more and more people are able to emulate such role models when the benefits become visible. In the specific case of the agricultural sector this process may have proceeded much more speedily had it not been for the enforced state subsidisation of intensive farming methods across most of the major democracies.

The classical liberal argument does not suggest that processes based on the 'exit' principle will necessarily throw up ideas 'good' for the environment, but that a process allowing for greater experimental adaptation is more likely to do so than a regime bound by majority decisions. Open-ended discovery processes such as markets necessarily allow mistakes and are characterised by an element of disequilibrium. 'Bad' decisions cannot be eliminated from evolution and are essential to a process characterised by trial and error learning. Ecosystems are themselves far from static entities. Rather, they are subject to constant change, both 'natural' and human induced, some of which may be beneficial, some of which may be harmful (Botkin, 1990; McCoy and Shreder-Frechete, 1994; Chase, 1995). The essentially unpredictable nature of such systems implies that collectives simply cannot know where they are supposed to be going. Experience suggests that governments are not in the best position to 'pick industrial winners', so there is little reason to believe that they will be able to select an appropriate development path, 'sustainable' or otherwise.

Now, it must be conceded that in the case of advertising there is probably a bias in the process of preference formation towards goods that can readily be supplied in markets, relative to those collective goods where the process of institutional evolution has not yet allowed for their supply via voluntary exchange.[8] There is, however, little reason to suggest that environmental or non-materialistic values per se would suffer from this bias, for there are a large number of growth-related consumption goods such as transport infrastructure that may be subject to similar problems in the organisation of supply. Moreover, the process of institutional entrepreneurship such as the formation of private communities discussed earlier is likely to allow an increasing number of environmental goods to be brought within the framework of market exchange and its attendant advertising and marketing procedures. That said, so long as the prevailing culture favours high levels of consumption those wishing to purchase property in order to live out a less materialistic lifestyle would have to compete directly in the market with those who prefer, say, new housing estates and shopping complexes to open spaces. This may, therefore, be an option confined to the relatively wealthy. From a classical liberal perspective, however, even if this turns out to be the case, the very fact that some people are able to make such choices can offer role models for others who may then be alerted to the benefits of alternative lifestyles – assuming such benefits do in fact exist.

Although people are undoubtedly influenced by the new consumption possibilities highlighted by advertising, this does not imply that their preferences are determined by the relevant information. In the final analysis, if people cease to derive benefits from additions to their consumption bundle then they must be assumed to be free to reject them. Social pressure may make choices of this nature very difficult, but for the reasons emphasised in Chapter 3 it may be easier to resist such pressure in an environment which relies on the 'exit' principle than under an alternative where choices must be justified in the context of a majoritarian forum. That the expression of alternative lifestyles may actually be discouraged by participatory politics is well illustrated via the experience of statutory land use regulation in the United Kingdom. Various 'travelling' groups, gypsies and 'deep ecologists' who reject much of modern consumerism and who happen to be relatively poor have purchased property with a view to creating camp sites in order to live out their particular cultural values. In many cases, however, they have been thwarted in their attempts to use their property accordingly by the system of nationalised development rights, which has allowed third-party 'stakeholders' to block what are seen as 'undesirable' lifestyles. A similar process was, in part, responsible for the initial nationalisation of development rights under the 1947 Town and Country Planning Act. During the 1920s and 1930s increasing numbers of the urban working class engaged in the speculative purchase of so called 'plot-land' developments, especially in South East England. The latter were informal housing settlements and self-sufficient agricultural allotments purchased by urban dwellers keen to escape the confines of city life. As Hardy and Ward (1984) show, however, the plot-lands movement was crushed by a coalition of middle-class rural residents demanding greater 'planning' and 'community control'.

Property Rights and Environmental Ethics

The remaining objection to the classical liberal focus on property rights raised by communitarians is that willingness to pay and 'bargaining' are simply not valid forms of decision-making in the context of goods deemed to reflect moral and ethical values. From a classical liberal perspective, however, this is a particularly weak line of tack. The fundamental reason for instituting property rights over environmental assets is precisely that they allow people to say no to inappropriate offers, whether on ethical grounds or for any other reason important to the property owner(s) concerned – and not to have such judgements made by bureaucrats or majorities of other 'citizens'. Just as one may refuse to sell the family home to the highest bidder because of personal history or identity, so a property right to a forest or waterway would allow individuals and groups not to sell extraction rights if the 'compensation' offered is judged inappropriate to the moral attachments concerned.

Communitarians complain that the use of a common denominator such as money is inappropriate where there are incommensurable moral ends involved, and where the aggregation of conflicting values is impossible. The classical liberal case for markets, however, does not claim that markets facilitate the aggregation of values into a yardstick of 'efficiency', but that in the absence of a consensus on ethical values they allow people with conflicting ends to engage in a process of mutual adjustment which increases the chance that any one of the relevant ends may be achieved. On a classical liberal understanding, what the 'common good' requires is a process of behavioural adaptation that takes into account a diversity of values and improves the chances of all concerned to achieve their respective ends. Critics of money prices appear to have no qualms about the use of a common denominator when it comes to their favoured 'deliberative designs', all of which resort to some form of majority voting (see, for example, Smith, 2003). Yet, for the reasons outlined earlier, such processes are far less likely to facilitate the necessary adjustments to variations in underlying ethics, changes in scarcity and local circumstances than a set of market generated prices.

That bargaining and mutual adjustment may also be required by those committed to 'green' values is apparent in the context of the debate within the United Kingdom over the ethical status of wind farms. For their proponents, such farms represent a more sustainable and 'socially virtuous' form of energy supply when compared to oil and natural gas. To their opponents, however, the prospect of hundreds of windmills atop previously open moors and hills is an affront to rural integrity and to the identity of those who live in the countryside. Unless one of these competing 'ethical ideals' is simply imposed on the relevant dissenting group, then some notion of bargaining and marginal adjustments between the holders of competing values must be accepted as the basis for deciding how many wind-farms there should be and where they should be situated. If property rights to land are specified then those who oppose wind-farms may seek to buy those sites which are thought most aesthetically sensitive, or if already owning them, they may attach private restrictive covenants which forbid any such development by a future owner. The latter move may, of course, reduce the marketable value of the property concerned. It is, therefore, erroneous to suggest that moral values cannot be reflected by the 'cash nexus', since every decision to engage in a transaction, for whatever reason, will be reflected in the price signals that emerge as a consequence. The choice, therefore, is not between the use of 'economic' or 'non-economic' forms of valuation, but between those that emphasise voluntary consent and those that rely on the coercive imposition of a particular scale of values.

EGALITARIAN OBJECTIONS TO CLASSICAL LIBERAL ENVIRONMENTALISM

In view of the above arguments, it may be conceded that property rights approaches are not incapable of accounting for the ethical dimension in resource use. Nonetheless, for egalitarians this dimension will not be fully reflected unless underlying matters of justice pertaining to the distribution of the relevant property rights are first addressed. Within this context, there are two distinct claims that are made by theorists who see the pursuit of social justice as an essential component of environmental protection objectives.

The first claim often made by egalitarian greens is that the existence of widespread poverty and, more specifically, inequality is a direct cause of environmental problems. According to the authors of the 'Brundtland Report', for example, poverty is one of the most important sources of 'pollution' in its own right (World Commission on Environment and Development, 1987: 28). This 'pollution' is thought to result from the fact that people who are poor – and especially those in developing nations – are more likely to act in ways that damage the environments in which they live, in order to secure basic survival or a minimum standard of economic well-being. In addition to problems wrought by absolute poverty, it is also argued that large-scale inequalities in wealth act as a form of environmental 'externality'. According to this view, the 'excessive' consumption habits of the rich prompt a process of competitive emulation by the poor and thus stimulate demands for ever higher levels of economic growth and its attendant environmental consequences. It follows that effective solutions to environmental problems require measures to end absolute poverty in both the developed and the developing world, and to secure a more egalitarian distribution of resources.

Distinct from these claims concerning the causal connection between poverty and environmental protection are a further set of arguments focused on the justice or injustice of the prevailing distribution of access to environmental quality. Distributive issues are said to lie at the heart of many environmental problems, because unless the distribution of environmental 'goods' and 'bads' is seen to be just then societal support for the behavioural changes that may be needed to avoid excessive ecological damage will not be forthcoming (for example, Barry, 1999; Eckersley, 2004).

From the perspective of liberal egalitarianism unequal access to environmental quality constitutes evidence of potential injustice. Though they may share the same abstract commitment to 'the environment' as the rich, faced with decisions over access to food or housing space those on lower incomes often exhibit a lesser willingness and/or ability to pay the opportunity cost of greater regulation. This phenomenon is, for example, witnessed in the propensity for wealthy residential areas to exhibit stricter controls than poorer equivalents which tend to be the primary recipients of environmental hazards such as waste treatment plants. The unequal ability of people to secure access to environmental quality may, on this account, only be justified if the relevant inequality maximises the position of the worst-off or is seen to reflect deliberate choices – rather than 'brute luck'. Such choices may include the conscious decision to favour growth over environmental objectives, the mistaken adoption of inefficient production techniques, or the failure to invest in ways that generate the wealth that may sustain material well-being and higher environmental standards. For egalitarian greens, however, it is self-evident that existing patterns of inequality exceed anything that might be justified in these terms. In addition, for those influenced by the 'politics of difference', lack of access to environmental goods reflects not only a maldistribution of resources but also a failure of institutional structures to allow those affected by environmental externalities to have sufficient control over the decisions that lead to their generation (for example, Pulido, 1996). From this perspective, environmental justice requires not only a redistribution of wealth, but also a move towards a more democratic form of social organisation where decisions that affect the distribution of environmental goods and bads are based on public deliberation rather than being left to emerge as an unintended consequence of individuals and organisations pursuing their own particular interests.

Though the existence of intracountry inequalities is a key concern for egalitarians, questions of environmental justice are thought to be even more significant at the international scale (for example, Shue, 1999). The fact that both individuals and governments in the developing world are in less of a position to 'afford' policies that might increase the level of environmental protection is considered as evidence of injustice. Low-income countries may adopt inferior environmental standards in order to maintain a competitive position in international markets or to attract foreign investment capital on the basis of low regulatory costs. In some circumstances, less developed nations may even 'import' pollution from the developed world by acting as waste processing locations in order to boost rates of economic growth. From an egalitarian perspective there is a double injustice in the resulting distribution of environmental costs. On the one hand, the existence of substantial inequalities between rich and poor nations is itself considered as evidence that the distribution of benefits and burdens between nations may be unjust. It may, for example, reflect unequal endowments of natural resources such as mineral wealth or climate. On the other hand, however, such a distribution is considered to result from a set of international economic institutions that are 'structurally unjust' because they prevent less-advantaged parts of the world from securing a greater share of resources through their own efforts (Eckersley, 2004).

The issues associated with the pursuit of global environmental justice are crystallised in terms of the responses that egalitarians propose to deal with problems such as anthropogenic climate change. The latter is held to include a requirement for large-scale transfers of wealth to less developed nations, because it is not they who have been responsible for the environmental problems wrought by the developed world (Shue, 1999). Solutions to global-level environmental dilemmas require cooperation from less developed nations and newly industrialising states, but these states cannot be expected to cooperate unless the distribution of benefits and burdens meets the requirements of social justice. Building on this perspective, it is often suggested that global environmental justice requires that 'ecological space' should be allocated according to principles of strict equality (see, for example, Hayward, 2006). The concept of ecological space refers to aspects of the environment that constitute a fixed stock – such as the capacity of the atmosphere to absorb CO_2 emissions without provoking catastrophic climate change. Owing to its finite character, greater use of ecological space in order to secure economic development by some actors is said to deprive others of their capacity to achieve an equivalent level of wealth without threatening the future of the planet. It follows, according to this line of thought, that developed nations that have exceeded their threshold by contributing to carbon emissions should compensate less developed nations which have yet to use the ecological space they would be entitled to under the principle of equal shares.

The Link between Poverty, Inequality and Environmental Protection

Though it is often taken as obvious by 'greens' that reductions in absolute and relative poverty are a necessary condition of environmental protection, there are few if any grounds to suppose that such a connection exists. It is certainly the case that there are instances where pressure on resources by people who lack adequate access to basics such as food and fuel have contributed to environmental degradation – increased desertification in sub-Saharan Africa being a potential case in point (Morris, 1995). Equally, however, it is possible for people who exhibit a very low standard of living not to exceed their environmental carrying capacity. Remote tribes in Amazonia live in absolute poverty and yet do not threaten the overall integrity of the resource base, in large part because their population is low relative to the resources available. The connection between environmental stress and poverty tends only to arise when population to resource ratios increase and/or people wish to rise above the level of mere subsistence. If people are willing to live in subsistence conditions and to limit their population accordingly then poverty may be entirely compatible with environmental 'sustainability' – albeit a form of sustainability which is hostile to economic development objectives.

There is of course no reason to suppose that people should be willing to trade off improvements in living standards and life expectancy for the sake of maintaining pristine ecological conditions. Rising living standards and life expectancy require that some environmental resources are sacrificed in order to create the material well-being that may then enable people to place a higher value on the remaining stock of ecological assets. It is in this context that there is indeed evidence that demand for environmental protection is related to absolute levels of wealth. Those who exhibit a higher standard of living and higher life expectancy appear willing to spend more resources on protecting environmental assets than the poor, for whom improving the standard of living may be more of a priority than reducing pollution or protecting scenic landscapes (Beckerman and Pasek, 2001). It may, therefore, be mistaken to imply that when lower-income groups receive fewer environmental goods this results from a deliberate 'injustice' on the part of the better-off. As Schmidtz (2001) points out, few would consider it an act of injustice if environmental hazards such as waste treatment facilities were sighted in wealthy neighbourhoods whose inhabitants then moved out, selling their houses to poorer people who were willing to live near the plant in order to access better homes than they could otherwise afford.

Within the above context, the problem for egalitarian greens is that there is little evidence that the best way of ending absolute poverty and hence raising the demand for environmental protection is to engage in large-scale programmes of income redistribution. If it is recognised that the demand for environmental quality is income-elastic – as people become wealthier they tend to place greater emphasis on environmental protection and other 'quality of life' variables – then it is true that transfers of income may raise the ability of low-income groups to pay for access to environmental goods. There may, however, be a simultaneous reduction in income and hence demand for environmental goods from the rich, as a consequence of such transfers. An increase in the total demand for environmental quality may require further economic progress and rising living standards for all social groups. This progress, however, is dependent on inequalities which signal to people where and how they can receive the best returns for their efforts. Similarly, the processes of competitive emulation that enable people to discover and to imitate the most successful ways of overcoming collective action problems depend on inequalities between actors to signal the need for change and to prompt social learning. Redistributive measures are likely to stifle this process by transferring assets away from those who have discovered ways to internalise costs efficiently, and by reducing incentives for those who have been less successful to modify their behaviour accordingly.

A second point to emphasise in the above regard is that many inequalities may continue to be necessary even if the relationship between income growth and the demand for environmental quality could be severed and the aim of policy were to shift towards maintaining a 'steady-state' economy where a constant level of output is produced for a lower environmental impact. It may not be possible, even in principle, for all people simultaneously to achieve the highest environmental standards. 'Clean technologies', for example, cannot be made simultaneously available to all but are dependent on a process of evolutionary change where high-cost environmental improvements are first delivered to a few before becoming available to a wider spectrum of people as the cost of technology falls (Wildavsky, 1989). In the specific case of measures to tackle anthropogenic climate change, 'low-carbon' technologies such as solar, wave or wind power cannot be made available to all parts of the world without first having been applied in a number of pioneering countries. Equally, it cannot be assumed that the process of industrialisation and contemporary technological advance could have proceeded on a 'low-carbon' basis. On the contrary, the ability to produce effective carbon substitutes today is dependent on an evolved capital structure of 'high-carbon' technologies which may have been necessary to enable sufficient production of the components and equipment required to bring low-carbon energy into fruition. In other words, inequality in the use of 'ecological space' may be a necessary condition not only for economic development, but also for subsequent environmental improvements.

The Mirage of Environmental Justice

If inequalities must be accepted as a necessary component of environmental protection, what of the demand to ensure that the relevant inequalities are structured to meet the requirements of social justice? From a classical liberal perspective, once the trade-off between environmental protection and equality is recognised then it is unlikely that there will be any basis for agreement on 'how much' equality should be traded off against growth, conservation or any combination of these objectives. If individuals, voluntary associations and states are able to make choices according to different weightings of these trade-offs, then the society-wide pattern of access to environmental quality that emerges cannot be accounted for in terms of the 'justice' or 'injustice' of any particular set of actions. Rawlsian principles are, for example, unlikely to be helpful when 'maximising the material position of the worst-off' may need to be traded off with other objectives such as reducing pollution. There is unlikely to be agreement on whether transferring billions in resources to secure relatively marginal increases to the per capita income of the poorest is worth sacrificing the large-scale investments that may be necessary to promote cleaner growth in the longer term. Similarly, Dworkin's 'equality of resources' is unworkable when the value of the natural resources that people hold is in constant flux owing to technical innovations and shifts in consumer preferences. And, where it is hard to find common ground in seeking to ascertain what proportion of the resources that people hold is due to their own efforts in discovering and developing the relevant assets, as opposed to the 'brute luck' of being born into an 'advantaged' or 'disadvantaged' socio-environmental context.[9]

In the absence of agreement on what social justice requires, far from helping to solve environmental dilemmas, a preoccupation with the desire to implement common distributive standards is likely to promote conflict. Such conflict may be particularly intense if inequalities are determined by deliberative democratic bodies of the sort favoured by the politics of difference. People may feel aggrieved at their inability to afford the level of environmental quality they may wish to purchase in a market, but since there is no individual or group which can be held responsible for their particular allocation this may be less likely to provoke resentment than under an alternative where public deliberators consciously determine which particular individuals and groups are to benefit or lose out from any necessary inequalities. Ostrom's work, for example, suggests that attempts to develop greater 'unity' with respect to the distribution of environmental goods may be more likely to undermine solutions to the collective-action problems that lie at the heart of many cases of resource depletion (Ostrom, 1990, 2006). Thus, while agreement on common distributive norms (such as performance-related pay or resource allocation lotteries) within groups that are relatively well known to one another or who share a common culture may enable them to overcome collective action dilemmas, large-scale redistribution conducted at the national level has tended to promote between-group conflict owing to an absence of shared norms of fairness.

The latter point may apply with equal if not more force in the context of the global distribution of environmental goods, such as the determination of who should pay the costs of responses to anthropogenic climate change. On the one hand, it is not self-evident that 'fairness' requires that poorer countries are 'compensated' for the environmental damage resultant from development in more prosperous parts of the world, because it is not usually the case that less developed nations have wanted to avoid economic growth and thus becoming 'polluters', but that their own development strategies have often failed. Neither will it suffice to blame such failures on the 'structural injustice' of the 'international system', for as the previous chapter showed, many of the countries that have embraced trade- and market-friendly institutions on a unilateral basis have had unprecedented successes in reducing poverty. The persistence of poverty across large parts of the developing world is often a reflection of internal policy decisions made by ruling elites.

Second, and contrary to the Malthusian doctrines of 'deep greens', the process of industrialisation in the developing world today does not require the same intensity of resource use previously required by developed nations. It requires less, because developing nations are now able to benefit from the capital structure and innovations that were arrived at in the developed world by an earlier process of trial and error learning. It is, therefore, far from obvious that developing nations are the environmental 'victims' of an unequal and 'unfair' use of 'ecological space' by the global rich. The 'excessive' use of ecological space by developed nations has opened up the possibility for developing nations to achieve higher living standards without inflicting an equivalent amount of ecological damage.

Now, it might be argued that the latter point does not hold very strongly because developing countries pay for many of the technological advances that they derive from the richer nations (Shue, 1999). The key point, however, is that they pay less for technological innovations both in economic and environmental terms than would have been the case were they to have evolved the relevant technologies on an independent basis. Thus, in a period when it was virtually alone in the process of industrialisation, it took eighteenth-century England 58 years to double its national wealth. One hundred years later, however, and owing to its ability to draw on technological developments elsewhere, Japan was able to double its wealth within 34 years and for a smaller level of resource inputs. A further 100 years of industrialisation saw South Korea doubling its wealth within a mere 11 years (Norberg, 2003: 134). A similar relationship also applies in those cases where poorer countries act as waste processing plants for pollutants produced in the industrialised world. For egalitarian greens, such transactions are manifestly unjust. The case in their favour, however, is that the income generated may enable developing countries to achieve a higher standard of living for a lower level of exposure to pollution than might be the case if the relevant countries sought to reach equivalent living standards via domestic industrialisation alone.

What matters in all of the above is that given the dependence of 'cleaner' growth on a history of 'dirtier' growth, it follows that the most environmentally advanced societies will at any given point either have a history of being the biggest 'polluters', or will profit from the technological advances developed by 'polluting' societies. There are, however, no common standards of justice, merit or desert to determine the position of different countries in the necessary evolutionary chain. The inequalities in access to economic and environmental goods that prevail today are a combined reflection of purposeful effort on behalf of specific individuals and cultural groups, different trade-offs reflecting a diversity of socio-cultural priorities, and accidents of history and geography. Unless the relative position of different people and countries is to be determined by a more or less random combination of such factors, then the only alternative would be for a global authority deliberately to assign shares of economic and environmental resources to specific actors. The latter process could not, however, be considered commensurate with social justice because there are no globally agreed criteria to determine what this would require.

The concept of 'corrective justice', it should be noted, is particularly ill-suited to determine an appropriate distribution of environmental goods and bads. As argued above, while it is true that technological and industrial developments that have occurred in some parts of the world have 'imposed' costs on others that are now seeking to develop in the context of climate change, it is also the case that poorer countries have received uncompensated benefits from this process. Crucially, it is not clear on what basis it could be determined whether the costs outweigh the benefits or vice versa. Any such calculation would require knowledge of what the pattern of economic activity in developing nations would have been were it not for the unequal use of natural resources by today's developed nations. Such a calculation would presuppose knowledge of countless different resource-allocation decisions made by a host of different governments, private individuals and organisations, and how the distributive results of those choices would compare with those seen in the world today. There is, however, simply no way of knowing how much better or worse off today the inhabitants of, say, Britain and the United States might be than the residents of India or Brazil if all had started off with an equal allocation of 'ecological space', because it is impossible to know which choices and trade-offs would have been made.

Property Rights, Power and the Mirage of Climate Justice

Insofar as individuals and organisational entities such as nation states are committed to the achievement of material prosperity as well as ecological protection, then from a classical liberal perspective there are no grounds to suppose that the distribution of environmental goods commensurate with the attainment of such prosperity can be determined according to criteria of social justice. Arguments concerning environmental injustice may be on stronger ground, however, with respect to the impact of industrial activity on those societies that do not desire to adopt a lifestyle conducive to prosperity, but who may suffer the consequences of decisions made by those committed to the pursuit of material goals. It is a clear breach of the 'non-interference' principle if some societies are faced with the possibility of severe disruption to their modes of life owing to externally generated phenomena such as anthropogenic climate change.

At root such issues come down to the question of the distribution of property rights and what the relevant domain of 'non-interference' should encompass in a specific case. From a classical liberal perspective 'externalities' are always 'double-sided' phenomena. It is not that 'polluters' are always the actors who impose external costs on a set of environmental 'victims'. On the contrary, those who wish to stop 'pollution' from taking place may also be interpreted as seeking to 'impose costs' on those who may suffer from the reduced opportunities to escape poverty that an 'excessive' concern with environmental protection may bring. Whether an actor or group of actors can be determined as the 'victim' is fundamentally a question of who possesses the relevant property rights and whether or not they wish to trade such rights in exchange for some form of compensation. With respect to climate change and the potential 'pollution' represented by CO_2 emissions the basic problem is that there are currently no enforceable property rights to the global climatic system. Crucially, however, even if the assignment of such rights was somehow practical it is not clear that their assignment could accord with commonly accepted standards of justice.

As noted in Chapter 5, in many contexts where resources are in an 'open access' state the establishment of property rights often involves the adoption of 'first-possession'-type rules (pp. 140–43). These rules benefit not only those who are the initial appropriators but also those who may not be in a position to secure initial possession. The advantage of first-possession rules is that they provide people with the security and incentives to expand or maintain the stock of resources by reducing the capacity for free-riding on acts of production or conservation. Consequently the range of available options for 'latecomers' is increased. The establishment of property rights also increases the potential for people to select between and to learn from a variety of modes of life. One of the strongest arguments for establishing secure property rights is that they enable people with conflicting values to coexist by securing a recognised domain in which they may exercise their own vision of a good life without needing approval from others. When there are a range of different owners of property, then there is greater scope for those who are not themselves owners to enter into and exit from a range of social and economic practices in order to best approximate their own particular schedule of ends. In the absence of property rights or where there is a single owner of all property – such as the state – conflict is more likely to arise as rival individuals and groups race to ensure that their own particular ends are achieved at the expense of those held by others. Seen in this light, property rules of the 'first-possession' variety may be a necessary requirement of the so-called Lockean proviso, which states that the appropriation of natural resources is only legitimate if the appropriators leave 'enough and as good for others'.

First possession may be an effective way of assigning property rights and reducing conflict where it is possible to draw boundaries that delimit the scope of particular resource parcels. In the case of the global climatic system, however, it is not clear how first possession or any other rule determining the distribution of property could be invoked in a satisfactory manner. Suppose, for example, that the right to an atmosphere 'unpolluted' by industrial CO_2 emissions and to a 'stable climate' was assigned to people who reject the idea of material progress. Such a right would represent the capacity to close down the global economy and to 'impose' a regime of relative poverty on the rest of the global population. Potential polluters could offer to 'buy' these rights, but such offers would most likely be refused because the very idea of monetary compensation would be frowned upon by people who reject materialistic progress. If, on the other hand, an effective right to 'pollute' were granted to those favouring industrial development then the position would approach the current status quo, which many people in the environmental movement consider unjust. How could it be just to require non-materialistic cultures to pay others not to pollute when the values of such people preclude the genera-tion of the wealth needed to make such payments?

What matters is that the global dimension to such questions precludes an 'exit' option. As a consequence, it is not clear how any mechanism for distrib-uting rights at the global level could meet the Lockean proviso because the beneficiary of the relevant assignment would be placed in a 'winner-take-all' position. The unfortunate conclusion to emerge is that any decisions taken with respect to the management of the global atmosphere are unlikely to reflect principles of justice but will depend on the underlying distribution of economic and political power. When there is no scope for the coexistence of conflicting values via an 'exit' option and when there is no room for compro-mise between those holding such values, then the likely result will be one of rule by the most powerful – and in the contemporary context, this means the majority of the industrialised nations.

Needless to say, classical liberalism does not claim that such a state of affairs is desirable or satisfactory. Rather, it points out that there are no stan-dards of justice to deal with such cases. The classical liberal emphasis on justice as 'non-interference' with property rights is unworkable, but so are egalitarian principles such as those of Rawls and Dworkin. To speak of 'maximising the position of the worst-off' is of doubtful relevance when there is no agreement on whether the 'worst-off' are those who wish to pollute the atmosphere as a route out of poverty, or whether they include those who may suffer the effects of climatic changes brought about by 'progress' of which they disapprove. Likewise, to speak of 'equality of resources' is questionable, when the underlying problem stems from an absence of agreement over whether it is legitimate to treat the global atmosphere as a marketable resource. Finally, it is doubtful that the processes of democratic deliberation favoured by the 'politics of difference' could result in decisions which reflect shared norms of justice. Those who wish to eschew economic progress in favour of a subsistence lifestyle are unlikely to consider it 'just' that their way of life may be impinged upon because a global majority has voted to take ecological risks – even if that same majority has offered to pay 'compensation' for its actions.

CONCLUSION

Environmental protection issues are seen by critics of classical liberalism as a sort of 'Waterloo' for an approach which emphasises private or several property rights and the importance of 'exit' over collectivist forms of decision-making. This chapter has sought to demonstrate that such critics are misguided. Though it cannot offer definitive solutions to all environmental dilemmas, classical liberalism is able to offer a clear set of principles against which to evaluate existing institutional practices and alternative proposals for environmental improvement. These principles include recognition that, wherever possible, environmental problems should be addressed through a decentralised, evolutionary process based on attempts to define and enforce property rights 'from the ground up'. The classical liberal approach also contends that where exit-based institutions cannot be adapted to a specific environmental problem, this should not be taken to imply the need for the 'top-down' imposition of regulations and controls, whether on economic or on ethical or moral grounds. Robust political economy analysis requires that the 'knowledge problems' and deficient incentives that may result from national or supranational systems of regulation and distribution are properly accounted for. In the latter instance it may often be necessary to recognise the unpalatable truth that no solution may be preferable to a misguided cure.

NOTES

1. Should crowding occur in the absence of exclusion technologies then the good becomes in effect a 'common-pool' or 'open access' resource.
2. There is no contradiction here between public choice analysis and the Hayekian account set out above. In the final analysis, the costs and benefits concerned are subjective and the 'socially optimal' pattern of policy interventions cannot be estimated accurately by an outside observer. It is not therefore possible to say that existing environmental interventions are 'inefficient' in some objectively definable sense. What one may do, however, is to examine

whether there are any structural biases within a set of institutions that prevent the interests of particular groups from being considered in the decision-making process. This is the sort of analysis that informs the Virginia school of public choice and its understanding of the differential effect of collective action problems facing various interest groups. It suggests that even if there are large numbers of actors who favour environmental objectives, there may be structural or incentive-based constraints that prevent these interests from being adequately reflected. Such an account may be in the best position to explain why politicians, though frequently claiming to promote environmental objectives, often introduce policies that contradict these very objectives.

3. It should be recognised here that 'open access' regimes are not necessarily inefficient from a conservation point of view. On the contrary, in conditions of relative abundance, where there are low population to resource pressures, open access may be optimal because the costs of defining and enforcing property rights in such cases are not outweighed by an impending scarcity constraint. The need to establish some form of exclusive ownership right only arises when access to the resource base becomes crowded and subject to the effects of free-riding.

4. In the case of 'public goods' subject to non-rivalrous consumption, the charging of entrance fees does not, contra the standard neo-classical analysis of Samuelson, necessarily undermine efficiency. When deciding how to use a resource, the relevant cost is its value in alternative uses and not the marginal cost of admitting additional consumers. The best way to discover whether consumers prefer the provision of the public good over some alternative may be to charge a fee for access. Even such criteria as non-rivalrous consumption may not be discernible without some form of pricing mechanism. What constitutes crowding for one person may differ for someone else, and without the capacity to charge for access to different degrees of exclusion (does one prefer an empty swimming pool to one with other swimmers? for example) it may not be possible to discern when one person's consumption of the good detracts from that of others (on this, see Minasian, 1964).

5. Russia in particular would likely be a net beneficiary owing to the improved agricultural productivity resulting from a warmer climate and fewer cold-related deaths during the winter months; China may also be a similar beneficiary from climate change (Nordhaus and Boyer, 2000; Lomborg, 2007). On some estimates there are currently far more deaths worldwide associated with cold-weather events than there are associated with excessive heat (Lomborg, 2007).

6. The recent fiasco surrounding overspending on the new Scottish parliament building and the 'Big Dig' public transport scheme in Boston, USA, are two of the most recent examples. The former had an original cost estimate of £40 million, but was completed for a total of £450 million, while the latter has seen costs rise from a projected $2 billion to $15 billion and is yet to be completed (Otteson, 2006: 183–4).

7. This section draws on the argument presented in Pennington (2005).

8. Supporters of deliberative democracy and the Habermasian 'ideal speech situation' are likely to object that such inequality arises from 'money power', is 'structural' in nature, and prevents alternative notions of life from receiving a fair hearing in the public discourse. So long as any form of commercial activity is allowed to coexist alongside those who reject material progress, however, it is difficult to see how this issue might be resolved, since by definition those who engage in activities which generate wealth are likely to have the wherewithal to propagate their own particular values. It would be odd to require that those who reject material progress – such as, for example, Buddhist monks – should be entitled to an equal share of advertising resources when their lifestyle precludes the generation of the necessary resources.

9. One attempt to apply Dworkin's principles which exposes their unworkability is Steiner's proposal that people in all countries should have equal access to a share of the aggregate global value of territorial sites (Steiner, 1999). The latter constitutes the difference between the aggregate value of sites and the aggregate value of those contents that represent improvements to the sites made by human activity (Steiner, 1999: 189–90). This proposal is similar to those advocated by supporters of the 'Georgist' movement who favour the taxation of land values on the premise that land rents constitute an 'unearned increment' – in effect the 'good brute luck' of living in a society which raises the value of the land one holds irrespective of

any improvements one makes to the land concerned. There are several problems with 'Georgist' arguments. First, it is not clear why the rationale for a land tax should not also apply to labour. The wages that people receive in the market reflect not only their own efforts but an 'unearned increment' reflecting the sum total of social and technological developments that contribute to the overall demand for labour services. Second, there is no basis for agreement on what proportion of an individual's wages or the rental returns to their land are due to the efforts of the owner relative to those which reflect the technological improvements and choices made by people in the wider society. Even in the case of natural resources it is far from clear what constitutes an 'unimproved resource' – 'resources' do not 'exist' as such but only come to be seen as useful assets through human perception and discovery; on this, see Simon (1981). Third, the taxation of 'idle' or 'unimproved' resources is likely to generate perverse environmental consequences. Specifically, it would constitute a disincentive to conserve natural resources because any individual or country thought to have more than their 'fair share' of 'unimproved assets' would be liable to taxation – thus inducing them to 'improve', that is, to use or develop the relevant resource.

9. Conclusion

Intellectual battle-lines in political economy are focused today, as ever, on determining the boundaries between the sphere of individual liberty and the coercive power of the state. Classical liberalism as it has been understood throughout this book bases its case for a movement 'towards the minimal state' on the principles of robust political economy. It suggests that given limited rationality and the need to constrain the behaviour of those motivated by self-interest, a framework that allows for decentralised experimentation and which holds people accountable for their experiments in living is more likely to promote socio-economic progress than one that centralises power in a coercive authority, democratically elected or otherwise.

At the time of completion in 2010, however, the pendulum of opinion appears to have swung decisively in the direction of a more state-centric approach. From responses to the financial crisis to concerns over income inequality and environmental protection, the notion that state power can deliver what liberty cannot is once again widely shared. Ideas matter in political economy, and for good or for ill, changes in the climate of opinion affect the direction of institutional change. The case for classical liberalism is held by critics to depend on the fanciful assumptions about human rationality that underlie the 'efficient markets' hypothesis of neo-classical economics. Classical liberals are widely thought to hold an asocial conception of the individual which has little or no appreciation for the communal identifications that shape human lives. And finally, classical liberalism is considered to be oblivious to questions of social justice and the unequal distribution of power and social status. The arguments presented in these pages have sought to show that, though they are widely cited, none of these charges stands up to scrutiny.

Though the scale of the movement towards liberalisation that has proceeded in recent years has often been exaggerated, the speed with which support for such measures has evaporated nonetheless raises serious questions about the viability of classical liberalism as a robust political project. Critics of the tradition have long argued that the notion of a society held together by a self-regulating spontaneous order is unstable and will itself generate 'spontaneous' demands for a growth in the power of the state. To some extent these criticisms appear well justified. On the one hand, the notion that a complex order can arise in society without some form of administrative control is

264

counter-intuitive. One need not accept Hayek's argument that the human mind has yet to adapt itself to life in the 'great' or 'open' society (see Hayek, 1988), to recognise that a tradition emphasising incremental improvement via signalling mechanisms and evolutionary selection may have less popular appeal than schools of thought which suggest that economic progress, solidarity and social justice can all be delivered at the stroke of a legislative pen. Equally, it is undoubtedly the case that politicians will continually come under pressure from organised groups representing economic and cultural interests who feel threatened by the process of evolutionary change. It may be unrealistic to expect that politicians motivated out of the desire to retain political power will always be able to resist such demands.

Granting these points, however, it does not follow that classical liberalism is unviable as a political project, for the question of viability in political economy is always a relative one. A 'pure' form of classical liberal order may well be unattainable, but the principles that inform the case for a movement 'towards the minimal state' may still prove more workable than any alternative. The arguments set out in these pages suggest that market-failure economics and the communitarian and egalitarian traditions lack a robust account of how the more extensive role they envisage for coercive authority can deliver their stated objectives. In a world characterised by uncertainty and imperfect knowledge, attempts to promote economic stability by centralising powers in the hands of regulatory authorities are likely to increase the possibility of 'systemic' failure. In a world where individual and communal identifications are in a state of constant flux, attempts to institutionalise a common identity by extending the scope of the 'public sphere' are likely to close off the process of cross-cultural interchange and understanding. And, in a world where people with different talents, histories and belief systems interact, attempts to implement social justice through the legislative powers of the state are likely to thwart ethical learning and to promote conflict rather then solidarity.

In a sense it would be accurate to describe classical liberalism as a utopian political project, but it is a very particular form of utopianism that classical liberalism is concerned with. Rather than assuming away fundamental features of the human condition, the case for a classical liberal order emerges from an exploration of the constraints set by the knowledge problem and the incentive problem, and the capacity of rival proposals for utopia to cope with these constraints. Classical liberalism aims, therefore, to discover which political utopias are unworkable and to delineate those universal conditions that a workable form of utopia must respect.

A consistent application of this 'modest' utopianism must, however, also inform any proposals for a movement 'towards the minimal state' – and it is here that classical liberalism faces its greatest challenge. While classical liberals offer a detailed account of the benefits that flow from an institutional framework that facilitates market exchange and allows for the decentralised evolution of civil society, the principles of robust political economy do not offer clear guidelines with respect to the processes and mechanisms that might bring such a framework about. Attention to the knowledge problem and the incentive problem suggest a sceptical attitude towards any efforts to introduce such a framework through legislative fiat. Legislators are unlikely to possess the knowledge to implement a process of institutional reform that is sufficiently sensitive to local contexts, and the greater the powers they possess to introduce such reform, the greater may be the incentive to act in an opportunistic vein. On the other hand, since hierarchical structures do, in certain circumstances, possess efficiency advantages over 'spontaneous orders' and may be needed to overcome collective-action problems, the case for legislative action to create a framework of private or several property rights within which the process of evolutionary growth may unfold also has its place.

The debate over the relative merits of evolutionary approaches versus those that seek to design the transition to a more liberal regime is most evident in the context of the developing world. Classical liberalism offers a coherent explanation for the almost universal failure of approaches that emphasise supranational structures and large-scale income transfers in promoting institutional reform. At the same time, however, the possibility that lower levels of government might be the agents of successful institutional change within the developing world cannot be ruled out. Though classical liberalism points towards a 'do no harm' philosophy at the international scale, beyond this it cannot specify at what level some form of government action may be required to create the framework of secure property rights that is the essential prerequisite of economic and social development.

The above tensions also afflict proposals to introduce liberalising measures in those parts of the world that do in fact possess the basic infrastructure of functioning property rights and a market economy. If there is to be a movement away from state-centric solutions to poverty and the supply of 'public services', then policy-makers will need to choose between an evolutionary and more 'constructivist' path. From an evolutionary perspective all that is required is for state-provided services to be open to competition from the private and voluntary sectors, and for people to be refunded a proportion of their taxes should they choose to receive these services outside of the public sector. The assumption underlying this approach is that 'inefficient' government agencies will simply 'wither away' in the face of open competition. Nonetheless, given the history of state monopoly power and the overwhelming advantages that incumbent tax-financed agencies possess, a case can also be made for the need consciously to 'break up' government monopolies in order to facilitate the desired process of 'creative destruction'.

Dilemmas of this nature are still more pronounced in the domain of environmental protection. On the one hand, the evolution of the new and more fluid structures of property rights required to cope with the complexity of environmental problems is unlikely to come about if governments play too active a role in seeking to 'design' the relevant institutions. On the other hand, with governments so heavily implicated in the current regulation and management of environmental assets it is difficult to see how any programme of classical liberal reform can avoid at least an element of institutional design.

In the final analysis, the advancement of classical liberalism, whether via an evolutionary or a constructivist route, will depend on questions of political judgement and knowledge of local circumstances. It will, however, also depend crucially on the role of 'events' in providing opportunities for reforms of different stripes and in generating obstacles to such reforms. There can be little doubt that the collapse of the socialist project in Eastern Europe and elsewhere provided a significant impetus for the liberalisation movement of recent years, modest though it may have been in practice. Equally, the crisis of 2008 has offered a new opportunity for those who wish to reverse the liberalising trend to advance a narrative that advocates a massive extension of state power. Whether classical liberalism can withstand the current storm in the political climate, and whether it can seize the future opportunities for reform that will arise as the contradictions of social democracy become more apparent, will depend on the clarity of its responses to the dominant opinions of the day. It has not been the purpose of this book to specify where and how a movement towards classical liberalism may occur, but to challenge those elements of the intellectual climate that point towards an increasingly illiberal future. From the current wreckage we may yet see the rebirth of classical liberalism as a political force. Where and how, is beyond the capacity of this classical liberal to predict.

References

Acemolgu, D., Johnson, S., Robinson, J.A. (2000) The Colonial Origins of Comparative Development: An Empirical Investigation, *American Economic Review*, 91 (5): 1369–1401.

Adaman, F., Devine, P. (1997) On the Economic Theory of Socialism, *New Left Review*, 221: 523–37.

Adsera, A., Ray, D. (1999) History and Coordination Failures, *Journal of Economic Growth*, 3: 267–76.

Akerlof, G. (1970) The Market for Lemons: Quality, Uncertainty and the Market Mechanism, *Quarterly Journal of Economics*, 97 (4): 543–69.

Akerlof, G. (2002) Behavioural Macro-economics and Macro-economic Behaviour, *American Economic Review*, 92: 411–33.

Akerlof, G., Shiller, R. (2009) *Animal Spirits: How Human Psychology Drives the Economy, and Why it Matters for Global Capitalism*, Princeton, NJ: Princeton University Press.

Alchian, A. (1959) Uncertainty, Evolution and Economic Theory, *Journal of Political Economy*, 58 (3): 211–21.

Alchian, A., Demsetz, H. (1973) The Property Rights Paradigm, *Journal of Economic History* 3 (1): 16–27.

Allison, P. (1992) The Cultural Evolution of Beneficent Norms, *Social Forces*, 71 (2): 279–301.

Anderson, E. (1990) The Ethical Limitations of the Market, *Economics and Philosophy*, 6: 179–205.

Anderson, T., Benson, B., Flanaghan, T. (2006) *Self-Determination: The Other Path for Native Americans*, Stanford, CA: Stanford University Press.

Anderson, T., Hill, P.J. (2004) *The Not So Wild, Wild West: Property Rights on the Frontier*, Stanford, CA: Stanford University Press.

Anderson, T., Leal, D. (2001) *Free Market Environmentalism*, New York: Palgrave.

Arne, R. (2002) Entrepreneurial City Planning, in Beito, T., Gordon, P., Tabarrok, A. (eds), *The Voluntary City*, Ann Arbor, MI: University of Michigan Press.

Arneson, R. (1996) Equality and Equal Opportunities for Welfare, in Pojman, L., Westmoreland, R. (eds), *Equality: Selected Readings*, New York: Oxford University Press.

Arrow, K. (1963) Uncertainty and the Welfare Economics of Medical Care, *American Economic Review*, 53: 941–73.

Arrow, K., Debreu, G. (1954) Existence of an Equilibrium for a Competitive Economy, *Econometrica*, 22: 265–90.

Axelrod, R. (1984) *The Evolution of Cooperation*, New York: Basic Books.

Ayittey, G. (2008) The African Development Conundrum, in Powell, B. (ed.), *Making Poor Nations Rich*, Stanford, CA: Stanford University Press.

Baden, J., Stroup, R. (1979) Property Rights and Natural Resource Management, *Literature of Liberty*, 2: 5–44.

Badhwar, N. (2006) International Aid: When Giving Becomes a Vice, *Social Philosophy and Policy*, 23 (1): 69–101.

Barber, B. (1984) *Strong Democracy*, Berkeley, CA: University of California Press.

Barr, N. (1992) Economic Theory and the Welfare State: A Survey and Interpretation, *Journal of Economic Literature*, 30: 741–803.

Barro, R. (1991) Economic Growth in a Cross-Section of Countries, *Quarterly Journal of Economics*, 106 (2): 407–43.

Barry, B. (1995) *Justice as Impartiality*, Oxford: Oxford University Press.

Barry, B. (2001) *Culture and Equality*, Cambridge: Polity Press.

Barry, J. (1999) *Rethinking Green Politics*, London: Sage.

Barry, N. (2004) Political Morality as Convention, *Social Philosophy and Policy*, 21 (1): 266–92.

Bate, R., Montgomery, D. (2006) Beyond Kyoto, in Booth P. (ed.) *Towards a Liberal Utopia?* London: Continuum.

Bauer, P. (1971) *Dissent on Development*, London: Wiedenfield & Nicholson.

Bauer, P. (1993) *From Subsistence to Exchange*, Princeton, NJ: Princeton University Press.

Beaulier, S., Subrick, R. (2006) Poverty Traps and the Robust Political Economy of Development Assistance, *Review of Austrian Economics*, 19: 217–26.

Becker, G. (1971) *The Economics of Discrimination*, Chicago, IL: University of Chicago Press.

Beckerman, W., Pasek, J. (2001) *Justice, Posterity and the Environment*, Oxford: Oxford University Press.

Beenstock, M. (2009) Market Foundations for the New Financial Architecture, in, Booth, P. (ed.), *Verdict on the Crash: Causes and Policy Implications*, London: Institute of Economic Affairs.

Beito, D. (1997) This Enormous Army: The Mutual Aid Tradition of American Fraternal Societies before the Twentieth Century, in Frankel-Paul et al. (eds), op. cit.

Beito, D. (2000) *From Mutual Aid to the Welfare State*, Chapel Hill, NC: University of North Carolina Press.

Beitz, C. (1979) *Political Theory and International Relations*, Princeton, NJ: Princeton University Press.

Benson, B. (1989) The Spontaneous Evolution of Commercial Law, *Southern Economic Journal*, 55 (3): 644–61.

Benhabib, S. (ed.) (1996) *Democracy and Difference*, Princeton, NJ: Princeton University Press.

Bereger, A., Udell, G. (1992) Some Evidence on the Empirical Significance of Credit Rationing, *Journal of Political Economy*, 100 (5): 1047–77.

Berggren, N., Jordahl, H. (2006) Free to Trust: Economic Freedom and Social Capital, *Kyklos*, 59 (2): 141–69.

Bergh, A. (2006) Is the Swedish Welfare State A Free Lunch? *Econ Journal Watch*, 3 (2): 210–35.

Bernstram, M. (1995) Comparative Trends in Resource Use in Market and Socialist Economies, in Simon, J. (ed.), *The State of Humanity*, Cambridge, MA: Blackwell.

Bessard, P. (2008) Challenges of Mixed Economy Solutions in Healthcare: The Examples of Switzerland and Singapore, *Economic Affairs*, 28 (4): 16–21.

Bhagwati, J. (2004) *In Defence of Globalisation*, Oxford: Oxford University Press.

Bhalla, S. (2002) *Imagine There's No Countries: Poverty, Inequality and Growth in the Era of Globalisation*, Washington, DC: Institute for International Economics.

Boettke, P. (1994) The Reform Trap in Economics and Politics in the Former Communist Economies, *Journal des Economistes et des Etudes Humaines*, 5 (2): 267–93.

Boettke, P. (1997) Where Did Economics Go Wrong? Equilibrium as a Flight from Reality, *Critical Review*, 11 (1): 11–64.

Boettke, P., Coyne, C., Leeson, P. (2007) Saving Government Failure Theory from Itself, *Constitutional Political Economy*, 18 (2): 127–43.

Boettke, P., Coyne, C., Leeson, P., Sautet, F. (2005) The New Comparative Political Economy, *Review of Austrian Economics*, 18 (3–4): 281–304.

Bohman, J. (1996) *Public Deliberation*, Cambridge, MA: MIT Press.

Bond, E.W. (1984) A Direct Test of the Lemons Model: The Market for Used Pickup Trucks, *American Economic Review*, 72 (4): 801–4.

Botkin, D. (1990) *Discordant Harmonies*, New York: Oxford University Press.

Bowers, J., Cheshire, P. (1983) *Agriculture, the Countryside and Land Use*, London: University Paperbacks, Methuen.

Brehm, J., Rhan, W. (1997) Individual Level Evidence for the Causes and Consequences of Social Capital, *American Journal of Political Science*, 41: 999–1023.

Brennan, G., Lomasky, L. (1993) *Democracy and Decision*, Cambridge: Cambridge University Press.

Brighouse, H. (2000) *School Choice and Social Justice*, Oxford: Oxford University Press.

Brighouse, H. (2002) Democracy and Inequality, in Carter, C., Stokes, G. (eds), *Democratic Theory Today*, Cambridge: Polity Press.

Browne, M., Dorphinghaus, H. (1993) Information Asymmetries and Adverse Selection in the Market for Individual Medical Expenses Insurance, *Journal of Risk and Insurance*, 60 (2): 300–312.

Buchanan, A. (1984) The Right to a Decent Minimum of Health-Care, *Philosophy and Public Affairs*, 13: 55–78.

Buchanan, J.M. (1969) *Cost and Choice*, Chicago, IL: University of Chicago Press.

Buchanan, J.M. (1986) *Liberty, Market and State*, Brighton: Harvester Press.

Buchanan, J.M., Stubblebine, C. (1962) Externality, *Economica*, 29: 371–84.

Buchanan, J.M., Tullock, G. (1962) *The Calculus of Consent*, Ann Arbor, MI: University of Michigan Press.

Buchanan, J.M., Tullock, G. (1982) *Towards a Theory of the Rent-Seeking Society*, College Park, TX: Texas A & M Press.

Buchanan, J.M., Vanberg, V. (2002) Constitutional Implications of Radical Subjectivism, *Review of Austrian Economics*, 15 (2–3): 121–9.

Butos, W. (2003) Knowledge Questions: Hayek, Keynes and Beyond, *Review of Austrian Economics*, 16 (4): 291–307.

Butos, W., Koppl, R. (1997) The Varieties of Subjectivism: Keynes and Hayek on Expectations, *History of Political Economy*, 29: 327–59.

Caldwell, B. (2004) *Hayek's Challenge: An Intellectual Biography of F.A. Hayek*, Chicago, IL: University of Chicago Press.

Caplan, B. (2007) *The Myth of the Rational Voter*, Princeton, NJ: Princeton University Press.

Caplan, B., Cowen, T. (2004) Do We Underestimate the Benefits of Cultural Competition, *American Economic Review*, 94 (2): 402–7.

Cawley, J., Philipson, T. (1999) An Empirical Examination of Information Barriers to Trade in Insurance, *American Economic Review*, 89 (4): 827–46.

Chamberlin, E.H. (1933) *The Theory of Monopolistic Competition*, Cambridge, MA: Harvard University Press.

Chamlee-Wright, E. (2006) Fostering Sustainable Complexity in the Micro-Finance Industry, *Conversations on Philanthropy*, 3: 23–49.

Chamlee-Wright, E. (2008) The Structure of Social Capital: An Austrian Perspective on its Nature and Development, *Review of Political Economy*, 20 (1): 41–58.

Chase, A. (1995) *The Fight Over Forests and the Tyranny of Ecology*, Boston, MA: Houghton Mifflin.

Chauduri, K.N. (1985) *Trade and Civilisation in the Indian Ocean*, Cambridge: Cambridge University Press.

Chiappore, P., Salanie, B. (2000) Testing for Asymmetric Information in Insurance Markets, *Journal of Political Economy*, 108 (1): 56–78.

Choi, Y.B. (1999) On the Rich Getting Richer and the Poor Getting Poorer, *Kyklos*, 52 (2): 239–58.

Choi, Y.B. (2000) Financial Crisis and Perspectives on Korean Economic Development, *Asian Financial Crisis*, 1: 357–78.

Choi, Y.B. (2002) Misunderstanding Distribution, in Frankel-Paul et al. (eds), op. cit.

Chong, D. (2002) *Rational Lives*, Chicago, IL: University of Chicago Press.

Chubb, J., Moe, T. (1990) *Politics, Markets and America's Schools*, Washington, DC: Brookings Institution.

Coase, R. (1937) The Nature of the Firm, *Economica*, 4: 386–405.

Coase, R.H. (1960) The Problem of Social Cost, *Journal of Law and Economics*, 3 (1): 1–44.

Coase, R.H. (1989) *The Firm, the Market and the Law*, Chicago, IL: University of Chicago Press.

Cohen, G. (1995) Incentives, Inequality and Community, in Darwall, S. (ed.), *Equal Freedom: Selected Tanner Lectures on Human Values*, Ann Arbor, MI: University of Michigan Press.

Cohen, J., Arato, A. (1992) *Civil Society and Political Theory*, Cambridge, MA: MIT Press.

Coleman, J., Hoffer, T. (1987) *Public and Private High Schools: The Impact of Communities*, New York: Basic Books.

Cordato, R. (2005) Market-based Environmentalism and the 'Free Market': They Are Not the Same, in Higgs, R., Close, C. (eds), *Rethinking Green*, Oakland, CA: Independent Institute.

Coulson, A. (1999) *Market Education: The Unknown History*, London: Transaction Publishers.

Coulson, A. (2004) How Markets Affect Quality: Testing a Theory of Market Education against the International Evidence, in Salisbury, D., Lartigue, Jr, C. (eds), *Educational Freedom in Urban America*, Washington, DC: Cato Institute.

Cowen, T. (1992) Law as a Public Good: The Economics of Anarchy, *Economics and Philosophy*, 8: 249–67.

Cowen, T. (2002) Does the Welfare State Help the Poor? in Frankel-Paul et al. (eds), op. cit.

Cowen, T. (2006) Poor US Score in Health Care Don't Measure Nobels and Innovation, *New York Times*, 5 October.

Cowen, T., Crampton, E. (eds) (2002) *Market Failure or Success: The New Debate*, Cheltenham, UK and Northampton, MA, USA: Edward Elgar.

Coyne, C. (2006) Reconstructing Weak and Failed States, *Journal of Social, Political and Economic Studies*, 31 (2): 143–62.

Curtin, P. (1984) *Cross-Cultural Trade in World History*, Cambridge: Cambridge University Press.

Curzon-Price, V. (2004) Switzerland: Growth of Government, Growth of Centralisation, *Economic Affairs*, 24 (2): 30–36.

Dahlman, C. (1979) The Problem of Externality, *Journal of Legal Studies*, 22 (1): 141–62.

Daniels, N., Light, D., Caplan, R. (1997) *Benchmarks of Fairness for Health-Care Reform*, New York: Oxford University Press.

David, P. (1985) Clio and the Economics of QWERTY, *American Economic Review*, 75: 332–7.

Davies, S. (1997) Two Conceptions of Welfare: Voluntarism and Incorporationism, in Frankel-Paul et al. (eds), op. cit.

Dawson, J.W. (2003) Causality in the Freedom–Growth Relationship, *European Journal of Political Economy*, 19: 479–95.

Dawson, J. (2007) The Empirical Institutions and Growth Literature: Is Something Amiss at the Top? *Econ Journal Watch*, 4 (2): 184–96.

De Alessi, L. (2003) Gains from Private Property: The Empirical Evidence, in Anderson, T., McChesney, F. (eds), *Property Rights: Cooperation, Conflict and Law*, Princeton, NJ: Princeton University Press.

De Alessi, M. (1998) *Fishing for Solutions*, London: Institute of Economic Affairs.

Deere, D., Welch, F. (2002) Incentives, Equality and Opportunity, in Frankel-Paul et al. (eds), op. cit.

De Haan, J., Sierman, C.J. (1998) Further Evidence on the Relationship between Economic Freedom and Economic Growth, *Public Choice*, 95: 363–80.

Demsetz, H. (1969) Information and Efficiency: Another Viewpoint, *Journal of Law and Economics*, 12 (1): 1–22.

De Soto, H. (1989) *The Other Path*, London: IB Tauris.

Dowley, K.M., Silver, B.D. (2002) Social Capital, Ethnicity and Support for Democracy in Post-Communist States, *Europe–Asia Studies*, 54 (4): 505.

Dryzek, J. (1987) Political and Ecological Communication, *Environmental Politics*, 4 (4): 13–30.

Dryzek, J. (1990) Green Reason: Communicative Ethics for the Biosphere, *Environmental Ethics*, 12: 195–210.

Dryzek, J. (2001) *Deliberative Democracy and Beyond*, Oxford: Oxford University Press.

Dworkin, R. (1981) Equality of Resources, *Philosophy and Public Affairs*, 10 (4): 283–345.

Dworkin, R. (1993) Justice in the Distribution of Health Care, *McGill Law Review*, 38 (4): 883–98.

Dworkin, R. (2000) *Sovereign Virtue: The Theory and Practice of Equality*, Cambridge, MA: Harvard University Press.

Easterly, W. (2001) *The Elusive Quest for Growth*, Cambridge, MA: MIT Press.

Easterly, W. (2006) *The White Man's Burden*, Oxford: Oxford University Press.

Easton, S.T., Walker, M. (1997) Income, Growth and Economic Freedom, *American Economic Review*, 87: 328–32.

Eckersley, R. (2004) *The Green State: Rethinking Democracy and Sovereignty*, Cambridge, MA: MIT Press.

Edwards, S. (2010) *Left Behind: Latin America and the False Promise of Populism*, Chicago, IL: University of Chicago Press.

Eggertsson, T. (2005) *Imperfect Institutions*, Ann Arbor, MI: University of Michigan Press.

Ellickson, R. (1991) *Order without Law*, Cambridge, MA: Cambridge University Press.

Epstein, R. (2003) *Scepticism and Freedom*, Chicago, IL: University of Chicago Press.

Feachman, R., Sekhri, N., White, K. (2003) Getting More for Their Dollar: A Comparison of the NHS with California's Kaiser Permanante, *British Medical Journal*, 324 (7330): 135–43.

Feser, E. (2005) There is No Such Thing as an Unjust Initial Acquisition, *Social Philosophy and Policy*, 22 (1): 56–80.

Folster, S., Henrekson, M. (1999) Growth and the Public Sector: A Critique of the Critics, *European Journal of Political Economy*, 15 (2): 3337–58.

Folster, S., Henrekson, M. (2006) Growth Effects of Government Expenditure and Taxation in Rich Countries: A Reply, *European Economic Review*, 1 (2): 219–22.

Frankel-Paul, E., Miller, F., Paul, J. (eds) (1997) *The Welfare State*, Cambridge: Cambridge University Press.

Frankel-Paul, Miller, F., Paul, J. (eds) (2002) *Should Differences in Income and Wealth Matter*, Cambridge: Cambridge University Press.

Fraser, N. (1993) Rethinking the Public Sphere: A Contribution to the Critique of Actually Existing Democracy, in B. Robbins (ed.), *The Phantom Public Sphere*, Minneapolis, MN: University of Minnesota Press.

Friedman, J. (1990) The New Consensus: The Democratic Theory of the Welfare State, *Critical Review*, 4 (4): 633–708.

Friedman, J. (2005) Popper, Weber and Hayek: The Epistemology and Politics of Ignorance, *Critical Review*, 17 (1–2): 1–58.

Friedman, J. (2006) Taking Ignorance Seriously: Rejoinder to Critics, *Critical Review*, 18 (4): 467–532.

Friedman, J. (2009) A Crisis of Politics, Not Economics: Complexity, Ignorance and Policy Failure, *Critical Review*, 21 (2–3): 127–83.

Fukayama, F. (1995) *Trust*, New York: Simon & Schuster.

Fukayama, F. (2001) *The Great Disruption*, London: Profile Books.

Gamble, A. (1996) *Hayek: The Iron Cage of Liberty*, Cambridge: Polity Press.

Gaus, G. (2003) Backwards into the Future: Neo-Republicanism as a Post-socialist Critique of Market Society, *Social Philosophy and Policy*, 20 (1) 59–91.

Gibson, C., Anderson, K., Ostrom, E., Shivakumar, S. (2005) *The Samaritan's Dilemma: The Political Economy of Development Aid*, Oxford: Oxford University Press.

Gjerstad, S., Smith, V. (2009) Monetary Policy, Credit Extension and Housing Bubbles: 2008 and 1929, *Critical Review*, 21 (2–3): 269–300.

Goodman, J., Musgrave, G., Herrick, D. (2004) *Lives at Risk*, New York: Rowman & Littlefield.

Gordon, P., Wang, L. (2004) Does Economic Performance Correlate with Big Government? *Econ Journal Watch*, 1 (2): 219–22.

Gray, J. (1998) *False Dawn: The Delusions of Global Capitalism*, London: Granta.

Green, D. (1985) *Working Class Patients and the Medical Establishment*, London: Temple Smith/ Gower.

Green, D. (1993) *Reinventing Civil Society: The Rediscovery of Welfare without Politics*, London: Institute of Economic Affairs.

Grossman, S., Stiglitz, J. (1976) Information and Competitive Price Systems, *American Economic Review*, 66: 246–53.

Grossman, S., Stiglitz, J. (1980) On the Impossibility of Informationally Efficient Markets, *American Economic Review*, 70: 393–408.

Guttman, A., Thompson, D. (2004) *Why Deliberative Democracy?* Princeton, NJ: Princeton University Press.

Gwartney, J., Lawson, R. (2004) The Impact of Tax Policy on Economic Growth, Income Distribution and the Allocation of Taxes, *Social Philosophy and Policy*, 23 (2): 28–52.

Gwartney, J., Lawson, R., Holcombe, R. (1999) Economic Freedom and the Environment for Economic Growth, *Journal of Institutional and Theoretical Economics*, 155 (4): 643–63.

Gwartney, J., Lawson, R., Holcombe, R. (2006) Institutions and the Impact of Investment on Growth, *Kyklos*, 59 (2): 255–73.

Haan, J., Sturm, J. (2000) On the Relationship between Economic Freedom and Economic Growth, *European Journal of Political Economy*, 16: 215–41.

Habermas, J. (1984) *The Theory of Communicative Action, Vol. 1, Reason and the Rationalisation of Society*, Boston, MA: Beacon Press.

Habermas, J. (1990) *Moral Consciousness and Communicative Action*, Cambridge, MA: MIT Press.

Habermas, J. (1992) Further Reflections on the Public Sphere, in Calhoun, C. (ed.), *Habermas and the Public Sphere*, Cambridge, MA: MIT Press.

Habermas, J. (1996) *Between Facts and Norms*, Cambridge, MA: MIT Press.

Hardin, R. (2000) Do We Want Trust in Government? in Warren, M. (ed.) *Democracy and Trust*, Cambridge: Cambridge University Press.

Hardin, R. (2001) Norms of Cooperativeness and Networks of Trust, in Hechter, M., Opp, K.D. (eds), *Social Norms*, New York: Russell Sage Foundation.

Hardin, R. (2004) *Trust*, Cambridge: Polity.

Harper, D. (2003) *Foundations of Entrepreneurship and Economic Development*, London: Routledge.

Hayek, F.A. (1944) *The Road to Serfdom*, 50th anniversary edition, Chicago, IL: University of Chicago Press.

Hayek, F.A. (1948a) *Individualism and Economic Order*, Chicago, IL: University of Chicago Press.

Hayek, F.A. (1948b) Individualism: True and False, in Hayek (1948a), op. cit.

Hayek, F.A. (1948c) Economics and Knowledge, in Hayek (1948a), op. cit.

Hayek, F.A. (1948d) The Use of Knowledge in Society, in Hayek (1948a), op. cit.

Hayek, F.A. (1948e) The Meaning of Competition, in Hayek (1948a), op. cit.

Hayek, F.A. (ed.) (1949) *Capitalism and the Historians*, Chicago, IL: University of Chicago Press.

Hayek, F.A. (1952) *The Sensory Order*, Chicago, IL: University of Chicago Press.

Hayek, F.A. (1957) *The Counter-Revolution of Science*, Indianapolis, IN: Liberty Press.

Hayek, F.A. (1960) *The Constitution of Liberty*, London: Routledge.

Hayek, F.A. (1967a) *Studies in Philosophy, Politics and Economics*, London: Routledge.

Hayek, F.A. (1967b) The Theory of Complex Phenomena, in Hayek (1967a), op. cit.

Hayek, F.A. (1967c) The Results of Human Action but not of Human Design, in Hayek (1967a), op. cit.

Hayek, F.A. (1967d) The Non-Sequitur of the Dependence Effect, in Hayek (1967a), op. cit.

Hayek, F.A. (1973) *Rules and Order*, Chicago, IL: University of Chicago Press.

Hayek, F.A. (1978a) The Pretence of Knowledge, in *New Studies in Philosophy, Politics, Economics and the History of Ideas*, London: Routledge.

Hayek, F.A. (1978b) Competition as a Discovery Procedure, in *New Studies in Philosophy, Politics, Economics and the History of Ideas*, London: Routledge.

Hayek, F.A. (1982) *Law, Legislation and Liberty*, London: Routledge.

Hayek, F.A. (1988) *The Fatal Conceit: The Errors of Socialism*, London: Routledge.

Hayward, T. (2006) Global Justice and the Distribution of Environmental Resources, *Political Studies*, 54 (2): 349–69.

Healey, P. (1997) *Collaborative Planning*, London: Macmillan.

Henrich, J., Boyd, R., Bowles, S., Camerer, C., Fehr, E., Gintis, H., McElreath, R., Alvard, M., Barr, A., Ensminger, J., Smith, N., Henrich, K., Hill, F., Gil-White, M., Gurven, F., Marlowe, J., Patton, Q., Tracer, D. (2005) Economic Man in Cross-cultural Perspective: Behavioural Experiments in Fifteen Small Scale Societies, *Behavioural and Brain Sciences*, 29: 795–855.

Hejeebu, S., McCloskey, D. (2000) The Reproving of Karl Polanyi, *Critical Review*, 13, 285–314.

Herzlinger, R. (2007) *Who Killed Health-Care?* New York: McGraw-Hill.

Hill, G. (2006) Knowledge, Ignorance and the Limits of the Price System, *Critical Review*, 18 (4): 399–410.

Hill, P.J. (2005) Market-based Environmentalism and Free Markets: Substitutes or Complements? in Higgs, R., Close, C. (eds) *Rethinking Green*, Oakland, CA: Independent Institute.

Hindmoor, A. (1999) Free-Riding off Capitalism, *British Journal of Political Science*, 217–24.

Hodgson, G. (1998) *Economics and Utopia*, London: Routledge.

Hoff, K. (2000) Beyond Rosenstein-Rodan: The Modern Theory of Coordination Problems in Development, in Pleskovic, B. (ed.), *Proceedings of the Annual Bank Conference on Development Economics 2000*, Washington, DC: World Bank.

Horwitz, S. (1992) Monetary Exchange as an Extra-Linguistic Communications Medium, *Review of Social Economy*, 50 (2): 193–214.

Horwitz, S. (2005) The Functions of the Family in the Great Society, *Cambridge Journal of Economics*, 29: 669–84.

Hoskins, W. (1993) FDICIA's Regulatory Changes and the Future of the Banking Industry, in Kaufman, G., Litan, R. (eds) *Assessing Banking Reform: FDCICIA One Year Later*, Washington, DC: Brookings Institution.

Huang, J. (2008) *Capitalism with Chinese Characteristics*, Cambridge: Cambridge University Press.

Hume, D. (1739–40/1985) *A Treatise of Human Nature*, London: Penguin Classics.

Husock, H. (1997) Standards versus Struggle: The Failure of Public Housing and Welfare State Impulse, in Frankel-Paul et al. (eds), op. cit.

Jablecki, J., Machaj, M. (2009) The Regulated Meltdown of 2008, *Critical Review*, 21 (2–3): 301–29.

Jacobs, M. (1992) *The Green Economy*, London: Pluto Press.

Jimenz, E., Lockheed, M., Paqueo, V. (1991) The Relative Efficiency of Private and Public Schools in Developing Countries, *World Bank Research Observer*, 6: 205–18.

Johanssen, D. (2008) Sweden's Slowdown: The Impact of Interventionism on Entrepreneurship, in Powell, B. (ed.), *Making Poor Nations Rich*, Stanford, CA: Stanford University Press.

Jolls, C., Sunstein, C. (2006) De-biasing Through Law, *Journal of Legal Studies*, 35: 199.

Kekes, J. (1997) A Question for Egalitarians, *Ethics*, 107: 658–69.

Kekes, J. (2003) *The Illusions of Egalitarianism*, Ithaca, NY: Cornell University Press.

King, P. (2006) *Choice and the End of Social Housing*, London: Institute of Economic Affairs.

King, R., Levine, R. (1993) Finance and Growth: Schumpeter Might be Right, *Quarterly Journal of Economics*, 108 (3): 717–37.

Kirzner, I. (1992) *The Meaning of Market Process*, London: Routledge.

Kirzner, I. (1997) Entrepreneurial Discovery and the Competitive Market Process: An Austrian Approach, *Journal of Economic Literature*, 35 (March): 60–85.

Klein, D. (2002) The Voluntary Provision of Public Goods: The Turnpike Companies of Early America, in Beito, D., Gordon, P., Tabarrock, A. (eds), *The Voluntary City*, Ann Arbor, MI: University of Michigan Press.

Knight, F. (1982) *Freedom and Reform: Essays in Economics and Social Philosophy*, Indianapolis, IN: Liberty Press.

Kukathas, C. (2002) The Life of Brian: And Now For Something Completely Difference Blind, in Kelly, P. (ed.) *Multiculturalism Reconsidered*, Cambridge: Polity Press.

Kukathas, C. (2003) *The Liberal Archipelago: A Theory of Diversity and Freedom*, Oxford: Oxford University Press.

Kukathas, C. (2006) The Mirage of Global Justice, *Social Philosophy and Policy*, 23 (1): 1–28.

Kuran, T. (1995) *Private Truths, Public Lies*, Cambridge, MA: Harvard University Press.

Kymlicka, W. (1990) *Contemporary Political Philosophy*, Oxford: Oxford University Press.

Laclau, E., Mouffe, C. (1985) *Hegemony and Socialist Strategy: Towards a Radical Democratic Politics*, London: Verso.

Ladd, E. (1996) The Data Just Don't Show a Decline in America's Social Capital, *Public Prospect*, 7 (4): 7–16.

Lal, D. (1994) *Against Dirigisme*, San Francisco, CA: Institute for Contemporary Studies.

Lal, D. (2002) *The Poverty of Development Economics*, London: Institute of Economic Affairs.

Lal, D. (2006) *Reviving the Invisible Hand*, Princeton, NJ: Princeton University Press.

Lal, D., Myint, H. (1996) *The Political Economy of Poverty, Equity and Growth*, Oxford: Clarendon Press.

Landa, J. (1995) *Trust, Ethnicity and Identity: Beyond the New Institutional Economics of Ethnic Trading Networks, Contract Law and Gift Exchange*, Ann Arbor, MI: University of Michigan Press.

Lange, O. (1936a) On the Economic Theory of Socialism, *Review of Economic Studies*, 4: 53–71.

Lange, O. (1936b) On the Economic Theory of Socialism, *Review of Economic Studies*, 4: 123–42.

Lavoie, D. (1985) *Rivalry and Central Planning: The Socialist Calculation Debate Revisited*, Cambridge: Cambridge University Press.

Lavoie, D., Chamlee-Wright, E. (2001) *Culture and Enterprise*, London: Routledge.

Leibowitz, S., Margolis, S. (1990) The Fable of the Keys, *Journal of Law and Economics*, 33 (1): 1–26.

Leibowitz, S., Margolis, S. (1994) Network Externality: An Uncommon Tragedy, *Journal of Economic Perspectives*, 8: 133–150.

Leibowitz, S., Margolis, S. (1995) Are Network Externalities a New Source of Market Failure? *Research in Law and Economics*, 17: 1–22.

Leeson, P. (2008) How Important is State Enforcement for Trade? *American Law and Economics Review*, 10 (1): 61–89.

Leeson, P., Subrick, R. (2006) Robust Political Economy, *Review of Austrian Economics*, 19: 107–11.

Lewin, P. (2001) The Market Process and the Economics of QWERTY: Two Views, *Review of Austrian Economics*, 14 (1): 65–96.

Lindbeck, A. (1997) The Swedish Experiment, *Journal of Economic Literature*, 35: 1273–1319.

Lindert, P. (2004) *Growing Public: Social Spending and Economic Growth since the Eighteenth Century*, Cambridge: Cambridge University Press.

Lomasky. L. (2005) Libertarianism at Twin Harvard, *Social Philosophy and Policy*, 22 (1): 178–99.

Lomasky, L. (2007) Liberalism beyond Borders, *Social Philosophy and Policy*, 24 (1): 206–33.

Lomborg, B. (2007) *Cool It*, New York: Knopf.

Lukes, S. (1997) Social Justice: The Hayekian Challenge, *Critical Review*, 11 (1): 65–80.

MacCallum, S.H. (1970) *The Art of Community*, Menlo Park, CA: Institute for Humane Studies.

MacFarlane, A. (1976) *The Origins of English Individualism*, Cambridge: Cambridge University Press.

MacIntyre, A. (1981) *After Virtue*, South Bend, IN: University of Indiana Press.

Marx, K. (1906) *Capital*, Vol. 1, Chicago, IL: Charles H. Kerr & Co.

Matsuyama, K. (1996) Economic Development as Coordination Problems, in Aoki, H.K., Okuno-Fujiware, M. (eds), *The Role of Government in East Asian Development: A Comparative Institutional Analysis*, New York: Oxford University Press.

McCloskey, D. (2006) *The Bourgeois Virtues*, Chicago, IL: University of Chicago Press.

McCoy, E.D., Shreder-Frechete, K.S. (1994) The Concept of Community in Community Ecology, *Perspectives on Science*, 2: 445–75.

Mathews, J. (2006) *Strategising, Disequilibrium and Profit*, Stanford, CA: Stanford University Press.

Meadowcroft, J., Pennington, M. (2007) *Rescuing Social Capital from Social Democracy*, London: Institute of Economic Affairs.

Medema, S. (1994) *Ronald H. Coase*, New York: St Martin's Press.

Miller, D. (1989) *Market, State and Community: Theoretical Foundations of Market Socialism*, Oxford: Clarendon Press.

Miller, D. (1990) Equality, in Hunt, G. (ed.), *Philosophy and Politics*, Cambridge: Cambridge University Press.

Miller, D. (1995) *On Nationality*, Oxford: Oxford University Press.

Minasian, J.R. (1964) Television Pricing and the Theory of Public Goods, *Journal of Law and Economics*, 7: 71–80.

Mitch, D. (1992) *The Rise of Popular Literacy in Victorian England: The Influence of Private Choice and Public Policy*, Philadelphia, PA: University of Pennsylvania Press.

Mitchell, W.C., Simmons, R. (1994) *Beyond Politics*, San Francisco, CA: Westview.

Montesquieu, Charles Louis de Secondat, Marquis de (1748/1961) *L'Espirit des Lois*, Paris: Garnier.

Morris, J. (1995) *The Political Economy of Land Degradation*, London: Institute of Economic Affairs.

Mouffe, C. (1993) *The Return of the Political*, London: Verso.

Mulberg, J. (1992) Who Rules the Market? *Political Studies*, 30 (2): 334–41.

Mutz, D. (2006) *Hearing the Other Side: Deliberative versus Participatory Democracy*, Cambridge: Cambridge University Press.

Myrdal, G. (1957) *Economic Theory and Underdeveloped Countries*, London: Duckworth.

Nelson, R. (2002) Privatising the Neighbourhood, in Beito, P., Gordon, P., Tabarrok, A. (eds) *The Voluntary City*, Ann Arbor, MI: University of Michigan Press.

Norberg, J. (2003) *In Defence of Global Capitalism*, Washington, DC: Cato Institute.

Nordhaus, W., Boyer, J. (2000) *Warming the World: Economic Models of Global Warming,* Cambridge: MIT Press.

North, D. (1990) *Institutions, Institutional Change and Economic Performance,* Cambridge: Cambridge University Press.

North, D., Thomas, R. (1973) *The Rise of the Western World,* Cambridge: Cambridge University Press.

North, D., Weingast, B. (1989) Constitutions and Credible Commitment: The Evolution of the Institutions of Public Choice in 17th Century England, *Journal of Economic History,* 49: 803–32.

Norton, S. (1998) Property Rights, the Environment and Economic Well-Being, in Hill, P., Meiners, R. (eds) *Who Owns the Environment?* Lanham, MD: Rowman & Littlefield.

Notturno. M. (2006) Economism, Freedom and the Epistemology and Politics of Ignorance: Reply to Friedman, *Critical Review,* 18 (4): 431–52.

Nozick, R. (1974) *Anarchy, State and Utopia,* Oxford: Blackwell.

O' Driscoll, G., Hoskins, L. (2006) The Case for Market-Based Regulation, *Cato Journal,* 26 (3): 469–87.

O'Driscoll, G., Rizzo, M. (1996) *The Economics of Time and Ignorance,* London: Routledge.

Ogilvie, S. (2003) *A Bitter Living: Women, Markets and Social Capital in Early Modern Germany,* Oxford: Oxford University Press.

Ogilvie, S. (2004) Guilds, Efficiency and Social Capital: Evidence from German Proto-Industry, *Economic History Review,* 58 (2): 286–333.

Olson, M. (1965) *The Logic of Collective Action,* Cambridge, MA: Harvard University Press.

Olson, M. (1982) *The Rise and Decline of Nations,* New Haven, CT: Yale University Press.

Olson, M. (2000) *Power and Prosperity,* New York: Basic Books.

Oorschot, W., Arts, W. (2005) The Social Capital of European Welfare States: The Crowding Out Hypothesis Revisited, *Journal of European Social Policy,* 15 (1): 5–26.

Ormerod, P., Johns, H. (2007) *Happiness, Economics and Public Policy,* London: Institute of Economic Affairs.

Ostrom, E. (1990) *Governing the Commons,* Cambridge: Cambridge University Press.

Ostrom, E. (2006) *Understanding Institutional Diversity,* Princeton, NJ: Princeton University Press.

Otteson, J. (2003) *Adam Smith's Marketplace of Life,* Cambridge: Cambridge University Press.

Otteson, J. (2006) *Actual Ethics,* Cambridge: Cambridge University Press.

Palmer, T. (2007) No Exit: Framing the Problem of Justice, in Bouillon, H., Kliemt, H. (eds), *Ordered Anarchy: Jasay and his Surroundings,* Aldershot: Ashgate.

Pejovich, S. (2003) Understanding the Transaction Costs of Transition: It's the Culture, Stupid, *Review of Austrian Economics*, 16 (4): 347–61.

Pennington, M. (2002) *Liberating the Land: The Case for Private Land Use Planning*, London: Institute of Economic Affairs.

Pennington, M. (2005) Liberty, Markets and Environmental Values, *Independent Review*, 10 (1): 39–57.

Pennington, M. (2008) Classical Liberalism, Ecological Rationality and the Case for Polycentric Environmental Law, *Environmental Politics*, 17 (3): 431–48.

Pincione, G., Tesson, F. (2006) *Rational Choice and Democratic Deliberation*, Cambridge: Cambridge University Press.

Pipes, R. (1999) *Property and Freedom*, London: Harvill Press.

Plant, R. (1994) Hayek on Social Justice: A Critique, in Birner, J., van Zjip, R. (eds), *Hayek, Co-ordination and Evolution*, London: Routledge.

Plant, R. (1999) The Moral Boundaries of Markets, in Norman, R. (ed.), *Ethics and the Market*, Aldershot: Ashgate.

Pogge, T. (2002) *World Poverty and Human Rights*, Malden, MA: Polity Press.

Polanyi, K. (1944) *The Great Transformation,* Boston, MA: Beacon Press.

Polanyi, M. (1951) *The Logic of Liberty*, Chicago, IL: University of Chicago Press.

Pomerantz, K. (2002) *The Great Divergence*, Princeton, NJ: Princeton University Press.

Postan, M. (1966) Medieval Agrarian Society in its Prime: England, in Poston, M. (ed.), *Cambridge History of England*, Vol.1, 2nd edition, Cambridge: Cambridge University Press.

Powell, B. (2005) State Development Planning: Did It Create an East Asian Miracle? *Review of Austrian Economics*, 18 (3–4): 305–23.

Prychitko, D. (1987) Marxism and Decentralised Socialism, *Critical Review*, 2 (4): 127–48.

Pulido, L. (1996) *Environmentalism and Economic Justice*, Tucson, AZ: University of Arizona Press.

Putnam, R. (2000) *Bowling Alone*, New York: Simon & Schuster.

Quian, Y. (2000) The Process of China's Market Transition (1978–1998): The Evolutionary, Historical and Comparative Perspective, *Journal of Institutional and Theoretical Economics*, 156: 151–71.

Rakwoski, E. (1991) *Equal Justice*, Oxford: Oxford University Press.

Ramsey, M. (2004) *What's Wrong with Liberalism*, London: Continuum.

Rawls, J. (1971) *A Theory of Justice*, Cambridge, MA: Harvard University Press.

Rawls, J. (1999) *The Law of Peoples*, Cambridge, MA: Harvard University Press.

Reynolds, A. (2006) *Income and Wealth*, Westport, CT: Greenwood Press.

Ricketts, M. (2000) Competitive Processes and the Evolution of Governance Structures, *Journal des Economistes et des Etudes Humaines*, 10 (2–3): 235–52.

Rizzo, M., Whittman, D.G. (2008) The Knowledge Problem and the New Paternalism, unpublished manuscript, Department of Economics, New York University.

Robinson, J. (1933) *The Economics of Imperfect Competition*, London: Macmillan.

Rodrik, D., Subramanian, A., Trebbi, F. (2002) Institutions Rule: The Primacy of Institutions over Geography and Integration in Economic Development, NBER Working Paper 9305, Cambridge, MA: National Bureau of Economic Research.

Romer, P. (1994) The Origins of Endogenous Growth, *Journal of Economic Perspectives*, 8: 3–22.

Rose, S. (1991) Is Mobility in the United States Still Alive? Tracking Career Opportunities and Income Growth, *International Review of Applied Economics*, 13: 417–37.

Rosenberg, N., Birdzell, L. (1986) *How the West Grew Rich*, New York: Basic Books.

Rosenstein–Rodan, P. (1957) Notes on the Theory of the 'Big Push', in Ellis, H. (ed.), *Economic Development for Latin America*, New York: St Martin's Press.

Rowntree Foundation (2007) *Tackling Educational Underachievement*, York: Joseph Rowntree Foundation.

Ryfe, D. (2005) Does Deliberative Democracy Work? *Annual Review of Political Science*, 8: 49–71.

Sachs, J. (2005) *The End of Poverty*, New York: Penguin Press.

Sachs, J., Warner, A. (2001) Natural Resource Abundance and Economic Growth, NBER Working Paper 5398.

Sagoff, M. (1988) *The Economy of the Earth*, Cambridge: Cambridge University Press.

Sally, R. (1998) *Classical Liberalism and International Order*, London: Routledge.

Sally, R. (2008) *Trade Policy: New Century*, London: Institute of Economic Affairs.

Schmidtz, D. (1998) Taking Responsibility, in Schmidtz, D., Goodin, R. (eds), *Social Welfare and Individual Responsibility*, Cambridge: Cambridge University Press.

Schmidtz, D. (2001) The Institution of Property, *Social Philosophy and Policy*, 11: 42–64.

Schmidtz, D. (2005) History and Pattern, *Social Philosophy and Policy*, 22 (1) 148–77.

Schmidtz, D. (2006) *Elements of Justice*, Cambridge: Cambridge University Press.

Schudson, M. (1995) What if Civic Life Didn't Die? in Verba, S., Scholzman, K., Brady, H. (eds), *Voice and Equality: Civic Voluntarism in American Politics*, Cambridge, MA: Harvard University Press.

Shapiro, D. (2007) *Is the Welfare State Justified?* Cambridge: Cambridge University Press.

Shue, H. (1999) Global Environment and International Inequality, *International Affairs*, 75: 531–45.

Silver, M. (1983) Karl Polanyi and Markets in the Ancient Near East: The Challenge of the Evidence, *Journal of Economic History*, 42 (4): 795–829.

Simon, H. (1957) *Models of Man*, New York: Wiley & Sons.

Simon, J. (1981) *The Ultimate Resource*, Princeton, NJ: Princeton University Press.

Skcopol, T. (1996) Unravelling from Above, *American Prospect*, 25: 20–25.

Smith, A. (1776/1982) *Lectures on Jurisprudence*, Indianapolis, IN: Liberty Fund.

Smith, G. (2003) *Deliberative Democracy and the Environment*, London: Routledge.

Smith, G., Wales, C. (2000) Citizens' Juries and Deliberative Democracy, *Political Studies*, 48 (1): 51–65.

Smith, V. (2007) *Rationality in Economics*, Cambridge: Cambridge University Press.

Snell, D. (1991) Market-less Trading in Our Time, *Journal of the Economic and Social History of the Orient*, 34: 129–41.

Snowdon, C. (2010) *The Spirit Level Delusion*, London: Little Dice.

Sobel, R., Leeson, P. (2007) The Use of Knowledge in Disaster Relief, *Independent Review*, 11 (4): 519–32.

Solon, G. (1992) Intergenerational Income Mobility in the United States, *American Economic Review*, 82 (3): 393–408.

Solow, R. (1956) A Contribution to the Theory of Economic Growth, *Quarterly Journal of Economics*, 70 (1): 65–94.

Somin, I. (1998) Voter Ignorance and the Democratic Ideal, *Critical Review*, 12 (4): 413–58.

Sowell, T. (1980) *Knowledge and Decisions*, New York: Basic Books.

Sowell, T. (1981) *Race and Culture*, New York: Basic Books.

Sowell, T. (1996) *Migrations and Cultures: A World View*, New York: Basic Books.

Steckbeck, M., Boettke, P. (2004) Turning Lemons into Lemonade: Entrepreneurial Solutions to Adverse Selection Problems in e-Commerce, in Birner, J., Garrouste, P. (eds), *Markets, Information and Communication: Austrian Perspectives on the Internet Economy*, London: Routledge.

Steele, D. (1992) *From Marx to Mises*, La Salle, IL: Open Court.

Steiner, H. (1999) Just Taxation and International Redistribution, *Nomos* 39: 171–91.

Stiglitz, J. (1994) *Whither Socialism?* Cambridge, MA: MIT Press.

Stiglitz, J. (2001) From Miracle to Crisis to Recovery: Lessons from Four Decades of East Asian Experience, in Stiglitz, J., Yusuf, S. (eds), *Rethinking the East Asian Miracle*, New York: Oxford University Press.

Stiglitz, J. (2009) The Anatomy of a Murder: Who Killed America's Economy? *Critical Review*, 21 (2–3): 329–41.

Stiglitz, J., Yusuf, S. (2001) *Rethinking the East Asian Miracle*, New York: Oxford University Press.

Storr, V. (2008) The Market as a Social Space: On the Meaningful Extra-Economic Conversations that can Occur in Markets, *Review of Austrian Economics*, 21 (2–3): 135–50.

Streit, M. (1984) Information Processing in Futures Markets: An Essay on Adequate Abstraction, *Jahrbuch f. Nationalok. U. Stat.*, 199 (5): 385–99.

Stringham, E. (2006) Overlapping Jurisdictions, Proprietary Communities and Competition in the Realm of Law, *Journal of Institutional and Theoretical Economics* 16 (2): 1–19.

Stroup, R. (2005) Free-Riders and Collective Action Revisited, in Higgs, R., Close, C. (eds), *Rethinking Green*, Oakland, CA: Independent Institute.

Sunstein, C. (2003) *Free Markets and Social Justice*, New York: Oxford University Press.

Sunstein, C. (2005) *Laws of Fear*, Cambridge: Cambridge University Press.

Sunstein, C., Thaler, R. (2003) Libertarian Paternalism, *American Economic Review*, 93: 175–9.

Svensson, J. (1998) Investment, Property Rights and Political Stability: Theory and Evidence, *European Economic Review*, 42: 1317–41.

Swan, T. (1956) Economic Growth and Capital Accumulation, *Economic Record*, 32 (3): 334–61.

Taylor, C. (1985) *Philosophy and the Human Sciences*, Cambridge: Cambridge University Press.

Tebble, A. (2001) The Tables Turned: Wilt Chamberlin versus Robert Nozick on Rectification, *Economics and Philosophy*, 17: 89–108.

Tebble, A. (2002) What is the Politics of Difference? *Political Theory*, 30 (2): 259–81.

Tebble, A. (2003) Does Inclusion Require Democracy? *Political Studies*, 51 (2): 197–214.

Tebble, A. (2006) Exclusion for Democracy, *Political Theory*, 34 (4): 463–87.

Tebble, A. (2009) Hayek and Social Justice: A Critique, *Critical Review of International Social and Political Theory*, 12 (4): 582–604.

Thomsen, E.F. (1992) *Prices and Knowledge*, London: Routledge.

Timberlake, R. (1993) *Monetary Policy in the United States*, Chicago, IL: University of Chicago Press.

Tooley. J. (1995) *Disestablishing the School*, Aldershot: Avebury.

Tooley, J. (1996) *Education without the State*, London: Institute of Economic Affairs.

Tooley, J., Dixon, P. (2006) De Facto Privatisation of Education and the Poor: Implications of a Study from sub-Saharan Africa and India, *Compare*, 36 (4): 443–62.

Tooley, J., Dixon, P., Gomathi, S. (2007) Private Schools and the Millenium Development Goal of Universal Primary Education: A Census and Comparative Survey in Hyderabad, India, *Oxford Review of Education*, 33 (5): 539–60.

Tooley, J., Dixon, P., Olaniyan, O. (2005) Private and Public Schooling in Low-Income Areas of Lagos State, Nigeria: A Census and Comparative Survey, *International Journal of Educational Research*, 43: 125–46.

Torstensson, J. (1994) Property Rights and Economic Growth: An Empirical Study, *Kyklos*, 47: 231–47.

Tragardh, L. (1990) Swedish Model or Swedish Culture, *Critical Review*, 4 (4): 569–90.

Tullock, G. (1994) *Rent Seeking*, Aldershot, UK and Brookfield, VT, USA: Edward Elgar.

Turner, D., Pearce, D., Bateman, I. (1994) *Environmental Economics: An Elementary Introduction*, Brighton: Harvester.

Uslaner, E. (1999) Democracy and Social Capital, in Warren, M. (ed.), *Democracy and Trust*, Cambridge: Cambridge University Press.

Van Parjis, P. (1995) *Real Freedom for All*, Oxford: Oxford University Press.

Van de Walle, N. (2001) *African Economies and the Politics of Permanent Crisis*, Cambridge: Cambridge University Press.

Vargos Llosa, A. (2005) *Liberty for Latin America*, Oakland, CA: Independent Institute.

Vedder, R. (2004) Taxes, Growth, Equity and Welfare, *Social Philosophy and Policy*, 23 (2): 53–72.

Von Mises, L. (1920) *Economic Calculation in the Socialist Commonwealth*, Auburn, AL: Ludwig Von Mises Institute.

Von Mises, L. (1949) *Human Action*, New Haven, CT: Yale University Press.

Wade, R. (1990) *Governing the Market*, Princeton, NJ: Princeton University Press.

Wallison, P. (2006) Moral Hazard on Steroids: The OGHEO Report Shows that Regulation Cannot Protect US Taxpayers, *Financial Services Outlook*, July, American Enterprise Institute.

Wallison, P. (2009) Cause and Effect: Government Policies and the Financial Crisis, *Critical Review*, 21 (2–3): 365–76.

Webster, C., Lai, L. (2003) *Property Rights, Planning and Markets,* Cheltenham, UK and Northampton, MA, USA: Edward Elgar.

Weingast, B. (1995) The Economic Role of Political Institutions: Market-Preserving Federalism and Economic Development, *Journal of Law, Economics and Organisation,* 11 (1): 1–31.

Weingast, B. (1997) The Political Foundations of Democracy and the Rule of Law, 91: 245–63.

Wenders, J. (2005) The Extent and Nature of Waste and Rent Dissatisfaction in US Public Schools, *Cato Journal,* 25: 217–44.

West, E.G. (1994) *Education and the State,* Indianapolis, IN: Liberty Fund.

West, E.G. (1970) Resource Allocation and Growth in Early Nineteenth Century British Education, *Economic History Review,* 23: 68–95.

Whelan, R. (1996) *The Corrosion of Charity,* London: Institute of Economic Affairs.

Whelan, R. (2008) British Social Housing and the Voluntary Sector, *Economic Affairs,* 28 (2): 5–10.

White, L. (1984) *Free Banking in Britain: Theory, Experience and Debate, 1800–1845,* Cambridge: Cambridge University Press.

White, L. (1989) What Kind of Monetary Institutions Would a Free Market Deliver? *Cato Journal,* 9 (2): 367–91.

White, L. (2009) The Credit-Rating Agencies and the Subprime Debacle, *Critical Review,* 21 (2–3): 389–99.

Whittman, G. (2006) WHOs Fooling WHO? The World Health Organization's Problematic Ranking of Health Care Systems, Cato Institute Briefing Paper 161, Washington, DC.

Wholgemuth, M. (1995) Economic and Political Competition in Neo-Classical and Evolutionary Perspective, *Constitutional Political Economy,* 6: 71–96.

Wholgemuth, M. (1999) Entry Barriers in Politics: Or Why Politics, Like Natural Monopoly, Is Not Organised as an Ongoing Market Process, *Review of Austrian Economics,* 12: 175–200.

Wholgemuth, M. (2005) The Communicative Character of Capitalistic Competition, *Independent Review,* 10 (1): 83–115.

Wildavsky, A. (1989) *Searching for Safety,* New Brunswick, NJ: Transaction Books.

Wilkinson, R., Pickett, K. (2009) *The Spirit Level: Why More Equal Societies Almost Always Do Better,* London: Allen Lane.

Wittman, D. (1995) *The Myth of Democratic Failure,* Chicago, IL: University of Chicago Press.

World Commission on Environment and Development (1987) *Our Common Future,* Oxford: Oxford University Press.

Yeager, T. (1999) *Institutions, Transition Economies and Economic Development,* Boulder, CO: Westview.

Young, C., Turner, T. (1985) *The Rise and Decline of the Zairian State*, Madison, WI: University of Wisconsin Press.

Young, I. (1990) *Justice and the Politics of Difference*, Princeton, NJ: Princeton University Press.

Young, I.M. (2000) *Inclusion and Democracy*, Oxford: Oxford University Press.

Index